STUDIES IN THE HISTORY
OF
POLITICAL PHILOSOPHY
BEFORE AND AFTER ROUSSEAU

STUDIES IN THE HISTORY OF POLITICAL PHILOSOPHY BEFORE AND AFTER ROUSSEAU

BY

C. E. VAUGHAN, M.A., LITT.D.

FORMERLY PROFESSOR OF ENGLISH LITERATURE IN THE UNIVERSITY OF LEEDS

EDITED BY

A. G. LITTLE, M.A., F.B.A.

VOLUME I

FROM HOBBES TO HUME

New York

RUSSELL & RUSSELL

1960

First Published, 1925

BY THE UNIVERSITY OF MANCHESTER PRESS

PUBLISHED, 1960, BY

RUSSELL & RUSSELL, INC.

BY ARRANGEMENT WITH THE UNIVERSITY OF MANCHESTER PRESS

L. C. CATALOG CARD NUMBER: 60–6034

PRINTED IN THE U. S. A.

PREFACE

PROFESSOR VAUGHAN was occupied with the history of Political Philosophy, and with the deeper problems—metaphysical, moral and religious—which lie behind it, from the time when he left Oxford to the beginning of his last illness. Though the work was frequently interrupted, and laid aside, sometimes for years together, the subject was constantly in his thoughts. The general plan of the book was recast from time to time, and most, if not all, of the chapters were re-written more than once. The one visible result of these labours so far published is his monumental edition of the *Political Writings of Jean Jacques Rousseau.* The present volumes contain the chapters before and after Rousseau.

The title *Studies in the History of Political Philosophy before and after Rousseau* is not Vaughan's. He does not appear to have decided on a title; when he referred to the book he spoke of it vaguely as 'a work on the History of Political Philosophy.' Had he lived to complete it, it would have contained the substance of his Introduction to the *Political Writings of Jean Jacques Rousseau,* and a chapter on Bentham and the Utilitarians. He was working on the latter at the time when he was taken ill, but it was not in a sufficiently advanced state to be made use of in these volumes. After consideration it has been decided not to reprint the Rousseau Introduction,[1] but to include in the present volumes only unpublished matter. It should, however, be understood that Vaughan's work on Rousseau comes between Volume I. and Volume II.

Volume I. represents Vaughan's final version for the period before Rousseau. The six chapters which it comprises were re-written between 1917 and 1921, as is explained more fully in the Memoir. They were left ready for press, and the work of the

[1] The Syndics of the Cambridge University Press were willing to allow the republication of the Introduction on generous terms.

editor has been confined to verifying references, correcting proofs, and compiling the table of contents.

The six chapters which form Volume II. have not had the advantage of the author's final revision. The bulk of the editorial work has been performed for Chapters I.-V. by Professor J. S. Mackenzie, and for Chapter VI. by Professor A. C. Bradley.

The chapter on Burke caused the greatest difficulty. Of this there were four versions: (1) an early and complete version (fair copy), written probably before 1890; (2) an incomplete version (also a fair copy) written probably before 1900; (3) an incomplete version (rough copy) written probably after 1900; (4) an incomplete version (rough copy) dated 1910.[1] These are not revisions of each other: each is a separate version, with a distinct method of approach and an arrangement of its own. It proved impossible to produce a combined version without an undue amount of repetition. Thus No. 3 contains an interesting account of Burke's relations to Montesquieu and the Utilitarians; but the inclusion of it would have involved repeating many quotations from Burke which occur in other connections in the other versions. The plan adopted has been to make the latest version (No. 4) the nucleus and to print it as it stands, to take the general introduction to Vol. II. from No. 3, and the conclusion from No. 1, the earliest but the only completed version. It must, however, be borne in mind that almost the whole of the chapter is printed from a rough copy, not from a manuscript prepared for press.

The remaining chapters are printed from fair copies prepared for press, but written probably before 1900. They are printed as far as possible as they stand in the manuscript, except that some quotations in the notes to Chapters II., III., and IV. (Kant, Fichte, Hegel) are omitted where the substance or a translation of the passage is given in the text, and that in Chapter VI. (Mazzini), English translations are substituted in the notes for the original Italian.[2]

In a book which has been so long on the stocks it is inevitable that there should be some inconsistencies and discrepancies, especially

[1] These two rough copies were written in a minute hand and were difficult to read. They were only made available by my friend, Miss E. N. D. Brewer, O.B.E., who produced accurate typed copies from somewhat baffling materials.

[2] See Professor Bradley's note at the beginning of Chapter VI.

when half of it has not been subjected to a recent revision by the author. Where there is evidence that the statement in the text did not correspond with Vaughan's final judgement, a note to this effect has been added. Such cases are, however, surprisingly rare.

The Index has been compiled by Professor Charlton. The bibliography by Professor Charlton is reprinted with some additions from the *Bulletin of the John Rylands Library*, vol. vii. No. 3 (1923), by kind permission of the Librarian, who has also allowed the reproduction of the portrait published in the *Bulletin*.

In writing the brief Memoir I have had the assistance of many of Vaughan's friends, besides those mentioned in the Memoir itself. To all of them I desire to give my sincere thanks.

A. G. L.

MEMOIR OF C. E. VAUGHAN

CHARLES EDWYN VAUGHAN was born at St. Martin's Vicarage, Leicester, on the 10th February 1854. He was the son of the Reverend E. T. Vaughan, who was then Vicar of St. Martin's, a living in the gift of the Lord Chancellor, previously held by his father (till 1829), and by his younger brother, afterwards the famous Dean of Llandaff, and subsequently by his youngest brother. Vaughan's father was a First Class mathematical and classical scholar, courteous, wise and sympathetic. In 1860 he removed to Harpenden, and became Canon of St. Albans in 1877, having previously been Canon of Peterborough. Among more distant relatives (all descended from Dr. James Vaughan of Leicester) may be mentioned Henry Vaughan, afterwards Sir Henry Halford, Baronet, the Court Physician (*d.* 1844); Henry Halford Vaughan, Professor of Modern History at Oxford from 1848 to 1858, who, in his philosophical view of history, his interest in literary criticism, the 'thrilling' character of his lectures, and his reforming spirit, seems to have resembled the subject of this memoir; and finally Professor T. H. Green, who was Vaughan's cousin.

Vaughan's mother was Mary, daughter of the Reverend J. Rose, Vicar of Rothley, and his wife Lydia, daughter of Thomas Babington, Esq., of Rothley Temple. Mrs. Babington, Vaughan's great-grandmother, was sister of Lord Macaulay's father. Mrs. Vaughan was of a peculiarly winning nature, 'and sweet attractive grace.'

Charles was the youngest child of the family and the only son. His youngest sister, Margaret (Mrs. Walter Smith) writes of his childhood: 'He had a very marked and leading character even as a small child, and I remember that at five years old he used to be called "the Governor-General" by our elder sisters. He was frail and delicate, but very keen in perception and quick in repartee. We moved to Harpenden when he was only five, and this was very happy for him, for he loved all country things, especially flowers. He did not go to school till he was thirteen, but was taught by our father, who took two or three other boys of the same age to teach and live with us. He went to Marlborough in February 1867, and had a very successful career there, getting scholarships, so that my mother has told me that his education cost them very little after his first year there. Games were not then compulsory, and I am afraid he was quite uninterested in that side of school life, except in running. I have been told he was the fastest "hare" at Marlborough. He became head of the "Junior House," and eventually head of the school, and these positions of responsibility consolidated his character and brought out the power of dealing with boys which afterwards proved so remarkable. His love of English literature was very marked through the later years at Marlborough, and still more at Oxford. I remember delightful readings of Wordsworth's lesser poems and of Browning on Sunday afternoons. Of foreign masters, Victor Hugo, both in verse and prose, took the first place. How many of his novels we used to discuss as we tramped for miles in the beautiful Hertfordshire country—with such passionate force of conviction on his side! All through these years we at home had the most delightful intercourse with him in holidays and vacations. He was so bright and affectionate—so ready to enter into home things—so brimful of ideas on all sorts of subjects which he delighted to talk over with our father, and even with my ignorant self, that after all these long years those days stand out crowned with a golden glory.'

From Marlborough, where he imbibed accurate scholarship from Bradley and literary enthusiasm from Farrar, Vaughan went to Balliol, by the advice of his cousin, T. H. Green, then tutor of the College. 'He will do best at Balliol,' Green wrote to Canon Vaughan (8th November 1871), 'the tuition there is more thorough than elsewhere and the general society better; nor is the liability to be "unsettled in belief," of which many parents now are not unnaturally afraid, greater there than it is everywhere else, where men meet who read the books of the day'; and with 'real carefulness,' the cost at Balliol could be kept down to £150 a year. Vaughan won the third scholarship at Balliol in November 1872. 'It was so good a year,' wrote Green to Canon Vaughan, 'that we have given an extra exhibition, but there was no question about his place. He wrote a very good essay, and was in the front rank on all the classical papers, though not absolutely first on any.' Among the successful candidates this year was Alfred (now Viscount) Milner.

Vaughan was at Oxford from 1873 to 1877; he obtained a First in 'Mods,' and a First in 'Greats,' and was twice bracketed for the College Jenkyns Exhibition, for which the leading 'Greats' men used to compete. He did not obtain any of the University Prizes, though he probably competed for some. The strongest influence under which he came at Oxford was that of T. H. Green; it was probably to him more than to any one else that he owed his abiding interest in political philosophy. It is indicative of the high opinion held of him by his tutors, Green and R. L. Nettleship, that both named him as executor.

College friendships are notoriously long-lived, and Vaughan's were no exception. With his old schoolfellow, J. M. Rendel, who came up to Balliol from Marlborough with him, he kept up an affectionate, if intermittent, correspondence to the end, in spite of the divergence in their lives. With other College friends he was kept or brought in touch by his work and subsequent career—with Professor A. C. Bradley (who was lecturing at Balliol when Vaughan was up), with W. W. Asquith, Principal J. V. Jones, Professor W. P. Ker, Sir Harry Reichel, Professor Tout and others.

Perhaps the man who attracted and impressed him most among his contemporaries was Arnold Toynbee; and the attraction seems to have been mutual. 'You are one of the best friends I ever had,' Toynbee wrote to him in 1878. During the long vacation in 1875 the two friends worked together in Whitechapel under the direction of S. A. Barnett—sharing a workman's lodging, which may be regarded as the nucleus of Toynbee Hall and many similar institutions. With Toynbee, too, he joined the gang of undergraduate navvies who were set to make a road at Hinksey by Ruskin. Breakfasts with Ruskin at Corpus were probably more attractive and perhaps more valuable than the work itself. And Vaughan came to the conclusion that neither 'slumming' nor digging helped a man who was reading for honours.

A wise and understanding letter from his father, dated 30th August 1877, shows that Vaughan's beliefs had been sufficiently 'unsettled' to make it impossible for him to take orders, if this had ever been intended. Vaughan's letter, to which this was an answer, has not been preserved (indeed, even at the time, Canon Vaughan had difficulty in recovering it, because 'Margaret had taken possession of the letter itself'). Vaughan did not often talk directly about religion, but his faith in an immortal purpose to be worked out in and through humanity shone out in his life, and formed the foundation or background of his philosophy. Nor did he find his beliefs inconsistent with the habit and practice of prayer, which he retained through life. And though he ceased to communicate for many years, he was a fairly regular attendant at church, and resumed the practice of attending communion in his later years at Manchester. But from what he counted the superstitions of ritualism of any kind he stood somewhat fiercely aloof.

After taking his Finals in 1877, he went to Switzerland to

study German, staying chiefly at Zürich, and spending spare time in learning Italian and 'improving himself on the piano.' These delights he reluctantly gave up to take the post of Master of the Upper Fifth at Clifton College, which was offered him by Dr. Percival, in May 1878.

Vaughan's friends and admirers have often expressed surprise that he did not obtain a tutorial fellowship at Oxford. He sat for a fellowship more than once. The following extract from a letter of T. H. Green to Canon Vaughan may explain his failure at Merton in 1878: 'C. has got into what is thought a crabbed, obscure, way of writing, and fails to make a due impression in consequence. The explanation, as I sincerely believe, is that the thoughts which he wants to express are more his own than is the case with most men; that thus they do not pass readily into phraseology acquired from books or lectures, and that under pressure of examination he has not time to beat them out fully and clearly. I trust he will do his best, when he tries at New College, to remedy this defect; though perhaps to say this is almost like asking him to change his skin. In the interval he had better be rubbing up Greek and Latin Prose, if he will condescend to that.' Two or three years later he made another—very half-hearted—attempt to obtain a tutorial fellowship; but on this occasion he was asked in an interview some questions which he interpreted as an attempt to probe into his religious beliefs and impose a test—and one may well imagine that his answers were not conciliatory.

He never regretted these failures in after years. Looking back towards the end of his life, he said once that he regarded his ten years at Clifton as perhaps the 'least unfruitful' part of his career. Certainly the beginning must have been trying enough. It was some time before he 'felt his feet'; a rowdy set of boys seemed determined to make the new master's life a burden to him. Vaughan was naturally sensitive, quick-tempered and impatient, but he kept control over himself, and before long won not only control over his class but their interest and admiration.

In his teaching he laid special emphasis on English literature and history, and the great questions underlying politics. And during his ten years at Clifton he did much to bring the teaching of these subjects into the ordinary curriculum, not only of Clifton, but of English Public Schools generally. A good many Clifton boys would endorse what one of them (an old Clifton and Balliol man) wrote to him later: 'As the years go on, I feel more than ever my indebtedness to you and Nettleship, as the two men who taught me not anything in particular, but everything.' 'Please do not think that my recollection of the Upper Vth at Clifton is too generous or in any way exaggerated—it is just the simple truth that you first turned my eyes to the light (by the by, I first read that bit of Plato with you).'

It is worth remarking that though he would hurl denunciations at the head of a delinquent, Vaughan never indulged in that sarcasm which withers the sympathies and makes one feel small.

He saw much of individual pupils out of school hours, and treated them as friends and equals—discussing the opinions of raw school-boys as if they were really worth something, and thereby both developing their intellectual independence and giving them a lesson in the truest courtesy. 'He used often to come to our house,' writes a Clifton boy, 'and I recall how on his first visit he seemed to my childish imagination the most gifted and beautiful of beings. When I sat for the first time in V*a*, I felt a sense of pride and exultation, and had sense enough to know that here was a spirit "touched to fine issues." He was an impassioned teacher, kindling quickly into flame at anything noble in literature or history, and into scorn and anger at all that was spurious and bad. . . . His Sunday breakfasts in Canynge Square were one of the joys of school life. I would gladly have watched him all the morning rolling his cigarettes, snapping his fingers at "Flip" (his fox terrier), and letting himself go in laughing comments on men and books and politics.' Often at the end of term he would take one or two boys for a walking tour, which opened out new sources of pleasure and interest and left lasting memories. He was fond of travelling, and paid many visits to Switzerland, Germany and Italy, and not a few of his pupils owed their first taste of that delightful experience to him.

During his time at Clifton, Vaughan published (in 1883 and 1884) in the now defunct *British Quarterly Review*, articles on two of his favourite authors—Victor Hugo and Robert Browning. Among his papers was found another article on Goethe and Victor Hugo, dating from about this time, which does not seem to have been printed. He was, however, already working at his *History of Political Philosophy*; and his literary output would probably have been greater but for the death in 1882 of Professor T. H. Green, and the work which consequently devolved on Vaughan as one of his executors. To a former pupil, who seems to have written to him professing weariness of life, he writes in 1887: 'The best pick-me-up which I can suggest, is that you should begin writing. I have always found that the surest refuge from boredom, so long as health holds out; a sure testimony to the natural vanity of man.'

About this time Vaughan himself was becoming restless. He was perhaps unduly sensitive to the moral atmosphere around him, and felt that he had lost the confidence of some of his colleagues. The circumstances are obscure, but a guess may be hazarded that his teaching of pure classics was suffering from his predominant interest in other subjects. What Old Cliftonians still remember of the Upper Vth in the eighties is Burke, and the French Revolution, Keats and Shelley—not Latin prose or Greek iambics. In later years Vaughan fought consistently against what he regarded as the excessive claims of the classics in the educational curriculum. At Leeds he championed the movement for allowing a modern language as an alternative even to Latin in the course for the ordinary B.A. degree. Some of the arguments he put forward in a memorial he drew up for the Council may be quoted as illustrating his attitude. 'Allowing for the sake of argument that Latin is the harder language, we are compelled to deny that hardness, in this connection, is an unqualified advantage. The harder the language, the more difficult it becomes for the student to break his way through the language to the meaning and spirit of what is written in it: the more apt he becomes to stop short with merely linguistic considerations and to neglect those of matter and literary beauty. And in our opinion this is to sacrifice the more to the less important. . . . It seems to us that the only right course is . . . to give the same freedom to those who prefer the study of modern languages and literature which we at present give to those whose preferences are for the ancient languages and literature. We permit students, after they have entered the University, to study Greek and Latin to the exclusion of all modern languages and literature. Why not permit them to study French and German to the exclusion of the ancients? Freedom of choice, should, we think, always be granted unless there is strong reason to the contrary.' This was written about 1910, but Vaughan was moving in this direction before he left Clifton. Yet for the masterpieces of classical literature he retained a deep affection, especially for the writings of Æschylus, Plato and Vergil. And though he fought against any exclusive claims made for a classical training, he rejoiced in the growth of the study of the classics in the younger Universities where he saw it competing freely with other subjects.

He resigned his mastership at Christmas 1888, took some temporary work at Rugby at the request of his old headmaster, Dr. Percival, and joined the ranks of Oxford University Extension Lecturers. He was already engaged to give five courses in the autumn of 1889, when he was induced by his friend, Principal Viriamu Jones, to apply for the Chair of English Literature and History at Cardiff, then vacant by the election of Professor W. P. Ker to the Quain Professorship of English Literature at University College, London. The appointment to a chair of English Literature of a man who had been for ten years a schoolmaster was unusual, but in Vaughan's case it was not a leap in the dark. It is true that he lacked some of the technical qualifications: as he told the Council, he had no knowledge of Anglo-Saxon. But he had proved his ability to teach History and Literature, and to inspire one generation of his pupils after another with a love of his favourite subjects. He possessed the necessary moral qualities,—pertinacity, sympathy, devotion to duty—combined with robust vigour of mind and body. He had a thorough knowledge of the great Greek and Roman writers, and a wide acquaintance not only with English but with foreign literature. He was a good linguist—knowing French, German and Italian, and something of most other European languages, including even Russian.[1] His memory was remarkably retentive and carefully cultivated. He had also the philosophic mind which enabled him to understand and bring out the mutual connection between history and literature. Though an exact scholar and scrupulous in details he was free from the limitations which often hamper the specialist, and of which he had a horror. To a former pupil he wrote in 1886: 'I should implore you not to specialise yourself—more than a decent respect for the main chance requires —at present. I am sure that something of philosophy is indispensable for a fruitful knowledge of history.'

Vaughan was Professor of English Language and Literature at the University College of South Wales and Monmouthshire from 1889 to the end of 1898. He was relieved of the History side of his Department in 1891. As a lecturer he had had some practice in speaking to large audiences at Clifton, but he was not naturally a fluent or easy speaker. It may be interesting to know that he achieved the art of seizing the right word by translating aloud (generally to one auditor) the novels of Victor Hugo. He spoke with few or no notes and generally destroyed such notes as he had used, in order that his mind might not be hampered by the shell of its past. Vaughan has often been credited with 'originality.' It is a dangerous word. Certainly his methods were all his own; and the matter of his discourses was fused in his own mind and came out stamped with his personality. The material for a lecture was always thought out afresh: the actual verbal form was left to the inspiration of the moment. This inspiration never seemed to be lacking: one could see the process of coining a phrase going on in the mind—fairly swiftly—and the phrase would be 'barked' out incisively. This method of lecturing was—and, especially in early years, seemed—an effort. The result was stimulating. It was difficult not to attend: it was impossible to go to sleep.

He adopted the same extempore method even in set public

[1] At Cardiff he learnt Welsh.

lectures, and in later years acquired a marked facility in speaking. When he delivered the Warton Lecture on English Poetry before the British Academy (1913), that august body was surprised to find he was speaking without notes instead of reading a paper. The lecture was delivered on the 29th October. On the 2nd November he writes: 'I have been toiling over the unwelcome task of reducing my unhappy lecture to writing. It is like flat champagne. But I have got the wretched thing nearly decanted now. I pity the poor victims who try to drink it.' These public lectures as given were in strictly literary, if rhetorical, form. The two lectures of Vaughan's which were taken down in shorthand—'Rousseau and his Enemies,' delivered before the Philosophical and Literary Society of Leeds on the 7th February 1911,[1] and 'Charlotte and Emily Brontë,' delivered at the Annual Meeting of the Brontë Society on the 20th January 1912,—could be printed from the reporter's transcripts with hardly any alterations.

The following extracts from an article which appeared in *The Western Mail*, 11th October 1922, give a fair idea of the impression he made on the Welsh students: 'No tutor was ever such an idol to his pupils as he. Gifted with brilliant intellectual genius, bubbling humour, boundless sympathy and kindness, fearless regard for truth, he was an incomparable lecturer and ideal teacher. His classes were easily the most popular in college, and always crowded the largest class-room among the "wooden shanties" in Newport Road. The Lecture-hall rocked with laughter at his witty sallies. In another moment the place was hushed to silence by some challenge made by Vaughan to the ancient traditions of his audience or some remark made which revealed the serious view of life that lay concealed by his "robustious" humour. His sense of truth was poignantly keen. He gave the necessary shock to hundreds of young Welshmen, and awoke them, as Hume did Kant, from their dogmatic slumbers. The present writer can testify this from experience. Brought up as a rigid Nonconformist and worshipper of the Puritans, one found it a difficult chunk to digest when Vaughan, with merciless criticism, unveiled the cant, the hypocrisy, the narrowness, and kill-joy bigotry which characterised some of the Puritans. . . . An invitation to dine with him and Professor Mackenzie—both living a bachelor life together at Llanishen—filled the inexperienced collier or farmer student with awe. An evening dinner of several courses was a new ordeal, and the joy of being asked to dine was curbed by a fear of a blunder at the professor's table. But once there, all fear vanished, Vaughan being as genial and kind a host as he was brilliant as a lecturer.'

Vaughan was naturally shy and did not love social functions.

[1] 'Lectured on Rousseau very badly,' is his note in his diary.

Indeed he could be at times exceedingly 'thorny' and difficult in society. He threw himself, however, into the social life of the College gallantly. When the students performed plays he generally acted as stage manager and dramatic coach. 'I remember,' writes a less theologically minded student than the one quoted above, 'the zest and energy he put into the rehearsals for the various dramatic entertainments in which I took part. On one occasion we performed Molière's *Les Fourberies de Scapin* in English, and he taught me to declaim the famous line, "What the devil did he want on board that galley?" with such gusto and emphasis, especially upon the word "devil," that all the theological students began to hiss.'

During this period the University of Wales was founded (the Charter was granted in 1893), and Vaughan took a prominent part not only in drawing up schemes of study in his own department, but also in the discussions which settled the general educational policy of the University. He represented the College Senate on the University Court, acted as a member of the Executive Committees both of the Court and of the Senate of the University, and was elected first Chairman of the Faculty of Arts. In general one may say that his weight was thrown on the side of freedom. He was a vigorous fighter ('I love a fight,' he admitted), but he never hit below the belt, and his attacks left no sting. By friends and critics alike Vaughan was sometimes dubbed the 'conscience' of the University. 'I never met another man who made me so uncomfortable if I differed from him on any point,' was the testimony of Principal Jones. Anything in the nature of a job roused his indignation. At least on one occasion a more worldly-wise Chairman strained the powers of the Chair to put him out of order and prevent him from blurting out unpalatable truths. He was, however, by no means an unpractical idealist. He was well aware of his natural impetuosity, and on guard against it. He was always ready to listen to arguments and consider them carefully and even humbly. The trust placed in him by his colleagues in one University after another is sufficient evidence both of his practical wisdom and of his single-mindedness.

The preaching instinct was strong in Vaughan. 'I have it in my bones,' he confessed. A flaming zeal for justice and liberty lighted his way through life and literature and politics. It never failed to blaze out in his lectures on Dante, Victor Hugo or Rousseau, and it inspires every chapter of his *History of Political Philosophy*. It also turned him into a democrat. He was an advanced Liberal in politics. But though he took a keen interest in public affairs, both domestic and foreign, and generally formed decided opinions on them, he did not take an active part in political controversies or political organisation.

There is another portion of his life which may be briefly touched upon—'his little, nameless, unremembered acts of kindness and of love.' Few people knew anything about them; none knows their number and variety. He would spend thought and time and labour and money to right wrongs, to help the unfortunate, to provide medical succour to the sick, and to assist poor students. If this generosity was sometimes abused, he was well content to take the risk. He referred to Macaulay's practice, and applied to himself on a small scale Macaulay's entry in his diary: 'I have been prosperous beyond the common lot of men, and may well assist those who have been out of luck.' But his generosity sometimes strained his resources. He came one day to a friend with a troubled face and a bank-book which he did not understand. The friend was not a financier, but knew enough to see that he had overdrawn his account.

Apart from 'gifts,' which often exceeded a quarter of his total income, he was careful about money matters. His personal expenditure was confined within narrow limits. He kept accounts methodically, and saved what he could; and his investments were well chosen. His nearest approach to a speculation was the investment of an unexpected legacy in the purchase of an annuity three months before his death.

While at Cardiff he published editions of Burke's *Reflections on the French Revolution* and Burke's *Speeches on America* in a series of which he was general editor, and of Webster's *Duchess of Malfi*. His principal publication in this period was *English Literary Criticism*, an edition of some of the more important texts on the subject from Sidney to Pater, with 100 pages of introduction on the development of literary criticism in England,—original in its conception, illuminating, suggestive and provocative, like his talk. It remains at once the best general introduction to the problems in the subject as a whole, and the best summary estimate of their relative values; and ought to be better known than it is. The wonder is that with his new teaching work and all his other engagements he should have produced so much. He was also writing and rewriting his *History of Political Philosophy*; while his duties as one of the literary executors of Nettleship (who died in 1892) took up much time.

Vaughan's health was not very good at Cardiff; he suffered from rheumatism, which was not remedied by a move to Llanishen. This, combined with natural ambition, led him to seek a change. Shortly after he came to Cardiff, the Chair of English Literature at Liverpool became vacant, and there is reason to believe that he would have been elected had he stood for it: he refused to stand, out of gratitude and loyalty to his friend, Principal Jones, to whose influence he attributed his election at Cardiff. In 1895 he was a candidate for the Chair of Rhetoric and English Literature in the University of Edinburgh, when Professor Saintsbury was elected. At the end of 1898 he was appointed to the new Chair of English Language and Literature in the Durham College of Science at Newcastle-upon-Tyne.

His words of farewell to his students after lecture on the 15th December 1898 may be quoted: 'I wish you every success in life; by that I mean not a life free from struggle, grief and sorrow; these come to all and for the good of all; but that you may meet them in a spirit of truthfulness and cheerfulness.

'I hope, too, that you may go through life with an ever-deepening sense of love to God and man; that your life may not only be strong, but a true and good life.

'I pray that you may go through life always keeping your eyes open to truth that offers itself from every quarter, however unpromising it may at first appear to be, and to the beauty spread lavishly around us on every hand; thereby your life will be keen, intense and enjoyable.

'These are my wishes for you, and such, I trust, are your wishes for me. I have only to add—God bless you.'

At a meeting of students who made a presentation to him, Vaughan's remarks were in a more humorous vein. But the ceremony was a moving one. 'It was,' wrote a student who was present, 'the largest assembly of students I ever attended at College, and the saddest.'

The six years he spent at Newcastle were perhaps the least happy period of his life. The death of his father, followed shortly afterwards by that of Principal Viriamu Jones, and the long and fatal illness of his housekeeper, who had served him devotedly for many years, all lent to this time melancholy associations. Vaughan, too, never reconciled himself to the subordinate position which the Newcastle professors held in the then constitution of the University of Durham. During his first year he was elected Vice-Principal of the College; his devotion to the interests of his students and their devotion to him were as great as ever; some popular lectures which he gave, especially one on Coleridge, seem to have produced a deep impression, and he found congenial friends in Spence Watson and Theodore Merz. When he had been some eighteen months at Newcastle, he became a candidate for the Chair of English Literature in the University of Glasgow, then vacant on the retirement of his friend, Professor Bradley. In 1904 he was appointed to the new Chair of English Language and Literature in the University of Leeds. He became one of those who at a critical time moulded the fortunes of the new University.

He strengthened the ties which bind it to the region which it serves. With the help of his colleague, Dr. Moorman, he created a school of English studies, which has already made its mark. And to his labour and generosity the University Library owes not a little of its present strength.

'From the first,' writes his colleague, Professor Arthur Smithells, 'Vaughan took a deep interest in the general affairs of the University. His work at Cardiff and Newcastle had of course given him familiarity with the life and problems of the modern universities, so that he had already clear ideals and definite and strong opinions on questions of academic and general policy. The maturity of his experience, the breadth of his sympathies, and the quiet cogency and gracious form of his participation in its discussions, gave him at once a position of authority in the Senate. On the major questions his feelings often acquired great intensity, and where the issues were to him those of justice or injustice he fired up at any suggestion of retreat or compromise. His influence may perhaps be fairly characterised as having been most conspicuously anti-pedantic. Whilst in the truest sense a scholar, he was in no way more easily inflamed than by arguments which adduced ancient customs, conventional proprieties, or vested interests as decisive considerations. He was ready and anxious to review every scheme of study or every proposal of university statesmanship in the light of modern knowledge and present-day conditions. He was one of the comparatively small number among men of letters I have known who have really felt continually and deplored truly their lack of a knowledge of natural science.

'For a short period Vaughan was Pro-Vice-Chancellor, and he was also for a time a member of the Council, but in those capacities he had scarcely time to grow into a new position of prominence in the larger regular administrative business of the University. He was, however, always sought whenever a small band of counsellors had to be called together at moments of emergency or on questions of more than usual importance. He took all such things almost too earnestly, or at least they perturbed him to a degree that made us reluctant to add them to his teaching burden, which his conscientiousness had made already a strain upon his vigour.

'The preparation which Vaughan thought necessary for any extra lectures of a public kind was extraordinary in its extent and thoroughness. The result was of course a work both of wisdom and of art, and in its delivery he seemed to assume and to give out the very spirit of the man whose thoughts or works he was expounding. His standards of professional duty in every relation to the University were an example to us all.' [1]

[1] The impression which Vaughan made at Leeds may best be seen in

Hitherto Vaughan had published little; his best energies were put into teaching and the preparation for it. His literary output now increased, though he was never a rapid writer. In 1907 his first considerable book appeared, *The Romantic Revolt*, which had been begun in 1900. The period of European literature which it covered (from *c.* 1778 to 1805)—a period when poetry, philosophy and politics were closely interwoven—was specially well suited to Vaughan's habit of mind. The book is a 'store-house of knowledge,' but it is much more than that. The important movements of the time are brought out clearly and vividly and truly. The greater part of the volume is devoted to Britain and Germany, and it would be hard to find anywhere a finer account of the deepest currents of that momentous generation than that contained in these 350 pages.

Next year, in 1908, appeared Vaughan's *Types of Tragic Drama*, probably the best-known and most admired of his books. This contains, among other things, the only contribution which he published on a favourite subject of his—the Spanish drama of the sixteenth century. The book represents a course of public lectures delivered in the University of Leeds in the winter of 1906. Vaughan gave the lectures extempore, but wrote out each within a week of its delivery. It is a brilliant survey of the drama from Aeschylus to Ibsen. The idea which runs through the book is that the whole movement of dramatic history has been from the external to the internal, from action to character: but the value of the criticism of the various 'types' is not dependent on this general view. The whole book is so fresh and stimulating that it makes one regret that no other of his courses of public lectures has been preserved. They were many. There was, *e.g.*, one at Cardiff on Dante, which lives in the memory of those who heard the lectures: there was another at Aberystwyth in 1921 on some French writers and thinkers of the eighteenth century, and their influence on English thought.[1] Of these nothing remains but a few fragmentary notes.

Between 1909 and 1914 he also wrote three chapters in the *Cambridge History of English Literature*, on 'Tourneur and Webster,' 'Sterne and the Novel of his Times,' and 'Coleridge,' and one in the *Cambridge Modern History*, on 'The Romantic

---

the sketch which his friend and former pupil, Professor Charlton, prefixed to his List of Vaughan's writings in the *Bulletin of the John Rylands Library*; this is reprinted in these volumes.

[1] The subjects were (1) Voltaire and English thought, (2) Helvétius and Diderot, (3) Montesquieu and Burke, (4) Rousseau and the Return to Nature, (5) Rousseau and the Social Contract.

Movement in European Literature.' His scepticism as to the worth of composite histories such as these did not detract from the value of his own contributions. Their brevity throws into high light his power of disentangling the essential from its massed encumbrances, and his genius for summary appraisement. During these years he published several literary articles in learned periodicals. A paper on 'Carlyle and his German Masters,' which he contributed to the first volume of *Essays and Studies* of the English Association (1910), was described by a very competent critic as 'the most interesting and valuable of the whole collection.'

In June 1900 Vaughan stated that he had 'brought a work on Political Philosophy—a work on which I have been engaged for many years—to the last stage of completion, and I hope to send it to the press before the end of the present year.' Yet that work was left unfinished at his death, and is only now published in an incomplete form. What is the explanation? His absorption in the 'Romantic Revolt' will only account for a delay of some years. The real explanation is twofold. Firstly, Vaughan felt the necessity of reconsidering the question of the value of expediency as a principle of political action (this may account for the existence of at least three unfinished versions of his chapter on Burke); secondly, he became convinced of the paramount importance of Rousseau in the history of political theory (as forming, so to speak, the bridge from the mechanic to the organic conception of the State), and of the need for working out anew the development of his ideas.

The next step, therefore, was to collect and edit or re-edit all Rousseau's political writings. For five or six years Vaughan spent a good part of the summer vacations at Neuchâtel and Geneva, copying and collating Rousseau manuscripts, and he was only prevented by the outbreak of the War from going to Cracow in August 1914 to examine a newly discovered manuscript of the *Gouvernement de Pologne*.

The result of these labours was the magnificent edition of the *Political Writings of Jean Jacques Rousseau* in 1915. It is a great book, whether regarded as a scholarly edition of texts, or as a study in political theory. Like the rest of Vaughan's writings on political philosophy, it is not merely a work of erudition, but is, and was intended to be, a direct contribution to the solution of the permanent problems of politics. In a lecture delivered during the War, and written out more fully than usual, on 'The Message of Rousseau to the Present Time,' he says: 'When the War is over, we shall have to set ourselves, as never before, to solve in practice the problem which neither Rousseau nor any other thinker has ever been able to solve more than half in theory: to work out the right relation—a relation right for us and for the given circumstances of our particular case—between the individual and the State. And when we come to do so, I must think that, taking all his works together, we shall find more help and guidance from Rousseau than from any one else. The two principles for both of which place must be found in our solution—the principle of individual liberty, on the one hand; the principle of State initiative or State control, upon the other—may not be, are not, fully reconciled in his writings. But they are both there; and each is stated with a force which no other writer has even distantly approached.'

Except the 'Epilogue,' which was finished in January 1915, the whole of the *Political Writings of Jean Jacques Rousseau* was written before the War: proofs of the Introduction were being corrected as early as January 1913. While the book was going through the press Vaughan unexpectedly sent in his resignation of his professorship in May 1913. The reasons were ill-health and a desire to devote the remainder of his life to political philosophy. He was at this time seized with a profound depression of spirits—a feeling of failure and unworthiness, which no doubt had its roots in some physical disturbance, but which made the strain of carrying on his teaching work unbearable. In course of time and in fresh surroundings he entirely recovered his mental serenity, though not perhaps his former buoyancy, and the last years of his life were as happy as his manner of life and increasing physical infirmities, and the anxieties of public affairs, permitted. The affection in which he continued to hold the University of Leeds is shown in the munificent bequests which he left in his will.[1]

Vaughan never took a long lazy holiday. He was always at work. Even after walking all day he would sit down to write at political philosophy, or read Aeschylus or Dante or Spinoza. He was enabled to bear the constant strain by his capacity to sleep for a few minutes at any time (sometimes at inconvenient times) and wake up refreshed. He loved the hottest sunshine, and would bask in it without a hat, while his companions took refuge in the nearest shade. His favourite recreation was walking (for a short period bicycling was a rival). He had an unerring eye for country, and was proud of his achievements in finding his way over moors or fells in the dark or in mist. There were few parts of England he had not trudged over. Of all parts the Lake District was that which he loved best—summer or winter. When the fine springy swinging gait of earlier days had been reduced by rheumatism to a

[1] He left £3500 to the University to found a Post-graduate research scholarship or fellowship in the Departments of English or History or Economics; and gave to the library his collection of Rousseau books and the right to select from his library any other books which they chose.

painful limp, he still contrived to enjoy tramps of twelve or fifteen miles—over Grisedale Pass or Shap Fells or on the Yorkshire Moors. But the effort led to over-strain of the heart. Gardening was perhaps the next favourite hobby: the growing of carnations in his Manchester garden was a source of pleasure and pride; his flowers must be sweet scented; for a kitchen garden he had no use, and rejoiced if he found flowers ousting vegetables in a friend's garden. Towards the end of his life he returned to an old love—the piano (a piano was one of the parting gifts of his friends at Leeds), though he never acquired much facility. He was not an indiscriminate reader of novels, but to his old favourites, such as *Quatrevingt-treize* and *Guy Mannering*, he returned again and again. He enjoyed reading aloud, and read with much dramatic force. He had other interests of a less intellectual kind. Though he never cared for games, he developed a keen pleasure in watching football matches, and the exhibitions of ' strong men ' had a curious fascination for him: he was a great admirer of Sandow.

In September 1913 Vaughan moved to Manchester, attracted partly by the John Rylands Library. The outbreak of the War stirred his passionate patriotism to its depths. Like many of the older men he became restless and dissatisfied with the daily round, and eager to give some more immediate service to the country. When he had got the Rousseau off his hands, he migrated to London and worked for a year (1915–16) in the War Trade Intelligence Department, where his knowledge of languages was of much value. His health suffered: from this time may be dated his chronic bronchitis. After this he gave his time and strength to help the Northern Universities in emergencies, giving courses of lectures at Liverpool during one winter, and at Leeds during another. In the University of Manchester he voluntarily gave two courses of lectures in the English Department, 1919–20; the next session he accepted an appointment as special lecturer in that department, and in 1921–22, again voluntarily, he held regular conferences with a group of students who were preparing theses on politico-literary topics. He was also, as usual, doing a great deal of examining. He received the Degree of Doctor of Letters, *honoris causa*, from the Universities of Liverpool (1913), Leeds (1914), Manchester (1919), and Wales (1921).

In 1917 he published a translation of Rousseau's *Paix Perpétuelle*, with an introduction which forms a valuable contribution to the history of the idea of the League of Nations, and in 1918 an edition of the *Contrat Social*, with a clear and closely reasoned introduction and admirable notes: the value of this as a text-book for the study of political theory has already been widely recognised.

He further gave a number of miscellaneous lectures to various branches of the English Association and other bodies.[1] He took a hand in the struggle for Woman Suffrage, to which he was an ardent, if somewhat late, convert. He was an active member of the Press Committee of the Manchester University, and a Governor of the John Rylands Library. As though this were not enough, he must needs form the plan of a new work on 'Literary Influences on the French Revolution,' and began collecting materials for it.

All this—and some, but not all of it, was inevitable—sadly interfered with the *History of Political Philosophy*. The entries in his diaries enable us to follow the course of his writing. Vaughan, as his diary shows, was working at Hobbes in 1916 on Sundays and Thursdays (the days he was not at the W.T.I.D.), and a version of this chapter was finished on the 17th August 1916. During 1917 the work was not touched till the 26th December, and then the whole was begun again on a new plan, as it appears in the first volume of this edition. The chapters on medieval political theory, Thomas Aquinas, Dante, etc., are scrapped, and the present short introduction substituted. Hobbes is again taken up and re-written on the new plan between the 25th April and the 14th June. Then follow the other chapters, each of which is re-written, not merely revised from the earlier versions—a rough copy being made first and a fair copy afterwards. This goes on till the 2nd January 1922, when the fair copy of Hume was finished. The next day Vaughan was at work on Helvétius; and he was writing steadily on Bentham from the 20th January to the 19th April, when the diary comes to an abrupt end. Fair copies of these two last articles were not made, and the rough copies discovered among his papers are incomplete.

From this time he was an invalid, suffering from over-strain of the heart, dropsy and intestinal troubles, some of which, as he laughingly said, formed 'a new bond of sympathy' between him and his 'patron saint,' Jean Jacques. He bore his afflictions with unfailing patience. 'After all,' he wrote, with some exaggeration, 'I have had the good fortune to enjoy unbroken health for nearly seventy years. And if I have only enough now left to go on with my work, I shall be perfectly content.' His chief anxiety was for his housekeeper, who nursed him with devoted care. 'I am longing (on the 17th August) for the time when I can get away for a change and release her from at any rate the heaviest part of the burden.' He became much worse early in September. But save when he was suffering from attacks of unbearable pain, which mercifully ended in unconsciousness, his mind was as vigorous

[1] The last lecture which he gave was one to the British Institute of Adult Education on 'The Place of Modern Languages in Adult Education,' in Manchester, March 1922.

and his memory as retentive as ever. Some ten days before his death, he remarked that one of the doctors reminded him of the line 'Physician art thou?—one, all eyes'; and as his visitor did not understand the allusion, he repeated the greater part of Wordsworth's 'A Poet's Epitaph.' In conversation with another friend about the same time, he quoted with a smile the humorous concluding line of Vergil's third Eclogue:

> Claudite iam rivos, pueri: sat prata biberunt.

The quotation not only threw fresh light on the subject under discussion, it was also strangely fitting to be a last recollection of a great teacher: the fields which his genius had watered had been richly fed. The end came on the 8th October 1922.

Vaughan did not in his lifetime receive the public recognition which he deserved. He certainly did not seek it. His influence on his pupils was profound, and through them is spreading farther and wider. His books are well known and highly valued by teachers of English literature. And it may be expected that some at any rate of his work on political theory will make itself felt more and more in thought and action, as the years go on.

A. G. L.

CONTENTS

CHAPTER IV

CHAPTER V

CHAPTER VI

CHAPTER I

INTRODUCTORY

POLITICAL theory goes hand in hand with history. As the conditions of the problem vary from age to age, so the solution of it must of necessity vary with them. Otherwise, theory in these matters would have little or no relation to practice; it would belong to a region almost as abstract as that of pure mathematics or astronomy. This, however, is far from being the case. The *Republic* or the *Politics* sprang from the City State, and would have been impossible without it. The rival claims of Church and Empire gave birth to *De Monarchia*; the first awakening of nationality—once more, in conflict with the Church—is reflected in *De civili Dominio* and *De Dominio divino*. The break-up of the old order in Church and State demanded a new statement of the first principles of political obligation: hence the whole line of thinkers from Hobbes to Rousseau and Burke. The industrial revolution, the sudden appearance of nationality as a dominant factor in the life of Europe, once more changed the whole face of politics: hence the Socialists on the one hand, the German philosophers and Mazzini upon the other.

This, of itself, is enough to put out of court those who would treat political philosophy as a purely abstract study, divorcing it wholly from the causes for which men have shed their blood and sacrificed all that would have brought them worldly happiness and ease. Is, then, political philosophy but another name for the philosophy of history? is its aim nothing more than to translate into terms of thought the successive struggles through which men have passed in their pursuit of the ideal? That would be to leap at once into the opposite extreme: to forget, as Hegel and Comte would sometimes have appeared to forget, that, in and behind all the movement of man's civic history, there are certain problems which, however much their outward form may vary, still remain essentially the same. The nature and grounds of political obligation, the relation of the individual to the State, the relation of one State to another—these are the questions which recur under all conceivable forms of political association, and recur in substantially the same shape. Other interests may drive them into the background; the special circumstances of the time may obscure, or even modify them, till they become hard to recognise. But, however overlaid, however modified, they are always present; always to be reckoned with; always the problems round which the speculative thought of any age must, in the last resort, inevitably turn.

Much the same thing, with a significant difference, is true of ethics. The moral code of one age is not that of another; the moral problems of one age differ from those of another. Yet the fundamental question—what is the nature of duty, what the sanction of the moral code?—remains invariable; it is to this that the moral philosophy of every age inevitably returns. Only, in the field of morals the circumstances vary infinitely less from age to age than in that of politics. The central problem therefore stands out far more clearly; it is less liable to be obscured, much less likely to be sensibly modified, by the circumstances of the moment than in the kindred realm of politics. Moral duties are comparatively unchanging. Political duties are determined mainly by expediency: in other words, by the circumstances—which, strictly speaking, are always unprecedented—of the given time and the given situation. Even in morals, no one not wholly inexperienced or grossly rash supposes that circumstances count for nothing. But in politics it is evident that the allowance to be made for them is infinitely larger: that, as Burke said, 'circumstances, which with some men count for nothing, in reality give to every political principle its distinguishing colour and discriminating effect.'

The central problem of political philosophy, the first and chief aim of political action, is, without doubt, to secure the right relation between the individual and the State. Conditions alter; new elements constantly force their way into the reckoning. But experience proves that, in the end, each in turn receives its value from the place it wins in regard to the more primitive elements; that, in the last resort, everything depends upon the rightness of *their* relation to each other, upon the courage and wisdom with which that relation is established and maintained.

Examples, both for good and for evil, abound in earlier as well as later times. One, from the last century, will suffice. At no time has an element more explosive than that of nationality been thrown into the crucible of political ideals. By no two men could it have been handled more differently than by Bismarck and Cavour. The one employed it as a means for reinforcing the already overgrown powers of the State—or rather, of a military autocracy masquerading as the State—at the expense of the individual. The other, under conditions beyond comparison more difficult, never forgot that, in making his people one and independent, it was his duty also to make them self-governing and free. The dream of the latter was a free Italy in a free Europe. The work, though not the conscious aim, of the former was to forge the slavish instrument by which others, more foolish than himself, have sought to bring all Europe under the yoke of their crazy hatreds and ambitions.

And if the contrast lay between the thinkers who, in each country, prepared the way for the action of the statesmen, it would speak more strongly yet. The memory of Fichte and Hegel is for ever burdened with the theory of the 'absolute State,' to which Bismarck harnessed the principle of nationality. Mazzini, the prophet of nationality, is also, of all writers, the one who has most truly defined the relation between the individual and the State. A nation ordered upon his principles would be not only the most ardent, but the freest and noblest, ever known. Before the 'stark congealment' of blood and iron, in which their theories have resulted, even Fichte and Hegel, it may be hoped in charity, would have stood aghast.

It is, of course, true that at some periods the influx of new elements has been more marked than at others; and at such times the main issue, in the field both of thought and action, is apt to be momentarily obscured. These, however, are just the moments when both thinker and statesman have most need to remind themselves of its importance. For history is there to show that those who have not done so have invariably had cause to rue their blindness. In the pursuit of other ends—ends in themselves, it may be, desirable enough—they have either reduced the State to impotence, or forged it into a machine without freedom, without ideals, without anything that deserves the name of life.

The period covered by these volumes—the period from Hobbes to Mazzini—offers both positive and negative proof of these assertions: more abundantly, perhaps, than any other period in the long story of political theory and practice. During the first two-thirds of it, from Hobbes to the close of the French Revolution, almost the sole question present to men's minds was what is here presented as the main issue: the struggle between the rival claims of the individual and the State. By the time of Rousseau and Burke, the solution to that issue was virtually accomplished. All that was left was to harmonise their results; to work them out in greater detail; above all, to apply them in the field of practice. With the tyranny of Napoleon, however, a new element, that of nationality, was called into being: or rather asserted itself upon a scale, and with a sense of its own rights and its own powers, never known before. And after his fall, the sudden irruption of industrialism brought yet another problem, Socialism and the various issues which sprang out of it, violently to the front. Each of these new issues—the one more, the other less, obviously—stood in the closest connection with the yet deeper and more vital issue between the individual and the State. Thus a double burden, a burden heavier than any which had yet fallen to them, was laid both upon statesman and philosopher. To deal with the new problem was a necessity from which no philosopher, and few statesmen, could possibly escape. But there was something more behind. Were these to be treated as isolated problems? or were they to be taken, above all, in their bearing upon the larger issue, already familiar in the sphere both of theory and of practice? That was the question which both philosopher and statesman were henceforth bound to answer. And by the answer which they gave to it, the soundness of their work, its influence for good or for evil upon their own time and the future, must necessarily be judged.

It will be seen that the period before us, from the middle of the seventeenth to the latter end of the nineteenth century, falls into two unequal halves: the one, roughly speaking, of a hundred and fifty, the other of less than a hundred years. During the first of these the issue is absolutely simple and clear-cut. It is the ceaseless struggle between the individualist and the corporate, or communalist, idea of the State; and it is virtually nothing else. During the second, the issue is complicated—at times, it may seem, darkened—in a hundred ways. There is the cross current of nationality, and there is the cross current of Socialism: not to speak of other issues which will disclose themselves, as we go further. All these new elements had to be set in their true light by the philosophers. They had to be drawn into the soul and substance, into the very life, of the State by the rulers, by the community as a whole. And while this twofold task was going forward, the old war between the corporate and the individualist ideals of the State was still waging; it had even taken a form more bitter than had ever been known before. In the sphere of theory it may have been fought and won by the end of the eighteenth century. In the order of action, which always lags behind that of theory, it is far from being decided yet.

It is just this, however, which gives so unique a significance to the period in question. Never, perhaps, has the main issue of man's political experience been presented so simply as during the earlier half of it; never has it been so strangely blended with other issues, so many and so vital, as in the later. A glance at the previous stages of the conflict, as they took shape in the speculative thought of the time, will set this beyond doubt. And nothing could enable us to see so clearly how the issue presented itself to those who, at the beginning of our period, were called upon to meet it.

In politics, as in all other fields of experience, philosophy begins with Greece. And the deepest genius which ever spent itself upon the subject is that of Plato. Yet the very keenness of civic life in Greece inevitably tended to blur the sharpness of the conflict between the community and the individual, as it presents itself to modern eyes. And at every page of the *Republic* we are driven to realise that what later thinkers have been forced to establish by reasoned proof—the 'priority,' and therefore the sovereignty, of the former—is assumed as self-evident by Plato. For good and for evil, the forces of the individual had not yet been fully let loose upon the world. And, though he foresaw their coming, it was thanks rather to the 'prophetic strain' in his nature than to the 'old experience' which time has brought to us. The problem was there for him, as it is for us; and it forms the background of all his reasonings and all his visions concerning the corporate destiny of man. Its solution was clear as day both to his reason and his heart. But it forms the hidden foundation rather than the visible fabric of his argument. It is presupposed, rather than logically beaten out. What appears upon the surface is that the quest for which he has taken the field is the quest of Right; and that, by the most unquestioned instincts of his nature, the right life for the individual is to him conceivable only in the rightly ordered State.

Both lessons were destined to be of the first importance for the future welfare of mankind. Both—for the two are, in fact, inseparable—form the starting-point of all that is most fruitful alike in the thought and in the practical endeavours of modern life. But for the ancient world they came too late. They were powerless to stem the tide of disintegration which, as Plato himself seems to have divined, was already threatening to sweep over Greece; while the genius of Rome was too little speculative—her mission, perhaps, too entirely alien—to allow of her gathering in the harvest which Plato left upon the field.

There are, however, two directions in which Rome did yeoman's service to the cause: by the creation and administration of her law; and by the Stoic conception—which, Greek in origin, found a second birth among the nobler spirits of the Empire—of the natural brotherhood of mankind. The latter, at least in its ultimate developments, was deeply influenced by Christianity. And both alike were inseparably bound up with the needs and cravings of an Empire which embraced the whole civilised world: a world, let it not be forgotten, of which a large part had been called out of barbarism by Rome herself.

In each of these services there is one point that calls for comment. Rome not only bequeathed to the world a code of Law which, save for our own country, is still accepted in all essentials by the whole of western Europe. She may also claim, and claim with justice, to have created the very idea of Law, as it is understood by all civilised nations whatsoever. Hers was the first attempt, and it remains the most complete attempt, to build up a coherent system of rules for deciding the contentions that may arise between man and man, for repressing all forms of fraud and violence which may be committed against society at large. The Roman Law is the 'living voice of reason,' as no Law had ever been before and as many have thought that none has ever been again. Once more, it is Roman Law which has stamped upon the conscience of the world the idea of unwavering uniformity: the sense that Justice, if she is not to belie her name, must be the same always, everywhere and for all. At Athens, as Rousseau remarks more than once, the Law was always liable to be overridden by decrees, specially devised to meet individual cases or serve the end of momentary passions. Since Rome has spoken, though such expedients may often have been thought of and even practised, they have never been adopted without shame.

Even more important for our purpose was the contribution of Roman stoicism to the conception of Right. In its wider aspects, this explains itself. We have here the germs of that faith in humanity as a collective whole which, from Rousseau onwards, has left so deep a mark upon political speculation. We have also the raw material out of which the whole fabric of international Law has been laboriously built up. The significance of both facts can be seen at a glance. It will become yet more apparent in the later stages of our enquiry There is, however, one specific idea, closely connected with the foregoing, which played a strangely large part in the political thought of the seventeenth and eighteenth centuries, and which, in a more valid form, will never, it may be hoped, lose its hold upon the reason and conscience of mankind. This is the idea of 'natural law,' which was handed on by the Stoics to the Roman jurists and, from them, became part of the common heritage of the world.

If natural law be conceived as a code of equity, a ready-made *Whole Duty of Man*, which, existing before all positive Law, embodies itself more or less completely in the positive Law of all peoples, yet is no more than faintly reflected in any one of them; if it be conceived as a code which is spontaneously recognised by all men, not idiots or hardened criminals, of all ages and all nations, as a code therefore which carries its own sanction and exacts its own obedience: then it may freely be admitted that such a conception is not only incapable of proof, but even contrary to all we know of human nature and development. That is the fatal flaw which runs, for instance, through all the reasonings of Grotius and of Locke. But if it be meant that a rudimentary sense of justice has been in man from the beginning; that all positive Law is at once the result of this and the cause of its further development; that the history of human society is the history of a constant interplay between man's inner sense of justice and the outward institutions in which it has progressively been embodied: then we have hold of a clue which will guide us through all the startling discrepancies between the 'justice' of one age and the 'justice' of another, between the Law of one community and the Law of another. We have also an assurance that, given good will and courage, the world, in this the most vital of all issues, will still continue to go forward in the future as it has done in the past; that the 'natural law'—that is the enlightened conscience, or even the average conscience—of the future may ultimately be as much above that of the present as that of the present is above the rude instinct which redeemed and purified the most primitive past.

The reign of Law, the idea of world-wide brotherhood—these were the bequests of Rome to the world which rose out of her ashes. Beyond this, her direct service to the corporate life of man can hardly claim to go. Her universal empire was a thing so unique, so utterly remote from all the world has seen or is likely to see again, that, apart from Law and administration, her history has little to offer for the practical guidance of mankind. In philosophy, with the one reservation mentioned, her record is a blank. It was only with the coming of the Barbarians that Europe once more woke to life.

On the side of speculative thought, indeed, there was little benefit from the change; and throughout the middle ages philosophy, for all deeper and wider issues, lay under a blight. But for the moment the practical side of the problem was far the more important. And never was there a time when new ideas were thrown into the common stock in greater plenty, or when new blood was employed with nobler energy to carry them into act. Saint-Simon was right in describing the middle ages as the seed-plot of modern Europe.

The first-fruits of the new order are to be seen in the coming, if we cannot yet say the triumph, of nationality. The old world, it may roughly be said, had divided its allegiance between the City State of the Greek communities and the vast conglomerate of such empires as Persia and Rome. The new world is built essentially upon the principle of nationality. And it is with the Barbarian invasions that this principle first began to take shape. Had the 'dark ages' left no other legacy, this alone would have sufficed to change the face of Europe.

The distinction between the Nation on the one hand and the City or the Empire on the other is, in the first instance, one of size. But other, and more searching, differences inevitably result. The Empire, as known to the ancient world, was, except in the more favoured municipalities of the Roman rule, entirely lacking in freedom; its existence was the very negation of all corporate life. The City on the other hand, under anything like favourable conditions, had an intensity of corporate life such as has nowhere else been even distantly approached. But this advantage was dearly bought by that equal intensity of blood feuds, political and personal, which Thucydides has recorded for all time. From these feuds the Nation, in the early stages of its growth, was wholly free; and even in later ages they have seldom, if ever, reached the deadliness of those known to the Greek communities or the cities of medieval Italy. And, given favourable circumstances, the Nation has inspired its members with a corporate purpose which, though far less keen than that of the City, is a thing different not only in degree, but in kind, from anything to be found in the Empires of the ancient world.

Nationality may have entered the common life of Europe with the Barbarian invaders. But centuries passed before it can be said either to have firmly rooted itself, or to have taken the shape which we now commonly associate with the name. For many centuries it is rather the tribe than the nation with which history has to deal. For many more, dynastic prejudices, the most irrational of all that have befooled man in the struggle to work out his own destiny, came in to thwart and shackle its natural growth at every turn. Nevertheless, it is from the fourth or fifth century that its origin must be dated. It is to the Teutonic tribes, which then broke their way into the Roman Empire, that its first dim appearance, as the shaping principle of European polity, is due.

Much the same must be said of Christianity, whose decisive entry into the world's drama must be traced to the same period. It was only when accepted by the Barbarians that it began to bear the fruit to which the apostle of the Gentiles had looked forward. And the one thing to regret is that it should have reached them not in the shape in which he preached it, but organised, secularised and largely sterilised by three centuries of Roman discipline and Roman sacerdotalism. This, however, was inevitable. And in the face of these drawbacks, the wonder is not that the Gospel should have borne so little fruit, but that it should have borne so much. As a civilising and purifying influence, as a power which works not only for personal righteousness but also for civic justice, it would be hard, even when all abatements have been made, to overestimate the debt which the world owes to Christianity. And the longer the time that passes, the more completely the spirit is liberated from the dead hand of the letter, the greater assuredly does that debt become.

During the first ten centuries, no doubt, much evil blended with the good which these new influences brought. The young nations were turbulent and plunged in endless wars among themselves and with their neighbours. The first effect of Christianity was to bring not peace, but a sword, to set up an irreconcilable feud between the spiritual and the civil power, between the Church and the State. Both results were inevitable; for neither of them was any remedy possible except from experience and the healing work of time. And, not unnaturally, this was a longer process with the issue of principle than with the purely natural, and therefore largely accidental, hostility of tribe to tribe or of nation to nation. Hence it was that the whole political thought of the middle ages turned round the controversy between Church and State. And, once it was admitted that the Church alone stood for the spiritual power, that controversy could end in no other way than in the logical, if not the material, triumph of the Church. Dante no doubt, with a few others, had the vision to recognise that the State also—or rather, the ideal State as represented by the Empire—is entitled to rank as a spiritual power. But even they were forced to admit that such a claim was to be put forward only with safeguards and reservations: that there was 'a certain sense' in which the supreme spiritual power—and, with it, the ultimate sovereignty—rested solely with the Church.[1]

Far more important than this controversy—which, at any rate in its extreme form, was only temporary, and which by the end of the fourteenth century had in fact burned itself to ashes—is the inward change which Christianity wrought upon men's minds: the overwhelming value, a value hitherto not even dreamed of, which it gave to the individual soul. Morally speaking, this is the greatest of all the services which it has conferred upon the world. But no mistake could be graver than to suppose that such a change either was, or could be, confined to the sphere of personal conduct. It has, in fact, transformed our view of life on almost every side. And there is no side where its influence has been stronger or deeper than in that of politics: than in our whole conception of the relation between the individual and the State.

[1] 'Quae quidem veritas [Monarchae auctoritatem a Deo dependere immediate] non sic stricte recipienda est ut Romanus Princeps *in aliquo* Romano Pontifici non subjaceat, cum mortalis ista felicitas *quodam modo* ad immortalem felicitatem ordinatur' (*De Monarchia*, iii.).

It was only with the Reformation, with the claim to the right of private judgement triumphantly asserted by the Reformation, that the spirit of Christianity, on this side, was definitely set free. Hence it is that the Reformation opens a new page in the political life of Europe. It does so in practical affairs; it does so also, though this was a later development, in the field of theory.

To bring about a political revolution was the last thing the Reformers desired. It was, however, among the first results of their teaching. They had thrown a gospel of liberty before an oppressed multitude, and how could they hope to limit its action to the world of the unseen and the divine? Might they not have foreseen that it would at once be applied to the world of human relations? above all, to a political and social order which treated the common herd of men as little better than the beasts which seemed to have been framed expressly to inflict injustice and suffering upon them? The one remedy the Reformers could suggest was to transfer to the civil magistrate, as the Lord's anointed, as much as might be of the mysterious sanctity which they had roughly torn from the Vicar of Christ. And this, though it opens a curious chapter in what may be called by courtesy political theory, was in no way calculated to calm men who were smarting under the sense of intolerable wrong. The Peasants' War and the fleeting reign of the Anabaptists at Münster are among the saddest episodes of history. None the less so, because the latter at any rate was marred by wild extravagances of fanaticism and wrong-doing.

These were perhaps no more than passing symptoms of the change which had come over the temper of men's minds. But before sixty years were out, they were followed in our own country by events which have left a lasting mark upon the political destinies of Europe. No sooner had Elizabeth, the last great figure of the old order, passed away than the Commons, themselves borne forward on a fresh wave of the Protestant revolution, began to demand a part in the government of the country which they had never claimed before. And within forty years they had swept all rival claimants, once the sole rulers of the nation, from the board. They seemed, no doubt, to have lost all for which they had striven when, twenty years later, the old order was summarily restored; and this was the judgement even of so wise an observer as Spinoza.[1] But appearances were a mockery. And from the moment of the Restoration, still more from that of the Revolution, the Commons began to take back piecemeal all that they had, for the instant, been forced to surrender to the Crown. And in this matter England set the model which sooner or later all Europe, with more or less

[1] *Tractatus Theologico-politicus*, xviii. 33-34 (1670).

of consistency, was to follow. Had that not been the case, the events referred to would have had no claim to be mentioned in this place. As it is, they are of typical significance.

The spiritual revolution which wrought these practical changes could not be expected to leave the field of political theory entirely untouched. And even before the end of the sixteenth century it was clear that, in this field also, a new era was about to open. The *Contr'un* of La Boëtie, the *Vindiciae contra tyrannos* of Languet—in a more general sense, the works of Rabelais and Montaigne—are all so many proofs that the individualist leaven, the natural outcome of the Reformation, was beginning to work. It is perhaps yet more significant that the doctrine, which was to be the battle-horse of the individualists, was already beginning to take challengeable shape. All the instincts of Hooker lay in the opposite direction: he was an Aristotelian, or he was nothing. Yet, in the midst of his subtle defence of Law as interpreted by tradition, he is unwary enough to slip in an argument which contains, if only in germ, the whole theory of Contract, and which a century later Locke, the starkest and most consistent of the champions of that theory, gleefully seized upon in support of his revolutionary plea: 'Laws human, of what kind soever, are available by consent.' Locke may have forced, perhaps not quite fairly, the meaning of these words. But it remains true that, when pressed to their logical conclusion, they point straight to the democratic form of government which Hooker would certainly have fought shy of, and even to the contractual theory upon which, during the next two centuries, all popular rights were commonly supposed to rest.

Once launched, the idea of Contract fairly took the world by storm. It not only won a wider popular acceptance than any speculative idea before or since, but, unlike all other such ideas, it was actually framed and shaped, not by the philosophers, but by the people. It was current coin among the men of action long before it was refined and minted afresh by the men of theory. It was an idol of the market-place long before it became an idol also of the lecture-room. What, we ask, was the secret of this extraordinary success? The answer is that the metaphor of Contract, once suggested, seemed to explain a great deal more than it actually does. It is of the essence of the State to combine freedom with restriction, law with liberty. But how to reconcile these two opposites? That has always been the chief problem for the theorist, as, on a lower plane, it has always been the chief test of the wisdom of the statesman. Now, the conception of Contract contains exactly the same apparent contradiction: on the one hand, perfect freedom to make it, or not to make it, in the first instance; on the other hand, an absolute obligation, enforced by outward penalties, to fulfil it, when once made. And directly it occurred to any one to put the two things together, to compare the remote, the unfamiliar idea of the State with a thing so simple, of such everyday experience, as the lease of a farm or a public-house, all difficulties seemed to vanish; the fortune of the analogy was made; and from that moment the belief that the State is founded on a contract between its members became an article of the Faith. The way, no doubt, especially in this country, was further smoothed by the prevailing habit of referring everything to the Old Testament: by the undoubted fact that the origin of the Jewish State is there traced to a covenant, or contract, between the chosen people and God. And at a moment when the discontent of the nation with its government was daily deepening, the doctrine that all government was, in the first instance, the result of a contract between the governor and the governed, as well as the still more fundamental doctrine that every Society is founded upon a contract between all its members, was far too useful a weapon of rebellion to be lightly thrown aside.

In this easy acceptance of a popular doctrine, one thing only was forgotten. This was that a contract is not possible, or indeed conceivable, except under the settled order of the State; that to assign the creation of the State itself to contract is therefore to assume the very thing which we are out to prove and to explain; that it is, in fact, a peculiarly flagrant instance of putting the cart before the horse.

The strange thing is that a doctrine which was tacitly assumed by the whole world should have had to wait for a century before its inspired theorist appeared. It is perhaps yet stranger that the first writer to formulate it in any detail should have perverted it to ends the direct contrary of those for which it was manifestly devised; that he should have forced a democratic theory into the service of autocracy. This, it need hardly be said, was the amazing feat of Hobbes; and in the whole history of philosophy there is none more ingenious—none, it must be added, more disconcerting—than his. That, however, was no more than a momentary diversion of the current. And with Spinoza and Locke, both of whom wrote in conscious hostility to the author of *Leviathan*, the stream once more resumed its natural course. Some seventy years after the publication of the *Essay on Civil Government* it was again diverted—this time, in a wholly different sense—by the genius of Rousseau. And with the appearance of the *Contrat social* the history of the doctrine of Contract, by a strange paradox, comes abruptly to an end.

The following chapters will offer a fuller discussion of these speculative matters. For the moment, the one thing needful is to fix our mind upon the unexampled readiness with which the doctrine of Contract was received. Whenever the dying creed of Divine Right was rejected, it would hardly be too much to say that the theory of Contract was at once accepted, as that which must inevitably take its place. To establish this, we must turn not so much to the jurists, from Grotius at one end of the period to Blackstone and the lawyers of the National Assembly at the other, as to those whose bent lay rather towards the beaten road of ordinary thought. As samples of these, we may take two men of great genius but little turn for abstract speculation: Dryden, that is, and Milton.

In a remarkable passage of *Absalom and Achitophel*, Dryden, half adopting and half confuting the arguments of the Country Party as to the relation between the 'subject' and the Government, speaks as follows:

> What shall we think? Can People give away
> Both for themselves and sons their native sway?
> Then are they left defenceless to the sword
> Of each unbounded, arbitrary Lord;
> And laws are vain by which we Right enjoy,
> If kings unquestioned can those laws destroy.
> Yet if the crowd be judge of fit and just
> And kings are only officers in trust,
> Then this resuming Covenant was declared
> When kings were made, or is for ever barred.[1]

And Milton, writing a generation earlier, is still more explicit. He applies the idea of Contract not only to the establishment of Government, but even—and this is far more important—to the very formation of Society. 'No man who knows aught can be so stupid to deny that all men naturally were born free . . . and that they lived so till, from the root of Adam's transgression, falling among themselves to do wrong and violence, . . . they agreed by common league to bind each other from mutual injury and jointly to defend themselves against any that gave disturbance or opposition to such agreement. Hence came cities, towns and commonwealths. And because no faith in all was found sufficiently binding, they saw it needful to ordain some authority that might restrain by force and punishment what was violated against peace and common Right. . . . When this would not serve, but that the law was either not executed or misapplied, they were constrained from that time, the only remedy left them, to put conditions and take oaths from all kings and magistrates, at their first instalment, to do impartial justice by law; who, upon those terms and no other, received

[1] *Absalom and Achitophel*, i. ll. 759-768 (1681).

allegiance from the people: that is to say, bond or covenant to obey them in execution of those laws which they, the people, had themselves made or assented to. And this ofttimes with express warning that, if the king or magistrate proved unfaithful to his trust, the people would be disengaged.' [1]

It is clear that the form of Contract which both writers had in view—the former with, and the latter without, qualification—is, in all essentials, the form subsequently expounded by Locke. That, indeed, is what was to be expected. The idea of Contract once given, the only natural application of it is that which turns it to purposes of democracy. To make it the charter of despotism was a freak which called for the sardonic ingenuity of Hobbes: nothing less would have served the purpose. And it is obvious that the democratic form of the theory must have been in the air before Hobbes could have thought of his sophistical distortion. Locke may have come after him in time; but the *Essay on Civil Government* is presupposed on every page of *De Cive* and *Leviathan*. All that Hobbes did was to turn the guns, which the enemy had painfully trained into position, against the enemy's own ranks.

The testimony of two such men as Milton and Dryden—neither of them a professed theorist, both of them keenly alive to the main currents of educated thought—is conclusive as to the prevalence, we may almost say the unquestioning acceptance, of the Contract theory, in one or other of its many forms, throughout the latter half of the seventeenth century.[2] And if further testimony

[1] *Tenure of Kings and Magistrates* (1649).

[2] A curious illustration of this statement is to be found in Bossuet's *Avertissements aux Protestants* (1689–91): 'Venons donc aux vrais auteurs du crime [le meurtre de Charles Ier]. C'est Cromwell et les Fanatiques. Je l'avoue. Mais de quelles maximes se servirent-ils pour faire entrer les peuples dans leurs sentiments? Quelles maximes voit-on encore dans leurs apologies? Dans celle de Midleton (*sic*) et dans cent autres libelles dont les Cromwellistes inondaient toute l'Europe. De quoi sont pleins tous ces livres et tous les actes publics et particuliers qu'on faisait alors que de la souveraineté absolue des peuples? de ces contrats primordiaux entre les peuples et les rois et toutes les autres maximes que M. Jurieu soutient encore après Bucanan (*sic*), que la Convention [de 1688] a suivies et où l'Eglise Anglicane se laisse entraîner malgré ses anciens décrets?' (*Avert.* v. § 62). The manner in which Bossuet mishandles the names of his British opponents does not say much for the thoroughness with which he had studied their writings. Who would recognise the author of *Paradise Lost* in 'Midleton'? It was an ill chance that led the Bishop to stumble over the name of a man still greater and still more famous than himself. His testimony to the point in question, however, is unimpeachable. The reference is to Milton's *Defensio pro populo Anglicano*, chaps. v., vi., vii.

—testimony drawn from a slightly different source—be wanted, it is supplied by the Act which dismissed James and cleared the ground for the choice of William and Mary in his stead. At that critical moment the Convention Parliament, casting about for grounds to justify its revolutionary action, was constrained to plead that, James having by his acts 'broken the original contract between king and people,' the throne was thereby rendered vacant. Other grounds are, no doubt, suggested: misgovernment, hostility to the national religion, and the rest. But the stronger those other grounds may be—and no one doubts that they were the grounds which actually determined the Revolution—the more impossible is it that 'breach of contract' should have been thrown into the same scale with them, unless Contract had been generally recognized as the foundation of all government and the breach of it by the sovereign as a crime worthy to be put side by side with the arbitrary suspension of laws and the infamies of the Bloody Assizes.

That the same acceptance of Contract, as the origin of all civil power, should be proclaimed two generations later in a book as little favourable to the popular cause as Blackstone's *Commentaries*, is only one more proof that the doctrine had now become an article of the faith.[1] And the less we think of the legal mind as a guide to speculative truth, the stronger that argument becomes. With Blackstone, we are within sight of the French Revolution; and the period with which we are immediately concerned is at an end.

The freedom of the individual soul, for all purposes and with no limitations, was asserted by Christianity. But the very vastness of the idea forbade that it should be conceived—much more, realised—otherwise than by stages and in fragments. The medieval Church did little more than drive it home, and that with countless restrictions and distortions, in the sphere of personal conduct. The Reformation, again most imperfectly and inconsistently, applied it to the field of doctrine and of worship. To work it out, again with many misconceptions and many extravagances, in the region of political practice and political theory was the task reserved for the French Revolution and the two centuries which preceded it. To correct those misconceptions and extravagances, to reconcile the claims of the 'individual' with those of the 'corporate' self, to show that the one cannot live without the other, that the full development of man's faculties is possible only in and through organised fellowship with other men: this was

[1] The first volume of the *Commentaries*, containing the passage in question, was published in 1765.

the mission of the two thinkers, Rousseau and Burke, who prepared or witnessed the Revolution. In a still fuller and wider sense, it was the mission not only of the thinkers, but of every civilised nation, whether in the old world or the new, throughout the century that followed And the end is not yet.

CHAPTER II

THE SOCIAL CONTRACT: HOBBES

THE Reformation was, in the first instance, a religious movement. But experience has shown—with a grain of speculative imagination, it might surely have been foreseen—that various political consequences, both speculative and practical, inevitably followed in its train. The main work of the Reformers—they themselves would have admitted it and gloried in it—was to lay a stress upon the individual responsibility of the Christian such as had never been laid before. The rebel leaders, Calvin excepted, may have thought of little beyond Church doctrine and Church government. But, once the principle was granted, no power on earth could limit its scope and application. And from the government of the Church, in particular, it was a short step to the government of the State. Two results—the one general, the other of a more special character—call for a few words of explanation.

The general result was to give a value to the individual citizen such as no other age had known. Hence, on the one hand, that sudden assertion of the Commons' claim to a determining voice in the government which has been already noticed; and on the other hand, the first appearance of individualism, as a reasoned theory of government, in the history of thought. Without the assumptions imposed by the Protestant revolution, the whole history of political theory from Hobbes to Godwin, indeed the whole history of philosophy from Des Cartes to Fichte, would have been inexplicable. We may go further and say, it would have been impossible.

The more special consequence is not so simple; but that does not make it the less real. So long as the medieval Church held sway over men's minds, it was possible, and even natural, that the State should leave the control of conduct for the most part in her hands. And the fact that the whole law not only of marriage, but even of testamentary disposition, was among the things so left is, of itself, enough to show how far the State was prepared to go in this direction. But the moment the ancient Church was either swept away or transformed out of all recognition, the question was bound to present itself: How are we to fill the gap which is left by the removal of the disciplinary powers of the Church? Is the State to step into the breach? or is this whole region—a region of vital importance both to the community and its several members—to be left purely to the individual conscience, restrained only by the terrors of the Law?

In the countries which remained faithful to the old religion, it is manifest that this question could not arise. In the Protestant countries, on the other hand, the difficulty was serious enough. On the whole, it may be said that those countries in which the Protestant feeling was strongest—Geneva and Scotland are the two typical examples—State and Church, more closely interwoven than they have ever been before or since in the history of Christendom, joined hands to tighten the discipline which in the old days had been wielded by the Church; and that the State, in this matter, acted mainly, though by no means solely, through the agency of the Church. Those countries on the contrary, which, like England, sought rather to transform the old system than to abolish it, after a half-hearted attempt to retain the Catholic discipline, were led by degrees to abandon all efforts at public control over the conduct of their members and to leave everything to the conscience of the individual, subject only to the forcible penalties of the Law.

And if this came to be more and more the practice of our own nation and of the organised institutions in which its life was constitutionally embodied, we must never forget that it came also to be more and more the theory of those smaller religious communities which, though cut off from the constitutional life of the nation, yet played a part altogether out of proportion to their size, or the social standing of their members, in moulding the national policy and building up the national conscience and ideals. As regards their own members, their discipline was commonly far stricter than that of the national Church. But it was enforced purely by moral suasion: by total or partial exclusion from communion with the rest of the body. And as time went on, even this weapon tended to fall more and more out of use. The Independents indeed, who did more than any other body to form opinion in this matter, were from the first shy of all outward interference with the liberty of their members and therefore more disposed than any other body to trust solely to the workings of the individual conscience. It is true that Milton, in his assault upon all State interference in such matters, is careful to reserve a right of excommunication to the Church. But it is clear that he is far more interested in the negative side of his argument than in the positive. It is equally clear that Erastus, in his assault upon the disciplinary powers of the Church, was far more concerned to overthrow the judgement-seat of the

Elders than to set up that of the civil magistrate. The argument of both writers, in fact, logically led to the abolition of all disciplinary power, ecclesiastical no less than civil.[1] And this, the natural consequence of the individualist principle, was the view which, on all sides, ultimately prevailed.

What were the effects of all this upon the theory of the State? The first and most obvious was to provide a seed-plot for individualism such as the most rebellious spirit of the old world could never have foreseen: an atmosphere under which it may fairly be said to have sprung unbidden from the soil. Under these conditions, the final triumph of the new theory was a mere question of time. And it is no accident that the first formal statement of it—embodied in Milton's republican pamphlets, embodied also, though under the most perverted form, in the opening arguments of *De Cive* and *Leviathan*—should have coincided with the throes of the Puritan Rebellion, or its final exposition with the fresh Protestant advance which followed on the revocation of the Edict of Nantes.

A theory, however, is no lifeless abstraction. If it be worth anything, it has consequences which stir the passions and give new power to the will. Individualism, in particular, was rich in practical results both for good and for evil. If on the one hand it deepened and widened the civic sense beyond all power of recognition, on the other hand it led to abuses and injustices which in the long run were bound to rouse the world to protest and revolt. A few words upon each side of the matter will suffice.

Until the sixteenth century, it may roughly be said that Europe, since the fall of the Roman Republic, had been content to be governed from above. And, so far as its rule was not intolerably oppressive, any government in possession was able fairly to count upon an indefinite continuance of its lease. But, with the Reformation, this comfortable reckoning was suddenly thrown out. Once cast himself athwart the religious convictions of any large class among his subjects, and the ruler, whether Catholic or Protestant, was henceforth liable to find himself face to face with armed resistance, with rebellion, or even with the prison and the scaffold. The history of England, France and Scotland, to say nothing of Geneva and the United Provinces, during the latter

[1] See Milton, *Treatise of Civil Power in Ecclesiastical Causes* (1659), and Erastus, *Quaestio utrum Excommunicatio sit ex divino mandato an excogitata sit ab hominibus* (1589). It may be observed that Erastus himself was no Erastian. His whole argument turns on the plea that it is an iniquity to rob a man of the aid of religion at the very moment when, *ex hypothesi*, he stands most in need of it. An English translation of his pamphlet was published in 1659. Milton describes himself as 'asserting the truth of Scripture against Erastus.'

half of the century is witness to the truth of this assertion. Still more so is the history of England during the whole of the century which followed. Nor can it be forgotten that the Thirty Years' War, one of the bloodiest upon record, had its rise in a rebellion which religious as well as racial differences—and both are equally germane to our argument—had conspired to bring about.

But this is not all. Behind all such specific grievances there lay, consciously or unconsciously, a growing instinct that the government is made for the people, not the people for the government; and even, though this was a more lingering process, that the only way of giving practical reality to such a maxim is to secure to the people some voice at least in the management of what, after all, is their own immediate concern. Nor was it merely a matter of expediency. The more men thought over these things, the more they were driven to the conviction that it was also a question of Right; that the State could have no powers save those which were conferred upon it by its members; and consequently that every individual member had an inherent claim—no less, if also no more, than any other member—to a share in its control. This conviction was, no doubt, in part due to the extreme difficulty of conceiving the original foundation of society as the result of anything but universal consent: a difficulty which goes far to account for the ultimate triumph of the theory of Contract. But it was still more the direct result of that faith in the indefeasible worth of the individual soul, in the equality of all men before God, which lay at the root of Christianity and which had for the first time come to a full consciousness of itself with the Reformation.

But, whatever the cause of the conviction, the result of it was to make a complete revolution in the common conception of the State. No man who held such a conviction could be content with a State in which the Government alone was active and the rest of the community a mere passive instrument in its hands. He could be satisfied with nothing short of a State in which the Government, not only in name but in deed, was responsible to the community; in which the community as a whole determined the course which the Government should take. In other words, the ideal was no longer, if indeed it had ever been, government from above; henceforth it was government, at least as to the broad outlines of policy, by the community at large. It was, in some measure at any rate, a return to the ideal of the Republics of antiquity: the ideal in the strength of which every citizen felt himself to be a living and active part of the being of the State. It was to replace passive obedience by active co-operation; to substitute a live organism for a cunningly devised machine. Doubtless, it was generations before such a conviction could work itself out to a clear consciousness of all that lay within it. But the history of our own country, still more that of the Revolution in France, shows that this was the goal towards which it ultimately led.

All this was a good, if not unmixed, at least as nearly so as it is possible for human things to be. But there is another side to the picture which it is impossible to overlook. The very virtues of such a theory lent themselves but too readily to perversion. The rights of the individual were pampered, his duties left absolutely out of sight. On the other hand, the rights and powers, to say nothing of the duties, of the State were assiduously starved. And this led to two kinds of evil which, in the long run, made it clear that the whole theory must be revised.

On the one hand, as Rousseau was the first to point out, to give unlimited power to the individual is always to establish the mastery of the strong over the weak, of the rich over the poor. The State is there, if not to prevent these inequalities, at least to keep them within bounds. And if, so far from checking them, it gives them sanction and encouragement, then it is false to the trust which has been committed to its hands.

On the other hand, while enlarging the borders of the State, as it does by increasing the number of voters, the individualist theory inevitably tends to limit and to beggar its scope. It is of the essence of that theory that the State has no powers beyond those explicitly entrusted to it from the beginning. And to restrict those powers within the narrowest possible limits has always, alike in theory and in practice, been the aim of those who start from individualist assumptions. The result is that, wherever those assumptions have prevailed, the State has been jealously stripped of all moral functions and left with no duty beyond that of preventing its members from picking each other's pockets and flying at each other's throats. From Locke to Beccaria, from Beccaria to Paine, from Paine to those who resisted the Income Tax, the Factory Laws, or the Old Age Pensions Act, this has been the invariable story. And if such be the only duty of the State, it is hard to see why either Poor Law or Education Expenses should appear upon the national budget; why the 'duty' of national defence should be anything more than a mischievous and costly prejudice; why, in short, when he has once paid his taxes—and that on the smallest scale conceivable—the individual should ever trouble himself further with what are pompously called matters of national concern. The truth is that, upon these premisses, both 'national honour' and 'social justice' are the vainest of delusions; and 'anarchy *plus* a policeman' is, as Carlyle saw, the only possible definition of the political ideal.

With these considerations in view, let us now turn to watch

the theorists at work, and observe the different purposes which the twofold assumption of an original state of nature and of a Contract, as the only possible door of escape from it, was successively made to serve.

The former of these two assumptions, under the familiar name of the golden age, is probably as old as the world. The latter, the social Contract, goes back at least as far as Plato, and possibly much farther. Plato, however, for the best of reasons, does little more than trifle with the notion. Epicurus has sometimes been credited with its adoption; but this would seem to put much more into his words than they can fairly be made to hold. And it was not until the Reformation and the strong bias towards individualism implanted by the Reformation that the hour of Contract can be said to have fully struck, that it can fairly be reckoned to have passed into the common currency of political thought. Even then, a century had to pass before it was formulated in any definite shape. It flits, as we have already seen, across the pages of Hooker. It reappears, but under the strangely different shape of a contract between already existing minor corporations, in the forgotten work of Althusius. And Grotius pays at least a passing tribute to it in the opening paragraphs of that learned medley,[1] *De Iure Belli et Pacis,* which, however valuable as a first attempt to lay the foundations of International Law—and even here it is vitiated by a perpetual confusion between fact and Right—is, for all speculative purposes, a nest of sophistries and contradictions.[2]

By a strange irony, it was reserved for the deadliest enemy of individualism to give the first formal statement of the theory upon which, in the heyday of its power, individualism was universally held to rest.[3] The whole work of Hobbes breathes the bitterest hatred not only of individualism as a theory, but even of those

[1] The work of Althusius, *Politica methodice digesta,* was published in 1603; that of Grotius, prompted by the horrors of the Thirty Years' War, in 1625.

[2] As, however, in the later part of the book, Grotius—it is sad to say that Locke follows him—accepts the 'right of conquest' and even the 'right of slavery' as valid foundations of civil power, it is clear that the idea of a free contract, as the foundation of all civil society, had taken no very deep hold upon his mind. See the unanswerable criticisms of Rousseau.

[3] The political theory of Hobbes is to be found in *De Cive* (1642) and *Leviathan* (1651). The latter, the English version, is the fuller and, if only on account of its style, by far the more important. He returned to the charge towards the end of his life in *Behemoth* (1679), a violent assault upon the political theory and the political practice of the now vanquished Puritans.

elementary rights which none but the most backward nations now deny to the individual in practice. Yet this preposterous system is itself based, consciously or unconsciously, on assumptions representing an extreme form of individualism: an individualism more uncompromising than that of Locke himself. And it rests upon the idea of Contract, as the only possible foundation of the civil state. Could anything prove more conclusively the extent to which the theory of Contract had taken hold upon men's minds? the enormous weight of resistance upon which any man who assailed the individualist scheme of politics must steel himself to reckon?

Hobbes was not wanting in courage for the task. Still less was he wanting in ingenuity. With uncanny skill he turns one part of the theory against the other, and avails himself of the premisses which all the world accepted to destroy the conclusion which eager spirits were coming more and more confidently to draw from them. Nothing could have been more baffling to his contemporaries, nothing more fascinating to readers of the present day. The latter have too often allowed the brilliance of his method to blind them to the inconsequence as well as the utter unsoundness of his argument. The former, so far as can be gathered from the evidence, fell into exactly the opposite mistake. In their bewilderment at the methods employed, they failed to recognise either the force of the blow which had been dealt by the audacious writer, or the genius of the man who dealt it. Locke, who thought it worth while to write a full-dress refutation of Filmer, never so much as mentions the name, and contents himself with two or three scornful allusions to the far more damaging assault, of Hobbes. And as for the champions of divine right, they preferred to lose their cause in the strength of Charles and Filmer, rather than gain it with the aid of artillery forged in the factory of the Devil.

The first thing to strike us in the argument of *Leviathan* is its preternatural ingenuity. The next is its amazing boldness and simplicity. After a long preface [1]—which, at first sight, may appear irrelevant, but which is soon seen to serve the useful purpose of pouring scorn on all the spiritual elements commonly attributed to man's being—we find ourselves suddenly face to face with a lurid picture of the 'natural condition of mankind': that is, of the state of nature. To most men, and not least to those of the seventeenth century, the state of nature is a state of innocence and, above all, a state of peace. To Hobbes, on the contrary, it is a state of war: a 'war of all against all,' a war in which each was as a ravening beast to his fellows: *homo homini lupus*. It was there-

[1] *Leviathan*, chaps. i.-xii.

fore a state in which 'nothing could be unjust'; in which the very 'notions of right and wrong, justice and injustice, could have no place'; in which, as must always be the case in a state of war, 'force and fraud were the two cardinal virtues.' In one word, it was a state of which the governing law was the law of the sword.[1]

At this point of his argument, however, Hobbes suddenly bethinks himself of another Law, a law of a very different, indeed directly opposite, character: that 'eternal and immutable law,' the law of nature; which, just because it is the law of nature, just because it is eternal and immutable, must, as he gravely assures us, have prevailed even in the unpromising state of things just described as the state of nature. This Law Hobbes, more generous by half than Moses, lays out into fifteen commandments; but, for all the purposes of his argument, he might well have stopped short with the first three. The first of these is, 'that men seek peace and ensue it'; the second, 'that men are obliged to transfer to another such rights as, being retained, hinder the peace of mankind'; and the third, 'that men perform their covenants made.'[2] Upon these three commandments, reinforced by the purely natural craving to escape from the 'force and fraud' of his neighbours, hang all the subsequent actions of man as a 'political animal.'

The only doubt left in the mind of the reader is, how such a Law can possibly have run in a world of which the cardinal virtues are deliberately stated to be force and fraud: how a 'state of nature,' in which 'the very notions of right and wrong, of justice and injustice,' are unknown, can possibly have been regulated by a 'law of nature' which, in the spirit—nay, in the very words—of the Gospel, lays down the commandment: *Do as ye would be done by*. For the moment, however, this difficulty may be left over; because, for the moment, Hobbes, in full cry after his original argument, has little time to spare for the new one; because, for the moment, he is much more concerned to prove that it is the interest, than that it is the duty, of man to surrender the natural for the civil state. In truth, for reasons that will appear in the sequel, it is not until civil society and Government are once established that the question of obligation, or duty, becomes in his eyes a burning question. For the first foundation of both he relies—mainly, if not solely—upon motives of expediency. And if he brings in the more compulsive motive at this stage of his argument, it is merely to give fair warning of what he has in store.

Hence it comes that, after a digression of two long chapters

[1] *Leviathan*, chap. xiii. [2] *Ib.* chaps. xiv., xv.

in exposition of the 'law of nature,' Hobbes takes up the thread of his former argument for all the world as though it had never been broken. Given such a state of things as prevailed under the law of the sword, what wonder, he asks, that man found his lot utterly beyond bearing? his soul swept by 'continual fear and danger of violent death'? his life 'solitary, poor, nasty, brutish and short'?

He would have been mad indeed, if he had not cast about for some door of escape from such a nightmare of wretchedness and terror; stupid indeed, if he had not recognised that the sole hope of escape lay in some common understanding with his fellow-sufferers, in some bargain with those who had as much reason for being in fear of him as he of them. A contract or covenant, in short, was the only conceivable means of putting an end to his misery. And that contract must be binding in deed, as well as word; or the misery would be left precisely as it was before.[1]

That being the case, it is manifest, we are told, that force and the fear which force inspires are the only possible means of riveting the contract, the one certain method of 'tying men to the performance of their covenant.' For 'covenants without the sword,' as we learn in a memorable phrase, 'are but words and breath, and of no strength to secure any man at all.'[2]

Accordingly, the first thing men had to do was to hand over all their individual rights and powers to 'some one man or assembly of men,' who should henceforth have the sole right and the sole power to act on their behalf: who should be trusted with the whole force of the community, as the sole means of coercing the disobedient and the sole means therefore of securing the peace and happiness of the community as a whole. The government thus set up must have absolute power, or sovereignty, over the actions of the governed; and the latter, by their own act, have lost not only the power, but even the right, to question or resist.[3]

More than this. Since action is largely determined by thought, the Government has the right, and any Government which knows its duty will take the power, to control all available avenues of thought. If the thing were possible—and Hobbes, a martyr to truth, admits that it is not[4]—it would, on this showing, have the still more precious right of controlling thought itself. Failing that, the least it can do is to make itself master, and sole master, of all the outward machinery by which the thoughts of men are influenced or directed; to suffer nothing to be publicly taught which has not been stamped with its own sanction, and no man

[1] *Leviathan*, chap. xvii.
[2] *Ib.* chaps. xvii., xviii.
[3] *Ib.* chaps. xvii., xviii.
[4] *Ib.* chap. xlvi.

to teach or preach who has not been at least tacitly authorised, and may not in case of need be summarily silenced, by itself.[1]

In all this, the sole purpose of government should be to stifle such doctrines as challenge the absolute sovereignty of the constituted authority, whether in the hands of 'one man, or one assembly of men,' and to foster, or rather actively to propagate, such doctrines as assert this sovereignty without hesitation and without limit. And this, among religious, no less than among secular, teachers. Otherwise, the whole fabric, so laboriously built up, will first be slowly undermined by seditious doctrine, often masquerading under the name of religion; and then, on the first chance offered, summarily blown to pieces. The toil of ages will be undone in an instant. And man will reel back into the savagery to which he was naturally born.

Thus, alike in matters of thought and of action, alike in theory and in practice, the sovereignty of the ruler is absolute, or it is nothing: absolute in its control of all public utterance and teaching; absolute in its power over the life and property of the subject. And if any murmurs are raised against conclusions so startling, Hobbes is ready with an answer which is as conclusive on the one side as on the other; which neither the champions of free thought, nor the champions of life and property, can, in his view, either challenge or refute. Such control, he replies, was conceded at the moment when sovereignty was granted; it is implied in the very act by which the State was called to life. It is therefore impossible for the subject to turn round at any later moment and quarrel with the inevitable consequences of the step which he, or his forefathers for him, deliberately took. Nor, however real may be his grievance, however inequitable the act by which he suffers, has he the smallest right to denounce it as either unlawful or unjust. As applied to any act of the ruler, such complaints are the grossest of contradictions: for every order of the ruler, however contrary to the Law of God and nature, must be accepted, simply because it *is* his order, as perfectly lawful and just. He has a right to the property of his subjects; because, if his sword were removed, there would be no such thing as property. He has a right, if so he wills it, to their lives; because, if his control were withdrawn, no life would be worth a moment's purchase: man's life—not one, but all men's—would once more be 'as cheap as beast's.'

Such, with the exception of the one point which has been held over for subsequent discussion, is an outline of all that is essential in the theory of Hobbes. Such is 'the generation of that great Leviathan—or rather, to speak more reverently, of that mortal god, to which, under the immortal God, we owe our peace and

[1] *Leviathan*, chaps. xviii., xxiii., xlii.

defence.'[1] It is manifestly, as the author himself never wearies of insisting, a theory of fear: an argument which, from foundation to coping-stone, is built upon the terror of the sword.[2] It is the terror of promiscuous rapine and slaughter which in the first instance impels men to submit themselves to the power of 'one man, or one assembly of men.' It is the fear of sinking back into that state of anarchy which impels them, in the face of a thousand 'incommodities,' to uphold the tyranny which their forefathers, under stress of dire necessity, had the wisdom and courage to set up.

The argument is so deep-reaching that, in fairness to the author, it must be stated in his own memorable words. After running over the 'twelve points' of sovereignty—they may all be summed up in the one phrase, *power arbitrary and unlimited*—Hobbes, with refreshing courage, turns round upon the opponent—it might be Vane, or it might be Milton—waiting ready for his spring. 'But a man may here object that the condition of subjects is very miserable, as being obnoxious to the lusts and other irregular passions of him, or them, that have so unlimited a power in their hands: . . not considering that the state of man can never be without some incommodity or other; and that the greatest that in any form of government can possibly happen to the people in general is scarce sensible in respect of the miseries and horrible calamities that accompany a civil war or that dissolute condition of masterless men, without subjection to laws and a coercive power to tie their hands from rapine and revenge.'[3]

This is the last word of Hobbes: his unfailing answer to every fresh protest of the adversary; a summary of the plea with which, as each outrageous consequence follows upon the other, his initial dilemma—either slavery or anarchy—is buttressed up. What, then, is the validity of that dilemma? How far does the theory which it embodies square with the facts? And how far is it consistent with itself?

A state of nature, a contract, a state of slavery, as at once the inevitable outcome and the only possible sanction of the contract: these are the three terms to which the whole argument is manifestly to be reduced. Let us take each of them in turn.

The idea of a state of nature has been a source of much merriment to historical rigorists. But much of their ridicule has been strangely beside the mark. The assumption that a state of nature—that is, a state without either settled society or government—ever existed has, of course, no historical foundation. It cannot be disproved; but neither can it be proved. And the burden of proof is evidently thrown upon those who go bail for its reality. That,

[1] *Leviathan*, chap. xvii. [2] *Ib.* chaps. xiv., xv., xviii.
[3] *Ib.* chap. xviii.

however, is not enough to bar out its use for the mere purposes of argument. And in so far as the idea of a state of nature has been employed to indicate not a historical reality, but the logical opposite to any recorded or conceivable form of the civil state, in so far as it stands not for a historical fact but for a purely speculative hypothesis, it is obvious that all criticism based upon historical grounds is entirely off the point. Even if it were far more certain than it is that a state of nature never existed in fact, the philosopher would still be entitled to use the idea for the sake of defining more exactly, by means of contraries, what is the true nature of the civil state.

No doubt, most, if not all, of those who professed to speak of the state of nature as a pure hypothesis were at least half inclined to believe that it was also a historical reality. The man who begins by treating the problem of political philosophy as, in the first instance, a question of origins has, in fact, virtually committed himself to this solution of it, and to none other. For to talk of the 'origin of civil society' is, strictly speaking, to imply that it sprang from a state of things which was not 'civil'; and that is the very definition of the 'state of nature.' This, however, is by no means an end of the matter. And to satisfy ourselves whether the man who does this is indeed the victim of his own hypothesis, we have only to ask ourselves whether any subsequent link of his argument depends upon the historical reality of the assumption, or no. If it does, then the whole chain of his argument is, so far, vitiated. If it does not, then we are once more thrown back upon tests of a purely speculative character. We have merely to ask: Is this theory, as a theory, a satisfactory explanation of the facts of political experience and of the implications which those facts, when duly sifted, can be proved to carry with them? or is it not? We may indeed have other grounds for supposing that a given writer did, in fact, believe in the historical reality of a state of nature. But, if this belief has no effect upon the subsequent march of his argument; if, on a fair examination, it can be shown that he does in truth employ the idea for purely speculative purposes; then the error is of no practical importance. It is by his argument that he must be judged, and by that alone.

Now the truth is that, judged by that test, several of the writers in question escape virtually unscathed. Spinoza and Rousseau, for instance, both believed, it is probable, in the reality of the state of nature. But it would be hard to show that the general tenor of their argument is, in the smallest degree, affected by the fact. Strike off, in each case, the first link of the theory, and the rest of the chain remains unshaken and untouched. The remainder of the argument is not vitiated, because it in no way depends upon the preface by which it is introduced. In neither case is the state of nature more than a picturesque frontispiece. It forms no integral part of the theory which follows And one reason for this is that both writers—Rousseau, indeed, even more markedly than Spinoza—are wise enough to tell us uncommonly little of what the state of nature was.

With Locke, no doubt, we are on different ground. His picture of the state of nature is only too full and definite. And in one point, if in no other, the rest of his theory depends absolutely upon the assumption that it is taken from the life. That point is his conception of natural law as a code accepted by the conscience of all men in the state of nature and providing a sanction for the contract by which that state was eventually swept away to make room for the civil state. This conception, in fact, is made to serve a triple purpose. It accounts for the continuance—it would hardly be too much to say, the very existence of the state of nature. It furnishes that sanction for the Contract which all other forms of the theory so conspicuously lacked. And it provides a standard by which the positive laws of all civil communities may be judged and on the model of which they may, if necessary, be reformed.[1] So far as the coherence of the theory goes, all this is purely to the good. But it manifestly assumes the state of nature, as so conceived, to have been a historical reality. And as there are no historical grounds for believing this, it is clear that the weapon with which Locke thought to slay the enemy is turned with fatal effect against himself.

But if this consideration is damaging to Locke, much more so is it to Hobbes. If there is one writer above all others who pins his faith to the reality of the state of nature, to the authenticity of the facts which he records about it, it is the author of *Leviathan*. The whole form which he gives to the Contract, the whole force of the reasoning which he builds upon it, depends upon the assumption that the state of nature was a terrible reality; that it was a state so 'brutish' that nothing worse is either possible or conceivable; that no price, not even that of unredeemed slavery, is too great to pay for the assurance that the barrier which a strong Government, and that alone, has set up against a possible renewal of these evils shall never be thrown down. Hence at every fresh turn of the argument, at each fresh revolt of the reader against the intolerable consequences which follow, Hobbes is at once ready

[1] We are entitled to add, though on this point there is a strange vacillation, that it also leaves the door open for a subsequent abrogation of the Contract: an eventual return, if the misconduct of the ruler so requires, to the state of 'good will, mutual assistance and preservation,' which is Locke's definition of the state of nature (see *Civil Government*, ii. §§ 19, 205, 211, 212).

with the retort: Either this, or a return to the miseries of ' nature ': in other words, either slavery or death. What force would be left in this dilemma, if the ' state of nature ' were a mere hypothesis, a pure freak of the imagination? How could the author have made use of it, unless he had accepted the ' war of all against all ' as a fact of the same order as the battle of Naseby, or the execution of Charles I.? And how much is left of his argument, when the historical reality of the initial assumption is given up? There is no other writer who is so deeply committed to the historical reality of that assumption; no other writer, accordingly, to whom the obvious impossibility of proving it is so fatal.

But, true though this may be, it is also true that all the other writers who dabbled in the idea of Contract are, in a more or less degree, tarred with the same brush; that they are all more or less caught in the maze of unreality and artificiality in which Hobbes had allowed himself to be ensnared. Even those who sat most loosely to that idea and to the whole train of thought inseparably connected with it were, at least partially, distracted from the real question: What are the conditions which must be realised before the life of the State can be set on a sound basis? They were, at least partially, diverted to the false question—a question probably insoluble and certainly irrelevant: What was the historical origin of the State? The ill effects of this may be traced even in Spinoza, in whom the idea of Contract, implied in the *Tractatus Politicus* and explicitly accepted in the *Tractatus Theologico-politicus*, is an obvious excrescence. They may be traced still more clearly in Rousseau, who was throughout hampered by assumptions which he had taken on trust from Hobbes and Locke, but which the whole tenor of his subsequent reflection manifestly impelled him to reject. They are to be traced most clearly of all in Locke, whose whole argument is vitiated by the conviction that the state of nature, as governed by a supposed ' law of nature,' is at once the original, and the eternal ideal, of man's existence; and that the more closely the civil state approaches to the state of nature, the better it will be. But, once more, no one of these writers, not even Locke, is pledged so deeply to these unproved assumptions, the state of nature and the Contract, no one of them has suffered from them so heavily, as Hobbes.

Having cleared this stumbling-block from the threshold, we are now free to return to the main thread of Hobbes' argument, and once more to ask ourselves: How far does it account for the facts, how far does it satisfy the requirements, of man's political existence? how far, as an argument, does it form a consistent whole?

That argument, as we have seen, may be summed up in the three terms: the state of nature, the contract, and the resulting civil state. Indeed, thanks to the amazing crudity of the author's solution, which is absolutism pure and simple, those three terms automatically reduce themselves to two: the state of nature and the contract. For the civil state of Hobbes contains nothing which was not already included in his contract. The terms of that contract once given, all the 'miseries' of the civil state mechanically follow. Absolute surrender on the part of the 'subject,' absolute despotism on the part of the 'sovereign'—the one is the inevitable counterpart of the other. And all the truculent rhetoric which Hobbes lavishes upon his description of the civil state in reality adds nothing to what we already knew from the plain, unvarnished tale delivered by the contract.

Let us now take each of these two stages in order: the state of nature, on the one hand; the civil state with its gloomy portal, the contract, upon the other. Or rather, without any attempt to separate two things which in the closely welded argument of *Leviathan* are inseparably bound together, let us consider that argument, so far as it relates to the passage from the natural to the civil state, as a connected whole.

As for the state of nature, there can, for the reasons already given, be no question of correspondence with the facts. Where the whole assumption is a freak of the fancy, there is obviously no room for quarrelling with details. In respect of this term of the argument, therefore, we are driven back upon the mere matter of consistency. And from this side two fatal objections at once force themselves upon our notice: the impossibility that the natural man of Hobbes should ever have become civilised; the impossibility that the same men should ever have been governed at the same time by two laws so directly contrary to each other as the law of the sword and the 'law of nature.' A few words on each point will put this beyond doubt.

The state of nature is, to Hobbes, a state of war, the 'war of all against all.' It is a state of which 'the cardinal virtues are force and fraud.' It is a state in which 'the notions of right and wrong, of justice and injustice, can have no place.' All this is consistent enough with itself. But who shall ever persuade us that it is consistent with the sequel? Who shall induce us to believe that the men of whom this is true could ever be capable of entering, or even desiring to enter, a state in which all these conditions are absolutely reversed: a state not of war, but of peace; a state in which force and fraud are deliberately laid aside; a state which is founded upon ideas of right and justice, and in which acts of wrong and injustice are put under the double ban of public disapproval and of positive prohibition? Given such men as Hobbes supposes, is it not obvious that the civil state, even if a miracle could have brought them into it, would have been to them both intolerable and impossible? that they would have entered it one moment only to leave it, with scorn and loathing, at the next? The Ethiopian cannot change his skin. Nor could the crafty cut-throat, the Machiavelli-Attila, of the opening chapters ever have become the peaceful labourer, still less the cringing Helot, of the close.

The truth is that, by persistently darkening his shadows, Hobbes ends by proving too much. In his desire to show that men were forced to fly from the state of nature, he has only succeeded in making it impossible for them to do so. The 'miseries' which make flight desirable are miseries that flow from the qualities with which he credits them, and from nothing else. And as they cannot escape from their own nature, so neither can they escape from the consequences which that nature, with its inbred, or rather inborn, lack of 'right and justice,' inevitably involves. The plain fact is that the natural man, as conceived by Hobbes, is radically anti-social; and no juggling with swords and contracts can ever make him a fit subject for society. How is it possible to believe that the same beings, who one moment have been flying at each other's throats, should the next moment, with equal eagerness, be flying into each other's arms?

Indeed, if primitive man were really the being presented in 'the odious picture of Hobbes,' then neither by instinct, nor by reason, would he ever have been capable of forming any union, of entering into any relation whatsoever, with his kind. Still less would he have been capable of acting upon anything which presents the most distant approach to a moral motive. The 'war of all against all' would be an inextinguishable instinct of his heart. So far from driving him into the civil state, it would for ever keep him fast bound in what Hobbes declares to be the state of nature. It would know no end until one man, the strongest or the craftiest, were left alone upon the earth, to enjoy a triumph the very completeness of which would bring destruction to the conqueror. Such a race—a race to which there is no counterpart in the 'lower animals'—would have been born only to destroy itself. Its very existence, let alone its propagation and continuance, would have been physically impossible. For such a being would be nothing less than a monstrosity: a being incapable of life; much more, incapable of morality, incapable of good fellowship, incapable even of that abject form of society for which he was expressly devised by his saturnine creator.

This, indeed, is the criticism of Rousseau; and no subsequent writer has ever been able to refute it. 'What a strange animal would that be,' he writes, 'which should find its well-being in the destruction of its kind! And how is it conceivable that a race so monstrous and so hateful should endure for so much as two generations? Yet that is the last word of a man of supreme genius: the logical issue of his passion, or rather his frenzy, for justifying despotism at all costs: an atrocious principle, well worthy of the purpose to which he puts it. . . . If this rage for mutual destruction had indeed been part of our nature, then it would make itself felt even in the civil state; in spite of ourselves, it would drive us to break all the chains which society has woven round us. The same hideous hatred of our kind would still be the recognised guide of all our actions. We should grieve at the birth of our own children and rejoice at the death of our own brothers. When we found any man asleep and helpless, our first impulse would be to kill him. The kindly feeling which makes us share in the joy of others, the compassion which makes us grieve over their sufferings, would be things unknown to us, and directly contrary to our nature. Pity and sympathy would be the marks of a monster; and we should *be* by nature all that our depraved surroundings can even now hardly force us to *become*.' [1] It would be difficult to put the case against Hobbes, on the first point that presents itself, more vividly than this.

This, however, is not the only inconsistency in the opening stage of Hobbes' argument; not the only flaw which destroys its coherence as a logical whole. A still more fatal defect is to be found in his treatment of the 'law of nature': in the two different, or rather contradictory, senses which he gives to this cardinal conception. For him the 'law of nature' stands, on the one hand, for a brute instinct; on the other hand, for a moral ideal. And the levity with which he passes from the one interpretation to its direct opposite is nothing short of astounding. In fact, the sense, which on any given page he puts into the words, is dictated purely by the convenience of the moment. When his object is to prove the misery of the state of nature and the consequent interest which all must find in escaping from it, then the law of nature is assumed to be brute force, qualified only, or rather still further envenomed, by treachery and fraud. When, on the other hand, it suits his purpose to supplant the blind, and therefore uncalculating and incalculable, workings of passion and selfishness by the presumably more discerning, and therefore more calculable, promptings of reason and duty, then it is a very different story. Then the 'natural man,' who the moment before was a mere animal, with no thought but of self-interest, with no power of conceiving, much less of recognising, duty, suddenly becomes aware that he is bound by a whole network of duties, held fast

[1] See Rousseau's early Fragment, *L'État de guerre* (*Political Writings*, i. pp. 305-6; compare p. 293).

by a long chain of moral obligations. Then—such is the virtue of this inner light—it suddenly becomes the command both of God and ' nature ' that, whatever his thirst for war, whatever his delight in force and fraud, he should bridle all such appetites and renounce all such habits; that he should change war for peace; that he should make a solemn covenant to this end with his inveterate enemies; above all, that the covenant thus made should for all time be religiously observed. In all the annals of religion, in all the ' fairy-tales of the Kingdom of Darkness,' there is no conversion so sudden, or so radical, as this.

Hobbes, no doubt, is not the only philosopher who has played fast and loose with the idea of duty; who has banished it from the foundations of his system only to smuggle it back, under a more or less transparent disguise, in the final result. All the utilitarians —after another fashion, most of the hedonists—are tarred with the same brush. Between them and Hobbes, however, there is this glaring difference: that whereas the utilitarians, and even the hedonists, seek, by a long process of elaboration, to distil the idea of duty from that of self-interest or of pleasure, Hobbes leaps straight from the one order of ideas to the other, reserving to himself the right to leap back again as often as it suits his purpose to do so.

For the argument of the utilitarians, and even for the more refined forms of hedonism, there is, at any rate upon the surface, something to be said. Given a sufficient amount of experience and reflection, it may plausibly be argued that enlightened self-interest, and even a prudent thirst for pleasurable sensations, may eventually be seen to find their true account in sacrificing the impulse of the moment to the cumulative profit or pleasure of a life-time; that such calculation may in time become a habit, almost an ideal; and that, as an ideal, it is hardly to be distinguished from what, in the loose speech of preachers and moralists, is known as a ' duty.' It is quite true that, with all these precautions, the process is, at bottom, no better than a juggle; and that, when the idea of duty, in however attenuated a form, has once supervened—allowing that such an idea could ever be squeezed out of materials so unpromising—the result is so different from the starting-point that the whole character of the motive, the whole nature of the agent impelled by it, is entirely changed. His world is no longer primarily a world of self-interest; it is no longer a world of pleasure. It is a world of right and wrong; a world of which the determining factor is obligation or duty. The truth is that here, as in so many other cases, the question of origins is a false question. The real question that has to be faced is not, How did the idea of duty take its rise in the mind of man? but, What is he to do with it when he has got it? What is the nature of the world—if we will, the new world—created by such a conception? What is the nature of the mind capable of forming it? Thus the very thing that gives plausibility to the utilitarian argument is at the same time the cause of its ruin. The moment comes when the true question, so adroitly replaced by the false, returns upon us as importunate as ever. Then the long delay, the elaborate argumentation, are seen to have availed nothing. The idea of duty, which has to be acceptable at the end of the argument, might just as well have been admitted from the beginning. All that has been gained by the long process of fencing is to put off the evil day when defeat has to be acknowledged.

From this particular fallacy, it need hardly be said, the argument of Hobbes is conspicuously free. His dangers did not lie that way. Neither on their safer, nor on their more perilous, side had theories of development any meaning—still less, any attraction—for him. They were reserved for a later and more sophisticated generation. And there is a further reason why it would be vain to look for any anticipation of such theories in *Leviathan*. To call attention to the contrast between the two orders of motive—and the existence of such a contrast is presupposed in the attempt to distil the one from the other—was manifestly the last thing to suit his purpose. On the contrary, his one object was to conceal the fact that there is a contrast: to keep the way open for sliding gracefully from the one order to the other. To have done anything to interfere with this manœuvre would have been a tactical blunder of which Hobbes was the last man to be guilty.

Yet the very precautions which he took on this side laid him doubly open to attack upon the other. And great as are the objections to the argument of the utilitarians and hedonists, they are as nothing to those which beset the reasoning of Hobbes. That, given a due amount of time and reflection, the idea of self-interest, or even of pleasure, should come to be confounded with that of duty; that, in the slow furnace of experience, the one idea, by a kind of spiritual alchemy, should gradually be, or at the least appear to be, transmuted into the other: this is one thing. The miracle postulated by Hobbes is quite another. He blandly asks us to assume that the change, which to the utilitarians is the slow work of generations, was in fact an instantaneous transformation; that the one order of ideas was at a moment's notice swept aside by the other; that the same men who all their lives had owned no law but that of blind passion or gross selfishness, whose whole outlook therefore was utterly unmoral, suddenly awoke to the consciousness that there was another law whose commands ran directly counter to all the promptings they had hitherto followed; that, at a single glance, they recognised their allegiance to be due not to the first law, but to the second; and that without hesitation they pledged themselves for all time, and under the most merciless sanctions, to obey it. All this is none the less of a miracle in that the second law, like the first, is described as a 'law of nature.' This is simply to palter with words in a double sense. For, however much Hobbes may strive to conceal the fact, it is clear that the law in question is essentially a moral, not a natural, law; that it is not a statement of what is, but of what ought to be; in short that it is a thing as different from the law of force and fraud, which in the opening stage of *Leviathan* is declared to govern the state of nature, as the law of England, or the law of the Ten Commandments, is from the law of gravitation.

Thus the opposition between the two orders of motive, which the later writers conceal under an infinite number of disguises, is presented by Hobbes in all its crudity and nakedness. And, under these circumstances, it is manifest that there could be no question of deriving the one order from the other: no question of that spiritual alchemy which, in the slow furnace of years, seeks to transmute the one into the other. The more subtle fallacy is, no doubt, excluded. But we are left face to face with a contradiction as glaring as the author's worst enemy could have desired.

Of all the contradictions in which Hobbes allowed himself to be entangled, none, in truth, was so fatal, so deep-reaching as this. The political philosopher has before him the choice between two roads. He may either rely upon purely natural causes: upon causes, that is, which exclude any motive beyond that of calculated self-interest, or the pleasure of the moment: in other words, upon the purely natural desire of man to provide security for life, limb and 'property'; or again, upon his desire to find scope for the free exercise of all his faculties, intellectual and emotional. Or he may admit that the individual was from the first prompted, more or less consciously, by some sense, however feeble, of duty and obligation towards his fellow-men; and that it was this which made some kind of political union a necessity of his being. In the former case, the philosopher will have, sooner or later, to account for the eventual emergence of the idea of duty as the guide which, however mistakenly, is acknowledged by most men to have the first claim upon their obedience. In the latter case, he will, no doubt, be accused of importing a mystical principle into man's nature: of taking for granted an 'ultimate fact of consciousness,' without making any effort to analyse it further or account for it. On the other hand, he will be free from the logical difficulties which beset the adherents of the opposite school; he will be more true to the facts; and he will not expose himself to the charge of explaining away facts which he is unwilling to recognise.

Neither of these roads was taken by Hobbes. He adopts a middle course; only to find in the end that it offers the advantages of neither and combines the disadvantages of both. His system is neither frankly utilitarian nor frankly idealist; neither wholly for 'force and fraud,' nor wholly for that idea of Right which, whatever the exact form it may assume, is in the field of politics what the idea of duty is in the field of morals. Had he stuck boldly to his main line of argument, had he persisted in recognising no motive power beyond self-interest or passion, he might have forestalled Spinoza by a generation; he might have anticipated Hume and the utilitarians by a century. Had he taken the opposite course, had he cloven consistently to the idea of natural Right, he might have forestalled Locke; he might—and it would have been a more congenial enterprise—have effected an unholy alliance between the champion of natural and those of divine Right. As it is, he falls between two stools. He imports just enough of Right to destroy the unity of a system which was essentially based upon brute force and the terror of the sword. He does not import enough to give any substance, or even any air of sincerity, to his plea for the sacred duty of submission to the image of lead and iron which his earlier argument had set up. The result is that, so far as the vital development of political thought is concerned, *Leviathan* has remained, and deserved to remain, without influence and without fruit: a fantastic hybrid, incapable of propagating its kind. It is a just nemesis for the vacillation which Hobbes permitted to wreck the argument at the critical moment; as that vacillation itself is a curious instance of the weakness which unnerves even the boldest spirits when, instead of seeking truth with a single mind, they suffer themselves to be swept away by the passion, or the apparent interest, of the moment.

For what was it that led Hobbes into this labyrinth of contradictions? It was the desire to justify a particular form of government at all costs, without regard to the truth, or even the consistency, of the speculative principles upon which he strove to base it. In appealing to force and the fear of force, he had worked out a wholly consistent, if strangely brutal, theory of government. It was indeed open to the objection that, of all the remedies against force, force itself is the least durable and the least to be depended on; that to lay the permanent foundation of government in it is therefore to build on sand, to move in a vicious circle of alternate despotism and anarchy. It was open to the further objection that, even with anarchy eliminated, the result of such a system would be not a community but an aggregate: in the language of Plato, the enthronement, not of the State, but of a Faction.[1] Such objections, however, are inseparable from the principles to which he was wedded; and as force was dear to him, and the very idea of a community of all things the most hateful, it is manifest that he was not the man to quail before them. Why then, we ask once more, did he flinch at the last moment from the argument which he had so cunningly built up?

Clearly it was no fear of the consequences, though they might well have appalled any spirit less stout, have daunted any purpose less resolute, than his. On the contrary, the consequences were the one thing on which his heart was set. And it was an uneasy suspicion that, after all, these consequences might in practice never result which was the cause of all the mischief. He was seized with a well-grounded fear that, in the last resort, self-interest will never be found to lie on the side of perpetual slavery; that no man in his senses will ever seek to secure life and property by setting up a despot with unlimited powers to take life and confiscate property at any moment that it pleases him to do so; that the fate of Uriah the Hittite is a warning to the subject no less than a condemnation —or are we to say a justification?—of the despot; [2] and that, however much men may have consented to such a prospect in a moment of discouragement and when it was no more than a remote possibility, they will never, on grounds of mere self-interest, consent to abide by their promises when the possibility has become a certainty and the remote prospect a matter of daily experience and hourly apprehension.

Accordingly, to secure his consequences, he cast about for some second string to his bow. He set himself to make sure that, if his victims should threaten to break the meshes of self-interest, they might at least find themselves held fast by the iron chain of duty. Hence the sweeping revision of the Contract and all that it carries with it. Hence a covenant, purely material in its origin, purpose and sanction, comes in the end to rest mainly, if not solely, upon a moral foundation and to be upheld mainly, though not solely, for its moral consequences. Hence the despot, established in the first instance for pure convenience, is in the final issue maintained merely as a painful duty. And what of the truculent maxims with which the author had spiced the original version of his theory? What of his solemn assertion that 'covenants without the sword are but words, and of no strength to secure a man at all'? [3] This and other challenges of the kind turn out to be the very reverse of his real meaning. In the light of his

[1] *οἳ δ' ἕνεκά τινων ἐτέθησαν, στασιωτείας ἀλλ' οὐ πολιτείας τούτους φαμέν* (Plato, *Laws*, iv. § 715 B).

[2] See *Leviathan*, chap. xxi.

[3] *Ib.* chap. xvii.

revised story, we are driven to the conclusion that it is the sword and the material interests represented by the sword which, to his second and riper thoughts, are mere 'whiff and wind'; and that the only thing really 'of strength to secure a man' or anything that he values is conscience and the sense of moral obligation. It is a kind of inverted rake's progress to which the reader has been witness. The author, who at the beginning was possessed by the very demon of force and fraud, presents himself at the end repentant, clothed, and in his right mind.

This, however, only serves to throw the radical absurdity of the theory into a still more glaring light. A despotism, which was at least not out of keeping with an argument avowedly based solely upon the idea of force, becomes the grossest of anomalies directly force is replaced by Right: directly the main motive for the formation of civil society is declared to be not terror, but the duty of obedience to the 'immutable and eternal laws of nature.' [1] Thus the very argument with which Hobbes strives to buttress up his crumbling consequences serves only to complete their ruin. Between despotism and force the simplest mind can see and recognise the connection. But once admit the determining factor in the political life of man to be not force but Right, then the case is altered. Then reason is there to tell us that the sword of the despot is the very negation of all Right. And all history is there to convince us that slavery is the last refuge in which men will voluntarily take shelter; submission to it, the last thing they will consent to regard as a moral duty.

With these considerations in mind, let us go back to examine some of the links of this curious argument in more detail than we have hitherto done.

When Hobbes started upon his enquiry, there is nothing to show that he intended moral considerations, scruples of conscience and the like, to find any place in the state of nature; nor indeed, except under a highly diluted, a strictly derivative, form, even in the civil state. Everything, in fact, points in the opposite direction. His opening chapters are devoted to proving that man is incapable of acting upon any motive save that of self-interest or of passion; and they have no other object. 'To this war of every man against every man this also is consequent, that nothing can be unjust. The notions of right and wrong, justice and injustice, have there no place. . . . Justice and injustice are none of the faculties neither of the body nor mind. If they were, they might be in a man that were alone in the world, as well as his senses and passions. They are qualities that relate to man in society, not in solitude.' [2] Could any repudiation of the moral law, any assertion that it had,

[1] *Leviathan*, chap. xv. [2] *Ib.* chap. xiii.

and could have, no existence in the state of nature, be stronger or more explicit than this? And who would have supposed that these sentences form the immediate prelude to a discussion of the 'natural laws' which 'bind' the Ishmaelites whom, but for this belated reminder, every reader, on the strength of the earlier description, would certainly have concluded to be absolutely free? [1]

Such, however, is the case; and such it was bound to be, if the subsequent argument of *Leviathan* was to be kept upon its feet. In order to rivet the yoke of the 'mortal god' upon the neck of his worshippers, it was necessary to prove not only that it was their interest, but also that it was their bounden duty, to remain, and to remain for all time, obedient to his will. And, as Hobbes rightly saw, this could only be done if it were established that, at the moment when they accepted the yoke, they were aware that all promises are binding, and that any subsequent attempt to repudiate them, however great the advantages to be expected from it, would be the most heinous of all crimes. Hence the glaring anomaly—to Hobbes, however, it was a stern necessity—of a moral law suddenly imported into a state of things which, on his own showing, is the very negation of all law and all morality. Hence the dilution of an argument, which had started from purely 'natural' premisses, by the infusion of a whole stream of non-natural—or rather, if the word may for once be used in the strict sense, of supernatural—obligations and ideals.

This flagrant inconsistency once granted, one can only admire the skill with which the alien element is insinuated, the innocent air with which the idea of duty is slipped into an argument where it is no better than a trespasser and a vagrant. The method employed by Hobbes for the purpose is, while apparently drawing a sharp, and very just, distinction between 'law' and 'right,' in reality to confuse the bounds between them at every turn. Thus, having started with the statement, only too well justified by his previous description, that the 'natural rights' of man may be summed up in one fell phrase, 'the right of every man to everything—even to one another's body'—he goes on to inform us that this right is at once limited and enforced by a two-edged 'natural law' which 'binds' man, wherever possible, to 'seek peace and ensue it'; but, wherever that is proved impossible, 'by all means he can to defend himself' against those whom he would otherwise have been under an obligation to embrace.[2] That the former of these two alternatives might be, and to all civilised beings is, the subject of a law, in the moral as well as in the civil sense of the term, will be universally admitted; though it is somewhat puzzling to find it figuring in the 'state of nature.' The

[1] *Leviathan*, chap. xiv. [2] *Ib.* chap. xiv.

latter alternative, however, stands on utterly different ground. It could never be the subject of a law. It is essentially and exclusively a matter of right: of right, that is, in the purely individualist sense of the term accepted by Hobbes: the sense in which it is opposed to duty.

Our suspicions once aroused by the discovery of this misuse of terms in the latter alternative, we go back to the former, only to find that here too, though in a slightly different shape, the same equivocation is at work. Though 'seek peace and ensue it' might be, as in the Christian doctrine it is, a law binding on the conscience, it may also be, and in the system of Hobbes manifestly is and must be, no more than a counsel of prudence. It carries no obligation with it. It does not say to man 'Thou shalt,' but 'If thou art well advised, thou wilt.' It is not a moral law binding on the conscience. It is merely a generalisation from experience—an experience, moreover, with which the 'natural man' of Hobbes could not possibly have been provided—suggesting certain practical conclusions to the intellect. In other words, it is no law, either 'natural' or moral. It is, at most, a maxim of worldly wisdom and of policy.

So much indeed, in a moment of unwonted candour, is admitted by Hobbes himself at the close of his discussion. 'These dictates of reason men used to call by the name of laws, but improperly. For they are but conclusions, or theorems concerning what conduceth to the conservation and defence of themselves; whereas "law," properly, is the word of him that hath command over others.' This is surely explicit enough. What words could say more plainly that the 'law of nature' is, after all, no more than a series of appeals to self-interest and worldly prudence? a *vade mecum* of self-help, claiming no authority higher than that of a 'theorem' of expediency? Mark, however, what immediately follows: 'But yet, if we consider the same theorems as delivered in the word of God that by right commandeth all things, then are they properly called "laws."'[1] Again, what words could speak more plainly? The very same 'laws,' which a moment before had sunk to the level of mere theorems of self-interest, are now exalted to the level of 'commands of God': they take rank side by side with the Ten Commandments. In other words: 'A command of God, a moral law, a counsel of self-interest—take your choice. It makes no difference. All three are simply fashions of speech; all three, merely different ways of expressing exactly the same thought. Once convince yourself that a given course is to your interest; and I am there to assure you that, by the same rule, it is the command of God, it is your moral duty, to adopt it.' After

[1] *Leviathan*, close of chap. xv.

this, what need of further discussion? Why indeed have discussed the matter at all? Discussion, like covenants, is but words and breath. It is of no strength to convey any meaning whatsoever.

Exactly the same criticism applies to the 'second law of nature,' which is indeed little more than a repetition of the first: 'that a man be willing, when others are so too, so far forth as for peace and defence of himself he shall think it necessary, to lay down this right to all things and be contented with so much liberty against other men as he will allow to other men against himself.'[1] Here again, under the guise of a 'law,' we are presented with what, when sifted, turns out to be nothing more than a 'theorem' of self-interest.

Having thus artfully prepared the ground by the subtle equivocation of his first and second laws, with the third Hobbes boldly unmasks his batteries and stoutly confronts us with the 'obligation'—an obligation which would have no sense, if it were not both presented and accepted as a duty binding upon the conscience—'that men perform their covenants made.'[2] It is true that, even here, he still makes play with the fear of consequences, still therefore palters in a double sense with the two contrary meanings of the 'law' which he invokes. But it is clear at the first glance that the balance is here shifted from the one scale to the other; that the whole weight of the argument is now thrown upon the appeal not to expediency, but to conscience; that his one anxiety henceforth is to nail his readers to that interpretation of his ambiguities, his one thought to persuade them that the Contract once made is a thing sacred and inviolable, that to lift a finger against its consequences, even the most hateful of them, is not only a blunder but a crime.

And what are the consequences in question? As has already been shown, they amount to nothing less than the total subjection of the community, all and several, to the arbitrary will of 'one man, or one assembly of men,' solemnly appointed for the purpose. And, as Hobbes makes no secret of his conviction that the former alternative, absolute monarchy, is the only certain means of securing the ends of the covenant—as the second alternative is clearly thrown in merely to save appearances—it is manifest that all may be summed up in one phrase: perfect, unmitigated slavery, alike in matters of speech and in matters of action, to the will of an irresponsible despot. And the covenant, which had at first seemed to be dictated solely by self-interest and expediency, is now discovered to be binding for all time as a matter of conscience and of duty.

It would be idle to follow the author through the remaining

[1] *Leviathan*, chap. xiv.

[2] *Ib.* chap. xv.

'laws'—there is a round dozen of them—which complete his natural code. They are all tinged with the same equivocation which has been pointed out in the first three. In this instance, however, the sting resides not in the tail, but in the head. And if the first three be once granted, the remainder follow as a matter of course.

All that is left is to ask ourselves: What right has Hobbes to invoke the idea of 'law' in any shape? in what sense, if any, are the men whom he has described in his earlier chapters as acknowledging no virtues save 'force and fraud' capable either of obeying a law, or even of recognising its existence?

Apart from the political meaning of the term, which in an assumed state of nature is obviously excluded and which indeed is equally absent even from the later stages of Hobbes' argument, there are two main senses in which the term *law* may legitimately be used. It may either mean a law of nature: that is, a generalisation of what is observed actually to happen, under certain circumstances, to inanimate objects, or to be done, again under certain circumstances, by inanimate agents. Or it may mean a moral law: that is, a command issued by God or conscience—for our purposes it is not necessary to pursue the distinction further—and recognised as binding, however little it may be actually obeyed, by a human agent.

In addition to these two main kinds of law, natural and moral, we may further distinguish, and the argument of Hobbes requires that we should distinguish, yet a third species which offers points of contact with each of them. It is possible, that is, though not perhaps altogether accurate, to describe as 'laws' those precepts or maxims of prudence which, being themselves based upon generalisations of the consequences observed to follow if a human agent acts in a certain manner, direct, advise, or warn him to act, or not to act in that manner, supposing him to desire the attainment of a particular end: his welfare in general, or any more limited end which he may happen to have set before him. As based upon considerations of men's actions and their consequences, such 'laws' have evidently something in common with the first sense of 'law,' as defined above. As precepts, or 'dictates,' drawn from such generalisations, they have also something in common with the commands embodied in the moral law. Indeed, the specific articles of the moral code of any age, so far as they are rational, take their rise from this source and from this alone. They might be defined as precepts which experience has shown to be necessary for the attainment of a predetermined end: the realisation of the idea of duty. They differ from prudential precepts only in the end, which is not self-interest but moral goodness; and in the motive which is desire not for pleasure or profit, but to obey the commands of our own conscience or of God.

Thus, in relation to the actions of men, there are three distinct senses which the term *law* is capable of bearing: an observed sequence between certain courses of action and their natural consequences; the prudential precepts founded upon such observed sequences—precepts, however, which are purely conditional upon the end which at any moment the agent may set before him; and lastly, a command of conscience binding the agent, whatever may be his personal inclination, to obey what he recognises as the law of duty.

Now, directly we examine the matter, it becomes clear that all these three senses of law are pressed into the service by Hobbes; that he rings the changes at pleasure upon them all.

In the 'war of all against all,' the law which regulates the acts of his imaginary beings is either a law of blind passion, by its very nature purely unreasoning and instinctive, or a law of calculated selfishness; and he does not even take the trouble to make clear which of these two very different motive powers he has in view. In point of fact, it must manifestly be the first. His miserable Ishmaelites pass their time in slaying and defrauding their neighbours not so much because they think it expedient, nor even because they are driven to it by outward circumstances, but because they are under an inward compulsion to do so, because it is their nature to, because, as we say, they know no better. On the other hand, when the stage of reflection comes, when it is borne in upon them that their life hitherto has been 'poor, nasty, brutish and short,' and when they set themselves to calculate all the advantages that may result from exchanging it for something radically different, then it is clear that they have passed under yet another law—still, however, a purely 'natural' law—the law of conscious reflection, of calculated prudence, of expediency, of self-interest.

Even this, however, is not enough for the purpose. And until their reflections have been reduced to a code of maxims or precepts, until self-interest has had time to exalt itself into a regulative principle—we may almost say, an ideal—of conduct, Hobbes instinctively felt that all was yet in vain, that his puppets would still inevitably remain wedded to the war of all against all to which they had been born.

It is at this point, be it observed, that the great break occurs in the history of their experience; it is at this point also that the fatal confusion begins to creep into the argument of Hobbes. For the moment that men begin to reduce their reflections to maxims, precepts, and what our author is pleased to call 'theorems,' the moment they begin to treat such theorems as guides for the regulation of their future conduct, from that moment it is clear that they have entered upon yet another stage of their pilgrimage. They have now passed avowedly into the region of ideals; they have now, however fitfully, accepted definite standards of action; they have now—in a sense, no doubt, which it is necessary to define very carefully—begun to recognise the existence of what Hobbes is determined that we shall call a 'law.'

The term *law*, in this connection, naturally suggests a moral law: a law recognised as binding upon the conscience of man; a law which, whether he like it or not, he feels himself to be under the obligation of obeying. That, however, is evidently not the sense which the whole tenor of Hobbes' argument demands. The law in question is, by his own avowal, no more than a mere collection of 'theorems,' of prudential precepts which it may be wise to follow, but which have no binding force, carry with them no obligation, whatsoever. Their appeal is not to the conscience—no conscience, no sense of moral obligation, is, in fact, possible to the beings who people Hobbes' Inferno of mutual destruction—but merely to calculations of individual self-interest. Every higher consideration, any appeal to the sense of Right and duty, is inexorably barred out.

Yet without the appeal to Right and duty, how was the desired result to be obtained? The beings assumed by the whole course of the argument are utterly unmoralised. They have, it necessarily follows, no inbred craving for concord. They have not the experience which alone could enable them to estimate its blessings. They have not the material—a material to be given only by experience—for framing those precepts and 'theorems' without which, as we shall see directly, the whole argument falls in pieces. It is therefore in the highest degree unlikely that they should ever even conceive the desire of entering into civil society. That they would withdraw from it at the first difficulty, at the first conflict between their immediate convenience and the will of an irresponsible tyrant, is absolutely certain. In one word, no society could ever be formed by such beings; and if it were, it would immediately be dissolved. If a slightly different application may be given to words originally quoted by Locke: *Intrarent civitatem, tantum ut exirent.*

Such were the fears which puzzled the will of Hobbes and drove him at the last moment to confound the boundaries which, in the opening stages of his argument, he had been careful to lay down. He was haunted by a dim sense that the appeal to expediency pure and simple was foredoomed to failure: a dark suspicion that, unless reinforced by the cry of duty, it must infallibly break down. And here, at any rate, who can doubt that he was in the right? How was it to be expected that men would submit to all the known miseries of slavery on the bare possibility—a possibility disproved for us by all the successful revolts of history—that rebellion might bring them to a yet more miserable pass? Even apart from the teachings of history—teachings repeated under his own eyes as he laboured over *De Cive* and *Leviathan*—might not the most elementary knowledge of human nature have saved him from nursing so childish a delusion? 'This is to think,' as Locke said in one of the few passages where we may suppose him to be writing with direct reference to Hobbes, 'this is to think that men are so foolish that they take care to avoid what mischiefs may be done them by polecats and foxes, but are content, nay think it safety, to be devoured by lions.'[1] Even to those who are still meditating the change from polecats to lions, who have therefore as yet no actual experience of the latter, this criticism is formidable enough. When the change has actually been made, when it is a choice between a lion ravening on the spot and a gang of polecats and foxes faintly clamouring in the background, who can doubt on which side the scales of expediency would be weighted?

Under these circumstances, the only thing left to Hobbes was to buttress up the principle of expediency by some other principle less shifty and more stubborn: to smuggle in by the back door that 'notion' of duty which, for good reasons of his own, he had in the first instance resolutely barred out from the front. If those who smarted under the war of all against all could only be persuaded that, quite apart from expediency, they were under a moral obligation to 'seek peace and ensue it'; if the subjects of the 'mortal God' could only be induced to believe that eternal submission was a matter not so much of self-interest as of conscience and of duty: then the breaches in the earlier part of the argument might not impossibly be made good; the theory of divine Right, adroitly stripped of its theological dressing, might be once more set upon its feet; the threatened victory of Behemoth might be staved off for generations; and all might yet be well. The attempt was at any rate worth making; and with imperturbable gravity Hobbes fights his way gallantly to the end.

It was, however, a lost cause from the very first. For the idea of duty not only had no place been left in the worshippers of force and fraud who throng the opening stages of his argument, but it had been explicitly barred out. It was therefore only by a subterfuge that it could subsequently be slipped in. It is, in fact, under cover of the double meaning attaching to the term *natural law*—as a code of theorems, of merely prudential maxims, on the one hand, and as a command of conscience on the other—that the new

[1] *Civil Government*, ii. § 93.

factor was brought into the reckoning. The two conceptions are sharply opposed. The one belongs to an order of thought poles asunder from the other. Yet the whole force of the argument, alike for Hobbes and for his readers, depends upon the silent replacement of the one by the other. By a stretch of compliance we may admit that Hobbes was entitled to the one. On every possible showing, he had debarred himself from invoking the other. It would be a miracle if men wholly without experience arrived at 'dictates of reason,' at prudential precepts, which, in the world as we know it, are to be reached only through and by a long discipline of experience. But no miracle in the world could convert these 'theorems' of self-interest into commands binding on the conscience.

Thus the effect of the sophism was exactly the reverse of that designed by its author. To call in the principle of obligation was a tacit acknowledgement that the principle of expediency had broken down. And the weapon which he himself admits to be useless is replaced by one to which he had manifestly no right. The second weapon was intended to rivet the despotism of Leviathan. Its effect was to shatter the whole argument upon which that despotism is built up.

It would be unjust to suppose that he was deliberately seeking to delude his readers; that he was himself aware of the equivocation which, while seeming to save his argument, in reality rent it from top to bottom. The charge against him is not that. It is that, blinded by the passion of the moment, he should have allowed himself to slip unobserved from one line of argument to another not only alien, but directly contrary to it; and that, having thus shifted his ground, he should have continued to pass from the one position to the other, as it suits his purpose, to the very end: betraying his sense of the weakness of the argument from expediency by taking cover behind the idea of duty, and unable to see that beings capable of recognising the bond of duty could never have been the inhuman monsters assumed, without any attempt at proof, in the opening stage of his argument and imperatively demanded by the whole tenor of the reasoning which follows.

That is the fatal flaw which Spinoza at once detected in the whole scheme of *Leviathan* and which he sought to repair in a theory where he starts with the undertaking to purge the political life of man from the last dregs of the idea of Right and duty, and where, but for faint visitings of human frailty, he almost redeems his promise. But, in order to obtain even this measure of success, the whole fabric of Hobbes' argument had to be taken to pieces and rebuilt from the very ground.

So much for the more speculative objections to the argument

of *Leviathan.* We now turn to the broader challenge which, alike by its doctrine of origins and its doctrine of sovereignty, it has never ceased to throw out to the reason and conscience of mankind. And here we need do little more than follow the lines long ago laid down by Rousseau.

Rousseau's criticism, which is embodied in the *Contrat Social*, in a number of Fragments written in connection with the *Contrat* and, to a less degree, in the *Discours sur l'inégalité*, may be summarised as follows. The theory of Hobbes is both self-contradictory and revolting; and even if these objections could be got over, it does not fulfil the ends with which it professes to set out. When all is said, it provides no basis for civil society: least of all, for a society which claims to rest upon Right. This criticism is applied in the first place to Hobbes' account of the origin of the State; and secondly to what he says of its claims upon the allegiance of its members.

'All the philosophers have attempted to reach back to the state of nature, but none of them has ever got there.'[1] This is the sweeping verdict of Rousseau upon the efforts of his predecessors; and on none of them does the blow fall so heavily as on Hobbes. None had made louder professions of reducing man to what he was when he came from the hands of nature; none had, in fact, failed more completely to justify his claim. The natural instincts of man, urges the apostle of nature, are limited by his natural needs: food, sleep, the gratification of his sexual impulse and—possibly, though by no means certainly—clothing. And as he is incapable of forethought, all care for the future must be jealously excluded. The instincts of Hobbes' man, on the contrary, are possible only to a being who 'looks before and after'; and they are limited, if this were indeed a limit, solely by vanity and a boundless lust of self-assertion. In other words, they are the product of a state of things which is purely artificial: of conditions which it must have taken centuries of settled society to bring about.

The result is a twofold contradiction. On the one hand, the being so pieced together is an unimaginable monster: combining in himself all the violence of a state of anarchy with all the calculated cunning peculiar to a decadent society; all the brutality of the sons of Nimrod with all the refined villainy of a Borgia or a Valois. The 'force and fraud' with which he is credited, even granting that each of them could exist separately, are 'virtues' mutually exclusive; the one belongs to an order of things which is wholly destructive of the other.

On the other hand, if the very existence of such a monster is impossible, still more impossible are the ends which are thrust upon

[1] *Discours sur l'inégalité* (*Political Writings*, i. p. 140).

him by the argument of *Leviathan*, the purposes for the attainment of which his life is every moment to be staked. The war of each against all is a war to the knife, or it is nothing; if carried to its ultimate consequence, it must lead to the extermination of all men, saving only the one who, in the final duel, is left master of the field. Thus the very attainment of his purpose would be the signal for his destruction; the moment of his triumph would inevitably also be the moment of his fall. 'The conqueror who, having slain all, should have the misfortune to be left alone upon the earth, would enjoy nothing, for the simple reason that he would be master of all. What good would he get from the possession of the whole universe, if he dwelt on it alone? How could he gorge his stomach with all the fruits of the earth? Who will gather for him the harvest of every climate? Who will carry the fame of his empire into the vast deserts which he will never reach? What will he do with all his treasures? Who will consume the food that he has stored? In whose eyes will he make boast of his power?' [1] His brutality, in other words, is the worst enemy both of his selfishness and his vanity. It drives him towards a goal, in the attainment of which selfishness, vanity—nay, even the craving for life itself—must inevitably work out their own destruction.

Once more: if this hateful combination of vices is really 'natural' to man, if these are really the qualities which lie at the root of his whole being, how can we account for the existence in man, as we know him, of qualities the very opposite of these in their essence and working? of the capacity for pity, love and self-sacrifice which, with the rarest exceptions, appears, if it be no more than fitfully, in the life of every human being and without which no society of men, not even that painted in *Leviathan*, could hold together for a moment?

In popular belief, and in the view of most of those who have thought seriously on the subject, the two impulses, 'good' and 'bad,' have jostled each other in man's nature from the beginning; and the history of the world is the history of the successive phases in the struggle of light against darkness, the successive efforts of the right to conquer fresh territory from the flowing sea of iniquity and wrong. According to Hobbes, on the other hand, the nature of primitive man is darkness unrelieved by one single streak of light. And how the light subsequently stole its way in, is a question to which *Leviathan* offers not even the semblance of an answer.

The difficulty—and it is insuperable—seems never to have crossed the mind of Hobbes. Or if it does, he takes refuge in

[1] *L'État de guerre* (*Political Writings*, i. p. 293).

the facile solution furnished by a peculiarly gross form of utilitarianism: in the impossible theory that unselfishness is, in the last resort, nothing more than a refined and enlightened brand of selfishness; that, on a balance of his budget, the man of ordinary foresight is ultimately forced to the conviction that he stands to gain more by a judicious reduction of his claims than by pressing them, as in the hot youth of the world he would have done, to the uttermost farthing; and that, by this means, acts which redound to the good of others can be distilled out of calculations which, alike in their direction and their motive, are purely selfish.

This theory must in no way be confounded with that worked out a century later by such men as Hume, Helvétius and Bentham. The later writers, whatever their other shortcomings, do at least assume the existence of the softer impulses as working from the very beginning of man's history. To them, therefore, such impulses have always been part of the self which it is his business to gratify. And there is some plausibility in the inference that, even without the aid of a sense of duty, they may, as mere impulses, prompt him from time to time, in the absence of any pressing motive to the contrary, to sacrifice his purely personal interests to the indulgence of such feelings as pity, sympathy or love.

But to Hobbes no such expedient is open. To him the softer impulses have been barred out from the beginning. And if in the later stages of man's growth there are signs which might be taken to suggest their presence and working, that, in Hobbes' view, is no more than an illusion. And those acts which we weakly suppose to be prompted by regard for others are, in reality, merely the product of a long-sighted selfishness which is found, by a long experience, to pay better than the craving for quick returns natural, and indeed inevitable, to man in the earlier stages of his growth. At best, they are the offspring of a 'magnanimity' which finds its reward in the sense of superiority it brings with it. And that is a quality which under no circumstances is to be looked for except in the stronger and more masterful natures; and which, even for such natures, is well-nigh impossible except after long generations of meek obedience on the one hand and of assured mastery upon the other.

Such acts and qualities, however, are of the very essence of man's nature; and what are we to say of a theory which can explain them only by explaining them away? The truth is that the political theory of Hobbes is buttressed up by a moral theory at least equally absurd. And the only valuable thing about it is the implied admission that, without it, the whole political argument—and, with it, the whole temple of the 'mortal god'—

would inevitably fall in ruins. Whether a buttress so crazy can do anything to avert that ruin, is a question which few men, utilitarian or otherwise, will have any difficulty in answering.

There is yet another, and a still more obvious, light in which the same objection may be put. The qualities which Hobbes attributes to the natural man are such as to make it for ever impossible for him to throw aside his savagery and establish terms of peace, much more of amity, with his neighbours. And the state of nature, as painted at the opening of *Leviathan*, could never have led even to the crude and barbarous form of civilisation which we are expected to bow down and worship at the close. Could any notion be more preposterous than that the men who one moment have been armed to the teeth against each other should at the next be making solemn leagues and covenants with each other? that men who hitherto had lived utterly without law should at a turn of the hand be found plunged into the legal fiction of 'mutually transferring their persons' to another? that beings who by nature were all for 'force and fraud' should in virtue of a sudden repentance voluntarily accept a contract which was to bind them for all time, by duty no less than force, to the paths of pleasantness and peace? Of all the dreams which have dazzled the vision of philosophers, surely none is so wild, so utopian, as this.

So much for Hobbes' theory of the formation of civil society. We now turn to consider the nature of the society which results. On this there are only two criticisms to offer. The society instituted by his Contract offers a state of things still more intolerable than the anarchy which it replaces. It is, in fact—and here we pass to the second criticism—no society at all; it is a herd driven together by sheer panic and held in the pen by nothing but the terror of the sword. The former is the criticism of Locke and Rousseau; the latter, which goes still deeper, is due to Rousseau alone.

On the former point, little need be added to what has been already said. The State of *Leviathan* is a State avowedly founded upon slavery: founded therefore upon a principle which is the very negation of all justice. And even apart from the 'hatefulness' of such a principle, who is weak enough to suppose that it offers any prospect of endurance? who is blind enough not to see that any society founded upon it is doomed from the very moment of its birth? Arguments from the fear of consequences, arguments from an alleged moral obligation, may be called in to stave off the inevitable revolt. But they are powerless for the purpose. If there is one thing certain, it is that 'no man will allow himself to be argued into slavery'; that every instinct, alike of self-preservation and of dignity, alike of expediency and of duty, bars the way to the submission which such an argument demands. Take the matter from the side of expediency; and Locke is there to remind us that the menace of the lion at the door will always prevail with men more than the fear of the fox and the polecat in the distance. Take it from the side of duty; and Rousseau is there to warn us that 'the gifts of nature, such as life and liberty, stand on a level far above those of fortune or convention; and that, as no worldly gain can make up for either of them, it is a sin both against nature and against reason to surrender either of them for any other supposed benefit whatsoever.' 'The man who renounces his freedom renounces his manhood, the rights which belong to him as man, nay his very duties. Such a renunciation is inconsistent with man's nature: to strip his will of all freedom is to strip his actions of all moral character.'[1] In fact, each of Hobbes' arguments—that from expediency no less than that from duty—breaks down, when taken by itself. And what is worse, the one, on his premisses, is not to be reconciled with the other. So far from supporting each other, the two wings of the theory are, in fact, mutually destructive.

Inconsistency, however, is the least of the objections which lie against the theory of Hobbes. Few are the thinkers, even of the greatest, who have a clean sheet on that score; and the more abundant, the more fruitful, their ideas, the less easy it may be to work them into a consistent whole. The fatal defect of Hobbes is that his ideas are not fruitful. They led, they were intended to lead, to nothing better than tyranny and stagnation.

If the history of mankind had really followed the lines laid down in *Leviathan*, consider what would have been the result. The fate of the whole world—not merely of a few backward races—would have lain in the grasp of a ring of despots. Not only political freedom, but all freedom, whether of thought or action, whether intellectual or social, would have hung upon their mercy. In other words, every single thing that makes life worth having would have been sacrificed; every one of the aims that have called forth the highest energies of man would have been either defeated or, more probably, never even conceived.

It is idle to urge that such a result is against human nature, and that the whole world would have risen to avert it. That, in truth, is to concede all that the author's worst enemy could desire. It is to admit that, from the first step to the last, he has misread the facts which he was there to interpret; that the principle by which he proposed to explain the past and guide the future of mankind could only be made tolerable, if that which is its direct

[1] *Discours sur l'inégalité* (*Political Writings*, i. p. 187); *Contrat Social*, I. iv. (*ibid.* ii. p. 28).

contrary were instantly smuggled in to counteract and thwart it at every moment of its operation.

In a modified form, that would seem to be the ground commonly chosen by those who still take up the gauntlet on behalf of a writer whose theory, as a theory, they are forced by mere shame to disavow. The instinct of freedom, they urge, is deeply planted in man's nature. Whatever happens, there is no fear that it will ever be rooted out. The real danger is just the other way: that it will run riot and choke itself, for lack of the pruning and guidance which are necessary for its growth. The control of a strong hand is indispensable for that purpose. And though it may at once be admitted that the despot, the hero, the divinely-appointed ruler—or whatever else we may choose to call him—will not invariably have wisdom or foresight, at least it will always be his interest to keep the rival folly, the innate lawlessness of the many-headed multitude, in check. The besetting sin of democracy is anarchy; and the best check yet discovered upon anarchy is the strong arm and, when necessary, the sharp sword of the ruler who is ultimately responsible only to himself. It is true that the motive power must commonly, if not always, be looked for from below; but the wild forces of nature, which furnish the raw material of the statesman, will in the ordinary course of things spring from the multitude and the soil. But what is motive power, or wild force, without guidance? and what is the worth of raw material until it is fashioned and worked up? At the lowest estimate, the second element is as necessary to the final product, the welfare and progress of mankind, as the first. And if, on the strictest construction, the rulers can claim no more than the second place, that is the worst of reasons for asserting that he has no place at all. In the language of Hobbes, Leviathan is the only possible corrective of *Behemoth*. Judged by a purely ideal standard, both may be evils; certainly, both carry many evils in their train. But in this imperfect world, both are necessary evils; and the one without the other would be ten times more evil yet.

There is no need to examine this statement of the case upon its merits. For, as a defence of Hobbes, it is manifestly beside the point. An argument which admits the ruler merely as a check upon the possible excesses of the multitude, but otherwise leaves the latter to their own freedom and their own initiative, has clearly nothing in common with a theory which entrusts the whole control both of thought and action to the arbitrary *fiat* of the despot and insists that every 'subject' holds his life, his freedom, his property, solely at the sovereign's will. To offer the gloss for the theory is not to defend the theory, but merely to degrade it. It is to reduce one of the boldest arguments ever put forward to the dead level of Whiggish timidity; to strip 'one of the greatest thinkers upon record' of all claim to our wonder and admiration. The theory of Hobbes is a theory of unadulterated despotism, or it is nothing. Freedom to him is not a horse who, with the aid of bit and bridle, can be made extremely useful; it is a wild beast to be chained and barred. The gloss may have all the merits in the world, as an independent theory; as an interpretation of *Leviathan* it is worth nothing.

But, if *Leviathan* is useless as a key to history, it is equally fruitless as a theory of the State. The 'society' called together by the 'covenant' is seen, directly we examine it, to be no society at all. All life is gathered in the 'one man' at the head of it; the rest of the body is a dead weight, a mere unprofitable mass. Is this what any man in his senses means by a community? Does it answer in the remotest degree to what even the most timid of reactionaries understands by the State? It is of the essence of every community that life should be more or less evenly diffused among its members; that every one of them should contribute his share, large or small, to the activity of the whole. And if it be objected that, in that case, the number of communities in the whole course of recorded history is comparatively small, the answer is that, on any rigorous interpretation, this is unfortunately too true; but that, while many communities have made some approach, more or less distant, to such an ideal, Leviathan, as conceived by Hobbes, is and is intended to be the very negation of it, the one infallible and perpetual bar to its eventual achievement; seeing that, apart from the 'one man or one assembly of men,' no single other person is admitted to any share, however paltry, in the life of the 'community' so established. Indeed, even the modicum of civic life conceded under the narrowest of the feudal monarchies would have been anathema to Hobbes. To find his ideal realised, or nearly so, we must go back to Babylon or Assyria. The assemblage of men supposed by him is, as Rousseau said, 'not a community, but an aggregate': [1] a mob huddled together by sheer terror, not that organised body which alone can be called a State.

That being so, it is manifest that, with two exceptions to be mentioned directly, Hobbes, with all his genius, contributed nothing to the theory of the State. By the mere perversity of his conclusions, he may have turned others—Spinoza, Locke and Rousseau—in the direction of the light; but his own face was set resolutely towards the dark. As an historical document, as a monument of the passions excited by the first stirrings of revolution in Europe,

[1] 'C'est, si l'on veut, une agrégation, mais non pas une association; il n'y a là ni bien public ni corps politique' (*Contrat Social*, I. v.).

Leviathan is of the last importance. As a step in the development of political philosophy, it is worth nothing.

There are, however, the two exceptions. Hobbes was the first writer to grasp the full importance of the idea of Sovereignty; and he was the first writer—this unfortunately is a much more questionable service—to attempt a complete severance of politics from morals.

Among the most notable omissions of Greek philosophy is the absence of any clear attempt to define the nature of Sovereignty, to determine its seat, or settle the ultimate sanction on which it rests. Its existence was indeed implied in Plato's and Aristotle's conception of Politics as the 'architectonic science': of the State as the ultimate authority for controlling and harmonising all the diverse energies of its members. But no effort was made either to fix the place where this power resides, or to define its limits, or to determine precisely what it is that obliges the community to obey it. Hints and fragments of answers to most, or all, of these questions—especially the last—are to be found scattered about their writings. But it is plain that the idea of Sovereignty had never presented itself to them as a clear-cut conception; and it follows that no clear-cut answer to such questions is to be looked for at their hands.

It is with the Roman jurists that the idea first takes definite shape, in the doctrine of *majestas*. But with these writers the idea was inevitably so closely interwoven with that of personal allegiance to an individual—they were, moreover, so completely free from any speculative impulse—that we owe to them little more than the coining of a name, the invention of an apt term, round which might be crystallised the conceptions already dimly recognised by the Greek philosophers and eventually to be defined, with ever-increasing clearness, by the course of history and the efforts of subsequent thinkers to interpret it.

So the matter virtually rested until the coming of Hobbes. The idea of Sovereignty which he propounded is, no doubt, utterly inadmissible. When pressed to its logical conclusion, it is, in fact, manifestly self-destructive. For, by reducing the whole herd to slavery, he has left no State for the sovereign to govern. By striking out one term of the relation, he has robbed the other of all intelligible meaning. Yet, in spite of this and other perversions, he must take the credit of being the first to see that the idea of Sovereignty lies at the very root of the whole theory of the State; and the first to realise the necessity of fixing precisely where it lies, and what are its functions and its limits. His solution of the three latter points may have been pernicious and impossible. But the first step towards a satisfactory solution of the problem was to perceive that it was there, and that an answer to it must be found.

The flaws of the answer which he himself offered have been already pointed out. The Sovereignty of Hobbes is placed solely in the ruler, who thereby becomes avowedly a despot. The sanction on which it rests, in the first and braver intention of the author, is nothing but terror; and if, at a later stage of the proceedings, the idea of obligation is brought in, that is merely to avert the impending ruin of his argument, to cobble up the breach which every moment was yawning wider and wider beneath his feet. The supplementary plea, as we have seen, is manifestly inconsistent with that originally brought forward: the argument from duty utterly irreconcilable with that from self-interest and fear. Finally, the functions of the sovereign are all-embracing, and his power without limits. The life, the property, the freedom of his subjects, alike in matters of thought and in matters of action, are absolutely at his mercy. In short, despotism pure and simple—that is the Sovereignty of Hobbes.

The attempt to divorce politics from morals has been fruitful of ill consequences. But, as the two fields are certainly not identical, it was bound to be made sooner or later; and here again Hobbes was the pioneer.

Against this claim two objections—the one historical, the other philosophical—might possibly be lodged. Historically, it might be argued that the honour, if such it is to be reckoned, belongs rather to Machiavelli. And philosophically, that what Hobbes did was rather to bring morals down to the level of politics than to mark out the frontiers between them.

The former of these objections rests upon an evident confusion. The question is not, Who was the first to divorce politics from morals in the field of practice? If that were all, no question could be more futile. The innovation is as old as the world. It goes back, doubtless, as far as Nimrod, or Cain, the first recorded builder of a city. It had been followed by every monarch and every republic upon record. And all that Machiavelli did was to reduce the time-honoured practice to system and illustrate it by examples profusely furnished by the Popes and Princes of his time. Of any speculative theory—and it is that alone which is here in question—he was entirely innocent. That was an honour thrust upon him, as an afterthought, by distraught professors in search of a reputable sponsor for their unchartered ravings. And if Machiavelli's is the only claim to the contrary, Hobbes may rest placidly upon his laurels. In him we have at least a stubborn attempt to base the whole political life of man, from first to last, upon nothing but self-interest; to admit none but self-regarding motives into the speculative origins and subsequent maintenance of the State.

It is perfectly true that he applies the same principle to the life of the individual: that, on his theory, the moral, no less than the political, life of man is governed solely by utilitarian—which, on his interpretation, means purely selfish—motives. And that, no doubt, is enough to distinguish him sharply from those later writers who admit disinterested motives—or, at any rate, motives which in long course of time have become disinterested—in matters of personal conduct, but steadfastly deny their legitimacy, and even their very existence, in matters of State: who are idealists, or something like it, in the region of ethics, but pure materialists in that of politics. Still, the main point for our purpose is not whether moral considerations are to be banished from morals as well as from politics, but whether they are to be banished from politics. And on this point Hobbes gives every guarantee that could be desired. What impels men, as he holds, to enter society is not any dim instinct of human kindliness, not any natural hatred of the 'force and fraud' to which they are driven by the truculence of their neighbours, but sheer terror of the bodily harm with which they are perpetually threatened, sheer disgust at the physical misery of the state of nature.

And the significance of this picture is clearly seen when we compare it with that offered by other chroniclers of the state of nature. All the others admit softer elements side by side with the more brutal qualities of primitive man. All the others, therefore—above all, Locke and Rousseau—allow for the working of moral, no less than of purely material, motives for the subsequent formation of the civil state. Hobbes alone confines the natural man to the lowest instincts of the brute. He alone, therefore, shuts the door to all but animal motives for his entry into civil society.

And that society, once formed, is inevitably true to its origin; it reproduces, and cannot but reproduce, the character of the rock whence it was hewn. The sole bond of union between the members of Leviathan is a common terror, the fear of relapsing into the state of nature. Or to speak more correctly, between one member and another there is no bond at all. The only cement provided is that which binds each of them, singly and separately, by sheer terror to the tyrant who stands above them all. It is quite true that this purely material bond, a bond of undisguised selfishness, is subsequently reinforced by a tie—that of obligation to fulfil their contract, to perform the covenant made between each of them and their common master—which claims to be a matter of duty; and that this tie is further supplemented by a whole code of 'natural laws' which are intended to carry with them the same implication. Not only, however, are these newcomers manifest intruders, but it is clear that Hobbes himself was shy of invoking them and more than half sceptical as to their value for his purpose. Even if that were not the case, it would still be true that between the members of the 'mortal god' there is no bond, moral or otherwise; that, after as before their embodiment, they are a mere agglomerate of atoms, held in their place not by mutual attraction, but solely by a compelling force exercised from above. In other words, the exclusion of all moral motive from the internal life of the community, the banishment of all sense of fellowship, is as complete as human ingenuity can make it. Between its members there is no moral relation, if only because, strictly speaking, there is no relation at all.

As for the external relations of the State, it was no part of Hobbes' plan to discuss them. He was so busy forging the chains which were to bind the subject within that he had no thought left for the policy which should be followed towards rivals, and possible enemies, without. Accordingly, the whole matter of foreign politics is dismissed in a single paragraph.

In that one paragraph, however, is contained all that is necessary for our purpose. We learn that 'the offices of one sovereign to another are all comprehended in what is commonly called the law of nations'; and that 'the law of nations and the law of nature is the same thing.'[1] By the 'law of nature' we are clearly to understand the code of laws—'To seek peace and ensue it,' 'By all means we can to defend ourselves,' and the rest—which Hobbes had laid out in two earlier chapters, and which he had there applied to individuals in the state of nature. It follows therefore that, whereas each State, as regards its own members, is under the law of Leviathan, they are all, as regards each other, solely under the law of nature. And our first inference would naturally be that the foreigner is to be let off far more lightly than the subject: that, while all the rigours of the system are to be reserved for the latter, all its more merciful elements are to be set in motion for the benefit—and, as it works out in practice, for the sole benefit—of the former.

If this were really the case, we should have to admit that the moral relations, which are, to all intents and purposes, excluded from the internal government of the State, are readmitted in all that belongs to its external dealings; and that, in all matters of foreign policy, Hobbes has conspicuously failed to carry out that divorce between politics and morals with which he has been credited. Such a result would be explicable only on the assumption that he was completely indifferent to foreign politics: so indifferent that

[1] *Leviathan*, chap. xxx. (close).

he did not even trouble to make his theory of them square with his theory of internal government. And even so, the inconsistency would be sufficiently disconcerting.

In fact, however, he is careful to mark that his reference to the natural law in this connection is to be taken as no more than a pious opinion; and that, in the absence of any sanction, such as in home affairs is afforded by the sword of the despot, this 'law'—even if we admit it to be a law, and not rather a counsel of prudence—is no better than 'words and breath.' Thus, if he reminds us that 'the same law which dictates to men that have no civil government what they ought to do and what to avoid in regard of one another, dictates the same to Commonwealths,' he insists in the same breath that the decision in this matter rests solely with 'the consciences of sovereign Princes and sovereign Assemblies,' and that, between States as between individuals, 'there is no court of natural justice but in the conscience only.' And this is to give away the whole position. For, if the conscience was of no avail as between individuals, how can we expect it to win more respect as between nations? If the sanction of force was necessary in the one case, how should it be any less necessary in the other? And if the state of nature is for individuals a state of war, the 'war of all against all,' in which it is explicitly asserted that 'nothing can be unjust,' that 'the notions of right and wrong, justice and injustice, have there no place,' and that in such a state 'force and fraud are the two cardinal virtues,' why, in the name of reason, should the picture be any different in the case of nations?

The truth is that all these questions had been answered by Hobbes himself with unwary candour, in an earlier passage of his treatise: in the crucial chapter 'Of the Natural Condition of Mankind concerning their Felicity and Misery.'[1] At a critical point of his argument, he supposes himself met by the awkward objection: 'Peradventure there never was such a time, nor condition of war, as this': in other words, that the assumption of an original war of all against all—an assumption, as we have seen, essential to his whole subsequent argument—is wholly unwarranted by the facts. While admitting that this may be so as regards individuals—in itself a sufficiently damaging admission—he turns round upon his imaginary opponent with the retort, obviously regarded as unanswerable, that such a condition is at any rate the normal and standing condition as between State and State: 'Though there never had been any time wherein particular men were in a condition of war one against another, yet in all times kings and persons of sovereign authority, because of their independency, are in continual jealousies and in the state and posture of

[1] *Leviathan*, chap. xiii.

gladiators, having their weapons pointing, and their eyes fixed, on one another: which is a posture of war.' [1]

After this, what need of further witness? We have from his own lips the confession that, when he talks of 'natural law,' he is trifling just as much with himself as with the reader; that, for nations as for individuals, the 'state of nature' is only another term for the state of war; and that which is true of 'particular men' in the days before the Covenant is true of all States at all times and in all circumstances: their 'cardinal virtues are force and fraud.' Could the divorce between morals and politics, in the field of foreign affairs, be carried out more completely? Could any description of the relation, the natural and normal relation, between State and State be more candid or more truculent than 'the posture of gladiators'?

In view of these facts, it will hardly be contended that Hobbes was not as bold a champion for the banishment of morals from politics as he was for the unlimited sovereignty of the State. And in both matters he may fairly claim to have led the way. In both alike his conclusions were lamentably wrong-headed. But in both alike he had the merit of fastening upon points which had hitherto been neglected, of marking out the ground on which, for the next century and more, the main struggle was to be fought out. And this is still more true of his plea for the severance of politics from morals than it is of his assertion of the unlimited sovereignty of the State.

As for the banishment of morals from politics, we must sharply distinguish between the plea itself and the argument by which it was supported. The former was undoubtedly disastrous. For the latter—the assault upon natural law, an assault none the less real because it was not explicitly avowed—there was a solid justification.

The belief in a common code of Right, existing above, apart from and prior to those tribal or national ethics which supply, and have always supplied, the moral substance of man's life—a code recognised as binding upon man as man, above all upon man in the 'state of nature'—this is an illusion, to which neither history, nor probable inference, lends any colourable support. Yet this was the assumption which, taken from the Roman jurists, had rooted itself firmly in the educated mind of Europe and found unquestioned acceptance with one political theorist after another.

Had Hobbes been free to follow the bent of his own genius, he would have rejected it root and branch. In a theory which based society upon force it could manifestly have no place. But even his spirit was not bold enough to cast off the faith of ages at a

[1] *Leviathan*, chap. xiii.

stroke. And besides, the idea of natural law came in as a useful rivet to the chains originally forged for the subjects of Leviathan by self-interest and fear. What he did, therefore, was to reduce it to a mere phantom: to retain it in words, but to strip it, save for the one purpose mentioned, of all intelligible meaning and all practical effect.

This was obviously a pure makeshift. And it is clear that the task left for his successors was either to recast the idea of natural law from top to bottom, or to get rid of it altogether. The former, the more difficult, task was that reserved for the writers immediately preceding and following the French Revolution. The latter—the heroic, but impossible, remedy—was the enterprise of Spinoza. In the next chapter we shall see him at work.

CHAPTER III

THE SOCIAL CONTRACT: SPINOZA

THE short life of Spinoza (1632–1677) was covered twice over by the ninety years of Hobbes. He was born more than a generation later than his English forerunner, and died two years before him. Yet within that brief space he had recast the whole fabric of philosophy: metaphysics, ethics and politics. And if Hobbes was in many ways the last of the schoolmen, Spinoza, at least in ethics and politics, was the first of the moderns. In metaphysics he must divide that honour with Des Cartes. But, whereas the French thinker represents the analytic element in modern speculative thought, Spinoza is the fountain-head of its more constructive, and therefore more vital, energies. His influence upon the systems of Schelling and Hegel, the extraordinary fascination upon both the character and the philosophical thought of Goethe, are facts which cannot be gainsaid. And there could be no stronger witness either to the depth of his genius or the fruitfulness of the vein which he opened up.

On political theory he has left no such memorable mark. Yet here too his achievement was notable enough. He was the first thinker since Aristotle to approach the subject without any personal prejudice, without any party passion, to bias his conclusions; the first to treat the facts of political experience as links in a purely natural order; the first, as has already been indicated, to purge political theory, so far as this was humanly possible, from the dogma—so misleading in the narrower, so indispensable in the wider, sense—of ' natural law ' or ' natural Right.'

This detachment of spirit had nothing to do with indifference, with coolness to the causes for which men have fought and died. No man had a deeper love of freedom; none could have branded the evils of tyranny in sterner words than he.[1] It was the fruit of

[1] 'Illa civitas cujus pax a subditorum inertia pendet, qui scilicet velut pecora ducuntur ut tantum servire discant, rectius solitudo quam civitas dici potest' (*T.P.* v. 4). 'Sed si servitium, barbaries et solitudo pax appellanda est, nihil hominibus pace miserius. . . . Servitutis igitur,

sheer intellectual honesty, of a fixed resolve to sacrifice everything, even his most cherished wishes, to the truth. In this we may fairly trace the influence of the community which surrounded him: the ideals of the nation which, having been the first in modern times to throw off the yoke of foreign bondage, was also the first to grant anything like freedom of conscience, to yield to all within its borders the right of worshipping, the still more hotly contested right of 'prophesying,' of speaking and publishing, as they pleased.[1] That is the debt of Spinoza to the land of his adoption; just as the religious fervour of the *Ethics*, where we hear the voice of the last of the Prophets, was a direct inheritance from the nation of his birth.

Spinoza's theory of politics is embodied in two treatises, both written in Latin: *Tractatus theologico-politicus*, published anonymously in 1670, and *Tractatus politicus*, left unfinished at his death and published in the course of the same year (1677). The latter, fragment though it is, is the more complete of the two; but there are certain points, notably those connected with the Contract and with the question of religious freedom, on which the earlier treatise is the more explicit.

No man has ever written with a clearer consciousness of the end he had in view. It was, as he expressly tells us, to recall the 'science' of politics from the pursuit of what ought to be to the study of what is; to clear the ground of the 'utopian dreams' with which the philosophers had cumbered it, and once more to base 'the most practical of all sciences' upon the facts of human nature as experience shows them actually to be.[2]

But what of the method which such a science should follow? In general terms, it is the method of intellectual contemplation, undisturbed by any attempt at moral assessment, by any award either of praise or blame. 'Others,' he says, 'have treated the actions and passions of men as matter for tears or laughter, for reprobation or loathing. It is my object to understand them. Accordingly, I have set myself to study them with the same disinterestedness that I should bring to any problem of mathematics. To me, as I contemplate them, love, hatred, envy, anger, boastfulness, pity and other emotions are not accidental vices, to which man yields by his own fault, but properties inherent in his nature; just as heat and cold, storm and thunder, are properties inherent in the nature of air. Inconvenient they may be, but they are not to be got rid of. They are due to definite causes,

---

non pacis, interest omnem potestatem ad unum transferre' (*ib.* vi. 4). The reference in the former passage is to Tacitus, *Agricola*, chap. xxx.; in the latter to Tacitus, *Hist.* i. 1. (*T.P.* = *Tractatus politicus*; *T.T.* = *Tractatus theologico-politicus*.)

[1] *T.T.*, Praefatio, § 12.

[2] *T.P.* i. 1-4.

by studying which we seek to arrive at an understanding of the properties themselves.'[1]

In other words, as it would seem, the methods of politics are the methods of science. And a modern reader might naturally jump to the conclusion that the sciences in question are the inductive sciences, and consequently that the method intended can be no other than the inductive method. This, however, would be a hasty inference. For there are various indications—such as the repeated use of the terms 'deduction' and 'demonstration,'[2] or again the analogy expressly drawn between politics and mathematics[3]—which show it to have been the deductive rather than the inductive sciences that Spinoza, at least in some of his utterances, had in mind. And this is confirmed by a reference to the *Ethics*, where the argument is marshalled as so many propositions of Euclid and the whole method is avowedly—not to say, defiantly—deductive. Spinoza himself is at the pains to rank politics in the same class with ethics.[4] And even if this were not so, it would be strange that the method of the one study should not also be the method of the other.

Yet here again we must be on our guard against rash conclusions. For the first thing to strike us in the *Tractatus politicus* —and the same thing applies to the earlier treatise also—is that the mathematical appliances of the Ethics—the Definitions, the Axioms, the Propositions, the Corollaries and the rest—have been thrown to the winds. Awkward enough as a framework for ethical discussion, Spinoza must have felt that they would be a thousand times more awkward when forced upon 'the most practical of all sciences,' upon the enormous complexity of politics. And this itself is enough to prove that he had more misgivings as to the fitness of the deductive method than, at first sight, he seemed willing to allow.

We go back, therefore, to probe more strictly than has yet been done into the exact terms of his utterances upon method. On the threshold, then, of the *Tractatus politicus* we are met by the

[1] *T.P.* i. 4. I have ventured to add 'accidental' and 'to which man yields by his own fault,' for the sake of clearness. They are to be justified by the whole argument of *T.P.* ii. 5-8 (compare § 18), which is a commentary on the text: 'Nihil homo, seu ratione seu cupiditate ductus, agit nisi secundem leges et regulas naturae, hoc est ex naturae jure' (§ 5). Indeed the words 'vitia in quae homines sua culpa labuntur' occur in the first sentence of the treatise.

[2] *T.P.* i. 4, 7; ii. 1; *T.T.*, Praefatio, § 29.

[3] *T.P.* i. 4.

[4] Thus he interrupts his ethical argument to insert, in a *scholium*, a sketch of his theory of politics: *Ethics*, iv. 37 (Sch. ii.).

statement that, unlike other philosophers, he has throughout set himself to bring his deductions 'into complete accordance with practical experience.'[1] 'I am clearly convinced,' he assures us, 'that experience has furnished us with all conceivable types of polity which enable men to live in harmony with each other: with all the various means by which the multitude may be guided and by which it may be kept within fixed bounds. Accordingly I do not believe that reflection can supply us with any results in this field that have not already been revealed by experience, unless indeed it were something utterly at variance with experience: that is, of no practical use whatever.' And that is the reason why the practical statesman—he was thinking certainly of Machiavelli, and perhaps of Bacon and Grotius[2]—have done far more by their writings than the men of theory, 'and above all, the theologians,' for the advancement of political science; 'for they have put themselves to the school of experience, and therefore have taught nothing which does not bear upon our practical needs.'[3]

The natural inference from all this is that the right method of political enquiry, in Spinoza's view, must be to start with an analysis of the facts—the facts of human nature on the one hand, of political society in all its varying forms upon the other—and to employ deduction solely as the means for establishing a rational connection between them: for showing how, when one or two cardinal principles are firmly grasped and the leading types of political society—that is, the leading ideals of political action—clearly distinguished, all the facts, so far as they are not the result of pure accident or of national caprice,[4] are seen to follow by an inevitable consequence, to justify themselves according to the law of reason. And, on the whole, he must be allowed to have carried out the method so announced with remarkable consistency.

But if this be a true account of the matter, it is clear that the 'deduction' of political theory is, to Spinoza, a thing very different from the deduction of mathematics. The one science is entirely independent of experience; the other, as he conceived it, draws all its material from experience, and its results have at every turn to be checked by experience. Deduction is the sole method open to the one science; into the other it enters, as it enters into all consecutive trains of reasoning, scientific or otherwise, only as one of two co-operating elements; and the part it plays, though possibly a larger, is not a conspicuously larger, part in it than it is in them.

[1] *T.P.* i. 4.

[2] For his view of Machiavelli see *T.P.* v. 7.

[3] *T.P.* i. 2-3.

[4] For instances of his allowance for historical accident or national caprice see *T.P.* viii. §§ 18, 37.

On a close scrutiny, it would seem that the same is true, though doubtless in a less degree, even of the *Ethics*. The deductive form in which, most unfortunately, Spinoza was there at the pains to cast his thought, is in fact largely an illusion; though an illusion which has necessarily left its mark on the reality which lies behind. That he should have bowed himself to the yoke is a curious instance of the submissiveness with which even the strongest minds will yield to the dominant studies of their day. And just as the moral and political thinkers of the last generation were misled by the masterful influence of chemistry and biology, so we have to admit that, in ethics at any rate, Spinoza was overborne—in externals, no doubt, rather than in essentials—by the then fashionable obsession of geometry. The wonder is that, in politics, he should have escaped almost unscathed.[1]

With these considerations in mind, what, we ask, were the first principles upon which Spinoza relied as the basis for his 'deduction'? For practical purposes, they may be reduced to one: the axiom that right and power are one and the same thing; that 'every natural object receives from nature, for all purposes of being and working, exactly as much right as it has power; that the natural right of nature as a whole, and therefore of every individual thing contained in her, extends as far as its power; and consequently that, whatever any single man does by the laws of his own nature he does in virtue of an absolute right of nature, and that his right over nature extends precisely as far as his power.'[2]

This, it will be remembered, was also the principle of Hobbes. But whereas Hobbes confines it to human beings—and to them only so long as they remain in the state of nature—and whereas political bias forbade him, even within that narrow range, to apply it with anything like consistency, to Spinoza it is a principle which embraces not only man but the whole world of nature, nay even God himself; and he works it out with a consistency which is proof against every scruple, however sacred, and quails before no consequences, however disconcerting. To him it is, in the fullest sense, a speculative principle which unravels the secret of the whole universe. To Hobbes it is no more than a political picklock which, as he speedily discovers, can be used just as well to break into his own house as to rifle the liberties of his neighbour.

[1] For a memorable defence of his method see *Ethics*, iii. (Preface): 'Mirum videbitur quod hominum vitia et ineptias more geometrico tractare aggrediar, et certa demonstratione velim ea quae rationi repugnare quaeque vana, absurda et horrenda esse clamitant. . . . Itaque humanas actiones atque appetitus considerabo perinde ac si quaestio de lineis, planis aut de corporibus esset.'

[2] *T.P.* ii. 2-4; *T.T.* xvi. 2-11.

Thus, as conceived by Hobbes, the principle that right is might is incomplete in itself, and it is not consistently worked out. It is upon the latter defect that Spinoza fastens in a letter which defines with perfect exactness the relation in which he stands to his English forerunner. 'In political theory, the difference between me and Hobbes is that I keep the principle of natural right absolutely watertight; and that, in every possible form of State, I conceive the rights of the ruler as against the subject not to exceed the limits of the power which he possesses in excess of the subject: that being a principle which is universally observed in the state of nature.'[1]

By 'keeping the principle of natural right absolutely watertight,' it is clear that Spinoza means consistently maintaining its absolute identity with power: the consistent refusal to contaminate it with those ideas of moral right and wrong—or again, of juridical right—which, as he held, have wrought nothing but havoc with the whole course of political speculation. The implied criticism of Hobbes, for failing to keep this principle 'watertight,' is perfectly just. So, when due allowance has been made for human frailty, is the explicit assertion of his own success in that delicate, not to say desperate, undertaking.

With this clue in his hand and with his eye steadily fixed upon the facts of human nature as he saw them, Spinoza sets out to unthread the labyrinth of man's political existence and of the conditions which led up to it. The traditional notions of his time—the state of nature, the social contract, the establishment of civil government in virtue of that contract—all reappear, however faintly, in the picture which results. But, in the light of the above principle, each of them in turn takes a strangely different colour, and the theory as a whole is transformed out of all knowledge. The following sketch of the argument will bear out this assertion.

As an integral part of nature, and no *imperium in imperio* standing aside from and above nature, man holds all his powers and all his impulses—the most irrational as well as the most rational, the most self-seeking as well as the most self-sacrificing—direct from God. 'Good' and 'bad' alike, they are a manifestation of God's power, and only through a continuance of that manifestation do they maintain themselves in being. That being so, it is idle to suppose that any human existence, any human institution, can be purely good, or purely rational; it is equally idle to quarrel with those elements of folly or evil which we discover, or seem to

[1] Epist. 50 (ed. Bruder, vol. ii. p. 298). The original of the letter, which is to an anonymous correspondent, was in Dutch; it has come down to us in a Latin translation.

discover, in them. All elements alike are due to natural, and therefore necessary, causes. All alike have their justification in the universal laws of nature; and if those laws were, as they are not and cannot be, fully known to us, we should ourselves admit the justification. Apply this principle to the chief phases of man's existence—to the state of nature on the one hand, to the civil state upon the other—and mark the consequences which result.[1]

In both states alike, man is 'led rather by blind desire than by reason'; and his powers—consequently, on Spinoza's principles, his rights also—are of necessity limited by this infirmity. If, therefore, it were in the power of man to exchange the one leading for the other, who can doubt that he would strain every nerve to do so? The instinct of self-preservation, the most primitive and most fundamental of all instincts, would inevitably drive him to that course. His powers, his rights, his liberty could all be extended beyond measure by the change. And the mere fact that he does not make it is unanswerable proof that he is incapable of doing so.[2]

Circumstances, however, may be either more or less favourable to the fostering of rational desires and the repression of those which Spinoza describes as 'blind.' And it is the endeavour of the wiser spirits to bring about such conditions as are likely to strengthen the one and discourage the other.

In the state of nature, the circumstances are undoubtedly at their worst. Each man individually is more completely the prey of blind desire and, owing to the lack of any common understanding, all alike are more completely the prey of each other's passions —anger, envy, hatred and the like—in one word, all are more completely in a state of 'natural hostility' toward each other than in the civil society which eventually follows.[3] In the absence of any restraining law, or social bond of any kind, the powers—and therefore the rights and liberty—of each individual may, in appearance, be greater than they become in civil society, as we know it; but, in reality, they are less. In fact, it may be fairly be said that, 'so long as the natural rights of men depend for their maintenance upon the unaided power of the individual to assert them, so long they have no existence.' And, as the state of things of which this is true is precisely what we mean by the state of nature, it follows that 'natural right,' in the sense in which it is the distinguishing mark of man, is hardly conceivable except in the civil state.'[4]

Here—and in the desire, perhaps not more than half conscious, to provide for the satisfaction of those wants which are not to be

[1] *T.P.* ii. 2, 3, 8; *T.T.* xvi. 2-11.
[2] *T.P.* ii. 5-6.
[3] *Ib.* ii. 14; *T.T.* xvi. 8.
[4] *T.P.* ii. 15; *T.T.* v. 18-20; xvi. 13.

satisfied 'without mutual aid between man and man'—lies the real motive for the origin of the civil state. And among such wants Spinoza is careful to reckon not only the physical needs which are obvious to every eye, but also the moral and intellectual needs which are involved in man's natural craving for the free growth —or, as the text quaintly says, the 'cultivation'—of his mind.[1]

Whether, then, by a formal agreement, or, as in the final form of his theory he would rather seem to believe, by a silent and gradual, indeed a half-unconscious, process, men are ultimately led—so Spinoza, like others before and after him, concluded—to abandon the natural, and to enter what is now universally known as the civil, state.[2] And what, we ask, are the distinguishing marks by which the civil state may be known? They are the formation of a community, or group of men, with a specified portion of land for tillage and habitation; the provision of a defensive force sufficient to drive off all aggressors; above all, the establishment of 'common rights and laws,' enabling or constraining all members of the community to live upon such terms as may be agreed upon between them. And all this is only possible if a Government be instituted with powers, recognised by all the members, to constrain each one of them to 'live according to the common will of all.'[3]

Of these conditions, it is manifest that the last two—the determination to live according to the common will of all and the establishment of a common Government for the formation and maintenance of that will—are by far the most deep-reaching. It is upon these, in fact, that the whole subsequent argument is built. And of the two, the former—the determination 'to live according to the common will of all, to be guided, as it were, by one mind'—is the more fundamental. It is the idea, of which the other, the institution of a common Government, is no more than the outward expression: the soul, of which it is the body.

The analogy would have been welcomed by Spinoza: and all the more, because it cuts both ways. For if the Government is, on the one side, no more than the outward form, the body, of the Community, on the other side it is a form which is absolutely essential to the very existence of the Community, a body without which the soul itself is impossible and inconceivable. And if Spinoza differs at all on this point from other writers, it is in attaching not less, but more, importance to the exact form assumed by the Government, the precise terms on which power is committed to its hands. There is a sense, no doubt, in which the same

[1] *T.P.* ii. 15; *T.T.* xvi. 13.
[2] For this curious divergency see below, pp. 115-16.
[3] *T.P.* ii. 15, 21; *T.T.* xvi. 13-25.

thing could be said of Hobbes. But whereas Hobbes admits only one form of government, that of the absolute and irrevocable despot, Spinoza, while maintaining his preference for one form, democracy, is willing to recognise at least two, if not three, others as hardly less legitimate. What he does insist upon is that each of these forms has its own specific dangers; and that, unless the utmost care be taken from the first moment to the last to guard against them, the whole history of the community will be one of weakness, strife, and ultimate civil war; thus defeating the very end for which all government is set up. Hence, while Hobbes sees but one danger, liberty, and provides one all-sufficing remedy, absolute despotism, Spinoza detects a whole army of perils and is ready with a safeguard against each of them. The panacea of Hobbes is simplicity itself; and just because it is a panacea, it is of no value whatever. The weakness of Spinoza, on the other hand, was for excessive subtlety. And if he erred, he erred on the side of attaching too much importance to constitutional checks, to guarantees which, at the first push, might too easily prove to be mere 'scraps of paper.' If he went wrong, it was because he placed too absolute a trust in outward forms of government and took too little thought of the great human forces which alone give them any meaning and by which the most cunningly devised of them may in a single moment be swept hopelessly away. Hence the curious stress which he lays upon the 'original contract' between the Government and the governed: a contract which, whatever he may have thought of the yet more original contract for the creation of the Community, he seems to have held indispensable to every legitimate form of government: as essential to aristocracy or democracy as it is to any monarchy which is not absolutely unlimited—that is, to any monarchy which he was prepared to recognise as permissible at all.[1]

This is the more curious, because on his principles it is manifest, and would be so even if he were not at the pains to remind us of it, that no such contract can be of anything but a one-sided character. Its sole sanction is 'power,' or force. And as the Government is expressly entrusted with the sole power of making the Law, the sole power of interpreting it and the sole power of enforcing it, who does not see that the force in question is wholly in the hands of the Government? and that the one check left to the 'multitude'—that is, the whole body of subjects or citizens—is the check of terror: the fear, never likely to be long absent from the mind of the ruler, that misrule, if carried far enough, will arouse a general revolt of the community, and the force, at one

[1] *T.P.* iv. 6; viii. 1; xi. 1; *T.T.* (but more vaguely), xvi. 58-67; xvii. 1-3.

stroke, be transferred back from the Government to the governed? How far such a check is likely to prove effectual, may well seem a doubtful matter: even more doubtful, it is probable, under modern conditions than under those which prevailed when the *Tractatus politicus* was written. In any case, as Spinoza ruefully admits, its enforcement, or rather the mere prospect of its enforcement, tears away the last pretence of Right and drives us back without concealment upon civil war: that is, upon brute force.[1]

So much for Spinoza's account of the beginnings of government and of the sanction on which it rests. Before continuing the thread of his argument, let us turn back for a moment to consider his far more notable account of the origin of civil society—of the State, as opposed to the mechanism of its Government—and of the change in men's whole outlook upon life which the entry into civil society brings with it.

'All men,' says Spinoza, 'are by nature enemies.'[2] Is this intended for an endorsement of *Leviathan*? does it mean that, to him as to Hobbes, the state of nature is a state of war, the war of all against all? At first sight, we might be tempted to think so. But a more careful reading will convince us that the 'war' of Spinoza, if indeed it can justly be called a war, is at least something very different from the war of Hobbes. To both alike, the state of nature is built upon a volcano. But, whereas to Hobbes the eruption is constant and deadly, to Spinoza it is smouldering and intermittent. It is, in fact, rather the fear of war, than war itself, which makes the scourge of the state of nature. It is a state in which each man is thrown entirely upon his own resources: a state in which, so far from looking for aid from his fellow-creatures, he cannot even count, for long together, upon freedom from their actual hostility. But it cannot be fairly described as a state of war. It is rather a state of settled distrust and of the weakness which distrust, together with his own natural imbecility, brings with it.[3]

Weakness, therefore—a weakness caused partly by distrust of others, partly by the violence of his own passions and the want of any curb to check them, either from within or from without—this is the real mark of man, as he is in the state of nature. And it is in the hope of escaping from all these things, from himself no less than from his neighbours, that he takes refuge in the civil state. It is not only to protect himself from the violence and aggression of his neighbours, it is also to increase the outward comforts of his life by co-operation with his neighbours; it is perhaps still more to win room for the growth of his intellectual and moral faculties by securing that settled peace which is to be

[1] *T.P.* v. 6. [2] *Ib.* ii. 14. [3] *Ib.* ii. 15.

laid and maintained only through the mutual consent of himself and his neighbours—in one word, it is for intellectual and moral, no less than material, objects—that he exchanges the natural for the civil state. Or, as Spinoza is careful to point out, if he renounces his freedom in the lower sense—the freedom of 'wild nature,' the freedom to act upon the impulse of the moment—it is that he may win it in the higher sense, by giving himself to that service of the 'perfect law of liberty,' which is possible only through the ordered development of all his faculties, intellectual and moral.[1]

It will thus be seen that not only is Spinoza's state of nature a very different thing from that of Hobbes, but also, and consequently, that the motives on which man quitted it are to him very different from those demanded by the whole argument of *Leviathan*. To Hobbes, the state of nature is a state of actual and constant war, of war in as deadly a form as it is possible to conceive; and the sole motive which induces man to enter the civil state is terror, the sense that any condition, however 'miserable,' must be less odious than that to which he is naturally born. To Spinoza, the war of the natural state is potential rather than actual; it is the fear, rather than the taste of it — the mistrust and suspicion, together with the sense of insecurity and weakness which these naturally breed—that weigh upon men's minds. Hence a corresponding change in the motives which lead men to the civil state. Fear, no doubt, is still present and working. But it is no longer the sole motive; it is now no more than an element, perhaps even a subordinate element, in the causes which bring about the transition from the natural to the civil state. Certainly, the points on which Spinoza lays by far the greater stress are the insufficiency of the individual, when left to himself, to provide for anything more than the bare necessaries of life, and the desire to escape from the 'almost brutish existence,' from the intellectual and moral vacuity, to which he was condemned in the state of nature. And this is an order of motive of which there is no vestige in the 'natural history' of Hobbes.

We pass to the last term of the comparison. Entered from motives so different, it is clear that the two kinds of society resulting can have nothing in common. The negative motive which Hobbes assigns for men's flight from the state of nature was bound to reflect itself, and does in fact reflect itself but too faithfully, in the character of the bond which clamps them together in the civil state. It was terror, terror of each other, that drove them together. It is terror, terror of the sword of the despot, which alone prevents

[1] *T.P.* ii. 15; *T.T.* v. 18-20. For Spinoza's doctrine of freedom see *T.P.* ii. 7; *Eth.* iv. 73.

them from flying instantly apart. The positive motives of Spinoza—not a blind flight from danger and misery, but a dim craving for betterment, intellectual and moral as well as physical—necessarily gives rise to a very different kind of State: a State in which the 'multitude' are in a position to make bargains or 'contracts' with their rulers, a power contemptuously denied to them by Hobbes; a State of which it is the first condition that all shall freely resolve to be 'guided by one will'; a State of which the ideal is—so Spinoza expressly assures us—that the service of all shall be actively enlisted in the attainment of one common purpose, that they shall live not as slaves but as freemen, and be bound together not by fear but by hope.[1] The 'city' of Hobbes, as we have seen, is at best no more than an aggregate, a mere herd. That of Spinoza, at least in ideal, is a living organism, a corporate body animated by one will, a community every member of which contributes, according to his capacity, to the common good. Whether the ideal thus boldly proclaimed is realised in actual working, whether the idea it embodies is consistent with other, and no less essential, elements of Spinoza's system—that, no doubt, is a different matter. But it is one that must be reserved for future discussion.

We take up the thread of Spinoza's argument at the point where, whether with or without a specific contract, he has safely brought his 'multitude'—in his conception, it must always be remembered, an essentially 'free' multitude—into the civil state.[2] How, we ask, are the rights of men affected by this change? The answer is: in the most various—not to say, conflicting—ways. There is a sense, but it is a purely abstract sense, in which they remain exactly what they were before: for in the civil, no less than in the natural, state the rights of man are precisely identical with his powers. There is a sense in which, seeing that the powers of the individual are strictly limited by those of the community, his rights, his power to act as he pleases, are reduced almost to nothing. Lastly, there is a sense in which the growth of his faculties and the newborn sense of security, both of which depend absolutely upon the corporate life of the State, infinitely increase the powers of the individual and, with them, his rights also.

As for the first point, it is, as we have seen, the cardinal principle of Spinoza's theory, the key with which he unlocks all the intricacies of the political problem. Hereafter we shall have to trace the most significant applications which he gives to it in

[1] 'Libera enim multitudo majori spe quam metu, subacta autem majori metu quam spe ducitur' (*T.P.* v. 6).

[2] 'Sed notandum imperium, quod in hunc finem institui dixi, a me intelligi id quod multitudo libera instituit, non autem id quod in multitudinem jure belli acquiritur' (*T.P.* v. 6).

practice. For the moment, there is no more to say about it. The second and third points give us respectively the negative and the positive side of his theory, so far as it touches the rights of the individual. They must therefore be taken together.

At first sight, Spinoza seems to assume as 'absolute a surrender' of the individual to the State as was subsequently demanded by Rousseau. He is careful, however, to point out that such a surrender is, of necessity, subject to sweeping limitations: that there are large tracts of man's life which, from the nature of the case, must always remain beyond the ken of the State; in regard to which, therefore, the individual must always 'remain in the state of nature.' Such is the period of infancy and youth: a period in which the future citizen cannot be supposed to have yet 'learned rational principles of living or have yet acquired the habit of virtue.' [1] Such again is the whole field of man's dealings with his neighbours, in so far—and it is far enough—as they are not, and cannot be, regulated by positive Law. Such lastly is the whole field of thought, of opinion: an impregnable citadel which, try as hard as it may, the State can never enter and even the outworks of which, speech and writing, in its own interests as well as those of the community the very strongest Government will do well never to threaten.[2] Indeed, so conscious is he of the wide field thus left open to individual freedom that he speaks of the 'reign and law of nature' as that 'under which all men are born and under which, for the greater part of their lives, they still continue to live.' [3] If this description errs at all, it errs in attributing not less, but more, freedom to the individual in the civil state than the facts may be thought to warrant.

Yet, however sweeping the limitations, it remains true that, in principle, the individual is rigorously subordinated to the sovereignty of the State. When once he has entered the State, 'he is no longer his own master; he is bound to obey all the commands of the sovereign authority, however unreasonable he may, in his own mind, consider them to be. He has lost all power of deciding for himself what is just and what unjust, what pious and what impious. His individual will, in fact, is replaced by that of the community at large.' [4] Rousseau himself would hardly have ventured to lay down the principle of sovereignty so defiantly as this.

But if Spinoza shows so little respect for the rights of the individual, it is not only because his theory demanded it; it is also because, on independent grounds, he held a strong control from

[1] *T.T.* xvi. 7.

[2] *T.P.* ii. 8. The sub-title of *T.T.* is: 'Quo ostenditur libertatem philosophandi non tantum salva pietate et reipublicae pace posse concedi, sed eandem nisi cum pace r.p. ipsaque pietate tolli non posse.'

[3] *T.P.* ii. 8; *T.T.* xvi. 7.

[4] *T.P.* iii. 5-6.

without to be for the interest of the individual himself. It is not only because, having identified 'right' with 'power,' he was bound to admit that the powers, and therefore the rights, of the community are incomparably greater than those of the individual;[1] it is also because he was convinced that the last thing to be desired for the individual is to be left free to follow his own caprices, to act as 'blind passion' may at any moment suggest. The liberty for which he craves is not licence. To him, the only true freedom is that which comes when man has won for himself the power—and when that power has become a constraining habit—of 'acting according to the law of his own nature': the law of 'virtue or perfection.' And 'this is hardly possible, or conceivable except in the corporate life,' and under the corporate control, 'of the State.'[2]

In all this, alike in what relates to the state of nature and in what relates to the transition from this to the civil state, Spinoza —so far as words go—may fairly claim to have kept his central principle 'watertight': to have held himself within the bounds of a purely natural process; to have maintained that strict identification of rights with powers which formed the starting-point of his argument; to have rigorously excluded all those ideas of Right—that is, of moral obligation to the community, its constituted authorities and its several members—which, to most men, lie at the root of the political, no less than of the ethical, history of mankind and which had forced so strange an entry even into the essentially materialist theory of Hobbes. Whether the consistency, so stoutly maintained in words, extends beyond words to the ideas which lie behind them, is another matter. That, however, is a question which must be held over for future discussion. All we are now concerned to notice is the astonishing grasp which Spinoza throughout maintains of his cardinal principle, and the enormous superiority which his consistent application gives to his theory over the fumbling argument of Hobbes. Hobbes could never make up his mind whether expediency suffices as the motive power of man's political and moral life, or whether it needs to be supplemented by the idea of duty. And by way of covering his confusion, he shuffles in the hybrid 'law of nature,' half prudence and half duty, to make a bridge between the two. Of this expedient Spinoza will have nothing. The 'law of nature' is, to him, merely a convenient phrase for the results yielded by considerations of prudence and expediency. As a law of moral obligation he rejects it root and branch.

Of the price which had to be paid for this consistency he makes no secret. It is not only that, except in organised society, the conception of justice can never take birth in the mind of man, that

[1] *T.P.* ii. 13, 16. [2] *Ib.* ii. 8, 15; *T.T.* xvi. 32.

'justice and injustice are inconceivable save in the State.' So far, he is saying little more than Plato had said before him; no more than Rousseau and a long line of subsequent thinkers were to say between his day and ours. And, so far, the conclusion is beyond assault. Spinoza, however, goes much further than this. So resolved is he to admit no kind of Right save that which flows directly from power that the only code of right and wrong which he is prepared to recognise is that framed by the community, or rather by its Government, and that even the promptings of religion—that love of God, which the author of the *Ethics* cannot refrain from acknowledging—are dismissed as the privileged possession only of the few, as entirely without validity for all those to whom God, 'in whose grasp all men are as clay in the hands of the potter,' has not willed to grant them. The inevitable effect of this is to establish a purely external—it may be, a wholly capricious—code of justice and injustice; to make the community, so far as all outward conduct is concerned, the one mint of moral values, the sole arbiter of right and wrong; to reduce not only 'justice and injustice,' but even 'sin and righteousness,' to a mere creation of the State.[1]

The rights of the State, in short, are, in these as in all other matters, unlimited against its members. And this consequence Spinoza, as we have seen, not only accepts but enforces without pity. To the criticisms which were likely to be launched against him on this account he was, doubtless, thoroughly alive. 'It may be objected,' he writes, 'that a total surrender of this kind to a judgement which is not ours is against reason and therefore that the civil state,' which cannot exist without such a surrender, 'is contrary to reason.'[2]

Spinoza's answer is twofold. It is, on the one hand, that the benefits conferred by the State are so vast, the curb it lays upon our own passions and those of our neighbours so salutary, above all, the interest of keeping the peace so universal, that no price can be too great to pay for them; and that even in the extremest cases, even where the suppression of our own deepest convictions is demanded for the sake of peace, we may rest assured that we have gained far more than we have lost by the surrender of our own will to the common will of all. The true freedom of the individual lies not in licence but in the power of developing all his faculties 'according to the dictates of reason'; and this power can only be secured in gross at the cost of some sacrifice in detail. Moreover, as the author proves at length in his earlier treatise, the wiser the Government the more clearly will it realise that, so far from losing, the State has everything to gain by 'liberty of prophesying'; and when this

[1] *T.P.* ii. 18-23. [2] *Ib.* iii. 6.

lesson is once learned, the worst of the trouble will have been cut off at the source. There may indeed be a handful of fanatics who, in their zeal for a particular religion, condemn the whole Law of the State as impious. The Law must assert itself against them; the resistance of one or two hotheads does not and cannot abrogate the Law of the land. And as for those 'fools and madmen' who defy all Law, as such, they are public enemies and must be proceeded against accordingly.[1]

Such is one half of Spinoza's answer to the enemy's objection. The other half is yet more in the direct line of his main argument and, perhaps for that very reason, still less liable to challenge. It must never be forgotten, he pleads, that the rights of the State, though illimitable in theory, are strictly limited in practice. They are limited by the fact that, whatever may be enforced in the sphere of outward act, the field of opinion and feeling is, by its very nature, beyond assault. They are further limited by the fact that, even in the sphere of action, the assertion of an unreasonable right, a right which affronts the whole community or even any large section of it, will inevitably bring loss of credit, and consequently of power, to the Government which attempts it. It will not impossibly provoke a revolt, in which the Government itself will be swept utterly away.[2]

This contention is vital to the whole argument of Spinoza. It is his answer, and the only answer he had left himself, to the charge that he was indifferent to the welfare and, in particular, to the freedom of the community; that, by identifying right with power, he had reduced all Governments to one dead level of legitimacy and allowed the same justification to the bad as to the good. The answer, upon its own plane, is complete. It is that, without reason and justice, there is no such thing as power; that the ruler who habitually tramples upon them will either be deposed by his subjects or find his power sink to a mere name; and that the life of the community which suffers from such misgovernment is no better than a lingering death. Mere brute force, in truth, is the weakest thing in the world. It is only when guided by reason—only, that is, when it ceases to be brute force—that it becomes power indeed. In other words, the powers, and therefore the rights, of the ruler are strictly measured by the degree of wisdom and insight, of justice and forbearance, which he brings to the task he has undertaken; and the same thing, with the necessary change of terms, is true of the community as a whole.[3]

It is in this last application that his argument is at its most original and its best. 'Human nature being everywhere the

[1] *T.P.* iii. 6-8; *T.T.* xvi. 58-63; xix. 21-25; xx. 1-46.
[2] *T.P.* iii. 8-9; iv. 4. [3] *Ib.*

same,' he urges, 'it follows that the civil man is not born, but made': that the difference between one community and another is due solely to the difference of their laws. If, therefore, it be found that crime or sedition is rife in any community, that is the fault either of its constitution or of the Government which administers it. And the same is true of those cases where sedition is either held down merely by terror, or staved off purely by the cowardice of the citizens. The Government may appear to be strong; but, in reality, it is miserably weak. So also is the community which submits to it. The powers of such a community are paralysed by strife or nervelessness. Its life is one long struggle against death. The peace it enjoys is not the true peace, which rests, and can only rest, 'upon courage and constancy, upon the persistent resolve to carry the will of the whole body into act'; it is, at bottom, no more than immunity from open war. Everything about it, in short, is negative, and nothing positive. The community itself is not a community, but a 'flock of sheep.' In the words of Tacitus, 'it is a wilderness,' not a State.[1]

This argument is driven home in the crucial chapter, 'Of the highest prosperity of the State,' which is subsequently explained to mean 'the highest prosperity of any form of State'; a prosperity, that is, wholly independent of the particular form—monarchy, aristocracy, or democracy—which a given community may assume. The object of this chapter is to prove that, in making the above distinctions, the author is true to the principles which he had proclaimed from the beginning; that they were, in fact, inherent in the identification of rights with powers which is the corner-stone of the whole system. And here his position is impregnable. Once admit, as the very force of the term compels us to admit, that the powers in question are not powers on paper, but powers which can be enforced in practice, and the rest of the argument follows of itself.[2]

The consequence on which Spinoza himself lays the greatest stress is the distinction between the free State, the State founded upon the will of a 'free multitude,' and the despotic State—in particular, the State based on the 'right of conquest'—which Grotius had justified and which was the ideal of Hobbes. This distinction does indeed follow directly from his cardinal principle, and it goes to the root of the whole matter. It is true, he allows, that there is 'no essential difference in kind' between the one type and the other. But the ends for which they are formed are so contrary, the means by which each is maintained so diverse, the powers and rights of which each is master so incommensurable, that it is impossible to regard them as governed by the same principle, or as belonging

[1] *T.P.* v. 3-4; vi. 4.   [2] *Ib.* v. 1-2.

to the same sphere. The one is founded to secure freedom, the free development of the powers both of the individual and of the collective whole; the other, to rivet the yoke of the conqueror or despot upon a community of slaves. The one is governed in the main by hope; the other, solely by fear. The one, therefore, stands for the highest, the other for the lowest, degree of power, and consequently of Right, conceivable whether for the whole community or for the individuals who compose it.[1]

It is true that a more complete unity and a more unbroken peace are claimed for the despotic State than for the free. That, however, as the above argument has shown, is a mere matter of words. Directly we pass beyond the words to the facts which lie behind them, it becomes evident that the truth is exactly the reverse: that the peace of despotism is either lethargy, or a veiled form of war; its unity, the unity not of life, but of death; its strength only another name for weakness; and consequently that to centre all the powers of the State upon an absolute ruler is to defeat the very ends for which the State is founded; that, once more to borrow the language of Tacitus, such a course is in the interest of slavery, not of peace.

Thus, in the end, the theory of Spinoza works itself out to practical issues strangely different from those which it seemed to threaten at the beginning. The Right, which was reduced to a phantom in its own name, returns to life and vigour under the *alias* of power. And the despotism, which we might have expected to see enthroned as the highest, because the strongest, form of government, is cast out with contempt, as an infallible source of weakness both to the despot and to the community he enslaves.

Such is the theory of Spinoza, so far as it concerns the inner working of the body politic; so far as it touches the relation of the community to its rulers, of the individual to the State. With a few reservations to be made later, it abundantly justifies his claim to have treated the political life of man as a link in a purely natural order, to have 'kept watertight' his original refusal to regard 'right' as anything but another name for 'power.' It is probably the boldest attempt ever made to build the inner life of the State solely upon expediency, to the total exclusion of obligation and Right. And the very consistency with which he applies this principle enables him to escape the degrading consequences which have too often been drawn from it: the worship of force, of which Hobbes was the unblushing champion; the tendency to bow down before the established order, just because it is established, from which Burke himself cannot claim to have kept entirely free. This, however, must not blind us to the fact that he does

[1] *T.P.* v. 6.

base his theory solely upon expediency; and that, so far as he differs from other champions of that principle, it is because he is not less, but more, consistent than they: not less, but more, stubborn in excluding considerations of Right.

The same principle is applied, as indeed it was bound to be applied, to the relations between State and State. Here, however, the conditions are widely different; and we must be prepared for a corresponding difference in the tone of the author's practical conclusions. The conditions differ, in that the relations between one State and another are necessarily of a more external, a less organic, character than those which exist between members of the same community, or between that community and its Government. It follows that not one of the arguments, which assumed the State to form an organic unity, has here the smallest application. The conditions there present are here, *ex hypothesi*, entirely lacking. Hence all appeals to the need of making the communal life at once as intense and as harmonious as possible—appeals which, as we have seen, play so large a part in Spinoza's handling of the internal life of the State and put so new a colour upon the whole principle of expediency—are necessarily banished from his account of its external relations. And he is left with nothing better than expediency in the baldest sense of the term: the self-interest of the moment, qualified only by the fear of consequences—of the evils that may spring from attacking a neighbour who may unexpectedly prove more powerful than ourselves, or from pushing an advantage against a weaker neighbour so ruthlessly that he has no choice but to bide his time for the day of vengeance.

It may be objected that Spinoza ought to have reckoned with the possibility of some more intimate relation between State and State; that such a relation—far short of organic, no doubt, but yet of a wholly different order from that denoted by his phrase, 'the state of nature'—has since been established, at least in theory, between the civilised nations of the world; and that, even within his own lifetime, a first step in this direction had been taken at the Treaty of Westphalia. And there is some force in the objection. There are, however, two things to remember. On the one hand, those who witness the first step of a new movement may fairly be pardoned for not recognising its significance: still more, for not foreseeing all that it may lead to in the future. In this case, indeed, all the most notable thinkers of the time—not only Grotius who wrote before, but also Hobbes and even Locke who wrote after, the conclusion of the Treaty—widely as they differed in other respects, were yet of one mind with Spinoza in regarding the normal position of one community to another as being the 'state of nature.' And the same admission—as to the fact, though not the right—was wrung, reluctantly enough, almost a century later from Rousseau, at the moment when, far in advance of his time, he raised his voice to declare that in a Federation of Europe lay the sole hope for the future. On the other hand, it is clear that nothing short of an organic connection—a connection, that is, as close between State and State as that which exists between different members of the same State—would have met the difficulties of Spinoza; and that such a union, inconceivable in his days, is no nearer practical realisation in ours. To say that the establishment of kindlier relations between State and State is a duty of our common humanity is to say nothing to Spinoza. He had rejected all ideas of duty from the inner life of the State. How could he be expected to admit them in a region where, according to ordinary standards, their validity is far more open to question? Even if there had been no such disparity between the two cases, he was the last man in the world to surrender a principle which he had adopted upon conviction and which, in the main field of his enquiry, had yielded such notable results.

With this clue to guide us, we pass at once to enquire what his doctrine of foreign policy actually was. All political communities, in Spinoza's view, are to each other as individuals in the state of nature. And as each of them, even in the least favourable circumstances, is far more capable of protecting itself than any individual can ever be, it is clear that the motives which drive the individual out of the state of nature can have little or no hold upon the State. Remaining then, as they normally do, in the state of nature, all States are 'natural enemies' to each other: unless special measures be taken to the contrary, they are in a settled state of potential war. They have no duties towards each other. They have no rights, except those conferred by proof or presumption of superior power, against each other. And in deciding whether they shall, or shall not, pass from potential to actual hostilities, their action is, and ought to be, determined purely by expediency: by the advantages which one of them may, or may not, hope to reap from attacking another.

For purposes of attack upon a third party, as for those of defence against possible attack, it is, however, clear that one State may find it convenient to make a treaty of alliance with another; to exchange, for those limited purposes, the state of war for a state of peace with that particular Power; and consequently, so far as that Power is concerned, to quit the state of nature and to enter into what, by a stretch of terms, may be called some approach to civil relations with it. Much the same conditions manifestly arise in the treaty of peace which concludes an actual war between one Power and another: with this difference, that on the part of the defeated

State, the motive behind the civil agreement, or treaty, is no longer hope, but fear; no longer expediency dictated by self-interest, but necessity imposed by force. In either case, it is clear that, as the contracting parties inevitably forgo something of their future liberty of action, the agreement lasts, and ought to last, only so long as the conditions which prompted the contract remain unchanged; that no treaty is binding on either party one moment longer than self-interest demands. It is idle to say that promises, once given, must be kept. For that is to appeal to standards which have from the first been barred out of the discussion: to standards of obligation and honour. And the Power which either holds itself bound to respect such standards, or acts on the assumption that they will be respected by others, is no better than a fool. Once more: in the matter of treaties, as in all other fields of political action, expediency, not duty, is the only guide. And between States it is a harsher guide than between one individual and another.[1]

This doctrine has been vehemently assailed by some whose judgement is not to be lightly set aside. It aroused Hallam, for instance, to a blaze of unwonted indignation.[2] And, even when the best face has been put upon it, it remains, in truth, sufficiently disconcerting. The real root of bitterness, however, lies far deeper than this. And there is little use in blaming one application of a principle, when it is the principle itself which is at fault. It is to the initial exclusion of obligation from the sphere of politics that exception should be taken; not to one of the many consequences, however startling, which that exclusion necessarily carries in its train. That Hallam himself failed to see the connection between the doctrine of treaties and the rest of Spinoza's system is hardly to be supposed. But it is not so clear that he was alive to its significance.

The truth is that much of the outcry against Spinoza in this matter of treaties is altogether misplaced. For three-quarters of the treaties in question, we may fairly reckon, it is entirely baseless; and for the remaining quarter, it has no more than a partial justification. Roughly speaking, such treaties fall under three heads. There is the treaty imposed by the conqueror on the conquered at the close of a war. And there are the treaties concluded by the spontaneous act of two States in time of peace:

[1] *T.P.* iii. 14.

[2] 'In this treatise of Politics, especially in the broad assertion that good faith is only to be preserved so long as it is advantageous, Spinoza leaves Machiavel and Hobbes at some distance and may be reckoned the most phlegmatically impudent of the whole school' (Hallam, *Literary History of Europe*, iv. § 76).

treaties which may be either offensive, or defensive, in their general character and purpose.

In the first case, the whole thing is avowedly a matter of compulsion; and no one in his senses has ever supposed that the terms of the treaty will be observed by the defeated nation 'one moment longer than its interest demands,' or its necessity compels. Who ever thought of blaming the Prussians for repudiating in 1813 the treaty imposed upon them by Napoleon in 1806? Who dreams of blaming the Allies for compelling Germany to tear up the treaties of Bucharest and Brest Litovsk? Before such a treaty can be binding, its terms must be intrinsically just; or, at the least, not flagrantly unjust. It is the justice of the terms, not the signature of minister or delegate, that alone constitutes the obligation.

The same appears still more clearly from the negative proof. And this is furnished by the second of our three cases: that of an offensive alliance between two Powers for the destruction of a third. Offensive wars are, by their very nature, unjust; and the more the Powers engaged in launching it, the more unjust it becomes. If, therefore, by a miracle such as probably has never happened, one of the Powers unjustly pledged to an assault of this nature should suddenly desert its accomplice and make such reparation as lies in its power to their intended victim, even to the extent of taking arms against its sworn ally, who can doubt that the breach of faith thus committed would be a return, however late, to the way of justice and honour? that the defaulter would deserve, not the blame, still less the execration, but the respect and praise of mankind?

Thus, of the two cases already taken, the one can hardly be said to involve the principle of obligation in any shape. It is a question, not of good faith, as that is binding between man and man, but of national interest and national passion; perhaps also, as men's minds become slowly humanised, of a just reluctance to disturb the peace of the world for any object not absolutely vital to the national existence. In the other—the offensive alliance—there is obligation in plenty; but it is against the treaty, root and branch. It commands not to fulfil the compact, but to annul it: not to keep the pledge, but to break it.

There remains the case of the defensive alliance. It is the only case in which the contract, as a contract, is morally binding; because it is the only case in which the engagements taken can hardly fail to be just. Whether they were originally promoted by self-interest, or by chivalry, makes no difference. Whatever the motive, it can never be unjust, though it may often be hazardous, and even impossible, to defend the weaker Power against the stronger. And when the promise to do so has once been given, when expectations and perhaps even actions have been based upon it, a refusal to keep it at the hour of need is sheer treachery. The betrayal of Serbia by Constantine in 1915 was an act as unjust as it was personally shameful. The invasion of Belgium by one of the Powers which had sworn to protect her marks a yet lower depth of infamy.

The upshot of all this is that the binding force of treaties depends only in a small degree upon the 'sacredness of the plighted word'; in an infinitely larger measure, upon the intrinsic justice of their terms. In other words, the obligation they impose is not absolute but contingent; and what governs that contingency is the reference to some higher principle—for instance, the welfare of Europe, as a commonwealth of equal and interdependent nations—which lies beyond.[1]

So far as Spinoza may be taken to uphold this view of the matter, the outcry against him is unreasonable. His error lay not in the 'broad assertion' that the obligation of treaties is a qualified and contingent obligation, but in his irrepressible tendency to replace justice, as the determining principle, by expediency: the welfare of the European commonwealth by the interest of any individual nation which, for the moment, may happen to be the stronger. That, however, is an error which is in no way confined to his doctrine of treaties. On the contrary, in one form or another, it lies at the root of his whole theory of politics.

This completes the more speculative part of Spinoza's theory. The remainder of the *Treatise*—unfortunately, the first two sections only were finished—is taken up with a discussion of the three chief types of government, Monarchy, Aristocracy, and Democracy; of the means to be taken for guarding against the abuses to which each of them is liable; and in particular, of the variations in subordinate institutions, such as property, which each such type

[1] As for commercial treaties, they are hardly to be distinguished from ordinary business transactions between man and man, and must be judged by the ordinary laws of individual morality. Hence, in modern times, there is almost always a provision for 'denouncing' them on due notice. Much the same applies to purely temporary contracts, such as an armistice. They are in the nature of a bargain—*quid pro quo*; and the victorious Power, having discharged his part of the bargain (the allowance of a breathing space to the enemy), is entitled to his equivalent. The ultimate sanction is his existing superiority: his power to punish any breach of contract by force of arms. He for his part is bound in honour strictly to keep his side of the bargain.

involves.[1] The details of the discussion are beside our purpose. Only the more general points of interest will be noticed.

First of these, without doubt, is the spirit in which the whole enquiry is undertaken: that spirit of absolute detachment, of which something has been said already. Whatever the writer's personal preferences may have been, they have left no trace upon his conclusions, nor upon the arguments by which he reaches them. As each form of government is placed upon the dissecting table, its merits and defects are laid bare without fear or favour; means for strengthening the one and curbing the other are impartially suggested; above all, each is accepted as a fact which carries its own justification and which, beyond certain easily reached limits, it is in no man's power to alter.

All this is a direct consequence of the cardinal principle that the political life of man is the product of purely natural forces, which human will is powerless to sweep aside, which are to be modified only in secondary points, and which it is therefore the first duty both of the theorist and of the practical statesman to accept, to analyse, and to 'understand.' To adopt this principle was to make a complete breach with the aims and methods pursued by political theorists throughout the Middle Ages and, under another—perhaps, a yet cruder—form during the troubled times which followed. It was to reject the passionate partisanship which had inspired both Papalist and Imperialist, both Monarchist and Republican, during the last four centuries, and to revert once more to the more prudent path marked out by Aristotle: to what, since Saint-Simon and Comte, has been known as the positive spirit and the positive method. It is true that this change of temper had in some degree been anticipated by two writers so different as Bodin and Althusius. But neither of these was enough of a philosopher to make the best of the opportunities which lay within his grasp. And it was reserved for Spinoza to gather the first-fruits of the principle after which they were dimly feeling and to point the way to the richer harvest which was to be reaped by Montesquieu and others in the future. But for one strange omission, of which more will be said hereafter, the results he achieved would have been still more notable than they are.

To analyse the facts was therefore the first task which Spinoza set himself. And it was a task demanding not only the insight of the philosopher, but also, in no small measure, the knowledge of the historian. As to the former, there could be no question. How far was he provided with the latter? In the then dearth of accessible information as to anything later than the fall of the Roman

[1] The section concerning democracy was cut short at the fourth paragraph by the author's death.

Empire, it is perhaps surprising that he should show so wide an acquaintance as he does with the relevant facts: all the more so, as he was the last man in the world to parade his knowledge. The history of the Jews, of Alexander the Great, of the Roman Republic and Empire, of Castille and Aragon, of the English Monarchy, of the Dutch Republic, of the Republics of Venice and Genoa—all these supply material for his argument.[1] And on the first and three last of these it is clear that he had bestowed much reflection. His model scheme of aristocratic government is, in fact, mainly framed upon the experience furnished, whether for good or for evil, by the history of the two Italian Republics and of the Dutch. From a man whose whole mind was given to philosophy it would be absurd to expect such stores of constitutional knowledge as were accumulated—and that, under conditions far more favourable—by an historian like Montesquieu. But, on the sum of the whole matter, he may fairly claim to have satisfied the requirements of the case up to the measure of his day and opportunities. Certainly, his analysis of these matters is more illuminating than anything which had been attempted since Aristotle.

What is the main purpose which underlies his discussion of the three forms of government? It is, as he tells us himself, to find out the means by which the abuses incident to each of them may most readily be corrected and the stability of each therefore most fully assured. Thus, the abuse of Monarchy being Tyranny, he sets himself to surround the monarch with a ring-wall of constitutional checks, intended to bar the path against the first approaches of autocracy. A prohibition against the levy of foreign mercenaries is one of these. Another, and a still surer, is the establishment of a representative Council, drawn from each of the 'families' or constituencies into which the community is divided for the purpose; and without some support from this body, the king is forbidden to pass any law, or take any executive measure of moment,

[1] For Rome see *T.P.* vi. 3-4; vii. 14; viii. 3; x. 1-4, 10. For Alexander, *T.P.* vi. 5; *T.T.* xvii. 19-24. For the Jews, *T.P.* vii. 14, 24-5, and *T.T.* xvii.-xx., *passim*. For Castille and Aragon, *T.P.* vii. 30. For England (the Rebellion), *T.T.* xviii. 32-34. For Venice, *T.P.* viii. 3, 18, 20-30. For Genoa, *T.P.* viii. 3, 18, 37. For the Netherlands, *T.T.* xx. 30; *T.P.* viii. 10, 31; ix. 14. The last reference furnishes a signal proof of Spinoza's strict impartiality. Although himself a personal friend of De Witt, he criticises the policy of hostility to the statholdership, with which his friend was identified, on the ground that, without Statholder or Count, the constitution of the Netherlands was reduced to a shapeless, nameless thing, a body without a head. The historian he seems to have studied most carefully is Tacitus, to whom his references and allusions are frequent.

whatsoever. By these and other means, Spinoza hopes to have 'bounded the power of the monarch by that of the community and, at the same time, to have put that power under the protection of the community itself. And that,' he adds, 'is the one aim I have set before myself in laying down the fundamental principles of this form of government.'[1]

In the same way with Aristocracy. The abuse of Aristocracy is Oligarchy. And to guard against this, Spinoza is ready with elaborate provisions for keeping the size of the governing class in a constant proportion—a proportion of one to fifty—to that of the community as a whole. And as he is keenly aware that the real, as opposed to the nominal, power in such a body will always be concentrated in comparatively few hands—two or three out of each hundred is his calculation—it follows that the number of 'patricians'—that is, of those who hold a seat on the Great Council—must be very large: five thousand for 'a State of moderate dimensions' is the estimate he gives. With a Council of this size, however, it is clear that the executive must be vested in a smaller body—four hundred, to be elected annually—which he calls the *Senate*. By this means, and by a further provision that no man under thirty may be co-opted on to the Council, he claims to have taken security against the gradual lapse of power into the hands of immoderately few families; while the institution of a small body of *Syndics*, manifestly modelled on the Venetian Council of Ten, with the duty of preventing and punishing all breaches of the constitution, is a still further guarantee against the designs of an oligarchical minority.[2]

The non-privileged classes, the 'plebeians,' are in little or no need, he considers, of constitutional safeguards against oppression: their very numbers are protection enough. Indeed his main fear seems to be that they will have too much power, rather than too little: that, in face of their numbers, the aristocracy will be hard driven to keep its place. And it is for this reason, among others, that he presses for a constant recruital of the governing caste, as well as for the appointment of Privy Councillors, from the ranks of the plebeians.[3]

There is, however, one form of tyranny against which he is jealously on his guard. That is the tyranny of the Capital over the provinces, of the large city over the small. The only sure check upon this, he holds, is a sweeping measure of Home Rule:

[1] *T.P.* vii. 4-5, 12, 31.

[2] *Ib.* viii. 2, 7, 13-15, 17, 18, 22, 28-29.

[3] *Ib.* viii. 4-6, 13-14, 41. But on the former point, the recruital of the Great Council from the ranks of the plebeians, he is, as it would seem, deliberately vague.

a drastic devolution of power—always, however, in a carefully guarded aristocratic sense—to the various cities, large and small, within the borders of the State.[1] This devolution is not confined to matters of local interest. By an elaborate scheme for taking the vote of each City Council separately and pooling the results, it is extended also—manifestly in a modified form—to matters of national concern. Into the details of this scheme it would be futile to enter. The object of it is to safeguard local liberties, without imperilling the unity of the State. It is obvious that the former purpose is attained much more completely than the latter.

On the subject of Democracy, we have no more than Spinoza's introductory remarks. There are two questions, however, on which he has placed his opinion beyond doubt: What are the distinguishing marks of Democracy, and what its merits, as against Monarchy and Aristocracy?

To the first question his answer is entirely his own. According to him, the vital difference between Aristocracy and Democracy is, or ought to be, that the former is based upon the principle of election, of co-option by the governing Council from a certain determined, though extensible, group of families; while the latter is founded upon the inherent right of all persons possessing a certain qualification—it may be age, it may be primogeniture, it may be the payment of a specified sum in taxes, it may conceivably be something different from all of these—to a place in the sovereign Council, and therefore to the full *status* of citizen. And this distinction holds good, so he expressly says, even if the result should be that those admitted to citizenship bear a smaller proportion to the total population in a Democracy than in an Aristocracy. In a word, the distinction is between personal choice and a qualifying right. It will be observed that this bars out, and is intended to bar out, what in fact has been the commonest form of Aristocracy: that based on the right of hereditary descent. Such a form of polity would, according to this rather freakish use of terms, be not an Aristocracy but a Democracy.[2]

On the second question, Spinoza is no less explicit. To him, Democracy is a better form of government than either Monarchy or Aristocracy. And the reason is that here, far more completely than in the other two forms, the community *is* the Government;

[1] *T.P.* ix. 2-6. It is clear that, in this Home Rule scheme, Spinoza writes with his eye upon the constitution of United Provinces, as against that of Venice or Genoa.

[2] *Ib.* viii. 1, 13; xi. 1-2. It may be noted that Spinoza thinks it worth while to argue the question whether women have not a right to citizenship on the same terms as men. He rejects the suggestion on the ground of their moral and physical inferiority (*imbecillitas*) (*ib.* xi. 4).

whence it follows that the chances of collision between community and Government are far less, the chances of maintaining that peace which is the end of all government far greater; above all, the identity between rights and powers is far more entire. For these reasons he is apt to describe Democracy as the most 'absolute' form of polity: a malicious use of terms, perhaps intended to mark the gulf which parted him from Hobbes and, prophetically, from other champions of the 'absolute State.'[1]

The most original thing in these closing books of the *Treatise* is the contention, again and again repeated, that a change in the form of government carries with it a change also in the dispositions required as to such crucial, but subordinate, matters as property, military service, religious establishments and the like.

Thus in a Monarchy, where discontent is always likely to arise over taxation and other necessary acts of government, it is expedient that the whole settled property of the community—land and, if possible, houses—should be vested in the ruler, leased (but never sold) to private applicants, and the proceeds of the rent devoted to the expenses of the State: all other taxes being prohibited, except in time of war. In an Aristocracy, on the other hand, such a provision would be a fruitful source of tyranny and oppression;[2] it would probably end in a general exodus of all who did not belong to the privileged body. Under this form of government accordingly, Spinoza demands that the land—which he still seems to conceive of as owned by the State, that is, the privileged caste—should be sold outright to such subjects as are in a position to purchase, with the sole condition that a yearly property tax be paid to the State. In a Monarchy, as in an Aristocracy, it may be noted that he regards all moveable property as being vested absolutely in the private owner: with the restriction that, in a Monarchy at any rate, all investments in foreign securities, all loans to foreign merchants, are prohibited.[3]

The constitution of the army under the two forms of government presents a similar contrast. In a Monarchy, one of the main securities against oppression is that enlistment of foreign mercenaries shall be absolutely prohibited and that troops shall be levied solely from among the subjects. In an Aristocracy, such a provision is neither necessary nor possible. The levy of troops should, indeed, be made mainly from natives, whether of the

[1] *T.P.* viii. 3; xi. 1; *T.T.* xvi. 25-38. Elsewhere, he makes a significant variation: 'Imperium democraticum ad statum *naturalem* maxime accedit' (*T.T.* xx. 38).

[2] It does not appear why the same danger, perhaps under a less extreme form, does not arise in a monarchy also.

[3] *T.P.* vi. 12; vii. 8; viii. 10.

privileged class or otherwise; and none should be admitted to the Great Council who has not proved himself skilled in the art of war: a provision intended to ensure that a sufficient proportion of the officers should be constantly furnished by the 'patricians,' from whose number, according to a further provision, the General-in-Chief is invariably to be drawn. But the levy of mercenaries should in no way be prohibited; and for several reasons, among which Spinoza is careful to specify the need of guarding against domestic sedition, it may easily prove desirable.[1]

The most curious, and certainly the least expected, turn given to the principle under discussion has been reserved till last: its application to the burning question of religious establishments. Of all causes, that of religious and intellectual freedom—the right 'to think as you will and speak as you think'—was that which lay nearest to Spinoza's heart.[2] It was in behalf of this that he had written the *Tractatus Theologico-politicus*: a more reasoned, if less passionate plea for freedom of thought and utterance than *Areopagitica* itself. Insisting, like Milton, on the impossibility of imposing limits upon thought and the disastrous folly of imposing them on speech—the injustice of such a policy, the strife and hypocrisy it inevitably begets[3]—he had also, like Milton, insisted upon the more positive, and therefore still more vital, side of the same truth. He had proved that the community from which freedom of thought and speech is banished is not a live community, but a dead: not a tree of life 'springing from a firm root,' but 'a stark and dead congealment of wood and hay and stubble, frozen together' at the will of a dull and timorous despot.[4] And he had pleaded that, if there is to be any limitation at all in such matters, the right of imposing it is far better vested in the civil government than in any privileged Church. The one is at least likely to be guided by a sincere, if mistaken, desire for the public good; the other will certainly be swayed by sectarian prejudices, not improbably by personal spites and resentments.[5] Indeed a good part of the treatise is devoted to laying bare the evils which fell upon the Jewish Commonwealth from the persistent efforts of the priests and other religious fanatics to make themselves masters of the State.[6]

Under a monarchical government accordingly, Spinoza, in the *Political Treatise*, expressly forbids the recognition of any one privileged Church; though, in accordance with the practice of the Roman Empire and many States of his own day, he seems to

[1] *T.P.* vi. 10; viii. 9.

[2] This quotation from Tacitus (*Hist.* i. 1) occurs both in the Preface to *T.T.* and in the title of the closing chapter (xx.).

[3] *T.T.* xx. 27-35. [4] *Ib.* xx. 11-13. [5] *Ib.* xx. 20-26.

[6] *Ib.* xvii.-xviii.

have reserved to the State the right of prohibiting certain forms of public worship, as pernicious. Such religious bodies as are permitted to worship in public are to put up their churches at their own expense; and, with the exception just mentioned, no restrictions on freedom of thought and discussion are to be allowed. When account is taken of the necessity, real or supposed, of yielding to human prejudice, which even in the United Provinces was still liable to violent outbreaks, all this is fairly in accordance with the principles laid down in the earlier treatise.[1]

What, however, are we to say of the corresponding provisions laid down for an Aristocracy? It is essential, in Spinoza's view, that all members of the governing Body should be of the same Confession, and that this Confession should be of the 'simplest and most catholic'—that is, most comprehensive—cast. Other creeds and other forms of worship are to be permitted on sufferance to members of the subject population. But the chapels appropriated to such worship must be restricted to a specified size and built—it need hardly be said, at the expense of their respective sects—on sites sufficiently scattered. The temples of the 'national Church,' on the other hand, are to be 'large and stately'; and although the duty of preaching may, in case of need, be devolved on 'plebeians' —a community of dukes was hardly likely to abound in oratorical talent or in unction—none but members of the governing Body should be permitted to administer baptism and other sacraments: to the end, as Spinoza expressly states, that the nobles may be recognised by all as the priests of the national religion, its champions and interpreters.[2]

The general purpose of these somewhat startling provisions, as the author explains, is to prevent religious dissensions among the members of the privileged class and, by the same stroke, to secure liberty of worship—it is true, with considerable limitations —for the unprivileged 'multitude': a liberty which might be imperilled if one sect were likely to find a backing among the aristocracy at the expense of the rest. Whether the means are well calculated to the end, is open to question. For our purposes, the significant thing is, on the one hand, that to secure liberty in the gross Spinoza should have been willing to make such trenchant sacrifices of it in detail; and on the other hand, that his conviction as to the need of adapting the whole life of the community to the ideal embodied in its form of government should have been strong enough to force his acceptance of a consequence which to many minds will seem so remote and which to his own mind can hardly have been anything but violently unpalatable.

No one of the applications which the principle receives from

[1] *T.P.* vi. 40. [2] *Ib.* viii. 46.

Spinoza appears to be especially cogent. So much must be frankly admitted. The importance of his argument lies not in the applications, but in the principle itself. Broadly stated, it is the principle that the life of the community is not a mechanism made up of isolated acts and formal institutions, but a vital organism, each one of whose parts reacts upon the others, each one of whose acts qualifies, and is qualified by, the rest. It would be idle to pretend either that he applied this principle as fruitfully, or even that he grasped its scope as fully, as many who came after him. After all, he was a precursor. But Montesquieu, and in another way Burke, were to build their fame upon the principle which he here implicitly lays down.

Spinoza's theory stands or falls by his identification of rights with powers: in other words, by his refusal to admit the idea of Right into the life of the State. If this initial assumption cannot be made good; if it can be shown that the idea of Right, as opposed to power, is essential to the existence of the State, that without it there can be no lasting and steady bond either between citizen and citizen, or between the Government and the governed, then the whole argument fails, the whole fabric crumbles to pieces. Our one business, therefore, is to ask: How far is such a theory in accordance with the facts of our experience? how far is it possible that any State should maintain itself without some sense, however imperfect, of obligation between its members, without some recognition of mutual duties between the Government and the governed?

It is the surpassing merit of Spinoza to bring this question swiftly and sharply to an issue. How swiftly and how sharply, is best seen by a reference to two other writers who, in a greater or less degree, have accepted the same principle, but who, for good or for bad reasons, have not carried it out with the same ruthless consistency. Hobbes, as we have seen, persistently confuses the issue by juggling with the utterly incompatible principle of 'natural law': that is, with the idea of duty. Burke again, while accepting the principle of expediency—and that, with infinite qualifications—in the sphere of politics, would, we may be very sure, have indignantly rejected it in the field of ethics. Spinoza, on the other hand, applies it with the same thoroughness in the one domain as in the other. He banishes the idea of duty, of Right, not only from the field of politics, but from that of ethics also. His exclusion is not limited to the relations between citizen and citizen; it reaches also to the simplest and most personal relations between man and man. It is clear that, by so doing, he reduces the problem to the most elementary form which it is capable of taking.

That, in itself, is enough to set the two *Treatises* in a place apart. Nowhere else — unless perhaps in the pages of Hume, whose Politics, however, are avowedly fragmentary—do we find the exclusion of Right enforced with such rigorous consistency; nowhere else do we find the utilitarian solution presented so fully or with such remorseless clearness; nowhere else do we find results so fruitful wrung out of the principle of expediency. Here, therefore, if anywhere, that principle enters the field with every chance in its favour that courage and genius can give it. And if even Spinoza's advocacy cannot carry it to victory, we may fairly conclude that the fault lies not in its champion, but in itself.

What we have to assume, then, is a community from which all belief in duty, in any kind of moral obligation, is rigidly barred out: barred out not only from its corporate life, from all relations between citizen and citizen, between the Government and the governed, but also from its purely social life, from all the countless and ceaselessly shifting relations which are for ever weaving themselves between one individual and another. We are forced to add the latter condition, partly because the idea of duty is as stiffly banished from the ethical system of Spinoza as it is from his political system: partly because that idea — even if it were admitted in words, which it is not — is, as an operative motive, inevitably barred out by the rigidly necessarian doctrine of the author; partly again because, as he never ceases to remind us, the 'life of reason,' the life laid before us in the closing Book of the *Ethics*, is the attainment only of the few, while 'by far the greater part of mankind judge of expediency purely by their lusts and are swayed solely by their passions': in other words, because, in practice as well as in theory, they renounce all bonds of obligation to others, so that the only check left upon their madness is to be found in the terrors of the Law.[1]

Given such a community, what chance is there, we ask, that even the terrors of the Law will long suffice to keep the peace between the warring passions of its members? How, even when most effectual, can the terrors of the Law touch anything but what is most external and least vital in the dealings of one man with

[1] 'Fit raro ut homines ex ductu rationis vivant' (*Eth.* iv. 35); see also *T.T.* v. 21; xvi. 6-7; *T.P.* ii. 5-8. It must be remembered, however, that in the next Proposition of the *Ethics* (iv. 36) he expressly says: 'Summum bonum omnibus commune est.' So it is, in the sense that all men would be happier, if they could only bring themselves to 'live by the light of reason.' But that is just what, in Spinoza's view, the majority of them will never do.

another? What other bond has Spinoza in reserve except the calculations of self-interest: the sense that, in the long run, it is for the advantage of the individual to put a bridle upon his own passions, lest he should be devoured by those of the 'natural enemies' who surround him? And is not such a bond even flimsier than that furnished by the terrors of the Law?

Before any answer to this question is attempted, one point at any rate must be made clear. It is not denied—no man who understands the first elements of the matter will ever dream of denying—that in morals as in politics, in politics as in morals, the exact course which it is our duty to take at any moment is determined purely by expediency: by what experience has shown, or what reason declares, to be in the true interest of ourselves, of our neighbours, of our fellow-citizens, of mankind at large. The part that mere intuition can play even in matters of individual conduct, much more in politics, is extremely small. And, even were it much larger than it is, intuition would still need to be checked by reason, or by that experience which is itself a record of past reason; else, how could we be sure that it was not a false guide? And reason, in these matters, is essentially a calculation of consequences, a balancing between the good and the less good: in one word, a reckoning of expediency.

So far, all who have a right to speak on the matter are agreed. So far, utilitarian and idealist stand on common ground. It is from this point, and from this point only, that the difference begins. To the utilitarian, here is an end of the matter. In expediency, self-interest, the 'greatest happiness principle,' everything is included. Every reasonable man is capable of learning to know his own interest, of being trained to see that, in cases of conflict, it is necessary, for the sake of that very interest, to sacrifice his 'lower' to his 'higher' self; and that, in the long run, it is for his greatest happiness to do so.

To the idealist, on the contrary, there is a further question behind. On the assumption that self-interest is all in all, he asks, how can we account for the very existence of the higher self? much more for the good man's conviction that it is this, and not the lower self, which has the higher claim? How can man ever have come to distinguish between his higher and his lower self, to regard the latter as a thing to be jealously controlled and the former as an ideal to be realised at all costs, unless he starts from the sense that it is his duty to do so? unless, from the first, he acts on the assumption that this sense of duty is at once the highest and the most binding thing within him? It is only in the light of this fundamental sense that he can detect what his own interest really is; only in the strength of it that he can discern where his true happiness is placed. Judged purely by tests of pleasure and self-interest—judged, that is, purely by its own standards—it is impossible for a man to foresee, at the moment of decision, in which of two courses his 'greatest happiness' will be. More than that: it is impossible for the onlooker to be sure, even after the event, that the full-blooded 'man of pleasure' has not secured more happiness to himself by fearlessly following the promptings of his lower self than the social reformer, the man of science, the poet, the martyr, has achieved by sacrificing his ease and comfort to win truth, to realise an ideal vision, to further the triumph of a cause which he believes to be just and wholesome.

To assert the contrary, the idealist argues, is to play, however unconsciously, upon the double sense of the term 'happiness': the common sense, in which it is hardly distinguishable from 'pleasure,' and the religious sense, in which it is equivalent to 'blessedness.' It is the former sense to which the word must be strictly confined in this connection; for it is in the former sense alone that 'happiness' has any reference to the natural impulses of man, any relation to beings who 'for the most part judge of expediency purely by their lusts and are swayed solely by their passions'; and it is with these alone that the utilitarian—above all, Spinoza—is concerned.[1] 'Blessedness' implies a faculty for conceiving moral ideals, a power of framing and striving to attain certain reasoned or imagined ends, which for the utilitarian man, who acts solely to gratify the desire for pleasure, to secure certain pleasurable sensations, high or low, is manifestly out of the question.

But the fundamental sense of duty once recognised, its claim to approve or reject every desire as it rises once admitted, then the idealist, no less than the utilitarian, will be eager to assert that the only test it can apply in each such case is that of expediency: of what experience, or reason, shows to be the surest way of attaining the end we have set before us. Let it never be forgotten, however, that expediency qualified by the idea of duty is something very different from the expediency of the utilitarian or hedonist: that is, from expediency pure and simple. We call it by the same name; but it now comes heavily weighted in favour not of the lower, but the higher, self: of the self which is capable of conceiving and striving for ideals; of the self which is what it is in virtue of the knowledge that it draws its life from its relation to a world of reason, of beauty, of ordered effort, of obligation to other selves—to our neighbours, to our fellow-citizens, to mankind.

[1] 'Omnes quidem suum utile quaerunt; et minime sanae rationis dictamine, sed perplurimum ex sola libidine et animi affectibus abrepti (qui nullam temporis futuri aliarumque rerum rationem habent) res appetunt utilesque judicant' (*T.T.* v. 21).

There is one more misunderstanding against which it is necessary to guard. The practical results which, under favourable circumstances, Spinoza expects to reach by the way of self-interest are, it need hardly be said, exactly the same as are commonly held to be attainable solely by the way of duty. To think otherwise, to charge him with lowering, or desiring to lower, the moral standard, is the grossest injustice. That is the last charge in the world that can be brought against the author of the *Ethics*. The question is not one of results, but of causes: not one of moral standards, but of motives. And if he holds self-interest to be the only motive of which man is capable, that is because he holds it to be a sufficient motive not only for the lower forms of action, but also for the higher: not only for those which are evil or indifferent, but also for those which the world has agreed to call heroic or good. Was he right in this estimate, or was he wrong? That is the sole question at issue between him and his opponents. To attack him on any other score is to open an entirely false scent.

He is at one with the idealists in the conviction that, without the 'good' will, bearing fruit in 'good' action, there can be no such thing as welfare either for the individual or the State. He differs from them in that, while they conceive the will to be determined to the good action mainly, if not solely, by the idea of duty, he considers such action, alike in the man and in the citizen, to flow solely from calculations of self-interest. To the idealist, the difference between the good and the bad action is that the one is determined by the sense of duty, by the will which has become what it is because it has been moulded by the abiding sense of duty; the other by self-interest, in the sense of selfishness, or the unthinking impulse of the moment. To Spinoza, both are determined purely by self-interest. But in the one case, that self-interest is enlightened; in the other, short-sighted, or wholly blind. In the one case, it takes long views; it reckons not only with the present, but with the future; not only with the most pressing desire of the moment, but with the wellbeing of a lifetime; it seeks not merely to snatch a passing advantage but to secure the lasting prosperity of a State, whose life is measured not by years but by centuries.

Thus the real question at issue is a question of probabilities. Is it likely that identically the same motive—self-interest, more or less enlightened—can be made to yield results so different as an act of deliberate selfishness on the one hand and an act of pure heroism, of deliberate self-sacrifice, upon the other? Is it likely that the result which Spinoza desires can be drawn from the motives which alone he is willing to recognise? Is it not morally certain that, to produce the result required, very different motives—the motives he expressly eliminates—must be called into the reckoning?

Or, to put the same thing otherwise, the self Spinoza speaks of may be either the lower or the higher self. It may be either the self which seeks to gratify the impulse, to strike for the apparent interest, of the moment; or it may be the self which lives in the abiding world of realities; the world of forethought, of justice, of respect for the needs and rights of our fellow-men. It may be the self, in virtue of which man is merely the first among the beasts; or it may be the self which is capable of conceiving remote ends, of framing high ideals, of enduring untold toil, suffering, perhaps even death itself, in the effort to attain them. Once again, which of these two selves is the more likely to profit by the balance of loss and gain which to Spinoza is the sole guide to action, both for the man and the citizen, and the sole test of its fitness? Is it not obvious that, but for rare exceptions, it will be the self which looks, mainly or solely, to the advantage, often merely the apparent advantage, of the moment: the self which is determined mainly, if not solely, by the most pressing desire of the moment? In other words, is it not clear that, for the vast majority of men, the scale will always be heavily weighted for the lower self?

There is one assumption, no doubt, under which this consequence might be expected not to follow. Let us suppose a man who has been trained from childhood to recognise an imperative law of duty: a man, therefore, whose 'conscience' has during long years been moulded and nurtured by an ever-present sense of that law, by constant efforts, however often defeated, to make it the law of his own life. Let us then suppose this conviction to be suddenly swept, as by a miracle, from his heart. Let us suppose that, from middle life onwards, he is thrown back, for the whole guidance of his life and conduct, upon mere calculations of expediency, upon what Bentham, athirst for the credit of 'moral science,' was pleased to call the *felicific calculus*.

Such a man, it may readily be admitted, might not unsafely be trusted to make much the same choice under the new conditions that he had been used to make under the old. He brings to the choice an experience of the higher, as well as of the lower, pleasures, which the man who has never had any guide except pleasure is only too likely to be without. He brings to it also a will moulded, however imperfectly, to judge between the two, to recognise the true nature of each, to esteem each at its proper worth: predisposed therefore, at least in his better moments, to give the preference to the one, to feel shame and remorse whenever he suffers himself to be hurried by passion into grasping at the other.

The same admission, though with much more of hesitation, might perhaps be made in favour of a community which, for all common or civic purposes, accepts no guide but expediency, yet whose members, as individuals and in all matters of private conduct, recognise a binding law of duty. There is at least some chance that the principle to which they do homage in their private life will make itself felt also, however illogically, in their estimate of civic prudence: that they will instinctively shrink from doing as citizens what it would be against their conscience to do as men. There is at least some hope that, in this case too, an echo from the one world, the world of duty, will make itself heard in the other world, the world of expediency, also. But, in this case, experience forbids us to feel any confidence. Instances to the contrary, examples of men perfectly honourable and dutiful in their private life, yet singularly lax—as borough-mongers, as slave-owners, as sweaters of labour—in their public standard, are far too frequent.

For neither of these admissions is Spinoza any the better. His assumption differs materially from either of those here imagined, and differs manifestly for the worse. His individual has never at any time recognised a sense of duty. His community is wholly made up of those who, as men no less than as citizens, have never at any time acknowledged any motive save that of expediency. His agent therefore, unless his endowment be exceptionally happy, will, from beginning to end, have to make his choice without any experience of what the higher pleasures have to offer, without any organ for discerning them or judging of their worth, without any 'higher self' to which either he himself, or his well-wishers, can possibly appeal.

That, in exceptionally happy temperaments, nature can do the work which, for others less richly endowed, is to be wrought only by a long and toilsome process, only by the slow growth of the sense of duty, is perfectly true. And it is probable that most of those who have pinned their faith to the 'felicific calculus' are among the few thus fortunately placed. Certainly, it was so with Spinoza. Few natures have been so saintly, few hearts so overflowing with love to God and man, as his. But to judge of others by himself is a strange error in a philosopher; and in a case of this kind, an error particularly fatal. It is not only to make a false induction; it is to employ a false method for drawing it. It is not only to treat the few—and those, manifestly exceptional natures—as a rule equally for the many. It is also to turn into a matter of logical necessity what is in fact a mere question of human probability. And in this matter, it must be said once more, the probabilities are all against him. The majority of us, if thrown back upon a pure calculation of profit and loss, are in no position to make it. We have no experience of what the higher pleasures have to offer; we have no organ for judging of their worth. We have not even the mental power required for casting up the sum

Under these conditions, how can we be expected to sacrifice the nearer and more assured pleasure to the more distant and uncertain? What chance is there that mere calculations of expediency will enable us to stand against the sweeping tide of passion and desire?

It may be pleaded that, whatever the motive which governs the action of the man, whether it be expediency or duty, the motive presented to the child will always be much the same. It will be the fear of displeasing, the hope of pleasing, his parents. It will be 'you ought' and 'you must': enforced, when necessary, by punishments and rewards. Thus, by the time he has come to youth, the habit of acting 'rightly' will have become a second nature. He will have gained some experience of the higher pleasures. He will have acquired, at least in some measure, the organ for discerning them and judging them at their true value.

Against this plea there are two obvious objections: one of practice, the other of theory. On the one hand, the time of liberation, the time when the child is released from leading-strings, is the most critical time of all; for of all times it is that most dominated by passion. Of all times, therefore, it is that when the strongest possible counter-motive is the most urgently needed, and a sudden change from the stronger to the weaker motive most jealously to be avoided. On the other hand, disguise it as we will, the discipline of childhood, at any rate as practised in the vast majority of cases, is at bottom essentially a discipline not of expediency, but of duty. The very warnings, 'you ought' and 'you must,' are enough to set this beyond doubt. And this means that throughout these crucial years—the years that, in many ways, set the key for the whole lifetime—the determining motive set before the child is not expediency, but duty. In other words, this is to give away the whole case. The motive which is shut out by the front door is smuggled in by the back; with the result that the number of men who have never known the appeal to duty, whose whole life has been governed by the principle of expediency, is extraordinarily small: so small as hardly to count. And the few exceptions—the few who, like the Edgeworths, have been brought up on a half-reading of Rousseau's *Émile*—can hardly be said to commend the system which it is their mission to set forth. Whatever their other virtues, they have always seemed to carry about them a faint flavour of the prig.

But after all, the strongest argument against the 'greatest happiness principle' is its incredible irrelevance. Thus the difference between the 'good' and the 'bad' man should lie in the success or failure of a purely intellectual operation, however often repeated; that the good man should be he who has mastered the 'felicific calculus' correctly, and the bad man incorrectly: this, for those who have learned by a bitter experience the incalculable difference between right and wrong, between the good will and the bad, will infallibly seem a cruel mockery, a theory which has hopelessly missed the mark. That any man, even in the grip of a system, should seriously accept it is a matter of blank amazement.

So far, we have been mainly concerned with the bearing of expediency upon the conduct of the individual. What about its application to the State?

The same things that make the idea of duty a necessity to the individual also make it, whether under its own name or that of Right, indispensable as a bond between citizen and citizen in the State. Without some sense, however rudimentary, of a common brotherhood, without some acknowledgement, however imperfect, of mutual duties and obligations, it is impossible that any community should hold together; and barely conceivable that it should even have been formed. It is this indestructible sense of brotherhood and of the obligations which grow out of brotherhood—a sense which has doubtless been strengthened by experience, but which is beyond experience and above it—that constitutes the fundamental fact in the life of every tribe, of every nation, of every State. It is upon this that the life of every civil community is founded. Withdraw this, and the whole fabric falls to pieces.

Were it not for this sense, why indeed should the individual citizen feel called upon to sacrifice his own convenience to that of his neighbours? Why should all of them acknowledge the necessity of surrendering their own immediate interests for the welfare of the community as a whole? It is idle to say, as Spinoza says, that they do these things because, by simple reasoning and by common experience, they know that in the long run it is for their own interest to do them: because they are aware that, if the settled order of the State were swept away, their own comfort would be destroyed, their own life not worth a moment's purchase. It may be perfectly true that these consequences would ultimately result. It may even be true that a considerable proportion, possibly a majority, of the citizens in any community is aware that they are likely to result. But it is also true that, in any given case, such consequences are, at worst, extremely remote; that the selfish or uncivic action would need to be repeated again and again before they are likely to follow; that, granted a reasonable amount of good fortune, they may even never follow at all. So, at any rate, a large number of individuals are pretty certain to argue; and it would be hard, perhaps impossible, to prove that their reasoning is false.

The actions in question are such as are avowedly uncivic, the selfishness of which no man can seriously expect to disguise: such actions as refusal to take one's share of the burden at a time of national danger, or a persistent effort to turn the public need to private profit: such actions, in short, as go by the name of 'shirking,' or 'profiteering.' Short of such manifestly indefensible acts, however, there is a whole host of others upon which it is possible to put a decent colour, but which, in his heart of hearts, the doer must know to be little better, whether in their motive or results. They may not threaten the 'end of all things.' But the less they do so, the better do they serve our present purpose. For the less their menace to society, the less can Spinoza's argument be invoked against them.

So much for the acts which are more or less avowedly selfish, more or less consciously uncivic. But the difficulty does not end here. Under another and more subtle form, it meets the citizen in almost every decision which he is called upon to take.

The most obvious difference between morals and politics, it will probably be admitted, is that in the former the weight attaching to considerations of pure expediency is comparatively small, in the latter immeasurably large: the good will, which in the former is almost everything, carries us but a small way in the latter. The reason is that the conditions in politics are both infinitely more variable and infinitely more complicated than they are in morals. In matters of individual conduct, long experience, guided by the sense of duty, has enabled men to map out the course almost by rule and plummet; so that, to the man who is honest with himself, the cases of doubt, the questions of legitimate casuistry, are exceedingly few; and the more honest he is, the fewer are they likely to become. In matters of politics, on the other hand, the course is very largely uncharted. Who can foresee all, who can foresee even the most fateful consequences involved in the imposition or repeal of a tax? much more of an act establishing a new form of government, or opening an era of friendship, or coolness, with a foreign Power? Did Cobden foresee the depopulation of the rural districts which has followed on, and is largely owing to, the Repeal of the Corn Laws? Did Bismarck foresee the ruin which has fallen on Germany as a result of his alliance with Austria and of the whole system of foreign policy, at first so apparently successful, of which that alliance was an inseparable part? Did he even foresee the consequences which have flowed, and in the long run were bound to flow, from his enthronement of the War Lords as uncontrolled arbiters of the destinies of Germany?

There may, or may not, be any blame attaching to the man who fails to discern all the elements of such problems. For the moment, that is not the question. The point is that the problems themselves, as problems of pure expediency are often extraordinarily intricate, and not seldom, as in the case of the Corn Laws, so intricate as to defy anything like complete calculation altogether. Who could have foretold that, within a generation after the Repeal, the home market would be flooded with inexhaustible supplies of corn, at prices immensely below anything previously known, from the virgin fields of the western States and Canada?

Under these conditions, what wise man will neglect any clue that may offer itself from without? any other principle which may serve to unravel, to expound, to interpret that of expediency pure and simple? Is it not the case, we ask, that many of these problems are difficult only so long as they remain mere matters of expediency? that, directly moral considerations are brought to bear upon them, their difficulty is either diminished or altogether disappears? In matters of individual conduct, this is a common experience. And when all allowance has been made for the greater intricacy of political questions, it is reasonable to suppose that something of the same kind must happen also in matters of national concern.

In fact, directly we look beneath the surface, we become aware that in many of these cases, perhaps in most of them, the difficulty of the problem, and consequently the false solution of it, was mainly due to the exclusion of certain moral elements: that their admission, so far from increasing its complexity, would have made it enormously more simple. It was because Napoleon trusted purely to material power that, at the first check to his arms, his whole fabric fell in pieces. It was because Bismarck had a false ideal of national greatness, an ideal from which all moral ends were rigorously banished, that he fell into those blunders for which his country is now paying the price. The *Real-Politik* on which he prided himself was, in truth, not his salvation, but his bane.

Both these were men of great intellect: one of them, a man of the highest genius. Both therefore saw certain elements of their problem—the purely material elements—with surpassing clearness. And as those were the elements which alone counted in the opening stages of the venture, both, so long as those stages lasted, achieved a dazzling success. But the moment that moral forces were once more able to assert themselves, the fabric that each had reared was shaken to its foundations; and in both cases—the one sooner, the other later—it fell hopelessly in ruins. Both men, it is probable, saw as far as it was possible to see by a process of mere material calculation; and little good it did them. With the same calculating genius and even a normal faculty for discerning moral issues, their work might have stood for centuries. As it was, riches in the one direction meant for both of them utter poverty in the other, and their work was doomed from the moment it was completed.

One more example must suffice. *The Prince* of Machiavelli is commonly thought to have been written in support of the theory which, with exemplary thoroughness, these two men put in practice. Yet the very hero of the book, on his worshipper's own showing, was a miserable failure. With all his 'vulpine faculty,' with all his skill in 'employing the beast' for the furtherance of his ends, he saw his work dashed into fragments at the first strain that befell it. And, by the author's own admission, the fault lay not with his bad fortune, but himself. All his calculations were based on the need of securing, if not a friend, at least a neutral as his father's successor in the Papacy. Yet, at the critical moment, he allowed a dangerous enemy to be chosen. 'It was the cause of his ruin.' [1]

The truth is that the Machiavellian scheme of politics makes greater demands on human foresight and persistence than even the wiliest can fulfil. The moves of the game are too intricate for even the stoutest brain to master. And 'a few strong instincts and a few plain rules,' drawn from the moral order of things, will commonly do more for a man than all the fine-spun calculations in the world. It is of course true that moral considerations are in no way excluded either by Spinoza or by any other respectable champion of the utilitarian system. On the contrary, both he and others make every effort to include them. But, by reducing moral considerations themselves to a mere matter of calculation, they inevitably confuse the issue. In spite of themselves, they weight the scales against the higher wisdom and in favour of the lower. They encourage others to draw the inference which they themselves strenuously reject. So that, whatever the theory may say, in practice the *calculus* of Spinoza leads straight to the ignoble schemings, the combined 'force and fraud,' of Bismarck and Napoleon. The gloss of Machiavelli is, in short, the natural, though assuredly not the intended, outcome of the refined and subtle reasonings of Spinoza. And this is still more true in the field of politics than in that of individual conduct.

Thus Spinoza's analysis of political motive, of the bond which holds civil society together, lies open to two fatal objections: the one of theory, the other of practice. By ignoring all sense of brotherhood, by rejecting all ideas of Right and duty, he makes it impossible to account either for the first formation of the State, or for its subsequent maintenance. And by reducing all motives, alike in morals and politics, to the single one of expediency, by refusing to allow for anything in human conduct but a ceaseless

[1] 'Essendo adunque un Principe necessitato saper bene usare la bestia, debbe di quelle pigliare la volpe e il leone' (*Il Principe*, cap. xviii.). 'Errò adunque il duca (Cesare Borgia) in questa elezione, e fu cagione dell' ultima rovina sua' (*ib.* cap. vii.).

calculation of loss and gain, he inevitably—though this was as far as possible from his intention—tends to lower the moral standard, to destroy the nerve of the will, to make men less capable of unselfish—much more, of heroic—action than they would otherwise have been. The two things are closely connected: they are, in fact, no more than two growths from the same root, two aspects of the same fundamental error.

With this clue in our hand, let us now go back to scrutinise more narrowly than we have hitherto done the main line of the theory laid down in Spinoza's *Treatises*. All that is necessary to say may be centred round two points: what is the bearing of his doctrine upon the formation and existence of the State? and what its bearing upon the relation between the Government and the governed?

On his account of the matter, self-interest is the one motive that leads men to quit the state of nature for the civil state; self-interest, the one bond that prevents them from returning to the state of nature. So far, we might suppose ourselves to be dealing with creatures of pure reason, with the calculating machines so dear to the age of Bentham and not altogether unknown even to Bentham himself. That, however, is very far from the thought and mind of Spinoza. As he looked out on mankind, the first thing to strike him was their miserable unreason, their enslavement to 'blind desire,' their helpless surrender to the raging blasts of passion. How, he asks himself, are the two things to be reconciled: defiance of reason, bondage to passion, on the one hand; and the fact that reason is the sole guide of life, the sole index to self-interest, upon the other? The very extremity of the evil, he virtually answers, is what compels men to discover a cure. The very violence of their passions makes it an absolute necessity for them to place a sufficient curb upon their ravages. And it is because they know the settled order of society to be such a curb, and the only one which can possibly serve the purpose, that they are willing to put up with all the inconveniences and all the sacrifices which that settled order inevitably brings with it.

It is plain at a glance that this is not the utilitarian system pure and simple. It is the utilitarian system strongly tinged, not to say contaminated, with the more desperate one of Hobbes. Spinoza may have one foot in the age of reason; but the other is still firmly planted in the age of war, the 'war of all against all' which forms the background, ever striving to thrust itself once more into the foreground, of *Leviathan*. It is a strange blend; and the question is whether, for every leak that it closes, it does not open another. The revised theory may be more true to the facts of life; but that does not make it square more easily with the argument. By his very insistence on the unreason of man, he makes it more difficult than ever to accept an account of human conduct which, even in its undiluted shape, makes greater demands upon the strength and firmness of human reason than are ever likely to be fulfilled. The more truculent the element which he inherited from Hobbes, the less readily will it suffer itself to be fused with the purely utilitarian elements which he contributed himself.

It may be urged that Hobbes himself had a strong dash of the utilitarian: that all modern forms of utilitarianism may be directly traced to his teaching. That is perfectly true. But it is also true that Hobbes is careful to guard himself against the particular embarrassments in question, and that Spinoza took no such precautions. Between Hobbes' state of nature and his civil state there is an impassable barrier. In a moment of weakness the savage of *Leviathan* allows himself to be frightened out of his natural state. From that moment he ceases to be a free agent. He has bound himself by an oath never to return; what is more to the purpose, that oath is enforced by the sword of the despot he has set over his head. Whatever his passions, he has no longer the power of indulging them. Against his will, he finds himself driven back upon self-interest, in which the terrors of the law play a commanding part, as the sole motive left him for the guidance of his life and conduct. And if this motive is reinforced in practice, as it should be in theory, by the duty of 'performing his covenant made,' so much the better. There is no conflict between the two. For his covenant binds him to nothing but to obey the law which his lord and master may lay down. It is all very unconvincing; but the later stages of it at any rate—and it is those alone which concern us at the present moment—offer a plausible account of the matter, with no very obvious discrepancies.

It is impossible to say the same of Spinoza's picture. His men are at once in a state of war, and in a state of highly sophisticated peace, with one another: at once the slaves of ' blind passion ' and the devoted servants of a deeply calculating reason. It is part of the price he had to pay for keeping his central principle 'watertight': for his relentless identification of rights with powers. Unfortunately, he forgot that even powers stand in need of some mediator to keep the peace between them: that nothing in the world is so little likely to listen to reason as a concourse of blind passions.

The discomforts and bareness of the natural state—such is Spinoza's calculation—are enough to drive man into the civil state; once in it, the memory of his past ills is enough to keep him there. But does it follow that familiarity is enough to breed good fellowship, or even mutual forbearance, between man and man? Is it not at least as likely to breed mutual hatred and contempt? And is not this above all likely to happen when the men in question are avowedly the slaves of blind passion, and when there is no stronger tie than self-interest, as interpreted by the mood of the moment, to bind them?

The truth is that, as Rousseau pointed out, the closer men are brought to each other, the more bitterly are their passions stirred against each other; so that the birth of society, so far from a blessing, may actually prove a curse.[1] And the only means of averting this consequence, the only hope of bridling these passions, is to throw some equally strong—if possible, some yet stronger—passion into the scale against them. Spinoza himself admits this as decisively as could be wished: 'except by an opposite and stronger passion, no passion can be either bridled or torn from us.'[2] Where, then, is such a passion to be found? Not in the ideal, one of the noblest ever conceived by the mind of man, embodied in the *Ethics*; for, as Spinoza knew too well, it is, for all but the purest spirits, only an ideal: a counsel of perfection which few men would desire, and fewer still be able, to make their own. Not in self-interest: which, on Spinoza's own showing, was at work even in the natural state and which, by his own admission, men will always interpret at the bidding of their passions. But in duty, and in duty alone. In the words of Rousseau, it is only through a tissue of 'moral relations,' it is only when 'the sway of natural impulse and appetite is replaced by that of Right and duty' that 'the stupid and limited animal of the natural order becomes at length a reasoning being and a man.'

Now of duty, on Spinoza's system, there can manifestly be no question. When the door was shut upon Right—and it was so from the moment that Right was identified with power—it was shut upon obligation also. The only bonds of cohesion left are expediency and necessity: in other words, self-interest, more or less liberally interpreted, and force. Spinoza, it is true, not seldom avails himself of terms which, on any strict construction, evidently imply obligation, in the sense of duty. Thus, in a crucial passage, he speaks of the individual citizen as being *bound* to obey all the commands of the State; and none the less *bound* in those cases where he considers them unjust.[3] And it is probable that many readers, it is not impossible that the author himself, may have been

[1] 'Nos besoins nous rapprochent à mesure que nos passions nous divisent.' *Contrat Social*, first draft, I. ii. (*Political Writings*, i. pp. 447-458); and, for the quotation at the end of the paragraph, final version, I. viii.

[2] *Ethics*, iv. 7.

[3] 'Videmus itaque unumquemque civem non sui sed civitatis juris esse, cujus omnia mandata tenetur exsequi. . . . Atque adeo, quamvis civitatis decreta iniqua esse censeat, tenetur nihilo minus eadem exsequi' (*T.P.* iii. 5; comp. *T.T.* xvi. 27).

misled by this unfortunate choice of words. What is certain is that the whole tenor of his theory forbids us to interpret them in their strict sense: that, on his principles, they can mean nothing more than either that it is, in the long run, for the interest of the individual to bow to the will of the community, or that the community, being more powerful than he is, will have no difficulty in compelling him to do so. These are the sole bonds that he provides for the cohesion of the State. Are they strong enough to hold together those conflicting interests which will surely be found in every community: which are, in fact, of the very essence of its being? And, even if there be no open disruption, what hope do they offer of that 'ready obedience,' that 'courage and constancy,' that 'unflinching resolve to carry out the will of the whole body,' which statesman and thinker alike have regarded as essential to the health, to the 'true life,' of the community and which are to be found, doubtless with more or less of imperfection, in all the higher examples of the State? Spinoza himself, in the words just quoted, declares this to be the true 'definition,' the effort to realise it the true end, of the State. What is to be said of the means by which he proposes to attain it? [1]

The end is, in the fullest sense, a moral end: an end involving the recognition of duties to others, and indeed to ourselves also: an end to be won, if at all, only by ceaseless sacrifice of our own convenience to the good of our neighbours and of the community as a whole. The motives proposed by Spinoza for its attainment are purely selfish motives: the hope of gain, the fear of loss, not to our neighbours, not to the community at large—for that would be to smuggle in ends of a wholly different nature—but to our single, naked self. For it must never be forgotten that it is not 'the greatest happiness of the greatest number' which is here put forward as the end and motive, but the greatest happiness of the agent himself. It may be perfectly true that Bentham's formula raises as many difficulties as it solves, or even more. But at least it has the merit of concealing, if only for the moment, the weakness which is common to all utilitarian theories of morals or politics: of staving off the evil day when the enquirer stands face to face with

[1] 'Pax civitatis non belli privatio, sed virtus est quae ex animi fortitudine oritur; est namque obsequium constans voluntas id exsequendi quod ex communi civitatis decreto fieri debet. Illa praeterea civitas cujus pax a subditorum inertia pendet, qui scilicet veluti pecora ducuntur, ut tantum servire discant, rectius solitudo quam civitas dici potest. Quum ergo dicimus, illud imperium optimum esse ubi homines concorditer vitam transigunt, vitam humanam intelligo, quae non sola sanguinis circulatione . . . sed quae maxime ratione, vera mentis virtute et vita definitur' (*T.P.* v. 4-5).

the awkward question: Why, in the name of happiness, should I be called on to renounce the very form of happiness on which I have set my heart?

It is not, however, with the 'hybrid but beneficent utilitarianism' of Bentham that Spinoza concerns himself, but with utilitarianism pure and simple: not with the utilitarianism which slips in duty to others under the fair name of the happiness of the greatest number, but with that which takes its stand boldly upon the enlightened selfishness of the individual himself. And this account of the matter, whatever may be said for it in the sphere of morals, is manifestly no explanation at all of the problems that meet us in that of politics. Whatever difficulties it may raise when applied to the conduct of the individual, conceived as isolated from his fellows, are multiplied tenfold when we set ourselves to consider him, first and last, as member of a community.

This condition given, what is the chance, we ask, that the individual will recognise as his own good what, primarily at least, comes before him solely as the good of others? that he will be ready to sacrifice his own immediate convenience for the remote benefit of the community at large? It may be quite true that the end proposed will, in the long run, bring gain, even priceless gain, to the individual himself. Such a gain, however, is a gain mainly if not solely to his higher self; and the price to be paid for it is the vigilant repression, the continual sacrifice, of his lower self. Now at the moment when the choice has to be made, the self which is to benefit from the sacrifice is, from the nature of the case, either undeveloped, or, in the early stages of the history of the community, even still unborn. It unfolds—or, on the less favourable supposition, it comes to birth—only after the sacrifice is made, or while it is in process of making. It is so far the result of the sacrifice that we cannot credit it with the strength to be its cause: to foresee its advantages, to balance them against those in the opposite scale, and to decide for their acceptance. The consequence is that the lower self is left master of the field. And with the only instrument at its disposal, the 'felicific calculus,' there can be but one answer to the sum. Evidently, all the gain lies on the side of continuing in the course which is the more pleasant, or the less troublesome, to the lower self; and all the prizes offered to the higher self must be thrust aside as illusions by the mind which is virtually without the organ for perceiving them, and absolutely without that for judging them at their true value.

It is quite true that, even when the appeal is not to expediency, but to duty, the issue of the choice must still remain uncertain. This is implied in the very term, 'choice': it is implied in the fact, which the experience of every moment compels us to recognise, that all action, so far as it is not either instinctive or habitual, is a conflict. The conflict remains, whether the appeal be made to the higher expediency or to duty. It is the motive power that differs. And the difference is wholly in favour of duty. It is one thing to surrender a near advantage, the nature of which is well known or easily to be calculated, in order to gain one which is incalculable, uncertain and remote. Quite another, to surrender it at a command, the authority of which we instinctively recognise, and recognise all the more readily just because it forbids us to haggle over the cost, just because it resolutely rejects, and bids us also reject, 'the lore of nicely calculated less or more.' This is to fling a motive of a wholly different order into the scale: a motive infinitely deeper and more powerful. Even this motive, of course, may not be strong enough to outweigh the attractions of those marshalled against it. But if this will not, it is certain that nothing else will. And it is in the strength of this motive, and of none other, that the victory, if victory there is to be, must be won. The commonest of experiences confirms this conclusion. And to any one who faces the facts, the utilitarian account of the matter, which is also Spinoza's account, can seem no more than an unreal and bitter mockery.

Has expediency, then, nothing to say in the determination of our duties? To suppose this would be an error only less fatal than that which assumes it to be all in all. The idea of duty—when abstracted, so far as it can be abstracted, from the other elements of the process involved in an act of moral judgement—tells us no more than that we are bound to seek the highest good of our neighbour and ourself; or, in the language of religion, that we are bound to obey the will of God. What that highest good, what that will of God, may be, is to be learned from experience, from considerations of expediency, from the adaptation of means to the given end, and from these alone. To have insisted upon this is the great and enduring service rendered by the utilitarians: by Spinoza among them, by Spinoza probably the earliest of them all. And it is little or no detraction from this service, if we admit, as experience compels us to admit, that the first perception of the course which duty commands has more often been the result of intuition than of anything that can fairly be called a reasoned calculation. For even where this is true of the first perception—and it is perhaps equally true of any discovery in mathematics, or even, which is far more startling, in experimental science—that perception has, sooner or later, to be verified by a calculation: a calculation, not indeed as complete and accurate as that of a mathematical demonstration or a scientific proof, but as full and careful as the rebellious nature of the subject will allow. But for this safeguard, there could be no warrant that, in adopting a new course—and if there is to be any progress, whether in morals or politics, it can only be through the adoption of new courses—we are not plunging into the wildest of adventures. The world would be at the mercy of every fanatic, or every charlatan, with a sounding specific for the cure of all its ills.

It may be objected that much of this argument is concerned with principles of individual conduct, and that such matters have no place in a *Political Treatise*, no bearing either upon the theory or upon the practical management of the State. In truth, however, it is just because they are matters of individual conduct that they are of supreme importance to the practical business, and therefore to the theory, of the State. Where indeed, if not in the moral relations between man and man, are we to look for the raw material upon which the ruler is to work? It may, or may not, be true that he can do nothing to change, and little to modify, them. That is a matter which has been hotly disputed and is likely to be so till the end of time. But what no man has ever denied is that the first duty of the statesman is to study them and, if he can, to understand them. For even if he has no power to change them, they at any rate have the power to execute sentence, with infallible certainty, upon him. Indeed, the very men who have most loudly proclaimed his inability to alter them are also those who have most stubbornly pressed upon him the duty of ascertaining them and framing his policy upon them. Spinoza, at any rate, was as keenly alive as any man has ever been to the necessity of doing so. To have insisted upon it is one of his chief services to the theory of politics. The sharp distinction which is commonly drawn between morals and politics, and which has wrought such havoc with both, was to him not only mischievous but unmeaning. And as he inserts a sketch of his political theory in the middle of his *Ethics*, so in his *Political Treatise* he incorporates the rudiments of his theory of morals.[1] And this perhaps is one of the reasons why the doctrine of expediency, so barren in most other hands, becomes so full of life and fruit in his.

With these things in mind, we return to the more strictly political side of Spinoza's argument: to the relation which he establishes between the Government and the governed. Here again, the identification of rights with powers, the consequent exclusion of Right in the accepted sense of the term, is carried out with unfaltering consistency. Such criticism as is to be passed on the details of his plea may be deferred for the present. Once more, the essential thing to ask ourselves is: Is it possible to base the claims of the Government solely upon expediency? is not the idea

[1] *Ethics*, iv. 37, 73; *T.P.* i., ii.

of Right necessary to the very existence both of the Government and the State?

The idea of Right—without which it is commonly held that no human association, large or small, can hold together—rests at bottom upon a sense of brotherhood and carries with it a corresponding sense of obligation towards all those to whom that feeling of brotherhood extends. Such a sense of brotherhood has spread itself, in the course of ages, through an ever-widening circle. It has spread from the family to the tribe; from the tribe to what the Greeks knew as the city; from the city to the nation. Beyond the nation, there are signs that it is now reaching out to the community of the civilised peoples; and beyond that again, as the nobler spirits have long realised, to humanity as a whole. In all these cases alike, the sense of brotherhood has come first; and in its train has immediately followed a sense—in the first instance, no doubt, rudimentary enough—of reciprocal obligation.

Whether the communities so formed are, in their first origin, voluntary or no, is a matter of little moment. What is certain is that, once formed, they have carried with them a host of moral obligations, some of which are, while others are not, enforced by outward compulsion; and that the health, indeed the very life, of the community depends upon the cheerful, ungrudging acceptance of them by a sufficient number of its members. The last is assuredly the most vital thing of all; for without public spirit, without a widespread readiness to spend and be spent for the common good, no community could long stand against the shocks which inevitably come from without or the constant tendency to disintegration from within. Yet even the element of compulsion is not to be despised; if only because it bears witness to the overmastering nature of the duties which it is designed to enforce, to the permanence and necessity of the relations upon which those duties are based.

In the case of distinctly political communities—the various forms assumed by what we conveniently call the State—the obligation is manifestly of a special kind. It is in the first instance not, as it is with the family or with friendship, to a certain number of individuals; but to an organised body, which is doubtless made up of individuals, but which for many purposes we regard, and rightly regard, as having a separate being of its own. Here, therefore, we have to reckon not only with the obligations created—or, rather, recognised as already existing—between one member and another; but also, and indeed primarily, with those prevailing, on the one hand between the given community and others which lie outside of and perhaps in rivalry with it, and on the other between the various members, taken as individual citizens, and those who, in a special sense, represent the corporate life of the community as a whole: in other words, with the obligations of the governed to the Government and of the Government to the governed. So that here, as elsewhere, here perhaps in a sense yet fuller and deeper than elsewhere, everything comes back to the principle of obligation: to the necessity that all members of the community, each in his own place, should feel themselves bound together by ties of duty as essentially moral in character as those which all recognise in the personal dealings of friend with friend, of neighbour with neighbour, of man with man.

Of all this Spinoza will have nothing. To him, there is no call for duty, no need of obligation. The sole motive power which he recognises, the sole tie binding either on the Government or the governed, is expediency: the hope of gain, the fear of loss: on the one side, an abiding sense of the priceless advantages, both to body and mind, to be gained from the peace and security of a settled Government; on the other, a ceaseless dread lest oppression, if carried too far, shall provoke a general rising against the yoke of the oppressor. It is quite true that, with uncanny insight, he makes this apparently meagre principle carry further, that he draws from it consequences both wider and more fruitful than any man, statesman or theorist, has ever done before or since. It is quite true that, given the same insight in those whose task it might be to put his theory in practice, most or all of these consequences would, under favourable circumstances, actually follow. But this would demand a community of Spinozas. And, to use his own words, what ' dream ' could be more ' utopian ' than this?

In default of such insight, what may be expected to happen? For the answer, we need only remind ourselves of what actually happens, or would happen if the above conditions were ever completely realised, in the parallel case of personal conduct. In the one case, as in the other, it will be admitted that everything depends upon the persistent acceptance of expediency at its highest value: the value which coincides, if such a thing be possible, with that yielded by the principle of duty. In fact, however, the infallible result of withdrawing the motive of duty is to reduce expediency to its lowest value: the value which is identical with self-interest in the most short-sighted, and therefore the most sordid, sense which the term is capable of bearing. It may be perfectly true that honesty is the best policy. But, as moralists have often lamented, it needs an honest man, a man trained on some other diet than policy, to see it.

And if this is true of the personal life of man, where, to a healthy mind, calculations of expediency play a comparatively small part and where, even apart from duty, they are liable to be kept in check by the more generous impulses, much more will it be so of his political life, where, from the complexity of the problems to be solved, they necessarily bulk extremely large and where what we take for generous impulses are often no more than class or sectional interests, cunningly disguised. Here, even more than in matters of personal conduct, the calculating faculty, if it is not to sink into the meanest quest of individual or sectional profit, needs to be checked and qualified at every turn by the keenest sense of duty. Deprived of this check, neither party to Spinoza's Contract, neither the ruler nor the subject, is ever likely to put any but the basest interpretation upon what expediency demands. The one will push the rights of power, the other the rights of passive resistance, to the furthest possible limits. And all those qualities in which Spinoza himself recognised the saving 'virtue,' the 'true life,' of the State will inevitably be crushed out. It was this apparently that Vico had in mind when, in one of the few references to the *Tractatus* discoverable for more than a century after the author's death, he described the State of Spinoza as 'a city of hucksters.' [1] That is the fatal flaw in Spinoza's system. No criticism could be packed into fewer words; and unfortunately, none could be more just.

There is one point on which it is necessary to return: so curious is the light it throws both on the strength and the weakness of the whole theory. No reader can have failed to notice the stress which Spinoza lays upon the supreme importance of peace: of tranquillity within the State, of freedom from war without. With the latter part of this doctrine we are not immediately concerned; and a generation which has drunk the horrors of war to the dregs may well be disposed to think that no words are too strong to brand its iniquity and brutality. Yet, when we are told that 'no price paid for peace can ever be too great,' [2] it is right to remind ourselves that there are horrors even worse than those of war; that moments may come in which war is the most sacred of all duties; that to shrink from war in a just cause, when the rights of mankind or the existence of our own nation are at stake, is the deadliest of all wrongs, a depth of injustice and cowardice which

[1] 'Benedetto di Spinoza parla di Repubblica come d' una società che fusse di mercadanti' (Vico, *Opere*, t. v. p. 138). It does not appear with absolute certainty whether the reference is to the *Tractatus politicus* or to the *theologico-politicus*. But in the absence of proof to the contrary, the former seems the more likely; especially as, for a reason to be given later, the former work lays itself more open to the criticism than the latter. Bayle and Pufendorf, on the other hand, refer explicitly to the latter treatise, but are, to the best of my belief, silent as to the former.

[2] *T.P.* viii. 31.

can never be forgiven. Spinoza himself was a citizen of a nation which for a hundred years had stood in the breach to defend the liberties of Europe against the tyranny first of Spain and then of France. Were these also among the wars which ought to have been avoided 'at all costs'? Thus, even when applied to foreign war, Spinoza's doctrine has its limits; and when the inner life of the State is judged, or seems to be judged, by the same principles, we have no choice but to ask ourselves: What exactly does the author mean by it? how much is he prepared to sacrifice for a quiet life?

The answer is to be found in page after page of the *Political Treatise*: above all in the passage which deals with the Contract between the ruler and his subjects. It is of the essence of that contract to hand over the sole power of making the Law and the sole power both of interpreting and of enforcing the Law to the Government—'one man or one assembly of men'—which is thus solemnly set up. No private citizen, not even the whole body of private citizens, has the right—because, in the ordinary course of things, neither the one nor the other has the power—to overthrow the authority which it has thus deliberately transferred.[1] And as they are powerless before it, so there is no peaceable check whatever upon its encroachments and oppressions. In other words, the city of Spinoza is not only a 'city of hucksters'; it is also, or at any moment may wake up to find itself, a city of slaves. Save in one feature only, it is an exact copy of the city of Hobbes.

That one exception, it need hardly be said, lies in his refusal to follow his master in imposing submission, as a moral duty. To bow to oppression, to submit to slavery, may be expedient; it may be a less evil than civil war. But a duty it is not and never can be: and that, for the simple reason that in no field of human conduct has duty any place; that, in politics as in morals, it must be set aside as a pure illusion. The inconsistency of Hobbes enabled him to add insult to injury in this matter: to enslave not only the body, but even the soul, of his destined victims. The consistency of Spinoza, his stubborn resolve to 'keep his system watertight,' to guard it at all costs from any intrusion of Right or obligation, saved him from this crowning enormity. Otherwise, there is little to choose between the practical consequences of the two theories, though in aim and spirit they are poles asunder.

Even for practical purposes, however, there is—at least on paper—one glaring difference in Spinoza's favour. The Helots of *Leviathan* are without remedy and without hope. Even given the power to free themselves, they have deprived themselves of the right. By their own act, by the act of their fathers with

[1] *T.P.* iv. 6.

ingenious cruelty imputed to them, their bondage is without respite and without end. The slaves of Spinoza are not sunk so low as this. Their limbs may be held fast in the fetters; but their soul at least is free. Should the chance of escape come their way, they are entitled to seize it. They have only to will civil war. And if their sword prevails, their bonds are broken; the old tyranny is swept away; there is nothing to hinder them from setting up a free Government, even a Democracy, in its stead.

But what of the spectre of anarchy, the haunting dread of chaos come again, with which Hobbes never ceases to appal the mind and puzzle the will of his disciples? Has Spinoza guarded himself on this side, as well as on the other? No one can say that he has not. To Hobbes, dissolution of Government is dissolution also of Society. To Spinoza, it is not; in his view the one naturally, and even necessarily, survives the destruction of the other. 'The State,' he explicitly tells us, 'is never, like other societies, dissolved by strife and dissension. What happens is that, if the strife cannot be healed in any other way, the State is remoulded into a fresh form.' [1]

Considering that, on Spinoza's showing, the State had no existence before the formation of the Government, that the Contract with that Government is the sole outward proof that the State has come into being, it may be doubted whether, in strict logic, he was entitled to this conclusion. Indeed, it may have been with an eye to this objection that Locke—who, like Spinoza and far more intensely than Spinoza, was anxious to keep the door open for rebellion—devised the plan of two separate instruments: the one, the 'social compact,' giving birth to the community and concluded between all those who desire to join it; the other, a 'fiduciary trust' conferred by the community, with provision for legal succession, upon certain persons who, so long as they remain faithful to the terms of the trust, cannot rightfully be removed. And that, as we have seen, is (with the substitution of *contract* for *fiduciary trust*) substantially the view that Spinoza himself must have taken, when he wrote the *Tractatus theologico-politicus*. In the interval, however, between that and the later treatise, he had apparently changed his mind, and the first of the two Contracts has been silently dropped. It is this which gives rise to the slight difficulty before

[1] 'Ex discordiis igitur et seditionibus, quae in civitate saepe concitantur, nunquam fit ut cives civitatem dissolvant, ut in reliquis societatibus saepe evenit; sed ut ejusdem formam in aliam mutent: si nimirum contentiones sedari nequeunt servata civitatis forma' (*T.P.* vi. 2). It is true that in another passage (iv. 6) he allows himself to say: 'Quod si tamen ejus naturae sunt leges ut violari nequeant nisi simul civitatis robur debilitetur, . . . eo ipso civitas dissolvitur.' But it is fair to regard this as a momentary inadvertence.

us. Spinoza would probably have replied that the difficulty, such as it is, is one purely of logical machinery; and that the real reason why the civic bond, once formed, is never broken lies not in any original contract between the members of the community, but in the 'natural law' that the blessings of civil society, once tasted, will never be willingly surrendered: in other words, that the interest of the members, though in case of extremity it may force them to break the original form of Government, is an absolute barrier to the dissolution of the State. And such an explanation may be allowed fairly to meet the needs of the case. It is one more proof how slight was the hold which the idea of Contract had upon the mind of Spinoza: how determined he was to bring everything back to the natural working of self-interest and expediency.

The *ultima ratio*, then, is left by Spinoza in the hands of the community; and freedom may be retained, or won back, if only at the price of civil war. It is something, if not enough. And as Spinoza himself, perhaps in an unguarded moment, admits that 'nothing can be more miserable than tyranny,'[1] it would seem that, in extremities, he was not unwilling for such a remedy to be enforced. On the other hand, he is throughout so intent in 'ingeminating peace' that it is hard to imagine the circumstances, however desperate, under which he would have been ready to give his approval to war. It is still harder to believe that any community bred upon his principles, laboriously trained to judge of everything by calculations of expediency, could ever nerve itself to the task of risking all for an end which may never be gained and which, if gained, may be found to bring at least as much inconvenience as advantage.[2] To draw the sword, so only it be in a just cause, is a heroic resolve; and in the 'city of hucksters,' heroism is but too likely to have been sawn through at the roots.

Spinoza's final conclusions as to the 'liberty of prophesying' throw a significant light upon this matter. There was no subject on which he felt so keenly: none therefore on which he might have been more readily expected to show a fighting spirit. He had written his earlier treatise solely for the purpose of demanding freedom of thought and utterance for all civilised nations. He had given unanswerable reasons for his conviction that such freedom, so far from imperilling the State, cannot be withheld without grievous loss to all that is highest in its life. Yet when, a few

[1] 'Sed si servitium, barbaries et solitudo pax appellanda sit, nihil hominibus pace miserius. . . . Servitutis igitur, non pacis, interest omnium potestatem ad unum transferre' (with a reference to Tacitus, *Hist.* i. 1) (*T.P.* vi. 4).

[2] 'Quae gens unquam tot tamque gravia vectigalia pendere debuit ut Hollandica?' (*ib.* viii. 31).

years later, he came to ask himself, What then is the practical duty of the citizen in cases where this primary 'right' is denied or limited by the Government? all he could offer by way of answer is that resistance must not be carried so far as to endanger the 'concord and tranquillity of the community'; that matters of outward worship, 'having nothing to do with the true knowledge and love of God,' are concerns of comparative indifference; and that, after all, no individual, unless by a special revelation such as was granted to the Apostles and Prophets, has the right to make himself the 'knight errant of religion.'[1] If this is his counsel in the most sacred of all causes, what is it likely to be when less serious and less certain interests are at stake? The strain of quietism, the noble side of which is revealed in the contemplative vision of the *Ethics*, here puts on the ugly shape which it always assumes when applied to matters of practical concern. It was not so that the great Reformers understood their duty; or the later champions who finally won for the world the freedom which to Spinoza remains no more than a pious aspiration.

From all this it appears that, when it comes to the point, the *ultima ratio* of Spinoza is little likely to be invoked. Yet, as we have seen, that, at least in a Monarchy or Aristocracy, is the one weapon he leaves his citizens against misgovernment and oppression. What then, it may be asked, of the constitutional checks which he provides for each of these two forms of government? are they to be thrust aside as worthless? are they to count for nothing in our estimate of his foresight and good will? Of his good will they leave no doubt. Of his foresight, nothing can be taken for granted.

On paper, no doubt, his guarantees are admirable: for a Monarchy, a consultative Council; for an Aristocracy (at least, in the form which he manifestly prefers) a large scheme of local government, amounting, though he is careful to avoid the term, to a Federation of Cities and Provinces on a footing of almost absolute equality. But in practice, it is easy to see that, in the case of Monarchy at any rate, they would come to nothing. In the first place, like so much else in Spinoza, they are merely counsels of perfection. In the second place, there is no security that, even if adopted in the first instance, they will ever be seriously maintained. As to Monarchy, so much is, in fact, admitted by Spinoza himself. What other meaning is it possible to put upon his assertion that the only judge whether the ruler is justified in breaking the terms of the Contract between himself and his subjects is the ruler himself? On this showing, no Constitution, however cunningly devised, is worth the paper on which it is written. The ruler has only to say, It is not for the public interest that this

[1] *T.P.* iii. 10.

instrument should be observed; and it is as though it had never been accepted and proclaimed. What more could the most faithless of despots wish for? What else did Ferdinand of Spain or Frederick William of Prussia demand? The only wonder is that, on these conditions, Spinoza should have thought it worth while to draw up any constitution for his Monarchy at all.

With an Aristocracy of the type commended by Spinoza—a type more or less, but rather less than more, modelled upon that of the United Provinces—it is true that the same objection cannot be pressed. Local liberties and local Assemblies once granted, the central Power, it may fairly be argued, is no longer in a position to force its will upon the constituent Provinces; and the check provided is therefore not illusory, but real. The only doubt is whether a fabric, so loosely compacted, is capable of standing at all. The independence of the parts is amply secured; but where is the cohesion, where is the possibility of any common life, for the whole? [1]

We are left with the other and more familiar type of Aristocracy, the type akin to that of Venice or Genoa, in which few or no checks are imposed upon the supremacy of the central Power. We are left also with the fact that, even in the more liberal form of Aristocracy, there is no protection for the 'plebeian multitude' against the tyranny of the governing caste; and this is still more true of the other and more centralised type. Spinoza contents himself with the mild hope that self-interest, especially in the more generous form of polity, will lead the Patricians to deal kindly with their defenceless subjects.[2] But what reason is there for supposing that this hope will be fulfilled? And as he expressly permits the wholesale massacre or deportation of conquered enemies, it is clear that his faith in the humanity of governing castes, or of monarchs either, can hardly have been intense.[3]

[1] Spinoza is careful to assure us that his conglomeration of Provinces and Cities is not to be regarded as a Federation but as an unitary State. His projected Constitution however, including as it does the provision that the central Parliament is never to be summoned save in extraordinary emergencies (*T.P.* ix. 6), by no means bears out this assurance. He seems, in fact, far more anxious to secure the freedom of the several parts than the unity of the whole. And without special circumstances, such as the dread first of Spain then of France imposed upon the United Provinces, it may be doubted whether a State formed on this model could hold together for a day. The United Provinces themselves notoriously found joint action extremely difficult; and Spinoza's criticism of their constitution (*ib.* ix. 14; comp. *T.T.* xviii. 36, 37) seems to show that, at moments, he was fully alive to its defects. Yet his own ideal Aristocracy does little to correct them.

[2] *T.P.* ix. 14.

[3] *Ib.* vi. 33; ix. 13.

For these reasons, we are forced to the conclusion that the constitutional checks of Spinoza are little more than a delusion; that they too, like everything else in his system, are helpless before the imperious law that right is the same thing as might. And after all, what else was to be expected? Any other solution would have been contrary to his cardinal principle; it would have rent his theory in pieces from top to bottom. The sum of the whole matter is that the one weapon left to the community against its Government is rebellion; that civil war is the sole security for freedom. And that Spinoza would ever have permitted this weapon to be unsheathed, this security to be put in force, there is grave reason to doubt. In the man who thought 'no price too heavy to pay for peace,' it is hardly to be believed.

But is not this, it may be objected, too harsh a verdict? is it not to ignore the distinction which Spinoza himself draws between a 'free multitude' and a nation of slaves? Does he not himself insist that, under any form of government that he recommends, it is a free multitude of citizens, and that alone, which he has in mind? because none but a free multitude—none but a community 'led not by fear, but by hope'—is capable of conceiving, still less of achieving, that ideal of 'reason and manly courage' without which there can be no 'real peace,' no 'true life,' for the State? [1] And even if it be admitted that, on his principles, such an ideal is little likely to be realised either in a Monarchy or in an Aristocracy, is it not fair to remember that Democracy still remains behind; that, by his own avowal, it is the 'most complete'—indeed, the 'absolute'—form of polity; and that his own principles, no less than common sense, assure us that here, if anywhere, the 'free multitude' is to be found? [2]

The objection well deserves to be considered. It is perfectly true that Spinoza does make all these statements; that he evidently

[1] 'Quum dicimus illud imperium optimum esse ubi homines concorditer vitam transigunt, vitam humanam intelligo, quae non sola sanguinis circulatione et aliis quae omnibus animalibus sunt communia, sed quae maxime ratione, vera mentis virtute et vita definitur. Sed notandum, imperium quod in hunc finem institui dixi a me intelligi id quod multitudo libera instituit, non autem id quod jure belli acquiritur. Libera enim multitudo majori spe quam metu, subacta autem majori metu quam spe, ducitur. . . . Et quamvis inter imperium quod a libera multitudine creatur et illud quod jure belli acquiritur, si ad utriusque jus in genere attendamus, nulla essentialis detur differentia, finem tamen, et praeterea media quibus unumquodque conservari debeat, admodum diversa habent' (*T.P.* v. 5-6).

[2] 'Transeo tandem ad tertium et omnino absolutum imperium, quod democraticum appellamus' (*ib.* xi. 1).

attaches much importance to them; and that some of them at any rate—those relating to Democracy—are fully in accordance with the cardinal principles of the theory which he sets himself to expound. For if, as is clearly the case, he accepts Democracy as the best form of government, that is for the simple reason that it is the form in which the citizens and their rulers are, from the nature of the case, most completely identified with each other: in which therefore the possibility of conflict between them is reduced to the lowest point, in which the 'power'—and that means 'the reason, the virtue, the vital force'—of the community has consequently the best chance of reaching the highest point, attainable.

So far, therefore, everything is in order. It is when we turn to the other, the earlier, statements that doubts begin to arise: doubts whether, considering his peculiar views of human nature, it is likely that certain things asserted will really happen; doubts whether the moral judgements which he seems to pass on them are consistent with the cardinal principles on which his whole theory is based. Each of these points must be taken by itself.

In face of the large part which he gives to 'blind passion' in human action and character, has Spinoza any right to assume the possibility of a 'free multitude'? Has he left himself any chance of obtaining the number of men—the 'ten, twenty, hundred, thousand righteous'—sufficient, even under the most favourable conditions, to give colour to the whole body, to leaven the whole mass? To claim this, and to claim it while excluding all those ideas of duty which have done so much to redeem the natural frailty of man, is to make large demands upon our hopefulness or credulity.

But the question must be pushed a stage further yet. Even supposing the miracle accomplished, even granting the due number of 'free men' collected, has Spinoza, on his own principles, any right to the preference which he gives them? What test has he left himself by which to distinguish them from an equal number of slaves? One test, and one test only; the test of efficiency: the fact, or presumption, that a community of free men is likely to be more active, more full of energy, than a herd of slaves. The moment he steps beyond this, the moment he passes to considerations of ethical motive (hope, as against fear),[1] the moment he appeals to our natural admiration for the 'free man' or the 'free multitude,' he is travelling beyond the record; he is reverting to a test which he had deliberately rejected; he is substituting the judgement by motives for the judgement by results. And that is to renounce the principle which lay at the root of his whole system: the principle which he had sacrificed everything in order to keep 'watertight.'

[1] *T.P.* v. 6.

This is the difficulty which besets all utilitarian interpretations of human action, and all hedonistic interpretations of it also. In order to squeeze out the desired answer, all alike are compelled to assume standards of judgement drawn from a wholly different order of thought: the very order which it is their central purpose to dispense with and denounce. And no one can read Spinoza's chapter, *On the best ordering of the State*,[1] without being driven to the conclusion that, in spite of all his efforts, he is perpetually crossing the line which divides one set of principles from the other. It is, of course, possible that, if he had lived to give his considered verdict on Democracy, which he obviously held to be the best—not to say, the ideal—form of government, he might have done something to correct this impression. But it is at least as likely that he would only have confirmed it. And the mere fact that it *is* an ideal—that, whenever he speaks of the qualities which divide it from other forms of government, he writes with a moral fervour which he has deliberately banished from the rest of his treatise—is enough to betray how far, at the bottom of his heart, he was from accepting the pure judgement by results, as apart from motives, as apart from 'final causes,' which lay at the foundation of his whole system.

A precisely parallel defection must have struck every reader of the *Ethics*. There too, he starts with a purely intellectual analysis of the ideas and processes involved in man's life, as a moral agent. There too, the bulk of his enquiry is concerned with a dispassionate account of the moral virtues and the moral vices to which these ideas and processes give birth. And there too, everything leads up to a fervid exaltation of one particular frame of mind—the 'intellectual love of God': in other words, the 'beatific vision,' with a difference—as the highest ideal which man is capable of attaining. And that, in a system from which all ideals are rigorously excluded.

But, even if this speculative objection be disallowed, there is still a practical difficulty which it is impossible to overcome. Even if Spinoza is not to be charged with treating political 'freedom' as an ideal, can he be said to have seriously considered its relation to the other object of his desires—an object in itself wholly consistent with his cardinal principles—the peace and concord of his citizens both with one another, as individuals, and with the rulers who direct them, or who act in their name? Is it not the direct reverse of the truth to say that freedom leads to peace? Is it not the fact that, at least as often as not, it 'brings not peace, but a sword'? Would not the very nature of freedom have led us to expect this result? And does not experience prove it beyond doubt? Once

[1] *T.P.* cap. v.

again, it is possible that, if he had lived to complete his treatise, Spinoza might have endeavoured to show how he proposed to reconcile the one ideal with the other. But in the face of experience—an experience based on far ampler materials in our day than in his—it is hardly likely that he would have succeeded. 'Might is right, right is might,' that, in truth, is the first and the last word of Spinoza. And on his own, as on all other systems, it led straight to despotism: a despotism to which, thanks to his divorce of peace from justice, his nominal citizens, by one degree only less than the avowed slaves of Hobbes, are consenting parties. This is the more disconcerting, because few men have been more keenly alive than he to the evils of despotism; few have regarded the temper and policy of the despot with greater aversion or contempt.[1] A man's natural instincts are a better guide in these matters than Spinoza was aware. Had he been willing to trust them, he would not have allowed himself to be caught in the net of his own system. He would have recast it from top to bottom; he would have reshaped it into something less cold-blooded and more human.

As it is, the *Tractatus politicus* remains a monument to the principle of expediency, in its strength and in its weakness: a standing proof, worked out once for all, of what can, and what can not, be accomplished in its name. As a secondary principle, guided by a sense of duty, a sense of honour and a sense of justice, it is beyond price. For it is expediency, and expediency alone, which has the power to fill in the blank forms furnished by those higher principles; to give shape and meaning to the inarticulate cry which they utter in men's hearts; to clothe the 'soul of goodness' with a body capable of determinate action at a given time and under definite conditions.

But attempt, as Spinoza attempts, to exalt it into a primary principle, to strip it of the guidance which comes, and can only come, from the elemental ideas of duty, honour and justice; and expediency at once loses all that is noble or generous in its capabilities; it sinks at once into a sordid calculation of self-interest; and though the outward form of a State which is founded upon such a principle may long survive, it is as a body from which the soul has departed, a lifeless burden cumbering the earth, without profit to itself or to mankind. This was not in the intention of Spinoza. His own ideal of civic life was not material comfort; still less was it 'bestial oblivion.' It was an active harmony of diverse effort, directed to the common good and inspired 'by courage, by reason, by that

[1] 'Illa praeterea civitas cujus pax a subditorum inertia pendet, qui scilicet veluti pecora ducuntur, rectius solitudo quam civitas dici potest' (*T.P.* v. 4). 'Servitutis igitur, non pacis, interest omnem potestatem ad unum transferre' (*ib.* vi. 4).

energy in which lies the true life of the soul.' His error lay not in his perception of the end, but in the pitiable disproportion of the means to which he trusted for attaining it.

In his own heart, and unknown to himself, the supreme good of the State included, and was inspired by, ideas which he expressly debarred others from recognising or appealing to. The same discrepancy, as we have seen, reappears under a slightly different form in the *Ethics*, the close of which is lit up by an ideal of union with God which, even in the most rudimentary shape, had been studiously banished from the purely naturalistic account of moral qualities set forth at the beginning. In this case, he was aware of the incongruity, and justified it on the ground that the mass of men are, and must always be, the sport of blind passion; that the higher life is the privilege only of the few. How did he not see that, if this is the last word on the matter, it is next to impossible that even the lowest form of civic community should stand against the warring passions of its members, and altogether impossible that a State even remotely resembling that foreshadowed in his crucial chapter should ever come to birth at all? How did he not see that civic life in any form—above all, in that intensity of courage and energy which is his own ideal—is inconceivable unless on the assumption that men are capable of mastering their blind passions? that they do, in fact, respond—and respond the more, the more boldly the appeal is made—to the higher motives which his own theory deliberately rules out?

Spinoza was, before all things, a precursor: and a precursor whose followers are to be found in the most different, not to say conflicting, camps. As the champion of expediency, it is manifest that he anticipates, and much more than anticipates, the utilitarians of the next two centuries: Hume and Helvétius, Bentham and Mill, to name only the best. Under his hands, indeed, the utilitarian theory takes a purer, as well as a bolder, shape than it does with most of his successors. It is more purely individualist: it is not watered by appeals—appeals which to the unwary may make it more plausible, but which, on the fundamental principles of the theory, are wholly unauthorised—to the 'greatest happiness of the greatest number,' to the good of the community at large. Moreover, his sense of all that expediency carries with it is so keen, his perception of the remoter consequences which flow from it so wide and penetrating, that, as we read, we are half persuaded to believe that it fulfils the promises so lavishly offered in its name. And this is especially true of the checks which, on his construction, it tends to place upon the ever-growing encroachments of the despot. It is true that, even when thus deepened and extended, the foundation is not strong enough to bear the fabric which is raised upon it. But it may well be doubted whether any of his successors, not even excepting Hume, caused anything but a progressive enfeeblement by their modifications.

With Burke, no doubt, the case is different. But that is because the doctrine of expediency is no more than an element in the theory, if indeed it can be called a theory, which he beat out for himself: and an element transformed out of all knowledge by the other, and more vital, elements with which it is qualified and transfused. It is not only that he admits those primary ideas of humanity, justice and duty which are absent, or rather expressly banished, from the system of Spinoza.[1] He also interprets expediency itself in the light of a whole host of other ideas and instincts—religion, national tradition, conscious reverence for the past and a conscious desire to perpetuate it in the present—which, in some form or other, have certainly had an influence wide and deep, though not always unresisted, upon the moulding of political instinct, thought and action, but which find no place whatever in the bleak, colourless chart here mapped out by Spinoza. This is perhaps the most gratuitous gap in Spinoza's *Political Treatise*: gratuitous, because it in no way conflicts with the principle of expediency; because, in the *Tractatus theologico-politicus*, he had shown himself acutely alive to the strength which the Jewish theocracy had drawn from precisely these elements of its growth; and because, having grasped the truth so firmly in the particular instance, he might fairly have been expected to find some room for its working in his general theory of the State. It is the absence of such deep-drawn springs of action—springs which are all the more potent just because they are largely unconscious, just because they come down, as it were in the blood, from the past and do not require to be struck out by each individual afresh under the shifting needs of the present—that makes the expediency of Spinoza seem so pinched and starved a thing in comparison with that of Burke; and even, if in a far less degree, with that of Montesquieu. It is this also, at least in part, which gives the sting to Vico's laconic criticism: 'a city of hucksters.'

We pass to the opposite point of the compass. The theory of Spinoza has startling affinities, as well as obvious contrasts, with that of Rousseau. In the first place, the essence of the Contract, though in neither of them does that conception play so large a part

[1] 'The question with me is not whether you have a right to render your people miserable, but whether it is not your interest to make them happy. It is not what a lawyer tells me I *may* do, but what humanity, reason and justice tell me I *ought* to do' (speech on 'Conciliation with America,' *Works*, i. p. 192).

as might have been expected and is in fact commonly supposed, is to both of them what Rousseau describes as an 'absolute surrender' of the individual: a surrender which Spinoza expresses in the words that 'henceforth all are controlled as it were by one mind' and 'all submit their lives to the common good of all.'[1] It is of course true that a kindred conception—or rather, one more or less remotely resembling it—underlies the despotism of *Leviathan*. But the form is so different, the picture of Hobbes so distorted, his aim so little concerned with the 'mind' and 'will' of his victims, except as a convenient means of securing their enslavement, that the total effect of what he says is almost the exact contrary of that produced by the two later writers. Spinoza, with his speedy (if not simultaneous) transfer of the 'common will' from the whole body of citizens to their authorised Government, supplies the connecting link between Hobbes and Rousseau. But he stands much nearer to the latter than to the former; and his whole argument, both in its speculative and its practical issues, gains accordingly.

The resemblance becomes clearer yet when, with the above words of Spinoza in view, we turn to Rousseau's doctrine of the 'general will.' It is this, and not the idea of Contract, which forms the kernel of his whole theory of the State; and that being the case, we must expect to find it an idea of many articulations, branching out in many different directions. To him, the general will, which he is careful to distinguish from the sum of the particular wills of all the citizens, is first and foremost at once the outcome and the expression of the organic, corporate life which he recognises in the State.[2] It is this which makes the State something different in kind from a mere aggregate of the individuals composing it. That, however, is far from being all that the 'general will' stands for to Rousseau, all that he meant it to convey to the mind of his readers. It is not enough to know that the community, like the individual, has a life and will of its own. We must also be assured that the general, like the particular, will has the power of striving for worthy ends and the strength which enables it to attain them; that it is capable of 'meaning intensely and meaning good.' These requirements Rousseau meets by insisting, on the one hand, that

[1] *C.S.* (*Contrat Social*) I. vi.; *T.P.* ii. 16. 'Ubi homines jura communia habent omnesque una veluti mente ducuntur, certum est eorum unumquemque . . . re vera jus nullum in naturam habere praeter id quod ipsi commune concedit jus. Ceterum quicquid ex communi consensu ipsi imperatur, teneri exsequi, vel jure ad id cogi.'

[2] *C.S.* II. iii. Unfortunately, in the next sentence, he proceeds to violate the distinction which he had just drawn. In the earlier draft the distinction is still more trenchantly expressed: 'la volonté générale est rarement celle de tous' (*Pol. Writings*, i. p. 462).

without a keen sense of duty, a strong public spirit, there can be no such thing as a general will, a will that expresses the life of the community as a whole; and on the other, that, unless all partial or sectional aims be jealously excluded, the so-called 'will of the community' at once ceases to be general and becomes merely the will of the parties or sections for the moment in the ascendant. So long as these conditions are fulfilled, he considers that the general will must of necessity be the good will: so long, but no longer, it is incapable of 'erring,' of going wrong.[1]

Now it is clear that this conception, which cuts down into the very heart of the life of the State, has, to say the least, strong affinities with Spinoza's doctrine of the community as 'controlled by one mind,' as 'living in obedience to the common will of all.' It is more precise, more vividly realised, more fully articulated; but, at bottom, the two thinkers are at one. It may even be pointed out that Spinoza also speaks of the State as 'incapable of error': that his 'an civitas peccare potest' finds a curious echo in Rousseau's 'si la volonté générale peut errer.'[2] This, however, is one of the cases in which the words are the same, but the meaning conveyed by them entirely different. To Spinoza, the infallibility of the State means that there is no Law, moral or otherwise, above that of the State; and that, however foolishly, however much against its own interests, the State may act, it is, in the strict sense, incapable of doing wrong; for, apart from ultimate consequences, which from the nature of the case cannot come into play at the moment, there is no power by which it can be brought to book. We have here, in fact, only one more assertion of his cardinal principle that the ideas of Right and duty have no meaning when applied to the State, or to the motives and actions of its members. The corresponding words of Rousseau mean that, though the will of the community is capable of going wrong, that is because, for easily discoverable causes, all of which may be reduced to faction, it has then, for the time at any rate, ceased to be general; and the only way of meeting this danger is to stand ceaselessly on guard against it. His analysis may not be complete; his solution may not afford any great practical help against the dangers in question. But at least he recognises, as Spinoza does not, that there is some law higher than expediency: some ideals of duty and justice which the State is bound to acknowledge and act upon, under pain of forfeiting all claim to respect from its own members and others, all title to the character which

[1] *C.S.* II. iii., vi.; IV. i.

[2] 'Si haec nomina—lex et peccatum—genuino sensu sumantur, nulla ratione dicere possumus civitatem legibus adstrictam esse, aut posse peccare' (*T.P.* iv. 5; compare *ib.* ii. 21. Rousseau, *C.S.* II. iii.).

alone can make its 'sovereignty' legitimate. Yet, in spite of this crucial divergence, it is only just to insist that Spinoza's doctrine of the 'one mind' and 'common will' contains at least the germ of that which was subsequently adopted and widened, as well as deepened, by Rousseau. And if Spinoza, largely owing to the initial exclusion of Right from his whole system, fails to draw all that later thinkers have drawn from this conception, that is the worst of reasons for refusing him the credit which rightly belongs to the man who first explicitly, however imperfectly, embodied it in the theory of the State.

The last point we need notice is the stress which both writers justly lay upon religion, as a cementing principle of the State. In both of them—but especially, it need hardly be said, in Rousseau—this acknowledgement may be bound up with the further assumption that, to be effective for the purpose, religion must take a single, definite shape and even be formally embodied in the national institutions. But this, though a natural, is not a necessary development. And experience, to say nothing of reason, has shown the evils which inevitably result from its acceptance.

'As soon as men join in civil society, they need a religion to keep them there. No nation has ever endured, or ever will endure, without a religion. And if none were given them, they would make one for themselves, or would quickly perish.' These are the opening words of Rousseau's chapter on 'Civil Religion,' in its original draft; and none could express more clearly the idea which underlies that courageous—though, in one sense, most unhappy—pronouncement. Spinoza, on his side, devotes two Books of the *Tractatus theologico-politicus* to showing that the whole strength of the Jewish State—the strength which, as Tacitus testifies, enabled it, when all human hope was dead, to draw courage from despair itself—sprang from the inseparable union of the civic and religious ideals which had become a second nature to its members and which, in the face of a thousand shortcomings, made their 'valour and constancy' one of the miracles of history.[1] It is true that, when he came to cast his reflections into a systematic theory of Politics, he deliberately refused to make his reckoning either with this, or with any other, historical element; and his theory suffers accordingly. The reason probably was that he realised how wide a breach any of these elements—above all, the religious—would make in the pure gospel of utility. But, once again, that is no reason why we should deny him the credit due for his first, and better, thoughts: no reason why we should not acknowledge the

[1] *T.T.* cap. xvii., xviii.; especially xvii. 80-82. The reference here is to Tacitus, *Hist.* ii. 4; compare *ib.* v. 13.

insight which prompted him, as it afterwards prompted Rousseau, to find place for instincts so deeply rooted in human nature, but so strangely at variance with the speculative prejudice of his time.

Such are the chief points of agreement between Spinoza and Rousseau.[1] They may be no more than coincidences; they may mean that the later writer was directly and consciously influenced by the earlier. It is impossible to say for certain; nor perhaps is it a matter of great importance.[2] What does concern us is to recognise the surprising genius of the man who touches the main lines of political thought at so many places: on the one hand, recasting the whole theory of Hobbes into a shape at once more fruitful, more consistent and less oppressive; on the other hand, anticipating much of what was most pregnant in the theories of men so different as the utilitarians of the next two centuries, and Burke, and Rousseau.

With all this width of vision, how is it that the direct and certain influence of Spinoza upon the course of political theory should have been so curiously small? Pufendorf had read him; Bayle had read him; Vico had read him: and all of them, only to disagree.[3] With these exceptions, there is, so far as I know, no

[1] Another point in which it is possible that Rousseau may have been prompted by Spinoza is his rather futile argument that the powers of the individual citizen are in inverse proportion to the size of the State. See *C.S.* III. i.; *Émile*, Liv. v.; and Spinoza, *T.P.* ii. 13, 16; iii. 2.

[2] Personally, I am disposed to think that Rousseau must have read one, or more probably both, of his *Treatises*; possibly being put upon the track either by Bayle (art. ' Spinoza '), or by Pufendorf. He had certainly read both these writers; in both, the reference is to the *Tractatus theologico-politicus*.

[3] Pufendorf (*De jure naturae et gentium*, II. ii.: ed. 1688, Amst. q°, pp. 108-10) writing in 1672, before the publication of *T.P.*, attacks Spinoza for his identification of rights with powers (*T.T.* xvi. 2-24). Bayle (*Dict. historique et critique*, art. ' Spinoza ': ed. 1720, Rott. fol. vol. iii. pp. 2631-49) assails Spinoza's determinism; the same assault is repeated in other articles of the *Dictionary* (*e.g.* ' Buridan ') and in the *Réponse aux questions d'un Provincial* (ed. Rott. 1704–7, 5 vols. 12mo, iii. pp. 732 *sq.*, 769 *sq.*); his references are mainly to the *Ethics*, but with a few (art. ' Spinoza ') to *T.T.* He informs us in the *Dictionary* that a French translation of *T.T.* was published in 1678, and two others (under different titles) before 1697; also that, by that same year, there had been eight reprints of the original Latin. Vico's criticism is confined to the ' city of hucksters.' In the text of *Scienza nuova* (*Opere*, v. p. 138) he gives no detailed reference. But in the *Proloquium* to *Jus universum* (*Op.* iii. p. 11) he mentions nothing but *T.T.* The *Jus universum* was published in 1720–1; the *Scienza nuova* (versione seconda) in 1730. To *T.P.* I have come across no reference whatever. This is the more strange,

proof that, before the nineteenth century, his political treatises were known even by name to those engaged in working the same field. The truth probably is that his *Politics* were completely thrown into the shade by his *Ethics*. And it may well be that the taint of 'reprobation' attaching to his memory, in virtue of his supposed atheism, may have deterred the few who read and admired him from acknowledging their debts. Whatever the cause, the result is beyond doubt. He lived before his time; and when, after two long generations, the world was at last ready to receive what he had taught, his name, except as a beacon of warning, had almost been forgotten; so that his successors were either compelled to rediscover the principles for which he had battled, or were tempted to suppress the fact that they were guided by his light. As metaphysician and moralist, his greatness has long been recognised. As political philosopher, he has even now barely come by his own.

---

because in the original edition (1677) *T.P.* follows immediately upon the *Ethics*. It is hard to see why the latter should have been read—and abused—by all the world, while the former passed entirely unnoticed. It is also curious that Locke, who spent some crucial years in Holland (1684–9), should be entirely silent as to Spinoza, who had died less than ten years before.

CHAPTER IV

THE SOCIAL CONTRACT: LOCKE

SPINOZA was before his time; at least two generations were to pass before the vein of thought which he opened was to be effectively explored. With Locke we return to the beaten road of seventeenth-century speculation. And the *Treatise of Government*, whatever its flaws as a piece of speculative reasoning, has a historical importance to which few theoretical writings can lay claim. It provided the theory for the 'glorious Revolution' which had been safely accomplished a year before its publication (1690). And it remained the gospel of freedom, both in France and England, for at least two generations after its appearance. In this country, indeed, it was still a power to reckon with for considerably longer; and its influence, though no longer consciously recognised, is even now not entirely dead.

Locke's *Treatise* is a gun with two barrels: the one directed against Filmer and Divine Right, the other against Hobbes. The champion of Divine Right is treated with light-hearted disrespect; he was indeed hardly worth powder and shot. And it is a thousand pities that it should never have been Locke's fortune to measure himself with Bossuet, whose *Avertissements aux Protestants* were appearing just at the same time and who, if he cannot be counted a great thinker, was at any rate a great master of controversy, a great writer and a very great man: on every ground, a foe worthy, as the pedantic and rather fatuous Filmer certainly was not, of the philosopher's steel.[1] The truth is that the doctrine itself does not deserve to be taken seriously: still less, its knightly exponent.

[1] It must be remembered that his *Politique*, though originally written between 1670 and 1680, was not published until after his death (1709); and then, in a revised form. The only political writing of his that could have been known to Locke when *Civil Government* was published, is therefore the *Avertissements*; and, as the bulk of *Civil Government* was clearly written in or before 1688, all question of Bossuet in this connection must, in fact, be dismissed. Filmer's *Patriarcha* was posthumously published in 1680, the author having died in 1653.

With Locke's refutation, and Bossuet's contemporary reassertion of it (or something not remotely resembling it) against Jurieu, the theory of Divine Right practically vanishes from history.[1] Always an impossible theory, it was hopelessly at variance with the prevalent thought of an age which gave birth to the Royal Society and Bayle's *Dictionary* and which was beginning to lose stomach for theological discussions. Even the genius of Bossuet was unable to give it more than a momentary respite from death. Even the talent of de Maistre was unable, a century later, to galvanise it into more than a semblance of fresh life. The kings themselves, in the interval, had been hard at work to kill and bury it.

The second part of the *Treatise*, the *Essay of Civil Government*, is made of very different stuff. Here Locke puts forth all his powers: he is no longer concerned to destroy, but to build up. Like Spinoza, he writes throughout with his eye on Hobbes; and, like Spinoza, he never once allows the name of the terrible enemy to escape his lips. Here, however, the resemblance ends. Their methods of dealing with the problem are entirely different.

There are two possible ways of meeting the argument of Hobbes: the one, direct and simple, to judge it by its consequences; the other, less direct and more subtle, to assail its speculative assumptions. The latter is the method adopted by Spinoza: especially in that denial of natural Right—or rather, of Right in

[1] It is just to point out that Bossuet is not, strictly speaking, an advocate of the divine right of kings. In his one complete work on political theory, *Politique tirée de l'Écriture Sainte*, he explicitly admits the legitimacy of other forms of Government ('Il n'y a aucune forme de Gouvernement, ni aucun établissement humain, qui n'ait ses inconvénients: de sorte qu'il faut demeurer dans l'état auquel un long temps a accoutum le peuple. C'est pourquoi Dieu prend en sa protection tous les Gouvernements légitimes, en quelque forme qu'ils soient établis. Qui entreprend de les renverser n'est pas seulement ennemi public, mais encore ennemi de Dieu:' *Pol.* II. I, 12); pleading only that monarchy is 'the commonest, the oldest, the most durable and the most natural': in other words, basing his plea not upon Right, but upon expediency and fact. And in the *Avertissements* (v. § 48) he takes this ground still more definitely and unequivocally. Yet throughout the bulk of the former treatise, he seems, most illogically, to assume a superior sanctity in Monarchy, to argue as though the person of a king were more sacred than that of any other magistrate ('Il paraît de tout cela que la personne des rois est sacrée et qu'attenter sur eux, c'est un sacrilège:' *Pol.* III. ii. 2). It might be urged in his defence that, writing as he did for a future king, the Dauphin, it was natural that he should lay a marked stress upon the privileges and duties of kings. But this is hardly convincing. Certainly, the general effect of his argument is to surround the Monarch with a halo of divine majesty.

all conceivable shapes—that exclusion of all standards save those provided by expediency, which forms the corner-stone of his argument. The former course—straight, obvious and practical—is that followed by Locke. This gives his plea an actuality which, for the moment at any rate, was lacking to Spinoza's; but, for that very reason, robs it of the speculative interest which makes Spinoza's *Treatise* so notable a landmark in the history of political ideas.

There was, in truth, a very good reason why Locke should eschew the speculative line of attack. The elements of his system are almost identical with those of *Leviathan*. The relative stress laid upon each of them is, no doubt, extremely different; the practical upshot of his argument almost diametrically opposite. But the ideas themselves have the closest resemblance: they are drawn from the same source, from the common stock of seventeenth-century speculation. The state of nature, the law of nature, the social contract—all these figure in *Civil Government*, as they had figured before it in *Leviathan*; and in the one treatise, as in the other, there is little else beside. Spinoza also, it may be said, makes play with two of these ideas: the state of nature and the Contract. But neither of them forms more than an ornament to his system. Both of them might have been dropped—the Contract, as we have seen, was in fact dropped in the *Tractatus Politicus*—and the general course of his argument have remained practically untouched. Moreover, his explicit rejection of natural law changes the whole issue at a stroke. It is with him not a question of the rights secured, or the duties imposed, by the law of nature and the Contract; but of expediency, as determined by the permanent instincts and interests of men and by the circumstances in which, from time to time, they find themselves placed.

Under these conditions, it would have been an extremely intricate task for Locke to assail Hobbes on speculative grounds. He would have had to fight *Leviathan* chapter by chapter, almost page by page, in the effort to lay his finger upon the exact spot at which Hobbes had gone astray in applying each of these ideas, the precise grounds on which he himself was prepared to base his own very different application of them. He did well to decline a task so irksome to himself and to his readers: to avoid direct controversy and devote himself solely to build up his theory as it had shaped itself in his own mind. In practice, this was the method of Spinoza also. Only, starting as he did from a conception so fundamental and so simple as the identity between 'rights' and 'powers,' it was inevitable that, in stating his own principle, he should at the same time confute those of his opponent. Like Locke, however, he does so merely by implication; and except to those who are in the secret, his two *Tractates*, no less than the *Essay of Civil Government*, are entirely constructive.

What, then, are the main lines of Locke's theory? What is the use he makes of the three strands—the state of nature, the law of nature, the social contract—out of which it is woven?

Briefly, it may be said that he interprets each of them in a sense the exact opposite of that which it bears to Hobbes. The state of nature, so far from a state of war, the famous 'war of all against all,' is a state of 'good will, mutual assistance and preservation': in one word, a 'state of peace.'[1] The law of nature, so far from a mere natural impulse upon which the idea of moral obligation is at a later stage illicitly grafted, is from the first a moral law which, though it lacks any outward and positive sanction, is yet recognised by all men, even by those who break it, as binding upon the conscience: a law to be observed by man, as man: a law, therefore, valid not only in the civil state, but also in the state of nature. Finally, the Contract by which men pass from the state of nature to the civil state is not an instrument of enslavement, but a charter of freedom, for the individual: who, so far from surrendering all his powers to a despot monarch, or a despot oligarchy, surrenders so much, and only so much, of them as shall provide a security, hitherto lacking in fact though not in right, for the free, untrammelled exercise of all the rest.

The practical effect of this interpretation is to restore the theory of Contract to the purposes for which it was originally framed: to overthrow the portentous fabric so ingeniously conjured out of it by Hobbes; to sweep away the absolute sovereignty of the 'one man or one assembly of men'; and to set the sovereignty of the whole community—a sovereignty, however, strictly limited by the prior claims of the individual—in its place. And the limitation just mentioned is of the first importance. For a sovereignty that is not absolute, a sovereignty which can only claim second honours, is, in the strict sense, no sovereignty at all.[2] Locke's argument has therefore a wider bearing than appears at first sight: even wider, it may be, than Locke himself was fully

[1] *C.G.* (*Civil Government*), § 19.

[2] Locke's ideal of sovereignty appears from a casual reference in the course of the *Essay*: 'Thus we see that the kings of the Indians in America . . . exercise very little dominion and have but a very moderate sovereignty' (*ib.* § 108). Compare: 'In commonwealths where the legislative is not always in being and the Executive is vested in a single person who has also a share in the Legislative, there that single person, in a very tolerable sense, may also (*i.e.* as well as the Legislative) be called supreme' (*ib.* § 151). The example he here has in view is, of course, England.

aware of. The *Essay of Civil Government* is, in fact, an assault not only upon the sovereignty of *Leviathan*, but upon the very idea of sovereignty. Its shafts are aimed not merely against one particular form of sovereignty—doubtless the most oppressive and the least endurable—but against any form, even the mildest, that sovereignty can assume. In other words, Locke is not merely anti-despotic, but also markedly individualist. At bottom, he is as much against the 'sovereignty of the people' as against that of the oligarchy or the tyrant. His argument, if sound, is as fatal to the ideal of Rousseau as to that of Hobbes: as damaging to the claims of the French Convention or the British Parliament of 1919 as to those of Caligula or Nero. It was the anti-despotic side of his argument which struck home most closely to the men of his own day, and probably of the century that followed. But time was to show that the other, the individualist, side of it was yet more important.

The controlling link in the chain forged by Locke is manifestly the 'law of nature.' It is that which determines the character both of the state of nature and of the civil state which eventually follows. Now, at first sight, Locke's law of nature may not seem to differ essentially from that of Hobbes. 'Do not that to another which thou wouldest not have done to thyself': such is the 'easy sum' into which the fifteen laws of nature, with all their solemn corollaries, are 'contracted' by Hobbes.[1] And with the simple conversion into the positive form—'Do unto all men as ye would they should do to you'—it is a sum that Locke would readily have accepted.[2] So converted, in fact, it is identical with that law of 'peace, good will, mutual assistance and preservation' which, as Locke himself assures us, governs the state of nature. And the difference between positive and negative, though important enough, is not so crucial as the glaring difference between the net results of the two theories would have led us to expect.

But if the Law of Locke, in itself, differs comparatively little from that of Hobbes, the same can by no means be said of its application: of those over whom he gives it jurisdiction. To Hobbes, by the strangest of contradictions, the law of nature is

[1] *Leviathan*, chap. xv.

[2] Indeed, when he comes to sum up the law of nature, Locke himself is content to cast it in the negative form: 'The state of nature has a law of nature to govern it, which obliges every one; and reason, which is that law, teaches all mankind, who will but consult it, that, being all equal and independent, no one ought to harm another in his life, health, liberty or possessions' (*C.G.* § 6). But 'mutual assistance and preservation' goes considerably beyond this. Hence (§ 5) he quotes with approval the words of Hooker which declare 'that it is no less men's duty to love others than themselves': an essentially positive conception.

precisely not that which governs the state of nature. It only comes into operation at the moment when man passes out of the state of nature into the civil state. The state of nature itself is given over to a very different law, the law of war: the law of which 'the two cardinal virtues are force and fraud.' To Locke, on the other hand—and who shall blame him?—it seemed absurd that the state of nature should be governed by anything but the law of nature. Indeed, that law once granted—and, as we have seen, both writers are at one as to its general character and principles—there is no reasonable course but to make it part and parcel of man's original constitution: no choice but to accept it as the law which governs the state of nature.

Thus on the assumption common to both writers—that there is such a thing as the law of nature and that, wholly apart from any civil bond, it is 'plain to all who will but consult it,' [1] and therefore binding upon all men 'simply as they are men'—it is clear that Locke has the best of the argument, and that, on the premisses which both accepted, it is not Hobbes, but he, who drew the correct—and indeed, the only possible—conclusion.

So much for the bearing of the law of nature upon Locke's picture of the state of nature. What is its effect upon his conception of the civil state?

If the individual brings with him into the civil state not only a full-fledged 'moral sense,' but even a complete code of moral duties, the code which he recognises as laid down for him in the law of nature, then it is evident that what the civil state, with all its machinery of positive laws and fixed penalties, can do for him is uncommonly little. He is indolent; and it can save him the trouble of helping his neighbour to right the wrongs that have been done to him by others. He is timorous; and it can save him the danger of fighting his own battles. He is sensitive; and it can save him the affliction of acting as judge in his own cause. But beyond this, it has no attractions to offer. And when against such gains as these are set off the corresponding losses which the change inevitably entails, we are left to wonder why that change should ever have been made.

Compare the theory of Locke with those of other contractualists in this matter. The theory of Contract, in all its forms, is a theory of motives: of motives consciously realised and deliberately followed out. That is of its essence. Now these motives may be either material or moral: either the desire to escape from the physical inconveniences of the state of nature; or the desire to

[1] Compare: 'It is certain that there is such a law: and that, too, as intelligible and plain to a rational creature and a student of that law as the positive law of the commonwealth' (*C.G.* § 12).

find freer scope than that state furnishes for the moral and spiritual instincts with which man is sent into the world, or to which, being there, he gradually awakens. And the main difference between the varying forms of the theory lies in the varying stress they lay upon the material, or the moral, causes which led man to exchange the one state for the other. According to Hobbes, the motive is almost exclusively material: an overmastering desire to escape from a life which, in his own words, is 'solitary, poor, nasty, brutish and short.' According to Rousseau, on the other hand, it is predominantly moral. The effect of the change, at any rate—for, with characteristic prudence, he says little about motives—is to 'replace mere physical impulse by the voice of duty and mere appetite by Right: in short, to give to man's acts the moral character which was lacking to them before.'[1] In Spinoza's version, finally, the balance is held as evenly as is humanly possible between the two: between the desire of the individual to guard against the encroachments of his neighbours and his sense that, 'without the aid of others, his mental'—under which must be included his moral—'powers can hardly be developed.'[2] It is clear, however, that the scale dips, though not very markedly, towards the more material inducements; and it may be noted that Spinoza, like Rousseau, keeps the question of motives, as distinguished from results, as far as possible in the background: a course which, in the absence of any specific reference to the Contract, was in his case comparatively easy.[3]

But, however much the three writers may differ among themselves, they are all agreed—Spinoza, doubtless, with decidedly more reserve than the two others—in painting the gulf between the natural and the civil state as both wide and deep. No one could say the same of Locke. Neither materially, nor morally, is there any marked barrier between his natural and his civil state. Neither materially, nor morally therefore, is there any sufficient motive for the individual to go to the cost and trouble of removing such slight fences as divide them. He already possesses, already owns allegiance to, the 'law of nature': a law which, on Locke's showing, is at least a very tolerable substitute not only for the 'law of the land,' but even for the Gospel. He is therefore fully armed upon the moral side. His neighbours, with some few exceptions, are in the same happy case; and this gives him comfortable assurance upon the material side also. The state of nature, in short, as the author himself comes near to admitting, is a golden age; and if the civil state, at least in its later stages, is by comparison

[1] *C.S.* I. viii. [2] *T.P.* ii. 15; *T.T.* xvi. 12-20.

[3] Accordingly, in *T.T.*, where he does bring in the Contract, his account of motives plays a considerably larger part.

to be reckoned an age of iron, that must be due, in part at any rate, to the wilful act by which men surrendered the freedom, to say nothing of the 'innocence and sincerity,' of the one state for the restrictions and burdens of the other.

Under these circumstances, it is only to be expected that the first object of the individual, in entering the civil state, should be to make it as like the natural state as possible: to keep as much as he can of the freedom which he enjoyed in the state of nature, and to avoid as many as he can of the burdens and restrictions which, unless the most watchful care be taken, are sure to await him in the civil state. Having but little to gain from the change on the material side, and nothing at all upon the moral side, it must be his aim to surrender as little power to the community, and to retain as much in his own hands, as can be done without condemning his new creation to death from the very moment of its birth. And this is precisely the conclusion drawn by Locke. It is still more markedly the conclusion drawn from his premisses by the more discerning of his disciples. Beccaria, Paine—from a very different point of view, even Herbert Spencer—all refine upon this element of his theory: all carry out the consequences which flow from the initial assumptions of the master with a remorseless logic which his practical sagacity would have impatiently disallowed.[1]

In following out the effects of the law of nature, it has been necessary to trespass in some degree upon the later stages of Locke's argument. We now return to trace the main course of that argument from its rise in the state of nature to its conclusion in the civil state and the various forms which, in his view, the civil state, organised under settled government, may legitimately assume.

To Locke, as we have seen, the state of nature is a state governed by the law of nature: a state, therefore, of 'peace, good

[1] The words of Beccaria, the most extreme and the most consistent of them all, are worth quoting: 'Nessun uomo ha fatto il dono gratuito di parte della propria libertà in vista dal *ben pubblico*: questa chimera non esiste che ne' Romanzi. . . . Essi ne sacrificarono una parte per godere il restante con sicurezza e tranquillità. La somma di tutte queste porzioni di libertà sacrificate al bene di *chiascheduno* forma la sovranità di una nazione; e il sovrano è il legittimo depositario ed amministratore di quelle. . . . Fu dunque la necessità che costrinse gli uomini a ceder parte della propria libertà: egli è dunque certo che ciascuno non ne vuol mettere nel pubblico deposito che la minima portione possibile: quella sola che basti ad indurre gli altri a defenderlo. L' aggregato di queste minime porzioni possibili forma il diritto di punire. Tutto il di più è abuso, e non giustizia; è Fatto, non già Diritto.' (*Dei Delitti e delle Pene*, §§ 1, 2. It was published in 1764, two years after the *Contrat Social*—probably the 'romance' aimed at in the opening sentence.)

will, mutual assistance and preservation'; a state as unlike the 'state of enmity, malice, violence and mutual distraction' imagined by Hobbes as it is possible to conceive.[1] Its cardinal virtues, so far from being 'force and fraud,' are justice and the spirit of brotherhood. It is, in fact, the direct contrary to Hobbes' natural state; and that, not only in the negative, but also in the positive, sense. For, as Locke is careful to explain, the law of nature—that law to which all men, even as they are men, owe allegiance—demands not only that every man be obedient to it on his own account, in his own life and conduct, but also that he hold himself ready to punish every breach of it, so far as this comes within his notice, on the part of others. He must uphold it, that is, not only when he himself, but also when any one of his neighbours, is the sufferer. Otherwise, the law of nature would be no more than a dead letter; and if it is to be a reality, each man must remember that it is not only his right, but his bounden duty, to act as its 'executor.' He is the servant of Right, but he is its avenging minister as well. He is his own keeper; but, by the direct ordinance of God, he is his brother's keeper also.[2]

The state of nature is therefore a state of innocence: of innocence vindicated, when the need arises, by the sword. In this state of innocence there are, however, certain drawbacks which forbid us to deem it the garden of Eden that, at first sight, we might be tempted to imagine. In the first place, little as Locke's previous description would have led us to suppose it, the law of nature, which is the sole source of all these blessings, is found on experience to fail man at the very moment when he stands most in need of it. He is ready enough to apply its restraining canons to the acts of others; he is not quite so ready to apply them equally to his own. In the second place, even when his will is honestly set on doing justice to others, he can never be sure that his judgement is not warped by unconscious selfishness: by the bias to which all men are subject in favour of themselves. No man with a sensitive conscience will care to be 'judge in his own cause.' Lastly, even supposing both these conditions to be satisfied, even allowing that his will is perfectly good and his judgement perfectly sound, he can have no assurance that, in the absence of any settled Law which is of the essence of the state of nature, he will be able to make justice triumph: that he will have strength to enforce the claims of Right,

[1] *C.G.* § 19. The words quoted in the text are Locke's, and are manifestly aimed at Hobbes.

[2] *Ib.* § 11-13. It is right to point out that, in these paragraphs, Locke does not go beyond the assertion that it is every man's *right* to act as executor of the natural law. But from the very nature of that law it surely follows that it is not only his *right* but his *duty*.

whether on behalf of himself or of his neighbour, against the might of a powerful oppressor.[1]

For all these reasons—and, as champion of an innate sense of moral law, Locke lays special stress upon the moral objection to 'being judge in one's own cause'—men must sooner or later, and rather sooner than later,[2] find themselves impelled to quit their original condition of pure freedom and to seek for further guarantees—which inevitably involve new, or further, restrictions —in the civil state. Two things, however, must be understood from the beginning: on the one hand, that in taking this step, no man either will, or ought to, accept any restriction upon his own freedom of action that is not necessary for the sake of guarding it against the encroachments of others; and on the other hand, that, after as before taking it, he remains subject to the law of nature: in fact, that the law of the land is, and ought to be, nothing more than a machine for executing the law of nature. Thus, if man makes some sacrifice of his natural liberties in detail, it is only to secure their exercise in gross; and if he slights the law of nature in appearance, it is only to rivet its supremacy in reality. So far as practice goes, he is, in fact, not less, but more, free after the change than he was before it; he is not less, but more, subject to the law of nature in the civil state than he was in the state of nature.[3]

There is, however, one condition more fundamental yet. It is that no man can be 'incorporated into' any nascent community without his own formal and active consent. And though the same formality is not required in any of the later stages of its history, still the tacit, though not the express, consent of all new recruits—the heirs and successors of the original members—must even then be to be presumed. For 'consent is that, and that alone, which did or could give beginning to any lawful Government in the world.'[4] Yet, according as the consent in question is express or 'secret,' it is clear that, on Locke's principles, there is the widest difference between the obligations incurred. If the consent is no more than 'secret,' if it is merely to be inferred from continued residence, the individual concerned is 'at liberty to depart at any moment and incorporate himself into any other commonwealth, or agree with others to begin a new one *in vacuis locis* in any part of the world that they can find free and unpossessed.' If, on the other hand, a man has once, by actual agreement and express declaration, given his consent to be of any commonweal, he is

[1] *C.G.* §§ 124-7.

[2] 'Thus mankind, notwithstanding all the privileges of the state of nature, being but in an ill condition while they remain in it, are quickly driven into society' (*ib.* § 127).

[3] *Ib.* §§ 126-30.

[4] *Ib.* § 99.

perpetually and indispensably obliged to be and remain unalterably a subject to it, and can never again be in the liberty of the state of nature, unless by any calamity the Government he was under comes to be dissolved.'[1]

Freedom to depart, so long as no express undertaking to join the 'commonwealth' has been given, obligation to remain until death brings release, from the moment it has been given—such is the Social Contract, as it presented itself to Locke. No metaphor, but a literal reality: no play of words, but deadly earnest. A contract which is binding throughout their natural lives upon all the individuals who are parties to it: a contract which is terminable, so we must suppose that Locke conceived the matter, solely by the common consent of all of them together. And that consent, so Locke expressly assures us, is not likely to be extorted save by one of those revolutions which, like the floods of ancient legend, sweep all before them in one common devastation: by one of those 'necessities which,' as Burke says, 'are not chosen, but choose' for us.

So far as the individual is concerned, then, the Contract of Locke is no less indissoluble than that of Hobbes; and it rests on a much firmer sanction. Both writers, no doubt, profess to base it upon the law of nature: upon the clause of that law which commands 'that men perform their covenants made.' But, whereas Locke has every right to that appeal, Hobbes, as we have seen, has none. He invokes the law of nature purely as an afterthought: solely for the purpose of riveting the chain upon the neck of men whose life, up to that moment, had been one long defiance of its precepts. To Locke, on the other hand, the law of nature is the very foundation of man's being; its commands are, from the first, recognised as 'binding upon man, even as he is man'; they are still more obviously sacred in the state of nature than they are in the civil state. They provide, therefore, an unimpeachable sanction for any contract that it may suit the natural man to make.

The necessity of the Contract being thus established and its sanction placed beyond reach of question, it only remains to ask: What are the obligations which it lays on those who unite to make it? what the explicit engagements which it pledges them to fulfil? Here again the answer of Locke is perfectly explicit: Those who make a social Contract bind themselves to two conditions, and two only: firstly, to form a political society—a condition which one would have thought hardly needed to be stated—and secondly, to regulate all their future proceedings by a bare majority: a provision imposed by that accommodating oracle, the law of nature, whose commands form the strangest assortment, ranging from

[1] *C.G.* § 121-2.

Thou shalt not kill to *The odd man shall have the casting vote.* That is all; but that is enough. All else may be left to common sense, and to the necessities of the new conditions which the Social Contract has created.[1]

First of all these necessities is that which drives men to begin by setting up a Legislative, and to make provision for its perpetual continuance. And the reason for this, Locke confidently assures us, is perfectly plain. The sole motive which induced men to quit the natural state was the insufficiency—and in particular, the 'uncertainty'—of the unwritten law, the 'law of nature.' To set up a 'declared' and 'standing' law, a law which should set the rights and duties of each man beyond all possibility of dispute, must therefore be their first care on entering the civil state. For the same reason, it follows that the supreme power in every 'commonwealth' must necessarily be the legislative power; and that one commonwealth is distinguished from another by nothing so much as by the difference between the various forms which the Legislative may assume.[2]

What, then, are the chief forms which the Legislative—and with it, the Commonwealth of which it is the 'soul' and essence—is capable of taking? The answer to this question involves a curious breach in the continuity of Locke's argument. Up to this point his method had been sedulously abstract. He now suddenly passes to a method which, at bottom, is nothing but concrete and historical. And the whole subsequent course of his reasoning is profoundly affected by the change. The forms in question, he tells us, are almost infinite in number. The legislative power may be lodged with one man and his descendants; and then the Government is a monarchy. Or with 'a few select men, their heirs and successors'; and then it is an oligarchy. Or with the whole community, which is explained to mean anything from the whole to a bare majority; and then we have a 'perfect democracy.' Or, finally, the power of making laws may be divided, in varying proportions, between all these, or any two of them; and then we have one of the 'mixed' or 'compounded' polities of which the historians and philosophers, from Aristotle downwards, have so much to tell us

[1] *C.G.* §§ 96-9. 'For that which acts any community being only the consent of the individuals of it . . . it is necessary that the body should move that way whither the greater force carries it, which is the consent of the majority. . . . And therefore we see that in Assemblies empowered to act by positive laws, where no number is set by that positive law which empowers them, the act of the majority passes for the act of the whole and, of course, determines as having, by the law of nature and reason, the power of the whole' (§ 96).

[2] *Ib.* §§ 134-6.

—generally, Hobbes vigorously protesting, in the way of praise.[1] But, whatever the exact form assumed by the Legislative, Locke is convinced that, from the moment it is established, it must remain 'sacred and unalterable in the hands where the community have once placed it.'[2]

Laws, however, are of no avail, unless they are obeyed: unless provision is made for maintaining them and putting them in execution. Accordingly, the next step follows of itself. It is to set up an Executive, charged with the duty of seeing that the will of the Legislative is effectively and constantly carried out. Whether this step belongs of right to the Legislative, or to the community as a body, is a point which Locke leaves in some obscurity. But, since he is quite clear that the Executive is and must always be subordinate to the Legislative, the matter is not one of great practical importance.[3]

In any case, it is certain that the form and powers of the Executive will vary according to those of the Legislative, for which it acts. If the legislative power is lodged in the hands of a monarch, then the executive power can hardly be placed anywhere but in the same hands; and it will be his for life, with remainder from father to son, from original holder to his heirs and successors, as determined by the instrument which appointed him. If, on the other hand, it is lodged either with 'a few select men,' an oligarchy, or with the many—that is, a democracy in either of the two main forms which we have seen to be admitted by Locke—then the appointment of the Executive must almost infallibly rest with the Legislative; and it is certain to be of a limited, almost certain to be of a temporary, nature. In the first case, that of monarchy, it is manifest that the executive power is as 'sacred and inviolable' as that of the Legislative itself. In the other two cases, oligarchy and democracy, the appointment, even when nominally made for life, is revocable at will; its holder, being 'visibly subordinate and accountable to the Legislative, may be changed and displaced at pleasure'—the pleasure of the Legislative.[4]

It is with some of the mixed forms of Government that the main difficulty, whether in theory or practice, is likely to arise. Under the English Constitution, for instance, 'where the Legislative is not always in being and the Executive is vested in a single

[1] *C.G.* § 132. [2] *Ib.* § 134.

[3] *Ib.* §§ 143-4. It must be observed that Locke rightly distinguishes between 'executive' and 'federative' functions, but remarks with equal justice that, from the nature of the case, they must always be united in the same hands. 'Federative' powers are, of course, those of making war, peace, treaties; and, in general, the whole conduct of foreign affairs (*ib.* §§ 145-8). [4] *Ib.* §§ 151, 152.

person, who has also a share in the Legislative,' it is evident that, even where a breach of trust has been committed, the Executive can hardly, by constitutional means, be wrested from the hand of the offender: that the terms of the trust are not to be vindicated by anything short of a revolution: in other words, by an armed rising of the people. So far as legal remedies go, he is, in fact, 'no more subordinate to the other, and more representative, branches of the Legislative than he himself shall think fit: which we may certainly conclude will be very little.' And the same thing, *mutatis mutandis*, applies still more obviously to those cases, as in the France of Locke's day, where both Legislative and Executive are wholly lodged in the hands of the same man: that is, to a pure monarchy.[1]

So much for the institution of Government, under its twofold aspect of Legislative and Executive. But, whatever the exact form of Government established by the community, there is always one condition which must be fulfilled, if it is to be recognised as legitimate. This is that both Legislative and Executive are bound to act for the benefit of the community from whom, and from whom alone, their authority is derived.[2]

For this principle, which is one of the main pillars of Locke's theory, there are two sanctions, an inward and an outward. The former, as was to be expected, is, once again, the law of nature, which is 'given for the preservation of mankind' and which 'stands as an eternal rule to all men, legislators'—and executive officers—'as well as others.' And this law operates for the restraint not only of the Government which receives the power, but also of the community—the individual associates, regarded as a collective whole—which grants it. 'For it being but the joint power of every member of the society given up to that person or assembly which is legislator'—or, we may add, which holds the executive power—'it can be no more than those persons had in a state of nature and gave it up to the community. For nobody can transfer to another more power than he has in himself; and nobody has an absolute, arbitrary power over himself or any other, to destroy his own life, or take away the life or property of another.'[3]

The outward sanction is to be found in the right of the community to offer forcible resistance to the Government, whether legislative or executive, which abuses its powers to ends contrary to those for which they were entrusted to it. 'For the power

[1] *C.G.* § 152.

[2] The first and fundamental natural law, which is to govern even the Legislative itself, is the preservation of the society and, as far as will consist with the public good, of every person in it (*ib.* § 134).

[3] *Ib.* § 135.

so transferred being only a fiduciary trust to act for certain ends, there remains still in the people a supreme power to remove or alter the Legislative, when they find the Legislative act contrary to the trust reposed in it.' And the same must obviously apply to the Executive also. 'For all power given with trust for the attaining an end being limited by that end, whenever that end is manifestly neglected or opposed, the trust must necessarily be forfeited and the power devolve into the hands of those who gave it: who may place it anew where they shall think best for their safety and security.'[1]

It may cause some surprise that Locke should set the possible misdeeds of the Legislative in the forefront; and that of the far more likely transgressions of the Executive he should, at any rate in the more speculative part of his treatise, have much less to say. But, apart from the necessity of covering those cases in which the Executive is avowedly subordinate to the Legislative, in which therefore the duty of vindicating the Law belongs, at least in the first instance to the Legislative, there are two reasons why this course was the natural one for him to take. On the one hand, having made the appointment of the Legislative the first task of the new-born community and having, for sound practical reasons, made the Legislative rather than the Executive the supreme body in every legitimate form of polity, he was forced, for consistency's sake, to give it the first place also in his calendar of indictments. On the other hand, he wrote with the memory of the usurpations of the Long Parliament still fresh in the mind of every Englishman. And though it is perfectly clear that he knew the real danger to lie not on the side of the Legislative, but on the side of the Executive, it is impossible not to admire the skill with which, 'in equal scale weighing delight and dole,' he holds an even balance between the misdeeds of the Rump on the one side and the iniquities of the Stuart tyranny upon the other.

Of one thing he is perfectly certain. Whether the usurpation comes from the Legislative or from the Executive, it is the usurper, and not the community, which rises in revolt against him, that is the true 'rebel.' For, 'rebellion being an opposition not to persons, but to authority, which is founded only in the constitution and laws of the Government, those, whoever they be, who by force break through and by force justify their violation of them are truly and properly rebels. For when men, by entering into society and civil government, have excluded force and introduced laws for the preservation of property, peace and unity among themselves, those who set up force again in opposition to the laws do *rebellare*: that is, bring back again the state of war and are properly rebels.'[2]

[1] *C.G.* § 149.

[2] *Ib.* § 226.

It has often been said that Locke represents the relation between the community and the Executive as one of Contract: the 'original contract between king and people' of the famous Convention resolution of 1689. This may not be very far removed from the spirit of his doctrine, but it is doubly wrong as to the letter. For, on the one hand, the appointment of the Executive is apparently conceived by him as belonging normally not to the community, but to the Legislative. And on the other hand, what is far more important, he never once uses the term *contract* to describe the instrument from which the Executive derives its authority. It is always a *trust*, or a *fiduciary trust*.[1]

Now, according to the strict sense of the term, this ought to mean that the power which confers the trust is entitled at any moment to revoke it. For the possession of such a power is the one obvious mark of distinction between a trust and a contract. That, however, is far from being the intention of Locke. In one passage, indeed, he says that the Legislative have the right to revoke the trust, 'when they find cause.'[2] But in all the other passages he definitely asserts that the trust conferred upon the Executive is revocable only when it has been broken by the trustee.[3] And we must take that to have been his considered opinion on the matter. Yet this appears to make the trust of Locke a thing hardly distinguishable from the *contract* of the Convention.

Why then, we ask, if he came so near to accepting the idea expressed by *Contract*, did he so studiously avoid the use of the term? Why, if he practically accepted the thing, did he eschew the word which, at the moment when he wrote, was on everybody's lips? There can be little doubt as to the answer.

The theory of Contract, as applied to the relation between Governor and Governed, was, and was intended to be, a counterblast to the theory of Divine Right. It roughly stripped the king of the halo of sanctity, of mystical majesty, cast around him by seventeenth-century theology.[4] It reduced him at one stroke to a position of equality with his 'subjects.' For a contract is between equals, or it is nothing. This, however, was not enough for Locke, who was sharp enough to see that the theory of Contract

[1] *C.G.* §§ 149, 156. 'The power of assembling and dismissing the Legislative, placed in the Executive . . . is a fiduciary trust placed in him for the safety of the people. . . . And where else could this be so well placed as in his hands who was entrusted with the execution of the laws for the same end—the public good?' (§ 156).

[2] *Ib.* § 153.

[3] *Ib.* §§ 149, 156, 160, 164.

[4] 'They'—the original associates—'never dreamed of monarchy being *jure divino*, which we never heard of among mankind until it was revealed to us by the divinity of this last age' (*ib.* § 112).

was, after all, a two-edged weapon: that, if pressed to its logical consequences, it might be turned just as well against the 'usurpations' of the community upon the monarch as against those of the monarch upon his subjects. It was his object, therefore, to set it beyond doubt that the position of the king towards 'his people' was one not of equality, but of manifest subordination. And this object he sought to attain by describing the power of the king as a thing held 'on trust' from his people, or from the Legislative which represented them.

With Locke, however, it is no mere speculative balance between abstract equality on the one hand and abstract subordination upon the other. It is on the practical consequences which flow, or may be expected to flow, from each of the rival theories that his eye was evidently fastened. If the relation between Governor and Governed is really one of Contract, then it is clear that the hands of the people are tied no less tightly than the hands of the king: that any such gradual extension of popular liberties as has been the mark and pride of the English constitution would have been impossible. From the moment the contract is concluded, the community will either be condemned to one prolonged scuffle between the two contracting parties, each steadily asserting claims which the other as steadily denies; or, failing this, its life, if indeed it can be called a life, will be one of absolute stagnation. There will either be perpetual disputes over the true interpretation of the contract; or each party will resign itself to leaving things exactly as they are, for fear of giving the other a pretext for annulling the contract altogether. Either constant bickering—and that, not on a question of right, but on a question of fact—or complete immobility: that is the logical outcome of the theory of Contract.

But once assume that the institution of government is in the nature not of a contract, but a trust, and the whole face of things is altered. The terms of the trust are liable to be revised at any moment by those who granted it; nay, on any strict interpretation of the analogy, the trust itself is liable to be entirely revoked. The latter consequence, as we have seen, is expressly repudiated by Locke, due exception being made for one moment of refreshing candour. But the former consequence he heartily accepts, and enforces with much gusto in a significant chapter on 'Prerogative.'[1] Moreover,

[1] *C.G.* chap. xiv. 'Prerogative,' according to Locke, is 'a power, left in the hands of the Executive, to act according to discretion for the public good, without the prescription of the law and sometimes even against it.' But 'they have a very wrong notion of government who say that the people have encroached upon the prerogative when they have got any part of it to be defined by positive laws. For, in so doing, they have not pulled from the prince anything that of right belonged to

as we shall see directly, he explicitly reserves to the community, or its Legislative, the right of cancelling the contract by force of arms—that is, by a revolution—in case of need; and he displays no particular concern at the prospect that such 'appeals to Heaven' will, from time to time, probably be made. Altogether, it must be allowed that, by adopting the analogy of a trust rather than that of a contract, Locke makes very fair provision not only for popular control of Government, but also—what is yet more important—for a progressive extension of that control, as experience may dictate; and that, on any reasonable interpretation of the analogy, his conclusions would have been at once more consistent and more 'liberal' yet.

From all this it results that those who suppose the Convention doctrine of an 'original contract between king and people' to have been either inspired by the *Essay of Civil Government*, or to represent its teaching, do scant justice either to the philosophy of the author or to the practical sagacity which was still more remarkable than his speculative genius.[1] What he did was to crystallise and justify the principle which the English people had in fact followed, with not a few backslidings, from the days of the Plantagenets to those of the Stuarts; and which, with clearer consciousness and ever-growing determination, they were destined to follow still more faithfully during the two centuries and more that have passed between his day and ours. And on the rival principle of Contract,

---

him, but only declared that that power which they indefinitely left in him, or his ancestors' hands, to be exercised for their good, was not a thing they intended him, when he used it otherwise.' . . . When he does use it otherwise, 'he gives the people an occasion to claim their right and limit that power which, whilst it was exercised for their good, they were content should be tacitly allowed' (*ib.* §§ 160, 163, 164). Did Locke quite realise how deep a gash he was making in the 'sacred and unalterable' character of his trust? It is clear from the above that Locke did not object to the 'dispensing power' as such, but only to its abuse by the two last Stuarts. He even proposes to leave to the Executive the right, already exercised by Cromwell, of Parliamentary reform, by means of a periodical redistribution of constituencies (*ib.* §§ 157-8). Later times have secured all these ends through the action of the *Legislative* by means of suspensions of *Habeas corpus*, Defence of the Realm Acts, etc.

[1] Of direct inspiration there can hardly be any question; and that, for the best of all reasons—that the *Essay* was not published until the following year (1690). And though it is not impossible that it may have circulated, to some extent, in manuscript before publication, it is certain that no English Parliament which ever existed would dream of drafting its Resolutions from rumours of what was in a philosopher's manuscript.

all this—one of the most notable achievements in modern history—would have been logically barred out.

And what of the provision made by Locke for the actual revocation of the trust: for the 'dissolution' of the Government which follows, or ought to follow, upon a clear breach of trust—a breach grave enough to constitute a 'rebellion'—on the part of the executive power? In considering this question, we must be careful to distinguish it from another question, the 'dissolution of Society,' which, as Locke rightly saw, has to be answered on quite different grounds.

As for the dissolution of Government, once grant his initial assumption that the trust is not revocable except when the trustee has manifestly broken faith, Locke's arguments are sound enough. Taking for granted, as both from the nature of the case and from the recent history of his own country he was amply justified in doing, that the blows of the Executive will be aimed first and foremost against the Legislative and will consist in an attempt either to curtail its recognised powers, or to govern without it altogether, he maintains that from the moment when such a design becomes apparent, from the moment when the acts of the 'supreme executor' manifestly declare that he is 'going about to set up his own arbitrary will as the law of the society,' he has thereby put himself 'in a state of war with the people.'[1] For, seeing that 'the constitution of the Legislative was the original and supreme act of the society, antecedent to all positive law and depending wholly on the people,' any endeavour to overthrow it or to tamper with it is to wound the people in their most vital interest, to rob them of the one outward and tangible right which they possess.[2] The constraint which is thus laid upon them by force 'they have therefore the right to remove by force.' For 'in all states and conditions the true remedy of force without authority is to oppose force to it.' And in the case supposed, the people, the whole 'society,' is the sole body capable of doing so.[3]

Exactly the same principle applies when, as in the case of the Long Parliament, not the executive, but the legislative power is the 'aggressor.' Here again, under however veiled a form, force is employed to undermine or destroy the rights of the society; and the society as a whole is entitled, and it is its duty, to 'oppose force' to the 'unauthorised' usurpation.[4]

Throughout this argument it is manifestly assumed that, when the Government—in particular, the Legislative, which is 'the soul that gives form, life and unity to the commonwealth'—is

[1] *C.G.* §§ 155, 222.

[2] *Ib.* § 157. Compare 'the first and fundamental act of society,' § 212.

[3] *Ib.* §§ 155, 168, 215.

[4] *Ib.* §§ 149, 222.

dissolved, the commonwealth itself remains intact. And this is the conclusion drawn in so many words by Locke himself. 'He that will with any clearness speak of the dissolution of Government ought in the first place to distinguish between the dissolution of the society and the dissolution of the Government.' [1] This was demanded by the whole tenor of his argument; it was demanded also as a counterblast to the opposite doctrine of Hobbes. It had been the sheet anchor of Hobbes' system that, directly the Government, the 'rule of one man or one Assembly of men,' is dissolved, the dissolution of the community, the great Leviathan, follows of itself: or, to speak more correctly, that the two things are absolutely inseparable, that the one stands or falls automatically with the other. 'Abolish the Government and, by that very act, you dissolve the society which rests upon it. Either keep the rule of the sword with all its hardships, all its possible miseries; or consent to break once more into your original atoms, to fall back into the anarchy from which the sword alone rescued you, from which the sword alone is able to preserve you': that is the dilemma which Hobbes discharges in the face of the reader, at every awkward corner which his argument has to turn. And that is the dilemma, the force of which Locke sets himself deliberately to destroy. Who shall say that he does not succeed in doing so? Who will not allow that his account of the matter is more reasonable than that of Hobbes? that, when once the fiction of Contract, common to both writers, has been conceded, it is more in accordance with Right? that, so far as the teaching of history goes, it is more in accordance with the facts? [2]

[1] *C.G.* § 211.

[2] The pity is that, having laid down this principle so clearly, Locke, like Spinoza before him, should once at least vacillate when he comes to its practical application. In dealing with the various circumstances under which dissolution of Government may come about, he allows himself to speak as if a dissolution of society, a return to the state of nature, were the inevitable result. What other interpretation can be put upon the following words: 'In some countries the person of the Prince by the law is sacred and so, whatever he commands or does, his person is still free from all question or violence . . . unless he will, by actually putting himself in a state of war with his people, dissolve the Government and leave them to that state of defence which belongs to every one in the state of nature'? (*C.G.* § 205). In view, however, of his explicit declaration to the contrary and of its importance to the general upshot of his argument, it is evident that these words are no more than a momentary slip. Certainly, in the main, he is strikingly faithful to the contrary principle: that the dissolution of Government, however much 'anarchy' it may produce, does not carry with it the dissolution of Society also; and that, with one exception (§ 211) to be noted directly, the dissolution of Society, so far as it happens or can ever happen, must be an entirely separate act and

It will thus be seen that Locke makes deliberate provision for the contingency of revolution: that he opens what, by a slight stretch of terms, may be fairly called a constitutional door for the 'sacred right of insurrection.' For so doing, he has been roughly handled by some subsequent theorists. But he himself has been careful to forestall the criticism. 'It will be said,' he writes, 'that this hypothesis lays a ferment for frequent rebellion, a perpetual foundation for disorder.' [1] And his reply, to which there is no answer, is virtually as follows:

'This, as an abstract consequence, lies in the very nature of the case. Unless you are prepared to accept the doctrine of Divine Right, of passive submission to all extremes of tyranny, you are bound to admit that, once a certain point of misgovernment has been reached, the community has the right of resistance. And my "hypothesis" makes no more allowance for this than any other. The only difficulty lies in deciding when that point has been reached; when the moment has come at which resistance, with all its dangers, with all its possible bloodshed and other miseries, has become a duty. And this, like all the other critical decisions of life, must be left to the common sense, the practical judgement, of those immediately concerned. To suppose that the consequence in question, possible as it is in the abstract, will in fact be drawn upon every trifling occasion, "upon every little mismanagement in public affairs," is to suppose something "quite the contrary" of what experience teaches. History shows that men are strangely patient, rather lazy and very reluctant to take desperate resolutions: that "people are not so easily got out of their old forms as some are apt to suggest. . . . Great mistakes in the ruling part, many wrong and inconvenient laws and all the slips of human frailty will be borne by the people without mutiny or murmur." It is only when "a long train of abuses, prevarications and artifices, all tending the same way," all betraying a settled design on the part of the Government to usurp upon the recognised rights of the community and establish an arbitrary tyranny, that "men rouse themselves . . . to secure the ends for which Government was first erected and without which ancient names and forms are so far from being better, that they are much worse, than the state of nature or pure anarchy."' [2]

---

one that can only spring from the deliberate consent of all the members. See §§ 203, 219, 225.

[1] *C.G.* §§ 168, 224.

[2] It will be observed that, here again, Locke slips for the moment into the fallacy of Hobbes: that the dissolution of Government means the dissolution of Society also. The references are to *C.G.* §§ 222, 223, 224. Compare also § 210, where, without mentioning names, Locke

Fault has sometimes been found with Locke for not defining more closely the means by which the community should act, the organ through which it should take its decision, on the rare occasions when action has become a necessity, when a revolution against either its Executive, or its Legislative, has become a duty.[1] And it cannot be denied that this constitutes a technical flaw in the completeness of his theory. It is, however, a technical flaw only. And, what is more important, it is a flaw of which Locke himself was clearly aware and which he deliberately put up with, because neither experience nor common sense would have allowed him to do otherwise. So far as experience goes, he had himself been a witness, and probably a consenting party, to the Revolution of 1688; the earlier troubles of 1642 to 1660 were well within his memory.[2] And even if this had not been so, common sense would have taught him that such revolutions are to be carried through, not by any constituted body, but by the courage and determination of a few resolute spirits; and that they are subsequently accepted, so far as they are accepted, by the rest of the community, partly from the same sluggishness which caused men to submit to the previous tyranny, partly because, once accomplished, they are seen to be both necessary and just. That is the reason why he refused to tie the 'appeal to Heaven' down to the hazards of a preliminary *plébiscite*: a method to which, so far as I can see, he was in no way committed by the general tenor of his theory and which his native sagacity told him would have made all revolutions, however necessary, for ever impossible.

As for the main point, Locke's principle might in the abstract,

---

gives a list of the wrongs which James II. had inflicted upon the nation, and to which the nation had replied by the Revolution. All this part of the treatise must surely have been written after the events of 1687 and the first half of 1688, if not after the Revolution itself.

[1] For an interesting discussion of the point, see *Works* of T. H. Green, ii. pp. 281-4. I must confess that the author seems to me to press the case too hardly against Locke.

[2] His father had fought in the Parliamentary army. His own dates are 1632–1704. The year 1690 saw the publication of both his main works, the *Essay on the Human Understanding* and the *Two Treatises of Government*. During the latter part of his residence in Holland (1685–1689), he seems to have been in pretty constant communication with the Prince of Orange; he certainly returned to England in the same ship which carried the Princess, now (by the Act of the Convention) become Queen of England. It is therefore difficult to suppose that he was not consulted by the Prince as to the expediency of the expedition which was to end in the flight and dethronement of James; and it is certain that his advice, if given, must have been in favour of the attempt.

no doubt, be used to justify a purely seditious rebellion: a rebellion, that is, for which no negligence, no misgovernment, on the part of either Legislative or Executive affords any solid ground or vindication: a rebellion kindled either by the ambition of a selfish adventurer, or the turbulence of a handful of religious or political fanatics. But, having left the decision in such matters to common sense and common equity, he was abundantly justified in maintaining that his hypothesis was no more exposed to this objection 'than any other.' And it is no afterthought, but a long foreseen and perfectly consistent consequence of his theory that, after denouncing the 'rebellion' of Kings and Parliaments, he applies the same measure to the equally culpable rebellion of factions or individuals: branding the one, no less than the other, as 'the common enemies of mankind.' 'This I am sure: whoever, either ruler or subject, by force goes about to invade the rights of either prince or people and lays the foundation for overturning the constitution and frame of any just Government, he is guilty of the greatest crime I think a man is capable of, being to answer for all those mischiefs of blood, rapine and desolation which the breaking to pieces of governments bring on a country; and he who does it is justly to be esteemed the common enemy and pest of mankind, and is to be treated accordingly.' Even so, however, he cannot refrain from adding the following significant reminder: 'But whether the mischief hath oftener begun in the people's wantonness, or in the ruler's insolence, whether oppression or disobedience gave the first rise to the disorder, I leave it to impartial history to determine.' That is Locke's parting shot at Charles I. and James II.; his parting tribute to the firmness of Pym and Hampden, the Convention and William of Orange.

It only remains to ask: What, on the rare occasions when the Government is dissolved, are the rights which revert to the community as a whole? When the old Government is overturned, how far do the rights of the people extend in setting up a new one? Are they limited to a mere change of persons, or do they cover a change of system, of constitution, also? As for the answer, Locke is in no manner of doubt. At such a moment the hands of the community are entirely free. It is under no obligation to maintain the old order of things: it is entitled, if such seems the wisest course, to set up a fresh order altogether. 'It can never, by the fault of another, lose its native and original right' of taking whatever steps it may deem necessary for its own preservation; and that is an end which, as all experience shows, is to be gained 'only by a settled Legislative and a fair and impartial execution of its laws.' 'The people, therefore, are at liberty to provide for themselves by setting up a new Legislative'—and, by the same rule, a new Executive—'differing from the other by the change of persons, or form, or both, as they shall find it most for their safety and good.'[1]

Once more, however, Locke is firmly convinced that, so long as the original Government lasts—so long, that is, as neither Legislative nor Executive is arraigned on the charge of 'breach of trust'—so long do its powers remain 'sacred and unalterable'; that so long, therefore, does this reserve power on the part of the community remain strictly in abeyance; and that it becomes operative only by the misconduct of the constituted authorities: in other words, only after the Government has been dissolved. 'Thus the community may be said, in this respect, to be always the supreme power: but not as considered under any form of government, because the power of the people can never take place until the Government be dissolved.'[2]

A century later, in the early months of the French Revolution, the Revolution Society, with Dr. Price for its mouthpiece, claimed that, by the principles of the 'glorious Revolution,' 'the people of England had acquired three fundamental rights: the right to choose our own Governors; the right to cashier them for misconduct; and the right to frame a new Government for ourselves.' It was this claim that roused Burke to fury and called forth the indignant—it must be confessed also, the sophistical—refutation which fills the opening pages of the *Reflections*.[3] How far, we may ask, is the claim put forward by Price in accordance with the principles laid down in the *Essay of Civil Government*? how far would it have been admitted by Locke?

The answer is that, so far as the ordinary course of events is concerned and so long as the constituted authorities are true to their trust, the claims of the Revolution Society are, on Locke's principle, absolutely false; and he would have heartily subscribed to Burke's assertion that 'no Government could stand for a moment, if it could be blown down with anything so loose and indefinite as an opinion of *misconduct*.'[4] But directly a 'breach of trust' has been brought home to those authorities, directly the people re-enter upon the rights of 'supreme power,' they become, by the same principle, absolutely true. On the former assumption, the reply of Locke would probably have differed little from that of Burke. On the latter, he would hardly have brought himself to treat the 'old Whig' with more respect than he showed to Barclay, or the champion of Divine Right.[5]

So far, as to Locke's view of what happens on the dissolution

[1] *C.G.* § 220.
[2] *Ib.* § 149.
[3] Burke, *Works* (ed. Rogers, 1850), vol. i. pp. 383-393.
[4] *Ib.* p. 391.
[5] *C.G.* §§ 232-239.

of Government. What, we now ask, has he to tell us of the other dissolution—the disruption of society?

'The usual, and almost the only, way whereby this union'—Society, as opposed to Government—'is dissolved, is the inroad of foreign force making a conquest upon them.' In other words, a Society, once formed, is hardly to be dissolved except by force from without.[1] But, as a loophole for other modes of civil death is apparently left open, and as Locke has expressly told us that the dissolution of Government is not one of them, we must suppose that he held a voluntary dissolution of partnership—a dissolution as voluntary as its original formation—to be theoretically possible, although in practice almost without example.[2] So much seems to be demanded by the general tenor of his theory; and if he never explicitly commits himself to this second alternative, that must be set down to the essentially practical character of his whole system: to his sense that, for man as we know him, such voluntary disruption is barely possible or even imaginable.

We come back, therefore, to 'the usual and almost only' method of dissolution: 'the conqueror's sword, which often cuts up Governments by the roots and mangles Societies to pieces, separating the subdued or scattered multitude from the protection of and dependence on that Society which ought to have preserved them from violence.'[3] And this brings us to one of the most curious—it is also one of the least satisfactory—parts of Locke's theory: his doctrine of foreign conquest.

If a voluntary dissolution of Society is to be justified on grounds of Right—and on Locke's principle this is not to be denied—are we to conclude that the converse is also true? that a forced dissolution, a 'mangling by the sword of the conqueror,' must necessarily be an act of wrong? A modern thinker, if not of Prussian leanings, would unhesitatingly say so. Locke, however, at any rate to judge from first appearances, speaks with considerable reserve. In his view, it all depends on the justice of the war by which the dissolution is brought about. If the conqueror was

[1] *C.G.* § 211.

[2] The break up of the Austrian Empire, one of the most hopeful results of the late war, is not a case in point: for it was neither founded, nor governed, on any principle but force. It is rather an instance of the principle involved in Locke's doctrine of foreign conquest: that the rights of conquered nations, however long suspended, are inalienable and at the first chance which offers may be lawfully redeemed (see below, pp. 155, 178–9). It is to be remembered that, even before Locke wrote, Leibnitz had passed sentence upon the iniquity of Austrian rule: 'The policy of the House of Hapsburg is one eternal conspiracy against the rights and liberties of peoples.'

[3] *C.G.* § 211.

the aggressor, then, however great his successes in the field, he has no rights whatever, neither individually nor collectively, against the vanquished. On the contrary, as Locke hints but does not expressly say, he is bound, by every analogy of equity, to pay damages to the individuals whose land he has overrun and presumably laid waste: though, as a matter of fact, it is perfectly certain that he will do nothing of the kind. If, on the other hand, it was the conquered community which provoked the war, then it must expect to pay the penalty. And the only question remaining is: What is the nature of the penalty? and on whose shoulders does it fall? [1]

At this point, thanks to the essentially individualist assumptions of the author, the argument takes an unexpected turn. The penalty, he tells us, must fall only on the individual authors of the wrong-doing: only on those who are personally responsible for the original aggression, or who themselves bore arms in support of it. All non-combatants, all again who, as members of Legislative or Executive, did not give their voice for the declaration of war, are entitled to go scot-free. What is yet more to our purpose, the community, as a community, remains by Right absolutely unscathed. It was the express consent of the individual members which called it into being: it is by their express consent alone that it can be dissolved. More than that: such consent, if it is to have any binding force, must be absolutely free. A forced consent, in this as in all other matters, is no consent at all; and no conqueror 'can ever have a title till the people are both at liberty to consent, and have actually consented, to allow and confirm him in the power he hath till then usurped.' [2] And this remains true, however long the 'usurpation' lasts. For 'who doubts but the Grecian Christians, descendants of the ancient possessors of that country, may justly cast off the Turkish yoke they have so long groaned under, whenever they have a power to do it?' [3] The Turkish conquest of Greece had taken place some two centuries and a half before Locke wrote. Would he have had the candour to apply the same principle to the case of Ireland, where the plantation of Ulster was not yet a century old and the Cromwellian Settlement, which has left a far more rankling resentment, was within the memory of men considerably younger than himself?

So much for the claims of the community. But what of those individuals who, either by vote or arms, have made themselves responsible for the wrong-doing? What is the nature of the penalty which they are justly called upon to pay? They have forfeited their life. If that is spared by the conqueror, they have forfeited their liberty. But, except in so far as they owe com-

[1] *C.G.* § 176. [2] *Ib.* §§ 177-96. [3] *Ib.* § 192.

pensation for damages done to the land of the conqueror, they have not forfeited their estates. Still less have they forfeited—for it is not theirs to forfeit—the claims which their 'innocent wives and children' have, by the law of nature, upon those estates: a claim which subsists, and is handed down from generation to generation, from all time, notwithstanding all that the conqueror may say or do to the contrary. Indeed, sturdily entrenching himself in the law of nature, Locke is disposed to whittle down the conqueror's bill of damages till it is hardly worth presenting at all. 'As to money and such riches or treasures taken away'—he assumes throughout an initial invasion of the conqueror's territory—'these are none of nature's goods; they have but a fantastic, imaginary value'; and on that ground they are struck out of the bill without ceremony, at the start. There remains only the damage done to land, crops, and possibly a few stores of food and other necessaries of solid value. But this, all told, will hardly amount to more than 'the destruction of a year's product or two—for it seldom reaches four or five'; and, as we have seen, even this claim is subject to a deduction for the innocent wives and children, until such time —four or five years appears to be the utmost duration—as the conqueror shall have been fully reimbursed.[1]

What, then, is the general result of Locke's enquiry as to the right of the conqueror to dissolve a vanquished Society by force, and to incorporate it anew in his own State against the will of those who compose it? It is the exact reverse of that which the opening stages of his argument would have led us to expect. It is that such forcible annexation, though 'in the corrupted currents of this world' it may pass for Right, is never anything but an intolerable wrong; that a Society, once formed, can never, except by the express consent of its members, be rightfully broken up; in other words, that the Social Contract, once made, is to be annulled in one way, and one way only: that is, by the free consent of those who made it.

Thus, by a roundabout road and with the aid of arguments which they would have scornfully rejected, Locke, the prince of individualists, arrives at the same conclusions as Mazzini and the nationalists. To him, as to them, a political union, once formed, is indestructible; or, if destroyed, is to be destroyed solely by its own act. They, no doubt, would have held this to be true in a special sense of those unions which rest upon an original community of race or blood; and they would have extended it to those bodies, or groups, of men in whom the union, so far from being an historical fact dating from the far past, is no more than a dream of the future. He, on the other hand, fixes his mind solely on the bond of express

[1] *C.G.* §§ 183-92; in particular, § 184.

consent, whenever given. He asks no questions as to the motives which lie behind it. He attributes no special sanctity, still less any binding obligation, to one particular class of motive: that which springs from the inheritance of a common race, or a common tradition. Yet that consent, once given, is as sacred to him as the bond of blood or memory is to them. To annul it by force or desertion, is to him as 'criminal,' as much an offence against Right, as to dissolve it, or even resist the attempt to embody it in outward fact, would be to them.[1]

This ends our survey of Locke's theory, which is entitled, though on very different grounds, to share with that of Spinoza the credit of being the most consistent ever built upon the theory of Contract. From beginning to end, its key-note is consent: consent, as formally embodied in the 'original compact'; consent, as necessary to the establishment and subsequent maintenance of the Civil Government which is the first and chief consequence of the compact; consent finally, as instinctively yielded to the law of nature which furnishes the indispensable sanction to the contract: that law which is known and read of all men, 'even as they are men,'[2] which exists prior to and in complete independence of any positive Law that a given political society may subsequently enact, and by which all such positive laws are to be 'interpreted' and judged. These are the ideas which lie at the root of Locke's theory and which, with an ever-diminishing stress upon the assumption of a formal Contract and an ever-increasing bias towards individualism pure and simple, remained, in this country at any rate, the staple of Whig and Liberal popular philosophy for nearly two centuries after Locke wrote. Let us now turn to examine their validity.

[1] *C.G.* §§ 103, 120, 121, 176.

[2] The phrase is not Locke's, but Hooker's (*Ecclesiastical Polity*, i. 10). Locke, however, adopts it (*C.G.* § 15) and makes it emphatically his own. It has sometimes been said that the whole of Locke's theory is to be found in germ in Hooker. And, as regards the law of nature, there is some truth in the assertion. But there is so much else in Hooker—above all, his doctrine of Law as part of the whole order of nature, and his doctrine of its progressive development under the stress of human needs and of man's desire to bring himself nearer and nearer to the divine order of the world—that, as a whole, his theory has a bearing quite other, and much wider, than Locke's. In fact, he is less memorable as precursor of Locke than of Burke. The main motive for Locke's frequent references to him was controversial. It was highly embarrassing to the champions of Divine Right to find their favourite political doctrine roundly contradicted by their favourite divine.

In the last resort, it may fairly be said, everything turns upon the law of nature. It is this which wholly determines Locke's conception of the state of nature; it largely determines his conception of the civil state also. What the law of nature is to him, we have already seen. Briefly, it is a law which proclaims itself to the heart of every individual not an infant or an idiot; a law which owes nothing to human institutions, social or political, but to which, on the contrary, those institutions owe everything that gives them any worth. It is a law which not only commands man to 'love his neighbour' in general, but which also lays itself out, so that he who runs may read, in a detailed code of specific duties covering the whole field of his conduct and governing his whole life in whatever circumstances he may find himself placed. And if we ask what is the general nature of this law, Locke is at once ready with his answer. It is a 'law of good will, mutual assistance and preservation': in one word, a 'law of peace': a law which might have been dictated—and, if we may believe the Scriptures, was in fact dictated—by the Prince of Peace.

Such a conception, no doubt, is abstractedly not impossible. It forms a logically consistent whole. It makes a strong appeal to some at any rate of man's deepest instincts: his craving for Right, his impatience at the sight of social injustice, his sense that human law, even at the best, commonly lags behind the moral ideals of its own land and generation. Yet none the less, as presented by Locke and other thinkers of the seventeenth and eighteenth centuries, it is a radically false conception: a conception which squares neither with the facts of experience and history, nor even with other elements of the theory in which it plays so dominant a part. Let us begin with the more historical aspect of the matter.

It may be quite true that certain primitive communities—for instance, the 'peaceful Ariphuras,' with whom Herbert Spencer makes such determined play—have been discovered by travellers, old and recent, in various quarters of the earth: communities to whom war with other tribes is unknown and who even live a life of peace and harmony among themselves. But before such communities can be called in support of Locke's 'law of nature,' there is more than one serious difficulty to be met.

In the first place, the tribes in question are admittedly 'communities': they are not the mere unorganised herds which alone can be considered as living in anything approaching to what Locke calls the 'state of nature.' They are, no doubt, nearer to the state of nature, real or imagined, than any communities now existing in Europe, or in the civilised parts of the other continents and adjacent islands. But they have some kind of tribal organisation;

they have a rich store of tribal customs: in other words, they have definitely crossed the frontier which, in Locke's view, separates the state of nature from the civil state. And this means that they live, not under the law of nature, but under that of civil society, however rudimentary may be its shape.

Again, the outside observer, in all such cases, of necessity stands at an immeasurable distance from those whose life and mind he seeks to watch and understand. He is therefore peculiarly liable to draw unwarrantable or hasty inferences. Without the greatest caution, he is even liable to put a completely false construction on the acts, customs and beliefs that come before him. Thus, to take an example which bears directly upon the present argument, it would be easy enough for a hasty observer—and some of them are extraordinarily hasty—to argue from the absence of war in a given tribe to the presence of peace and harmony, as between one member and another. The one fact is extremely easy to verify; the other—it is, in reality, a highly complicated tissue of facts—is extremely difficult. One would wish to be more certain than it is easy to be that, in the case of the 'peaceful Ariphuras' and others, some such confusion has not been made.

But, even if the existence of peace and harmony among the members of such tribes be taken as proved, our difficulties are by no means at an end. Before the 'peace' in question is to be of any use for Locke's purposes, it must be shown to spring not from any merely negative quality, lack of energy or the like, but from an active desire to show 'good will,' to promote 'mutual assistance and preservation' among the members of the community: as Locke would say, to 'obey the law of nature.' And on probing into the matter, it might well be found that, in the more positive and assertive temper needful for this purpose, the less amiable and sterner qualities—the qualities which, in their perversion, lead to war and tumult—form an ingredient no less necessary than the softer and more submissive qualities for which these tribes have won their fame. In a word, all human excellence is based upon conflict; and, much as we may shrink from owning it, without the combative qualities, there is little virtue and no such thing as progress.

And this brings us to the last point on which it is necessary to touch. The cases which, as some have thought, tend to confirm Locke's theory of natural law are avowedly exceptional cases. The tribes in question fill a comparatively small space on the map of the earth. What is more, they stand apart from the main stream, or streams, of civilisation. They have contributed little or nothing to the progress of the world: least of all, to that of Europe. Yet it is the conditions of Europe, the beliefs and practice of Europe, which an European writer is bound first and foremost to reckon with and, if possible, to account for. And, with all his obvious conviction that his theory was a theory for all time and for all places, it is clear at a glance that Locke was, in fact, writing with his eye fixed upon Europe alone; though, in obedience to the fashion of the day, a few references to Palestine, and to other Asiatic countries whose traditions have come to us by way of Palestine, are here and there obligingly thrown in. Yet, though he has no eyes except for Europe, his state of nature transports us bodily to the banks of the Susquehanna or Ohio; and it is only with the entry of the civil state that he brings us back to the scene where his drama is laid and which his shadowy personages are supposed never to have left.

This initial inconsequence involved him in contradictions of which he seems to have been totally unaware. In the first stage of his argument, the state of nature, he peoples his Europe with nothing but 'peaceful Ariphuras,' who are all for 'good will, mutual assistance and preservation' and other such amiable services. But in all its later stages, those which deal with the civil state, these innocent Arcadians—they are, in reality, early Christians masquerading as aboriginal shepherds—have become men in every respect of like passions with ourselves. Their hearts, like ours, are filled with 'vain ambition, *amor sceleratus habendi* and evil concupiscence.' Their communities, like ours, are torn by civil and religious strife, by enmities between class and class, by the usurpations of grasping rulers and sometimes, though not too often, by the riots of mutinous subjects. We 'looked for judgement, but behold oppression; for righteousness, but behold a cry.'

And if we ask what is the cause of this lamentable change; what the root of this deplorable corruption, there is one answer, and one only, that it is possible to give. The real root of the evil is to be found in the institution of civil government; the great corrupter in civil Society itself. That is the answer which, with a notable variation, was to be given some sixty years later by Rousseau. It is the answer which, all unknown to the author, is inevitably suggested by the apparently innocent theory of Locke. The wonder is that two generations had to pass before any one had the wits to see it.[1]

Thus Locke is left face to face with two difficulties which he makes no attempt whatever to solve. How is it logically possible that the ideal beings, the 'minds naturally Christian,' of the opening

[1] See Rousseau, *Discours sur l'inégalité* (1755). To Rousseau it is not only civil society but society in any form—that is, any state other than complete individual isolation—which is corrupt. The relation of this idea to that which lies at the root of the *Contrat Social* (1762) will be discussed later.

pages of *Civil Government* should become the grasping hucksters, the quarrelsome tyrants and rebels, of the close? And, assuming such a change to have come about, how is it possible to deny that it is retrogression and not progress, that civil Society is not a blessing but a curse?

In an inverted and doubtless far less vicious form they are substantially the same difficulties which confronted us in the parallel reasoning of Hobbes. What is yet more important—for Hobbes' theory was, after all, nothing more than an ill-tempered caprice—they are precisely the same difficulties which confront, and must confront, every theory that starts from the assumption of a state of nature governed by an alleged law of nature, the epitome of all righteousness, and proceeds to supplant that law by a positive code, of man's making, in the civil state. The difficulty here, however, is not, as in Hobbes' theory, the physical impossibility of a sudden transition from war to amity, from the 'force and fraud' of the primitive state to the *Seek peace and ensue it* of the supervening Covenant. On the contrary, the change from the law of nature without any outward sanction to what is charitably supposed to be the same law with such a sanction may, at first sight, seem comparatively slight; and Locke does everything in his power to make it seem slighter yet. The real objection to the change declares itself only when we begin to ask: What is its moral justification? Then it at once becomes evident that to suppose the positive Law of any State either is, or can be, the same thing as the law of nature, that it differs from that law only in having armed it with a fresh sanction, is nothing better than a pleasing fiction; that, in place of the divine law, we are in fact fobbed off with an extremely imperfect human copy; that the sanction we now appeal to is no longer the moral sanction of duty, but the physical one of force; and that this double germ of infection is bound to spread itself with ever-increasing virulence, until it poisons the whole life both of the individual and the State.

So much, indeed, is incautiously admitted by Locke himself, when he tells us that 'the innocence and simplicity of the golden age'—an innocence and simplicity which he conceives as still lingering in the earlier stages of the civil state—have long ago been driven out by the 'vain ambition and evil concupiscence,' above all by the *amor sceleratus habendi*, which we see working everywhere around us, in spite of—the critic will rather say, as a direct consequence of—all the efforts of 'civil Government.' And if that be so, where is the moral justification of the change which, by substituting positive law for the law of nature, brought civil Government about? [1]

[1] *C.G.* §§ 110-111.

'Government in its best state is but a necessary evil,' said the outspoken author of the *Rights of Man*, 'but in its worst state, an intolerable one.'[1] And this is the unavowed feeling, the unspoken thought, of all who, however unconsciously, accept Locke's doctrine of the law of nature. Their only mistake is that they do not go far enough. On their principles, they are right in thinking that Government is an evil. They are wrong in adding that it is a necessary one. On their showing, all that is done by Government and human law was already done, and done better, by the law of nature. Why, then, should the law of nature ever be put away?

Thus Locke's theory of origins is not even consistent with itself. Still less is it consistent with the facts. Compare his glowing picture of original righteousness with the harsh reality, as we spell it out from such facts as history has handed down to us, from such inferences as the observations of modern travellers enable us to draw. In Locke's picture, the earliest stage of man's history—call it the state of nature, call it primitive anarchy—is not merely an 'age of innocence.' It is an age of conscious obedience to a divine law: a law which, without any outward sanction, not only enjoins the duty of justice as an abstract ideal, but even lays out that ideal into exactly the same practical precepts as would have commended themselves to the most enlightened minds of the seventeenth century: to such a philosopher as himself or Spinoza, to such divines as Tillotson or Fénelon. The history of man, on this showing, is a history not of progress, but of backsliding. For not only is the ideal of the seventeenth—or, for that matter, of the twentieth—century, as an operative and generally accepted ideal, below that of the state of nature; but, in the mass, men fall still further short of its practical attainment.

The truth, if any trust is to be placed in history, is almost exactly the reverse. The moral code of primitive races—even if we take them to include such half-civilised and, in fact, far from primitive communities as the Greeks of the *Iliad*, or the Hebrews of the *Judges* and the *Books of Samuel*—seems to later ages the strangest blending of good and evil, of justice and injustice, of cruelty and mercy. And the progress of the world—for, on the moral no less than on the intellectual side, there has demonstratively been progress—has lain in the gradual purging away of the baser elements, the gradual strengthening of all that makes for freedom, brotherhood, and a wider sense of individual responsibility. Such results as have been achieved have been won not by the easy method that Locke imagined: not by instinctive acceptance of a 'law of nature, plain to every rational creature' from the beginning. They have been won by bitter experience, by hard struggle, by cruel

[1] Paine, *Common Sense*, p. 3.

suffering, by the self-sacrifice, the courage and constancy which, if the need comes, will not shrink from the 'purification by fire and blood.' And by the same means only are they to be maintained.

But if the law of nature, when pressed to its logical consequences, works havoc with the political system of Locke, what are we to say of its place in his philosophy as a whole? The *Essay concerning the Human Understanding* opens with a vigorous assault upon the doctrine of innate principles and ideas. Few parts of the *Essay* were more fundamental than this; none was more loudly applauded by those who, in the next two generations, regarded themselves and were universally regarded as his authorised disciples. Now, if there ever was an innate idea, it is the law of nature, as expounded in the *Civil Government* of Locke. It springs fully armed from the brain of man, at the very dawn of his history. It owes nothing to experience. It is the gift of intuition, pure and simple. And when Locke compared the mind of man to a blank sheet, a *tabula rasa*, he must have forgotten that one side of that sheet, at any rate, was filled to very good purpose: filled with a code which prescribes the whole duty of man, and which no rational creature can fail to decipher, the moment he 'looks within his own breast.' The *Human Understanding* was published in the same year as *Civil Government*. Yet the whole argument of the latter may be said to rest upon the acceptance of those innate ideas which are vehemently repudiated in the former.[1]

So much for Locke's law of nature in its bearing upon his

[1] It may be objected that Locke professes to confine his attack to ideas 'innate' in the strictest sense of the term: *i.e.* ideas consciously realised by the mind from the moment of birth; and that he has nothing to say against the existence of certain principles which are recognised as true by every person, not an idiot, directly he comes to years of discretion. This objection, however, is to be admitted only with sweeping reservations. For, in the later stages of his argument, he goes on to question the existence—except with such limitations as to render it useless for all practical purposes—of the latter kind of principle also. And it is significant that his blows fall much more heavily upon those principles which concern—and which, if they can be proved to exist, obviously lie at the root of—the moral life of man than upon those which concern his intellectual activity. And it is precisely the former, the moral, principles which figure in *Civil Government* as the 'law of nature.' The inconsistency, therefore, seems to me to be undeniable. And the only question remaining is: how is it to be accounted for? The most probable answer seems to be that *Civil Government*—at least the earlier part of it (say, to the end of chap. xvii. § 198)—was written shortly after the publication of Filmer's *Patriarcha*, to which the first *Treatise* is avowedly an answer: that is, in or shortly after 1680, while Locke was still living in England. The *Human Understanding*, on the other hand, is known

state of nature. Let us now turn to consider it in another aspect: the colour which it inevitably gives to his whole conception of the civil state. As has already been pointed out, the theory of Locke is, and it is its historical importance to have been, markedly individualist. In fact, of all forms taken by the individualist doctrine, apart from such as are purely anarchical, his is probably the most consistent and the least easily assailable. Now such individualism was doubtless largely the result of personal bias: a bias from which no Englishman of his time and antecedents could fairly be expected to escape. But it was also largely—and, on the speculative side, almost wholly—a direct consequence of his deep-seated belief in the law of nature.

If man comes into the world with a ready-made knowledge of good and evil, if the individual, purely as an individual, finds the law of right and wrong, with all its specific commands and prohibitions, its *shalt* and *shalt not*, written on his heart from the beginning, then it is clear that what civil society can do for him is, at best, uncommonly little. It can do nothing for his moral nature; for that is, and must always remain, a matter solely of individual concern. Under God and the natural law, it is created and is to be maintained solely by the individual. With the individual alone rests the power of making or of marring it. Punitive measures excepted, the State has one duty, and one only, in regard to it; and that is to leave it rigorously alone.

As little can the State do for the intellectual life of the individual. Born into the world with such faculties as God has given him, he has only himself and his parents to thank for such use as he may learn to put them to. The State, so far as is to be discovered from Locke's utterances, is under no obligation to provide the means of educating him. For anything that Locke tells us, it is a matter of complete indifference to the State what kind of education he is provided with, or whether he is left with

---

to have been written (mainly, if not entirely) during his residence in the Netherlands (1684–Jan. 1689). It may well be that, until he began his *speculative* enquiry (into the principles of the 'human understanding') he had taken on trust the existence of 'innate principles,' at least in the wider sense of the term; and that it was only as the result of that enquiry that he came to reject them. Even so, it is strange that, when he came to publish *Civil Government* (which he did in the same year as the *Human Understanding*, though, according to Dr. Fraser, a few months earlier), he should not have noticed the discrepancy. It is the more strange, seeing that chapters xviii. and xix. (probably xx. also) must almost certainly have been added not long before the time of publication: certainly not later than 1687, by which time the *Human Understanding* must have been largely written.

no education at all. It is true that later individualists have thrown over this particular article of Locke's creed. But whether, on their premisses, they are entitled to do so, whether education at the public expense, or even under public supervision, is to be justified on individualist principles, is a very doubtful matter. It is hard to believe that, on this point, Locke is not more consistent than his humanitarian disciples.

Thus, the two higher ends which, in common belief and practice, the State exists to further—the satisfaction of the moral and intellectual needs of the community—are on Locke's 'hypothesis,' and probably on any hypothesis which starts from the assumption of a full-fledged law of nature, definitely barred out. We are left with only two motives for the formation of civil society: the desire for a more unbroken security of life and property than experience has found to be possible in the state of nature; and the desire for a fuller supply of the physical conveniences of life: such conveniences, to take an example from more modern conditions, as the building and maintenance of 'the king's highway,' or the lighting of public thoroughfares and other places of general resort.

The latter demand—but it is a mere matter of 'gas and water'—presents no difficulties. As to the former, the question at once arises: Can it be made to cover, as an indirect result, that pursuit of moral and intellectual ends which, on Locke's principles, is excluded as a direct motive for the formation of the civil state, but which, as Spinoza held, is only possible when peace of mind, as well as of body, has been reasonably assured to the individual—only possible, that is, as he rightly concluded, in the civil state? [1] On Locke's system, this is by no means so clear as it is on Spinoza's. It is one thing for men who live wholly without law, moral no less than positive, to make sacrifices for a peace which, under actual circumstances, is denied to them at every moment of their existence. It is quite another for men who are actually blessed with a moral law, as a curb upon their own and their neighbours' passions, to see the necessity of making any such sacrifice, merely for the sake of arming that law with an outward and positive sanction. The better that existing law is, the more complete is the peace, both inward and outward, which they already enjoy. And the greater the peace they already enjoy, the less need is there to put themselves about for the sake of winning more. We have here, in fact, an acute form of the dilemma which confronts Locke throughout the whole course of his argument: Either the law of nature is not so effective an instrument as you would have us believe, for curbing the passions of man and securing his peace and welfare; or the

[1] Spinoza, *T.P.* ii. 15.

change from the state of nature to the civil state is an unnecessary, and therefore an unwarrantable, revolution.

It will be observed that much of the above has rather to be collected from the general tenor of Locke's argument as to the motives which led man from the natural to the civil state, than drawn from the explicit statements which he makes on the matter. This, however, is inevitable. For—wisely enough, from his own point of view—he is extremely cautious not to commit himself too closely on this cardinal point. The only two things he is sure about are: firstly, that the law of nature, written only on the heart of man, needs to be reinforced by an outward sanction, which is obviously to be supplied only by the joint force of the whole 'commonwealth'; and secondly, that men rebel against the necessity, inherent in the natural state, of being 'judge in their own cause.' The first of these brings him face to face with the dilemma of which we have just spoken. The second—considering that the talk is not of Christian neophytes, but of primitive man, Red Indian or early Briton—is too grotesque to need serious discussion.[1]

The only further information he vouchsafes on the subject is to be found in his account of the 'original compact.' And it is vague enough. 'Whosoever out of a state of nature unite into a community must be understood to give up all the power necessary to the ends for which they unite'—that is, the two ends just mentioned—'to the majority of the community. And this is done by barely agreeing to unite into one political society: which is all the compact there is, or need be, between the individuals that enter into or make up a commonwealth.'[2]

It is manifest that this amounts to a blank cheque drawn in favour of 'the majority,' and eventually filled up either to tens or millions, as fortune may decide. Thanks to this device, Locke is enabled to escape, at least for the moment, from the difficulties in which other champions of Contract incautiously entangled themselves: Hobbes, for instance, by his call for the unconditional submission of the individual to the sword of 'one man or one assembly of men'; Rousseau, by his parallel demand for the 'absolute surrender of the individual, with all his rights and all his possessions, to the community at large.' But this advantage is bought at a heavy price. It plunges Locke still more deeply than other writers of his school in that atmosphere of historical fiction which, to a greater or less degree, clings around all forms of the theory of Contract. It involves the assumption that men capable of 'looking before and after' will willingly take a leap in the dark, careless of what they commit themselves to in the future, so long as no very definite demand is made on them in the

[1] *C.G.* §§ 87-90.

[2] *C.G.* § 99; compare § 96.

present. It involves the further assumption that these innocent savages are by instinct familiar with those constitutional refinements, the rule of majorities and the like, which the modern world has reached only after a long and hard experience. The personal despotism of *Leviathan*, the communal despotism of the *Contrat Social*—and the latter, as we shall see, is conceived rather as an ideal for the present and future than as an order of things ever established in the past—are, after all, imaginations less improbable than this.

Locke's description of the actual Contract, however—if that which has no terms can rightly be called a contract—has little direct connection with our immediate theme, his doctrine of the law of nature.[1] To that doctrine we return with the next stage of his argument, his account of the conditions to which any commonwealth, founded on a contract of this nature, is bound to conform.

The conditions to be met by any sound theory of the State may, in the last resort, be roughly reduced to two. It must provide for the freedom, the spontaneous action, of the individual; and it must provide for a general control over the individual by the community at large. Or, to put the same thing in the negative form, it must provide against the tyranny of the State on the one hand, and against the tyranny of the individual upon the other. Of these two conditions, the first is beyond question amply satisfied by Locke. Is it possible to say the same thing of the second?

The sole purpose for which Locke considers the State to have been founded is to prevent any individual from doing 'harm to life, health, liberty or possessions' of his neighbours: a purpose which, by a stretch which for the present may be allowed to pass unchallenged, is held to include the protection of the new 'commonwealth' from the sword of foreign assailants. Taken by itself, no doubt, the above formula might be made to cover almost any form of political union, not avowedly socialist in character. But there are at least two indications which determine the sense that it actually bore to the mind of Locke. The first is that, throughout the subsequent discussion, the one function of the State over which he betrays any serious concern, the only one which he commonly even deigns to mention, is the protection of individual property. And the second, that, when challenged to prove that the 'liberty' of the civil state, as he conceived it, is not to be confounded with 'licence,' he replies—aptly enough, as far as the immediate question is concerned—that it is the liberty to live in obedience to a 'standing rule or law,' which alone he has in mind. And as this law is expressly declared to be 'only so far right as it is founded on the law of nature, by which it is to be regulated and interpreted,'

[1] Except that involved in his assumption that the rule of the majority is prescribed by the law of nature: see above, p. 132.

it is clear that the liberty in question is the liberty to live in obedience to the law of nature. Both these matters demand a few words of explanation.

'The chief end of the State,' as Locke repeatedly assures us, 'is the preservation of property.' It is quite true that, by a curious straining of terms, he uses the word 'property' to include the 'life, health and liberty,' as well as the 'outward possessions' of the individual. And, so far as he remains faithful to this extension of meaning, only a word-catcher would be ready to find fault with the licence he has taken. The worst, however, of such freaks is that the writer is seldom able to keep them up to the end of the chapter, that his thought is nearly always coloured by the natural meaning of the words which he has chosen to distort. From this danger Locke can hardly be said to have entirely escaped. Insist as he will upon man's property in 'life, liberty and health,' it is clear that it is property in land and commodities which he has primarily in view. Why else, indeed, should he have been at the pains to use the incongruous term 'property' at all? It is a curious instance of the ineradicable tendency of the individualist theory—and Locke is an individualist, or he is nothing—to confine the functions of the State to the 'protection of life and property' and for all practical purposes to treat the former object as of much less importance than the latter. The train for all this had been laid in that earlier chapter of the *Essay*,[1] in which he had set himself to prove that property, in the usual and narrower sense, had already taken full shape under the convenient 'law of nature': that it was, therefore, one of the inalienable rights which man brought with him from the natural to the civil state. And, whatever the intention of Locke, the inevitable effect of it all is to set up a tyranny of the individual in one of the most deep-reaching, and therefore one of the most odious, forms which it is capable of taking: the tyranny of the economically strong over the economically weak, of the rich over the poor.

The other provision, that which determines the relation of the law of the State to the law of nature, has no such one-sided operation. It does not split the community into two standing factions, the smaller of which, under cover of the Law, is able to cast its yoke over the neck of the larger. But, none the less, it lays the State at the mercy of the individual, by enabling any minority, however small, to challenge the moral justification of any law which the majority has passed. It thus throws a slur upon the law of the State from the very beginning and 'lays a perpetual ferment for rebellion' against the State, on the part of any and every individual. For, if the law of the State is to be 'regulated

[1] *C.G.* ch. v.

and interpreted' by the law of nature, and if, as Locke also assures us, 'the law of nature is as intelligible and plain to every rational creature as the positive law of commonwealths—nay, possibly plainer,' what is to prevent every rational creature—that is, every individual citizen—from setting up for his own 'regulator and interpreter' and pronouncing, upon his soul and conscience, that the other law, the law of the State, fails to pass muster: fails, that is, to come up to the very standard which Locke himself has pronounced to be necessary and right? And if he goes a step further, if he draws the inevitable conclusion that the law of the State, being unjust and unnatural, is not entitled to his allegiance, that it is his duty to meet its commands at least with passive—and very possibly with active—resistance, who shall say that he is wrong? Certainly not Locke, who expressly reminds us that 'the law of nature ceases not in society, but stands as an eternal rule to all men, legislators as well as others,' and that 'being a declaration of the will of God, no human sanction can be good or valid against it.'

This is the very principle of antinomianism, transferred to politics. It is to commit, without reason, the very mistake which, for strong (if not altogether sufficient) reasons, was committed by the Constituents of 1789, when they began their task by laying down sweeping principles in their Declaration of Rights and then found themselves compelled to violate the most fundamental of them in the working Constitution which followed: as Burke scornfully said, to 'limit logic by despotism.' And if Locke's revolutionary procedure bore no such inconvenient fruits a century earlier, that, as has been well pointed out, is because the spirit of the 'sectaries,' so strong in the days of the long Parliament and Protectorate, had been broken by a generation of reaction: because the men of 1690 lived in a world poles asunder from the men of 1650. It is quite true that men will always test the legislation of the moment by the standard of equity which has shaped itself in the purer minds of their generation. It would be a poor outlook for progress if they did not. But that is no reason why the Legislator himself should roundly challenge them to do so; and unless he wishes to increase his own difficulties a thousandfold, he will do well to refrain. Above all, he will refuse to assume that there is an 'eternal law' of right and wrong, known to all men, 'plain to every rational creature' from the beginning of the world: a law, by which every human law, with its necessary limitations of time, place and circumstance, must necessarily stand condemned. And this, for the best of all reasons, because such an assumption is absolutely false.

Thus, of the two chief consequences which flow from Locke's conception of the law of nature at this stage of his argument, the first is bound, in the long run, to destroy the inward peace and harmony of the State; while the second, if carried to its logical issue, is such as to make the very existence of the State for ever impossible.

Is then the 'law of nature' an idea absolutely invalid? Were Locke and others under a total delusion when they pinned their faith to its reality? In the particular form which they gave to the idea, there can be no doubt as to the answer. To assume a law the same 'always, everywhere and for all,' a law which carries conviction to 'every rational creature'—saint or sinner, savage or civilised, worldling or moralist, 'foolish gentleman' or philosopher—is to fly in the face of all experience and history, to say nothing of all probability and reason. And when such a law is taken, as Locke takes it, to include not only moral relations, which are comparatively simple, but such social and political usages as the institution of Property or the rule of the majority, which are highly complicated and questionable, the absurdity becomes yet more glaring.

But if by the law of nature we mean that, from the beginning, there have been the germs of what we conveniently call the moral sense in man; that, with experience and reflection, these germs have constantly expanded, have become more and more consciously realised, have grown into fuller and ever fuller articulation, the root of the whole ethical life of the individual, the source of all his social energies—above all, of the State, which is at once the crown and mainstay of them all—then our answer must be very different. Then, so far from there being anything to say against the idea of natural law, there is everything to be said for it. Without it, all history, all experience, would be an unintelligible riddle. Only, let there be no misunderstanding. The natural law, so conceived, is a thing not only alien from the thought of Locke, but utterly repugnant to his whole teaching. The principle of growth, which is the life and soul of it, is not only not present in Locke's law of nature: it is directly and deliberately excluded. And this initial difference reflects, or rather intensifies, itself at all the main turning-points of the argument which follows: above all, in that which brings us face to face with the beginnings, the foundation, of the State. To Locke, however much he may disguise the fact, this was no less than an act of treachery to the law of nature. To his opponents, it is the first step towards the fulfilment of that law: the indispensable condition, without which no further development would have been either possible or conceivable.

What is the bearing of this upon our immediate argument? How does it affect the relation of the individual conscience to the Law of the land? To suppose that, either on this or on any other theory, the possibility of conflict between the two is abolished, or even seriously reduced, would be a mischievous delusion. The Law of the land, even at the best, can never hope to do more than reflect the average conscience of the community. Too often, it is the conscience of yesterday rather than to-day, of our grandfathers rather than ourselves. The fact is plain; and nothing but harm can come of trying to disguise it. The inevitable consequence of this is that, even under the most favourable conditions, a man of sensitive conscience is apt to find himself face to face with a law which, rightly or wrongly, he honestly believes to be unjust. He may recognise that, all Law being relative, the particular law which offends him had its justification in the past, may even have it in the common opinion of the present. He may admit that the Law of the land is entitled to respect: that only in the most extreme cases is the individual justified in disregarding or defying it. Yet, none the less, the point will come when he knows that, however it may be with others, for him there is no choice but to disobey, and take the consequences: to face the storm of indignation with which his neighbours will visit him; to submit to the punishment which the State—and that too has its rights—may feel bound to inflict upon him. It is probable that these occasions will arise less often as public opinion becomes more enlightened and as Locke's law of nature, eternal and unbending, falls more and more into discredit. It is almost certain that, when they do arise, they will be met, on both sides, in a less bitter spirit. But the conflict is in the nature of things; and so long as men are what they are, it can never wholly be done away. It is not always a sign of growth; for individuals, like States, are liable to obstinacy and error. But without it, all growth would be impossible.

Apart from the law of nature, all that is vital in Locke's theory, whether for good or for evil, is summed up in one word: individualism. And as we have seen, the connection between the two things is, to Locke's mind, extremely close. Having disposed of the one, let us now turn to see him at work upon the other.

Everything in Locke's system revolves round the individual; everything is disposed so as to ensure the sovereignty of the individual. Entering the civil state with his moral sense already fully trained, his moral code perfectly articulated, the individual owes nothing to the State on that side of the account; as little, on the side of his intellectual development. The consequence is that both these fields—and they are the fields in which the spirit of man finds its highest expression—are definitely excluded from the ken of the State. For the State to meddle with either of them is an unwarrantable impertinence. Indeed, in moral matters at any rate, the individual is entitled to dictate his own will to the

State: to refuse his assent—and we can only conclude, his obedience also—to any law or executive act that does not square with the divinely ordained code which each man finds written in his heart and which he alone has the right to 'interpret.'

Property again, like the moral code, is brought by the individual ready made into the State. It is the inalienable right of the individual. The State has one duty, and one only, in regard to it: and that is jealously to watch over it, as a sacred trust committed to its care; inviolable, unalterable, the very ark of the covenant of the commonwealth. To regulate it—much more to redistribute it or to nationalise it—would be the grossest of usurpations, the most flagrant of wrongs. In default of any moral or educational duties, the protection of private property—of the right of every man to do what he will with his own—is indeed the chief, and almost the only, function left to the State. Even the defence of the common territory from foreign invasion seems to be regarded rather as the discharge of a duty to the private proprietor than to the community as a whole.

The same supremacy of the individual which dominates the whole life of the State is no less conspicuous in the act by which it is created and in that—if such an act can be conceived as possible—by which it is dissolved. Consent, the express and formal consent, of every individual concerned is necessary to the foundation of the State: 'nothing can make a man member of any commonwealth but his actually entering into it by positive engagement and express promise and compact.' And the same consent, express and formal, is necessary to its dissolution. Such a dissolution, as we have already seen, can hardly be brought about except by the sword of a foreign conqueror. And that conqueror 'can never have a title till the people are both at liberty to consent, and have actually consented, to allow and confirm in him the power he hath till then usurped.' Until that moment the community, founded as it is upon the explicit consent of its members, can never be dissolved.

Such are the consequences of the individualist principle, as it shapes itself in *Civil Government*; and, with a few vacillations, they are clearly recognised and deliberately driven home by the author. There is hardly one of them which does not call for a searching examination.

And first, for the assertion that no political community can be rightfully established without the 'express promise and compact' of every individual concerned. It is obvious at a glance that this condition has not been fulfilled by more than a handful—if indeed by a single one—of the commonwealths at present existing upon the face of the earth; nor, so far as can be learned from history and probable inference, by any that preceded them. Even in those cases where consent may be charitably assumed—such, perhaps, are some of the Greek and New England Colonies, or again the barbarian tribes which overran large parts of the Roman Empire—that consent accounts only for the primitive nucleus of the commonwealth. It does not account for the gradual accretions which conquest, or some more veiled form of compulsion, has subsequently brought about.

Locke of course would reply, as Rousseau did in a like case: 'I am in search of Right and reason; I am not concerned to wrangle over facts.'[1] And there is some force in the answer. It must be observed, however, that a theory which disregards, or rather violently tramples on, all the facts can hardly be treated as a satisfactory theory: least of all, when the general tenor of the argument assumes, as Locke's argument clearly does, that we are dealing not with fiction, but with historical fact. A yet more fatal objection remains behind. Supposing that Locke's principle, the principle of express and unforced consent, had actually been applied from the dawn of history to the present day, then it is morally certain that mankind would never have passed beyond the stage of purely tribal organisation. Incessant feuds between tribe and tribe might have been safely trusted to bar the way to further progress. Would Locke have been willing to accept this consequence? Would he have consented, for instance, to see England stop short with the Heptarchy, with the endless and fruitless 'battle of the kites and the crows'? or, to speak the plain truth, with something far more primitive than that? with herds of naked savages wandering among primeval forests and held together by nothing better than a common faith in a tribal god, a common acceptance of certain tribal customs and a common hatred of all who did not embrace both the one and the other? If he would not—and no sane person will believe that he would—then he has no right to be counted the champion of consent. His faith in consent is, in fact, of a strictly limited order. It is consistent with availing himself—without any acknowledgement, and probably without any consciousness that he was doing so—of every advantage which history had put into his hand from the rival and opposite principle of compulsion.

Given the abstract method which Locke shared with all the writers of his school—even Spinoza is only a partial exception—given also the conception of natural law which he shared with most of them, this inconsistency was inevitable. Try as hard as he will, no man can altogether escape from his historical surroundings, nor from the assumptions which they insensibly breed even

[1] *Contrat Social*, first draft, I. v. (*Political Writings*, i. p. 462).

in the wariest mind. Yet, try as hard as he would, no ingenuity could avail to bring the actual beginnings of Government, as we know or divine them from history, under the principle of consent. However much we may hate to own it, history compels us to admit that force played a large part in the foundation, as it has certainly played in the subsequent life and growth, of every State. And the wiser course is to admit manfully, with Burke, that 'a sacred veil is to be drawn over the beginnings of all Governments.'[1] It is only as the idea of Right slowly wins its way to acceptance and, in doing so, slowly works itself out into a more and more consistent code of practice, that the consent of the governed comes to be recognised as essential to any form of Government which can claim, in the full sense of the term, to be legitimate. In other words, for the greater part of recorded history, it has rather been an ideal to be painfully attained in the future than an operative principle which has been at work from the beginning. Of Locke's successors, Rousseau was probably the first to win even the faintest glimmering of this truth.[2] Certainly, Locke himself was totally blind to it. It is only by a back door and in a blissful absent fit that he admits even the most beggarly elements of history. It never occurred to him that to leave even a chink open for them was to destroy his whole argument from top to bottom. Hence the strange contradictions in which he allowed himself to be ensnared.

Take, secondly, Locke's theory of Property. It is the theory of 'formation,' pure and simple, reinforced by a doctrine of hereditary right independent of all positive law and as unqualified as any that the most extreme of individualists has ever ventured to lay down. And, as we shall see in the sequel, his statement of this theory is not even consistent with itself.

According to the doctrine of 'formation,' the mere bestowal of labour upon any product of nature, not already appropriated by another, suffices to give a man the ownership of that which he has thus shaped or 'formed.' And this holds good of the simplest as well as the most complicated forms which such labour, or formation, is capable of taking. It is as true of the acorn which a man takes the trouble to pick up by the wayside, and then eats or plants, as of the gold which he refines and shapes into a chain, or of the cotton which he spins into a yarn and then weaves into a

[1] Opening Speech in the Impeachment of Warren Hastings. *Speeches* (ed. Bohn), i. p. 60.

[2] See his refutation of 'natural law' (in Locke's sense of the term), *Contrat Social*, first draft, I. ii.; and compare *ib.* II. iv. (*Political Writings*, i. pp. 447-454, and 494). It will be seen from the next chapter that Vico also had a dim perception of the truth: *Scienza Nuova*, ii. pp. 130-134.

piece. In all cases, he is by Right and the law of nature, quite apart from any positive legislation, full owner of the product which his labour has turned out. By Right and the law of nature, he is entitled to do with it what he lists. And the same applies—though it is admitted that this carries the principle a stage further yet—even to the land which yields the raw material upon which his labour or industry is spent: to the soil which a man ploughs, harrows and sows, and without which none of the fruits of the earth could be made amenable to his use. 'As much land as a man tills, plants, improves, cultivates and can use the product of, so much is his property. He by his labour does, as it were, enclose it from the common.'[1]

This is the theory of Property—the words just quoted are enough to show it—which Locke makes his own and which, Property being a test question, becomes one of the main bulwarks of his individualist theory of the State.

This, however, is not all. And Locke is as much bent on applying the law of nature to the tenure and transmission of property as he is to its original acquisition. Once acquired, he holds, the law of nature demands that, so far as it is not perishable, it be held for life; and that, on the death of the holder, it pass to the children—in default of children, we must apparently suppose, to the next-of-kin—for whom, by the law of nature, it is his duty to provide.[2]

Thus the rights of Property, so far from being the creation of the civil state, are, in Locke's view, part and parcel of the law of nature. All the prescriptions which civilised nations, or the majority of them, have established as to the acquisition, tenure and succession of property are, in fact, a link in the eternal order of things. They are as binding on the conscience as the Ten Commandments. It is one of the most curious, as it is one of the least pleasing, results of Locke's teaching as to the law of Nature.

It is true that, at one stage of his enquiry, he makes some feint of limiting acquisition by 'the extent of labour and the conveniency of life': that is, by the principle that no man has a right to appropriate more than he can win, or form, by his own toil and consume within the bounds of his own family.[3] The result of such a restriction, if maintained, would be to fix a deep gulf between the law of nature and the law which prevails in what, to disciples of Marx, are known as 'capitalistic States': that is, all existing States, with the doubtful exception of Russia under its present Government. We all know that it has not been

[1] *C.G.* § 32.

[2] 'His goods which Nature . . . hath made to belong to the children to keep them from perishing, do still continue to belong to his children' (*C.G.* § 182; compare § 183).

[3] *Ib.* §§ 36, 46.

maintained. And the change, which according to Locke had been carried through while men were still in the state of nature, is traced to the joint action of two causes: the 'desire of men to have more than they needed,' which 'altered the intrinsic value of things'; and their 'agreement that a little piece of yellow metal, which would keep without wasting and decay, should be worth a great piece of flesh or a whole heap of corn.'[1]

The fact is beyond dispute. Whether it is to be justified on grounds of abstract Right, the grounds on which Locke's argument is wholly based, is another matter. And the reader, conscious that all the restrictions hitherto imposed by Locke on the 'rights of Property'—restrictions obviously demanded on any conceivable interpretation of the law of nature—are swept away at a blow by this revolutionary innovation—looks to see it indignantly rejected. He looks in vain. With unruffled composure, Locke goes on his way as if nothing had happened. And from this time onward the new principle, with all its arbitrary conventions and all its certain injustices, is tacitly incorporated in the 'law of nature.' It is carried by group after group of men from the state of nature into the civil state. It is accepted as one of those individual rights which no civil society is permitted to touch: which, on the contrary, it is 'the chief end' of all civil society to protect and maintain.

'All the philosophers,' said Rousseau, 'have seen the necessity of going back to the state of nature; but none of them has ever got there. . . . Primitive man is on their lips; but the portrait they paint is of civil man.'[2] And of none of them is this so true as it is of Locke; of no part of his argument perhaps is it so true as of that which gives his theory of Property. The truth is that, from beginning to end of it, he credits the state of nature with ideas and practices which could only have arisen in the civil state. This is the case even with the doctrine which lies at the root of his whole argument: the doctrine of formation. It is still more the case with his doctrine of natural succession.

As for the former, no one will deny that in its original shape—that which excludes the storing of goods with a view to anything beyond the immediate future—it is equitable enough. Locke, however, is concerned not merely with equity, but with the historical fact. Unless he can prove that this was the way in which the notion and usage of Property actually arose, he has proved nothing: his whole argument, both as to the state of nature and the law of nature, falls to pieces. Now, what was or was not the fact, it is impossible to say for certain. It is admitted, and the

[1] *C.G.* § 37.

[2] *Discours sur l'inégalité* (*Political Writings*, i. pp. 140-41).

admission itself is sufficiently damaging to Locke, that we can get no further than probabilities. And who will believe it even probable that, in any primitive state, men were really guided by notions so equitable as these? Is it not likely that force, the right of the stronger, played a far larger part in the beginnings of Property than Locke shows the smallest intention of allowing? than, without ruining his whole theory, he could ever have thought of allowing? And if so, how can we say that the theory of formation is anything but an *ex post facto* explanation? a palpable transference of ideas, only conceivable in the civil state, to an imaginary state of nature?

But if this be true of the theory of formation, still more obviously is it so of the theory of natural succession. We may admit at once that the idea of succession—that is, of the transmission of property after the death of the owner—once granted, it is both natural and in the main equitable that the persons to benefit by it should be the children of the dead owner. He had an interest in them that he had in no other claimant; he had duties towards them that he had towards no other claimant. And this remains true, even when all allowance has been made for the probable weakness of such ties in a primitive state of things, as compared with that which is familiar to us at the present day.

That, however, is not the real point at issue. The question for Locke is not, who in equity the successors ought to be; but whether, in the state of nature—that is, by his own definition, a State without any form of civil government—there can be any such thing as succession at all. It is one thing that a man should enjoy what he has won, during his own life. It is quite another that he should have the power of willing it to others after his death. The very idea of succession is purely artificial. It could never have originated, still less could it ever have taken practical shape, in anything but the civil state. Except in the settled life of the State, it could never have been thought of. Without the whole force of the State behind it, it could never be carried into act. Other writers, far inferior to Locke, had already seen that this was so; and how Locke came to think otherwise, is not easy to understand. It is one more instance of the fallacy upon which Rousseau laid his finger: 'Primitive man is on his lips; but the portrait he paints is that of civil man.'

The truth is that, for all practical purposes, the 'law of nature' is no better than a phantom; and the only way in which Locke could give flesh and blood to it was to transfer to it bodily all that strikes him as rational in the positive law of England or of Christendom. 'He begins by casting about for the rules which, in their own interest, it would be well for men to agree upon; and then, without any further proof than the supposed advantage thus resulting, he proceeds to dignify this body of rules by the name of *natural law*. All the other philosophers of his school have followed the same method. The result is that all the definitions of these learned men, in standing contradiction with each other, agree in this conclusion only: that it is impossible to understand, impossible therefore to obey, the law of nature without being a very deep reasoner and a very great metaphysician. And that is only another way of saying that, for the establishment of society, men must have made use of the wisdom which is, in fact, only gradually acquired by a small minority of men, and that with the utmost difficulty, in the bosom of society itself.'[1]

That is Rousseau's criticism of the law of nature. No writer perhaps is so hard hit by it as Locke; and to no part of his teaching does it apply with greater force than to his theory of Property.

There are two further points which throw a curious light upon Locke's theory of Property. The one is connected with his doctrine of foreign conquest; the other arises out of an unexpected restriction which he places upon ownership.

The assumption which lies behind his whole argument as to the rights conferred by conquest is that the community has no collective responsibility for the acts of its Government and army: that no claim for damages can lie except against the individuals, soldiers or ministers, to whom the original wrong can be brought home. With this fundamental assumption we are not directly concerned at the present moment; it falls under the general criticism of Locke's theory with which this enquiry must close. It is only when he comes to apply the principle in detail that he begins to trench upon the theory of Property; though, having once entered upon this ground, he commits himself more deeply than perhaps there was any call for him to do. To the reader, however, the light thus furnished is serviceable enough.

Assuming, then, that an indemnity may justly be claimed by the conqueror from those immediately responsible for the wrongdoing, Locke promptly proceeds to neutralise this admission by proving that, according to the law of nature, the wrongdoer has, in fact, nothing, or next to nothing to give. By that law, no man has more than a life-interest, and that of a strictly limited character, in his estate. It is chargeable with the support of his wife and children during his life. It descends to his children, presumably with a suitable dowry for their mother, after his death. To all appearance, therefore, the dispute ends in a deadlock. The conqueror, *ex hypothesi*, has a positive claim upon what may well amount to the whole of the wrongdoer's estate. So, by the law of nature, have his wife and children; and the claim of the latter

[1] *Discours sur l'inégalité* (*Political Writings*, i. p. 137).

is both juster and 'more pressing.' It is one of those matters which can be settled only by equity, or an amicable compromise. The conqueror must abate something of his full claim; he must leave to the wife and children, if not to the man himself, enough for 'their subsistence.' [1]

If this argument is to be pressed home, it is clear that we have here more than one sweeping limitation upon the rights of Property, as commonly understood: upon the right of a man to do what he will with his own. If a man's wife and children 'have a title to the goods he enjoys, and their share in the estate he possesses,' it follows that his right to dispose freely of his property is laid under considerable restrictions. If the extent of their 'title' and the amount of their shares are to be reckoned on a liberal scale, then the restrictions become severe. Again, it is impossible to limit the rights and title of the owner in chief, without also limiting the claims of his creditors; the two things stand and fall together. The only creditor considered by Locke is the foreign conqueror. Would he be willing to put the native creditor on the same footing? And if not, by what argument would he justify the distinction? Once more: if the claims of the creditor are to be limited on grounds of equity and humanity—and the principle is two-edged, seeing that, after all, the creditor too may have a wife and children—how can we refuse to judge the claims of the wage-earner—this time, it is a question, not of limitation, but of extension—by the same rule? Would Locke have been willing to adopt the principle of a 'living wage'?

To the modern reader such inferences from Locke's statements will seem both logically necessary and morally just. But it is more than doubtful whether Locke himself would have accepted them. If he would, it is strange that nothing is said of them in that detailed discussion of Property, its origin and justification, with which the *Essay* opens. If he would not, what are we to say of his consistency? In either case, what becomes of his assertion that the law of nature, to which he makes explicit reference in this very passage, is 'plain and intelligible to every rational creature'? Some of the hottest disputes among economists have raged round these very points; and 'high and reverend authorities lift their heads on both sides.' Sufficient proof, if proof were needed, that neither in this, nor in many of its other applications, is the law of nature so simple a matter as Locke would have us to believe.

Another, and still more trenchant, limitation on the rights of the conqueror—and consequently on the rights of Property—remains behind. In estimating the amount of the damage done

[1] *C.G.* § 183. Compare *Treatise I.* (Refutation of Filmer), §§ 87-90.

to his territory, it is solely that inflicted on his real property—his land, crops and houses—that he is entitled to reckon. His personal property—'his money and such riches and treasures, being none of nature's goods'—must not be thrown in. 'They have but a fantastical, imaginary value ; nature has put no such upon them. They are of no more account by her standard than the Wampompeke of the Americans to an European prince, or the silver money of Europe to an American.'[1] The effect of this obviously is to reduce the conqueror's bill of indemnity to an indefinite extent. The conqueror will, no doubt, reply that such an argument cuts both ways : that, if he is at no loss from the 'money and such treasures taken from him,' neither will the thief be at any loss, if he is forced to restore them. Locke, however, and with much prudence, takes no heed of this obvious retort. At this stage of his argument, it is the law of nature with him, or it is nothing.

That indeed is the weapon with which he would doubtless have returned the blows of his critics in this matter. 'All commonwealths,' he tells us, 'are in a state of nature one with another';[2] and on that principle, it would seem, he may fairly claim to have his argument judged by the 'law of nature,' and by that alone. Such a plea has a great appearance of reason; and in the mouth of some writers—Hobbes, for instance—it would be conclusive. Locke, however, had expressly debarred himself from using it. For, in a passage to which reference has been made already, he had said in so many words that the revolution which gave this 'fantastical value' to gold and silver had been accomplished before men quitted the state of nature : that 'out of the bounds of society and without compact'—that is, before the 'original compact' which is the foundation of all civil society—they had already 'tacitly agreed in the use of money' and in the 'inequality of private possessions' which naturally, if not inevitably, follows.[3] It is therefore impossible for him to turn round at a later moment and declare that the use of money is a thing purely 'fantastical': a thing which is not justified by the law, and has no existence in the state, of nature.

It may be said that this is no more than a momentary inadvertence on Locke's part, that in the fundamental principles of his theory there was nothing which made it necessary for him to treat the convention of money, with its resulting 'inequality of private possessions,' as having arisen in the state of nature and as forming an integral part of the law of nature. A moment's reflection will show that this is not the case. The inequality of private possessions and, with it, the convention of money, are integral parts of the 'rights of property,' as they exist in practice. And to preserve

[1] *C.G.* § 184. [2] *Ib.* § 183. [3] *Ib.* § 50.

those rights, to prove that they are rights which man brought with him into civil society and which all civil societies are therefore bound to regard as sacred and inviolable, was one of the chief objects which Locke had in view as he thought out his whole theory of Civil Government.

'The preservation of Property' is 'the end of Government.'[1] And though, as we have seen, he often includes under the term a great deal—'health, life and liberty'—which, according to strict usage, does not belong to it, yet, as we have also seen, Property, in its obvious sense of 'goods and chattels,' is always that which is primarily present to his mind. In fact, in the passage from which the above words are drawn, the context shows this to have been the only sense which he had in view, as he wrote it.

If then there is any inadvertence on the author's part, it is manifestly not to be found in his acceptance of the money convention, or the consequent 'inequality of private possessions,' but in the contradictory assertion that the value attributed to 'money and such treasures' is a thing purely arbitrary, 'fantastical,' and in no way justified by the law of nature. And the inadvertence must be set down to a motive in itself entirely honourable: to his manifest hatred of war and of the vicious usages summed up under the vile phrase, the 'rights of conquest': usages, it may be remembered, which had been revived on a vast scale in the very year before the publication of his *Essay*, by the devastation of the Palatinate at the orders of Louvois and of Louis XIV (1689). None the less, it is a logical blot upon his theory of Property and his exposition of those individualist ideas with which his theory of Property is inseparably bound up.

The inconsistency does not stop here: it has a further rebound upon his presentment of the law of nature. We are forced to the conclusion that there are, in fact, two distinct conceptions of the law of nature struggling for the mastery in his mind. The one, that which comes to the front in his discussion of Property, is nothing more nor less than a transcript of the usages which he found established in his own country, or in what claimed to be the civilised world of his own day. The other—it is that which prevails in his chapter on the rights of conquest—is, at least in the main, governed by considerations of pure equity: though of equity determined, as it must always be, by the most humane standards of the author's own day and country. Both of them, no doubt, claim to be wholly independent of time, place and circumstance: to be 'plain and intelligible to every rational creature.' Neither of them is so, in truth. The former is an exact replica of the usages which prevailed throughout Europe at the time when *Civil*

[1] *C.G.* § 138; compare § 222.

Government was written. The latter is little more than an echo of the ideal which the best minds of the seventeenth century had dimly formed upon certain points of social duty, and by which they strove to correct the injustices of established fact and historical tradition. The latter, therefore, has a fair claim to call itself the 'law of nature.' It is an ideal which represents the best thought of the time, and which might eventually become embodied in the outward institutions of one community or another. The former has no such pretensions. It is a mere copy of the positive law which Locke found in force around him. To call it natural law, even in the very modified sense which alone can properly be given to the term, is a pure confusion. And how Locke came to be entangled in it, it is difficult to say. That he should ever have confounded the one of his two 'laws' with the other is still more surprising.

There is one more inconsistency in Locke's theory of Property: an inconsistency so glaring that it cannot fail to strike any reader who is not wholly blinded by individualist preconceptions. 'Government exists for the preservation of Property'; and Property, as we have seen, is a right existing before the foundation of Society, a right brought straight by the individual from the natural into the civil state. Starting from these premisses, we should expect to find Property treated as the sacred right of the individual: as something which, without the express consent of each individual concerned, it is sacrilege for the State to question, touch, or tamper with in any way whatsoever. What we actually find is something strangely different. The property of the individual is taxable by the State under conditions to be specified directly. What is more, it is tenable only so long as, at least by the implied consent of residence, he remains a citizen of the State in whose territory it is placed.

As for the former provision, it must at once be admitted that the payment of a tax to the State, in return for protection rendered by the State, is, in itself, reasonable enough. And if the consent of the individual were declared to be a necessary condition of such taxation, there would be nothing more to say on the matter. This, however, is far from being the case. Some consent is indeed demanded by Locke. It is the consent, however, not of the individual, but of his 'representatives'; and that is a very different thing. It is true that, to save appearances, Locke does throw in the individual—now reduced to a miserable fraction—as an alternative to his representatives: 'It must be with his own consent—*i.e.* the consent of the majority, giving it either by themselves, or their representatives chosen by them.'[1] But this is only

[1] *C.G.* § 140.

to make matters worse. For he must have known that to be one of a minority which, by a direct vote, opposes the imposition of a tax and yet has to pay it when imposed, is at the opposite pole from paying a tax to which I have heartily assented; and that, when the vote is indirect, the chances of misrepresentation are indefinitely increased: so that, when my official representative has the effrontery to vote for a tax which I personally condemn, the height of absurdity is reached and the plea of 'my own consent' is reduced to a mere farce. Under such circumstances I shall not be consoled by the assurance that 'the Legislative which imposes the tax consists wholly, or in part, of Assemblies which are variable, whose members, upon the dissolution of the Assembly, are subjects under the common law of the country, equally with the rest.'[1] I shall still feel that I am suffering from an act of tyranny, a gross violation of my 'natural rights.' And on Locke's principles, who shall say that I am wrong?

The truth is that, on individualist assumptions, taxation, as commonly understood, is in no way to be justified. The only legitimate form of it, when such assumptions are once granted, is that 'voluntary taxation' which was advocated by a fantastic, but logical, individualist in this country some forty years ago. And there is nothing risked by the prophecy that any State which adopted his system would be reduced to beggary within a fortnight. That, in the face of his pronouncements on the sacredness of Property and the inviolable rights of the individual, Locke should have found himself driven to fall back upon an inviolability violable at the convenience or caprice of other individuals, of a sacredness which is liable to be profaned at any moment by the sovereign will of 'the majority,' is one more proof of the impossibility of framing any individualist theory which does not contradict itself upon the very threshold. It is one more example of the way in which, after laying down principles that claim to be drawn from the unadulterated law of nature, Locke proceeds to fill up all the working details from the rough and ready practice of his own day and his own country: a practice which, if it is to be justified at all, is to be justified only on principles the very opposite of those he had chosen to assume in the first instance.

The same method, the same inconsequence, reappears in his handling of the second point above mentioned: the last point there is any need to consider in connection with his theory of Property.

'The preservation of Property is the chief end of civil government.' How then does it happen that, in the very act of joining any civil society, the owner not only submits his property to any

[1] *C.G.* § 138.

tax, large or small, which the society shall see fit to impose upon it in the future, but even exposes himself to forfeit the whole of it, so far at least as it consists in land, if at any future time either he or his heirs after him should renounce their citizenship and transfer their allegiance to another State?[1] On this point Locke is no less explicit than he was in the matter of taxation: 'Every man, when he at first incorporates himself into any commonwealth . . . annexed also and submits to the community those possessions which he has, or shall acquire, that do not already belong to any other Government. . . . By the same act therefore whereby any one unites his person, which was before free, to any commonwealth, by the same he unites his possessions, which were before free, to it also; and they become both of them, person and possession, subject to the government and dominion of that commonwealth, so long as it hath a being.' And again: 'Whenever the owner, who has given nothing but a tacit consent to the Government, will by donation, sale or otherwise, quit the said possession, he is at liberty to go and incorporate himself into any other commonwealth, or agree with others to begin a new one *in vacuis locis*.'[2]

What are the implications of this curious pronouncement? They are, firstly, that every citizen, at the moment of joining a given commonwealth, in effect alienates his land to that commonwealth; but is left in possession, though no longer in full ownership, of it and enjoys the usufruct of it, subject to the payment of a quit-rent, infinitely variable in amount, under the form of taxation. Secondly, that his right of possession, or usufruct, lasts only so long as, at any rate by tacit consent, he remains a citizen of the commonwealth. Directly he ceases to be a citizen—which, supposing his consent to have been no more than tacit, he has a perfect right to do—the commonwealth re-enters into the direct enjoyment of all its rights, as sovereign owner. Unless he has been able to dispose of his estate by private 'sale, donation, or otherwise,' it is, in short, confiscated without a penny of compensation; and thereafter—so we are left to suppose—is either resold by the commonwealth to be the private property of another individual under the same conditions, or is retained, under the form of domain land, in the hands of the State. Thirdly, and as a necessary consequence, that any

[1] So far as he himself is concerned, the forfeiture can only take place if his citizenship is of that 'tacit' and imperfect kind implied in mere residence. According to Locke, no man who has once expressly become a party to the contract of 'incorporation' is ever free subsequently to withdraw from it. He is 'perpetually and indispensably obliged to be and remain unalterably a subject to it' (*C.G.* § 121). But then, what becomes of his liberty—which, by Locke's definition, is a part of his property?

[2] *C.G.* §§ 120, 121.

land which has once been brought into a given commonwealth by a free and independent owner remains 'annexed' to that commonwealth for all time. Surely a strange method of preserving the inalienable rights of Property to the individual.

It is clear that, in the main, all this is simply taken over from the practice—or, if not that, from the juristic theory—with regard to Property which Locke found in force at the time when *Civil Government* was written. It was, in fact, the principle which underlay the fiscal measures taken both by the French Government against the Huguenots at the time of the Revocation and by the English Government against the Catholics under the Penal Laws; although, in justice to both Governments, and especially the latter, it must be remembered that many alleviations were admitted in practice. It is true that in both cases the application was abominable; for what right has any Government to treat its own subjects as aliens, or rather enemies? Yet the principle itself, if applied solely to genuine aliens—not to those who, for a special (and in this case, an illicit) purpose are made so by the Government—is not unjustifiable. Indeed, apart from the flat confiscation which Locke appears to contemplate as a possibility, it must be pronounced essentially sound.

That, however, is not the point. What Locke had to consider was not whether the principle is sound in itself, but whether it is consistent with the ideas which he had assumed at the start and which form the foundation of his whole theory alike of Property and of the State. And a glance is enough to show that it is not: that it is only to be justified on a theory of Property and a theory of Sovereignty which are in flat contradiction with those that lie at the root of his whole system. It is only to be justified on the assumption that Property is the creation, not of the individual, but of the State; and Locke had asserted exactly the reverse. It is only to be justified on an extremely rigid theory of Sovereignty; and Locke, in fact, had no theory of Sovereignty at all. The true sovereign of *Civil Government* is the individual.

This brings us to the last stage of our enquiry: How far does the State, as pictured in *Civil Government*, correspond to the State as we know it from experience? how far could a State, built upon Locke's principles, achieve the ends for which, on any reasonable showing, all civil Society exists? The question is unfortunately complicated by the inconsistencies of which we have just spoken. And it is necessary to hold the two strains of the theory, the abstract and the practical, carefully apart.

The State, as Locke originally conceived it, exists for two purposes, and for two purposes only: for the protection of the rights of the individual, or, as defined more closely, of the life, health, liberty and property—above all, the property—of the individual; and, as a necessary consequence, for the settlement of any disputes between one individual and another which may arise from a clash of claims or a doubt as to their extent. These rights all exist prior to the formation of the State; they are brought into the State, ready made, from the state of nature. All that the State does is to provide a positive rule for interpreting them, namely the municipal law of a given commonwealth, and a positive sanction, a sanction supplied by the joint force of the community, for their maintenance and execution. The moral sanction behind all positive law lies, as we have seen, in the law of nature; and by that law all positive laws are to be interpreted and judged.

The form of government which best—or rather, which alone—answers to these demands is manifestly pure Democracy: though a point might possibly be stretched, so as to cover those representative institutions which the size of the modern State, at least such examples of it as Locke apparently had in view, practically necessitates. Locke, however, goes a long way further than this in acceptance of the fact which he found in possession of the field. A limited Monarchy, tempered by more or less popular Assemblies, such as he knew in England; even an absolute Monarchy, so long as it could be credited with more or less benevolent intentions, such as he saw in France: these are the things that he is willing at least to put up with. And this easy-going tolerance, much as it furthered the practical influence of his teaching, is a serious flaw in its speculative consistency.

The main result of this rather unfortunate compliance is that the 'consent' of the individual, which he had emphatically declared to be the sole foundation of all civil society, is in effect whittled down to something far less substantial than we had been led to expect. It amounts to little more than a formal adherence to the 'original compact' which constitutes the given commonwealth; and thereafter, to a mere acquiescence in the laws from time to time passed by the Legislative and in the general policy of the Executive. What we expect to find is a self-governing Democracy, limited only by the rights which each individual brings with him from the state of nature. What we actually find is the system of shifts and compromises, of checks and counter-checks, so familiar to Englishmen, from their past history and present experience: a system which, as experience shows, may leave little or no initiative to the popular will, and pay little or no regard to those abstract rights of the individual which Locke had embodied in the 'law of nature.'

Such are the concessions to the established fact with which Locke's primitive theory is clogged. To the practical man, they may seem to make everything run smoothly; but, if the test is to be speculative consistency, they work havoc with the whole argument. It is not in them that the historical importance, the real originality, of *Civil Government* is to be sought. It is not by them, but by his primitive theory, that Locke is to be judged.

The first thing to strike us in that theory is that the ends for which the State is founded are strictly limited ends; and consequently, that the authority entrusted to the State is an authority jealously restricted. The protection of life, liberty and property is practically the sole purpose for which the State is created; and if it sets itself to pursue any object beyond this, it must, on any strict interpretation of Locke's principles, be guilty of unpardonable usurpation. The individuals who compose it must, in that case, have the right, and indeed the duty, to overrule and, if necessary, to dissolve it. It is pursuing ends which are not covered by the articles of association: ends which, sooner or later, are bound to threaten, or even openly conflict with, the rights of the individual: ends therefore which, on any strict construction, the individual members have no right, even if they have the wish, to consent to or permit. Let us consider what is the bearing of this principle, if accepted, upon our conception of the State: what it means to the life of the community on the one hand, and of the individuals composing it, upon the other.

On the appeal to history and common experience, we find that there are at least two marks which distinguish the State from any other form of association: a corporate life which draws upon, if it does not exhaust, every conceivable activity of its members; and an authority, a coercive power, a 'sovereignty,' on which it is impossible to set any definite limits. As its ends are far wider, so the powers it wields over its members are far greater, than can be claimed for any more partial, and therefore more limited, organisation.

The first point can hardly be disputed. Not only are all the faculties of the individual — moral, intellectual and physical — thrown into the common stock of the civil community, as they are not and cannot be into that of any more partial and limited association. But the corporate life resulting is something very different from a mere aggregate of the lives of the individuals in question: very different even from the corporate life which shapes itself, or may shape itself, in any of those more partial organisations. Striking its roots deep down in the past, it surrounds its members from birth with traditions, customs and institutions which, imperceptibly but none the less surely, go to mould their character, their will, their whole outlook, in the present. It is in them, but not of them; one with them, and yet apart from them; just as the air which is the breath of their being, or the brute matter out of which, cell by cell, their bones and flesh were first moulded and are still unceasingly renewed. Even when they rise in revolt against the outward forms which the past has given to it, they are still deeply dominated by its spirit. No revolution enables them wholly to escape from it any more than a sudden conversion enables the single soul to escape utterly from its own self.

Thus, to think of the individual as a pure abstraction, combining with others to make the State, but himself existing wholly apart from and independent of the State; still more, to think of him as the born enemy of the State—and the one assumption is of the essence, the other a common exaggeration, of the individualist theory—is to ignore the very first elements of the problem. And any theory based on such assumptions is built on a foundation of sand.

It is of course true that each generation, as it passes, has both the right and the duty to form its own judgement on the heritage it has received from the past and to take its own decisions, as best it may, accordingly. To suppose, as Burke in his weaker moments may be accused of supposing, that such a heritage is by its very nature inviolable and unalterable, that it comes down through the ages 'locked as in a sort of family settlement, grasped as in a kind of mortmain for ever,' is to deny to the present that very creative power which he had rightly conceded to the past.[1] It is to say that growth has been arrested; and that is the certain prelude to decay and death. Nevertheless, the judgement which the present pronounces on the past is itself largely determined—is, to say the least, strongly coloured—by the traditions, by the ideals, of the past. And the more those ideals are consciously before the mind of the present, the sounder in all probability will be its judgements and the wiser its practical decisions.

It has been natural to speak first of the corporate spirit as embodying itself in the traditions and institutions which have come down from the past. But, for the reasons just given, it would be the grossest of delusions to forget that the same spirit, under yet subtler forms, is constantly at work also in the present: shaping the will of the individual at every fresh turn of civic experience, moulding his judgement of each fresh situation that presents itself, rendering it impossible for him to say, in any decision he may be called upon to take, how much of his final verdict is due to the sectional, how much to the public opinion, the 'general will,' which surrounds him as the air he breathes, and how much to his own native intelligence and temperament, to his own individual power of reacting against the influences which flow in upon him from without.

It may, no doubt, be objected that all this holds good not only

[1] *Reflections on the French Revolution: Works*, i. p. 394.

of that corporate body which we call the State, but also, though possibly in a less degree, of any other form of association, wholly voluntary, avowedly partial, though it may be: a Trade Union, a Guild, a Society for the prevention of cruelty to children; that it is even true of a purely commercial or financial association, such as a Bank, or a Limited Liability Company for the manufacture of cotton, or the acquisition and sale of rubber. All such associations, it may be said, have their corporate sentiment, their traditional policy, their collective atmosphere. In all of them the individual is apt to be no more than a cog in a vast network of wheels and bands, for ever turning while he is powerless to control them or to save his individual self from being merged and lost in the general movement of the whole.

And when we come to associations founded for deeper and more spiritual ends, to Churches and religious bodies—above all, when we come to an institution as all-embracing as the medieval Church—then, it may be urged, we are face to face with something whose corporate life, if not altogether so wide-flung, is, by its very nature, still deeper, still more intense than that of a secular body like the State; and all attempts to distinguish in principle between the State and other forms of association must consequently be given up.

In this objection, if indeed it is to be called an objection, there is much that may be admitted at once. And, when rightly considered, it will be found not to weaken, but strengthen, the argument here put forward against Locke. It would be strange indeed if there were no analogy between the simpler, more partial, forms of association and the supreme association which, with certain possible qualifications, embraces them all and stands above them all. But, in all cases except that of religious bodies, the difference is so great as to leave no more than a distant resemblance between the one species and the other: so deep-reaching as to be a difference of kind rather than degree. And the one glaring exception, that of the medieval Church, is, in truth, the exception which proves the rule. For the Church of that day not only performed many of the functions which we now attribute to the State; it also claimed a sovereignty over all Christians—indeed, over all available pagans and infidels also—which rivalled, or rather outshone, the sovereignty of the State. It must be observed also that many of the conflicts which, at first sight, seem to involve an appeal from the sovereignty of the State to that of the Church arise, in truth, rather from an assertion of the rights of the individual conscience, of the generally recognised claim that 'opinion must be left free.' And the two things, though closely connected, are clearly of very different stamps.

So far then as the corporate spirit goes, we are entitled to say that, neither in degree nor in kind, is it, at least under modern conditions, the same thing in any more limited form of association that it is in the State.

The second mark which distinguishes the State from other forms of association is what is universally known as Sovereignty. To define the precise implications of the term is, no doubt, uncommonly difficult. The truth is, they have varied from age to age and from State to State. But every State asserts some kind of coercive control not only over its own members, but also over all those who reside, or even travel, within its borders; and no State could exist without it. The fact is admitted by all. And the only questions for us are: On what principle is it to be justified? and how far does it extend?

It is clearly not to be justified on grounds of consent; and that for several reasons. In the first place, the consent of the criminal or the law-breaker to the punishment that falls upon him is, at best, of that highly modified sort which the law-abiding citizen in his turn yields, or may yield, to the blackmail of a gang of thieves whom, from curiosity or otherwise, he has chosen to visit in their den. In either case the sufferer has acted 'at his risks and perils'; and having happened to lose the game, he must needs pay the penalty. But of consent, in any sense that is not a bitter mockery, there is as little in the one case as in the other. It follows that, on Locke's principle, there is as little of justice either.

Again, in the original formation of all civil communities, it is probable that there was at least as much of compulsion as of spontaneous consent. And that, as Rousseau points out, applies not only to single individuals, but to whole communities at a stroke. 'From the formation of the first community necessarily follows that of all the rest. There is no choice left but either to join it, or league with others to resist it: to follow its example, or be engulfed in it.' This is undeniable, and it is fatal to the whole theory of consent.

Take, lastly, the question of territory. On individual principles, it is clear that the land must be regarded as tied to its owner. It was his, before he joined the community. It must therefore remain his, or his heirs', whether they continue to be members of that community or no. The common sense of all nations, however, has established a practice exactly the reverse. And, as Locke himself ultimately admits, the sovereignty of the State extends to the land, even after the original owner has withdrawn. Indeed, the same admission must manifestly be carried back a stage further yet; and on the first formation of the community, the land of any owner who refuses to cast in his lot with his 'incorporated' neighbours must—by the same rule, the sovereignty of the State—

be handed over, 'by sale, donation, or otherwise,' to one of the contracting members, or to the community at large.

Thus, by the practice of all nations, the land is seen to be tied not to the individual, but the State. Citizenship is the first condition of its tenure; unless that condition be satisfied, there can—at least, in the full sense—be no ownership at all. That is the universal practice; yet, on Locke's original principles, what practice could be more unjust? Once again, and this time by his own admission, the principle of consent breaks down; and breaks down at a point, the matter of property, which he had chosen to place in the forefront of his whole system.

What is it that, in the face of these obvious difficulties, has made men cling so long and so stubbornly to the theory of consent? to that which is, in the last resort, the theory of individual rights? There are two reasons, a speculative and a practical. On the one hand, by tracing the birth of civil society to some prior principle, the supposed rights of the individual in a state of nature, this theory seemed to provide the State at once with an intelligible historical origin and with a firm foundation of Right. On the other hand, with regard to practical consequences, it seemed to provide the individual with an impregnable bulwark against the possible encroachments of the State. On neither ground can the claim be justified; but its failure is far more complete in the former case than in the latter. In the former, not only is the particular answer given delusive, but the question itself opens a thoroughly false scent. In the latter, the solution offered may be no solution; but the problem it strives to solve, the defence of individual freedom, is a very real problem; it is one which no tolerable theory of the State can by any possibility elude.

In the one case we are plunged in a question—partly historical, partly speculative—the answer to which, even if one could be given, would, on neither side, be anything but irrelevant. Even if we knew all about the first beginnings of civil society, and it is little likely that we ever shall, we should still be not one step nearer the knowledge of what it has come to be in the later stages of its growth. And even if we knew all about the rights of the individual in the state of nature, and it is absolutely certain that we never shall, we should still be not one step nearer the knowledge of what either his rights, or those of the community, are in the civil state. And it is with the civil state, not with an imaginary state of nature, that political philosophy is concerned. More than that: it is not from any prior rights—the rights of the individual—but from its own nature and the ends it is there to fulfil, that the rights of the State must be derived. Any other derivation, however seductive in appearance, is in reality off the point.

But with that side of the theory which treats of practical consequences it is a very different matter. Of such vital importance is it to safeguard the freedom of the individual that any theory which offers reasonable promise of the fulfilment of that end will always receive, and deserve to receive, a respectful hearing. And such promise the theory of individual rights, if on other grounds it could be proved a valid theory, does undoubtedly afford. It flies straight at the mark; it is concerned not with side issues of more than doubtful relevance, but with the essential nature of the State. The misfortune is that, on other grounds, it is demonstrably not valid: that the very foundations on which it is built, the historical and speculative assumptions just mentioned, are utterly unsafe.

This may serve to put us upon the track for determining the true foundation, and with it the true nature, of sovereignty. If the rights of sovereignty are not to be derived from any prior rights, from any rights existing before and apart from the creation of the State, then they can only be drawn from the needs of the State itself, from the purposes which, in universal practice, the State exists to accomplish. These are, roughly, to protect its members from any injury which may be offered to them by wrongdoers, and consequently to impose certain restrictions upon individual conduct; to provide the freest possible scope for the development of all their faculties, moral, intellectual and physical—and this involves further restrictions upon individual negligence or recalcitrance; to furnish protection against external enemies and facilities for industry and trade at home and for commerce with foreign lands; and lastly, to exercise a general supervision—the bounds of which it is difficult, or rather impossible, to specify in advance—over the whole of their dealings both with each other and with the world outside.

In all these things the one guide of the governing authorities, whether for action or forbearance from action, must be the public welfare. That is the sole, but sufficient, justification for any decision they may take. And if it be asked what is the speculative ground for conceding so indefinite an authority to the State, the answer is that nothing less than this will suffice to cover the infinite diversity of the ends which the State is there to fulfil. The members of the State have thrown their whole nature, the whole sum of their faculties and energies, into the common service. The State must reserve to itself the ultimate power of controlling them all: the eventual right of preventing individual passion, or individual interest, from running violently counter to the welfare of the whole body. When and where it should actively assert that right, is a matter to be decided purely by expediency. The essential thing is that the right should be acknowledged.

To this principle, however, one crucial qualification must be added. In any conflict, or apparent conflict, between the spiritual and material interests of the community, the preference must without hesitation be given to the former; and this test must be applied as rigorously to those decisions which affect foreign nations as to those which concern only the community itself. In other words, the sovereignty of the State is in all matters, foreign as well as domestic, limited by the moral law: by respect for the duties which one man owes to another within the borders of the same community, which one community owes to another throughout the world.

It is because States in the past have too often flagrantly overridden this limitation that the very principle of sovereignty has fallen into suspicion with many men who would otherwise have accepted it. And that suspicion has been still further deepened by the shameless theories of certain philosophers — Hobbes, for instance, at the beginning of our period, Fichte and Hegel at the close—who have treated the sovereignty of the State, particularly in its relations with other States, as something 'absolute' and uncontrollable, bound by no law, human or divine. The consequences are before us, in characters of fire and blood; and they have justly aroused the scorn and hatred of the whole world. No theory which does not bar the door against such abominations deserves to be considered for a moment. On the other hand, no theory which does not, in some form or other, admit the sovereignty of the State can claim either to square with the facts, as experience and history present them to us, or to block the road against the tyranny of the individual. The qualifications here urged—the limitation of sovereignty not by a system of checks and counterchecks, which in any case can have no application to foreign policy, not by the assertion of certain rights inherent in the individual, however helpful such a conception may be as a rough-and-ready rule of practice, but by the law of justice and humanity as understood by the best thought of each generation —these provide the necessary safeguard. With these restrictions, the principle of sovereignty is robbed of the sting which otherwise lurks in it. Without them, it inevitably becomes the instrument of tyranny and aggression.

But, if the foregoing plea is sound, it follows that Locke's theory, which takes account of none of these things, is, at best, utterly insufficient. To him, the State, so far from being a corporate body with a distinct life of its own, is a mere aggregate of individuals, who agree to act together for certain specified and limited purposes, but reserve their primitive freedom in all other matters whatsoever. The State therefore is, at the most, no more than a Limited Liability Company; the real sovereignty resides in the individual. Upon this individual sovereignty, it is true, he seems to place one sweeping restriction: the binding force of the 'original compact,' from which, when a man has once adhered to it, he is morally powerless to withdraw. This however, upon reflection, is seen to be a mere phantom: a restriction totally inconsistent with that individual 'consent,' that inalienable freedom of action, which Locke again and again asserts to be the corner-stone of his whole theory. With that restriction removed, as it manifestly must be removed, the individual is as free to withdraw from the commonwealth at any moment, as he was to join it in the first instance. And as other individuals enjoy the same freedom, there is nothing to prevent the State from breaking up into as many petty Statelings as the caprice of the moment may suggest. There is no true cohesion, still less any organic unity in the whole body. The only sovereign power accordingly is the will, the passing fancy, of the individual.

And what are the consequences of this to the life and activities of the State? The first, and most fatal, of them is that the life of the State is emptied of all moral content, the will of the State stripped of all moral purpose. The whole moral life of the community, if indeed it can be called a community, is centred in the individual. The State is jealously warned off from trespassing upon the rights of the individual conscience. The one tangible function left to it is the purely negative one of protecting the life and property of its members: of preventing them from cutting each other's purses or flying at each other's throats. How they spend their lives, how they employ their property, so long as they abstain from open violence towards each other, is a matter of profound indifference to the State. Let but the bare forms of justice be observed, let but the 'equality of all before the Law' be technically maintained: and the State has no right, even if it had the wish, to enquire further. All else must be left to the individual conscience: to the sacred right of the individual to do what he will with his own.

It matters nothing that this ends, as any one might have foreseen that it would end, in the virtual enslavement of the weak to the strong, of the poor to the rich. The State has done its duty. It has upheld the equality of all before the Law. It has abstained from any violation of the sacred rights of Property. It has maintained the sovereignty of the individual conscience. And if anything goes wrong, it is the individual conscience, not the State, that must bear the blame. We have only to recall the state of things symbolised by the Enclosure Acts and the Industrial System as it was from the introduction of steam power to the passing of the Factory Laws, and indeed much later, if we wish to realise to ourselves how such a principle, when pushed to its logical consequences, inevitably works out in practice. And if the same results did not follow, or did not follow with the same virulence in other countries, that is because the individualist theory had nowhere struck roots so deep as it had in Britain. Had Locke lived to see his country as it was at the close of the eighteenth and during the first half of the nineteenth century, he would have been the first to renounce the theory which was used, and fairly used, to justify such iniquities and which for more than a century after his death was, in this country at any rate, regarded as the last word of political wisdom.

In things more distinctively intellectual it is precisely the same story. Not a word is said in *Civil Government* about the education of the young; not a word about those foundations for the furtherance of science, art and letters which from time immemorial have been created and upheld by all civilised States. More than that: the right of the State to concern itself with such objects seems to be explicitly barred out by what may fairly be called Locke's articles of association. None of these things can by any possibility be brought under the 'life, health, liberty or property' of the individual. It cannot even be argued that he intended to include them under the one remaining article: that of 'rights.' His very silence on the point is enough to drive us to that unwelcome conclusion. His relentless insistence on the rights of Property affords more positive evidence to the same purpose. It is quite certain that no State can pursue such ends without making great and constantly increasing additions to its taxation. It is equally certain that the burden of this will fall upon the comparatively well-to-do, who, from the nature of a 'capitalist society,' necessarily form a minority of the population, though a minority strongly entrenched in political power and influence. Then these people—we have seen it in our own country—will loudly complain that they are being fleeced for the benefit of those who have no claim upon their purses, and for ends with which they have no sympathy whatever: ends, moreover, which the State has no right whatever to pursue. And, on individualist principles, there is no answer to their lamentations. Once again, we may be sure that Locke himself would have been the first to condemn the consequences which these men draw from the principles of *Civil Government*. But once again, he would be unable to prove that, the principles once granted, these consequences do not follow.

There remains the question of war. And here we are met by a difficulty on the very threshold. At the moment when men 'incorporate themselves' out of the state of nature into the civil state, it is hardly conceivable that they should contemplate the possibility of war, under any form whatever. Without States, there can be no war; and until they are taught better by experience, how can men—above all, the peaceable beings of Locke's fantasy—foresee the rivalries, the disputes, the wars and tumults which, as history tells us, the State almost inevitably brings with it? And if they did not foresee this and provide for it, how can so portentous an innovation be subsequently smuggled into the articles of association? And if these doubts be well founded, it would seem that war as such, war under any shape or form, is impossible on the principles of *Civil Government.*

But, even if this objection were put aside, there remain others which no ingenuity can dispute. War is of many kinds; and it is impossible to avoid the question: Which of these, if any, is permissible on the principles of *Civil Government*? Clearly, not offensive: not war undertaken for the sake of conquest or national aggrandisement. That—on Locke's principles, or indeed on any principles which, in our day, deserve a hearing—is manifestly barred out.

Even of defensive war, however, there are at least two clearly distinguishable types. There is the war which is defensive, pure and simple: the war waged by men in defence of bare life and personal liberty. And there is the war which is accepted in defence of some national interest, real or imaginary; or in support of that very intangible, yet utterly indispensable ideal: national honour. A moment's reflection will show that, for the last two centuries, the former type has been almost unknown. Five years ago, who would not have asserted that, in our day, it was impossible and inconceivable? And if, since then, the horrors of savage warfare have been let loose on Europe, at least the crime has called forth the execration of mankind; and it is the duty of the world to insure and reinsure itself—there are wise, as well as foolish, ways of doing this—against the possibility of its renewal.

On Locke's theory, on any theory, a defensive war of this type—a war in which the individual is, in the strictest sense, fighting for his 'hearth and home'—is beyond question to be justified. And it is fortunately a war of which we may now hope to have seen the last. But what of the other main type of defensive war, the most familiar of all wars—the war of national interest, of national honour, of national as opposed to individual defence?

It is more than doubtful whether, on the individualist principles that lie at the root of Locke's theory, a war which falls under any of these descriptions could ever be legitimate. All alike involve a conception of the nation, as a corporate body, which is wholly foreign to such principles. In all alike, the State, which to the individualist exists merely as a means to a given end, the security of the individual, has become an end in itself: an end to be realised only with certain loss to the property and often, indeed almost always, with certain risk to the life of the individual. Under these conditions, the individual may fairly ask himself: What interest of mine is it to prevent a certain strip of outlying territory—say Alsace or Ireland—from passing under the rule of the enemy? How is my honour concerned in saving my neighbour's land—say France or Belgium—from being overrun and his coal-fields or industrial districts from being annexed by an ambitious—if you will, a grasping—Power upon his borders? And to such a question no satisfactory answer can be given.

But what is to be said when the question is of defending not an outlying frontier, but the very core of the national territory? of preserving the very existence of the State, as an independent and sovereign body? To Locke himself, as we have seen, the bare question would have seemed sacrilege. But on his own principles it is almost certain that he would have been wrong. On those principles the one test is: Will the individual enjoy more, or will he enjoy less, of personal liberty under the foreign, than under the native, rule? If, on a balance of probabilities, it seems likely that he will enjoy more—even if it seems likely that he will enjoy as much—then there is no reason why he should resist the foreign invader. National feeling, love of country, devotion to the State of which he is a member can have no place in his scheme of life. They belong to an order of things wholly foreign to his way of thought. To foist them upon him, to expect him to be moved by them, to make sacrifices for them, is a pure impertinence. It is to credit him with ideals, feelings, aspirations to which he is an utter stranger. Once more, it is to bring back at the end of the argument a whole world of ideas and motives which, however little he may have been aware of it, Locke had effectively barred out at the beginning. It is quite true that they are ideas and motives without which no State has ever existed: without which no State worthy of the name could ever—even for purposes of peace, much more for those of war—hold together for a single moment. That, however, is no proof that Locke is entitled to the use of them. It may only prove, it does only prove, that his State—a State based on the sovereignty of the individual—has no place in the world of realities. And what criticism could be more damaging than this?

Two examples will serve to clinch the argument: Spain and Belgium. When Napoleon overthrew the old monarchy of Spain and imposed a new Government framed on the French model, the material interests of the country stood to benefit by the change. All the ends for which, according to *Civil Government*, the State exists were likely to be better met under the rule of King Joachim or King Joseph than under that of Charles IV. or Ferdinand VII.

The subsequent exploits of the 'restored' Ferdinand are enough to set this beyond doubt. On Locke's principles therefore, on the pure gospel of individualism, no Spaniard ought to have shown a moment's hesitation. On the one hand, decadence, corruption and superstition; on the other, a settled order, the Code Napoléon, an administration conducted according to the newest lights: on the one hand, certain loss of property and probable loss of life; on the other, peace, security and the 'road open to talent': this was the balance of the account; these were the respective fruits of resistance and submission. How could there be any doubt? To the Spaniard there was none. In an instant he had made his choice; and, if judged by Locke's tests, he had made it ridiculously wrong. Yet the whole world is now at one in praising his decision.

Take again the case of Belgium. When she was invited to waive her neutrality in favour of Germany, it was no question of national interest, it was nothing more than a point of national honour, that she was called upon to judge. The arguments for submission were still stronger, the arguments against it were incomparably weaker than in the case of Spain a century before. Once again, she ought not to have hesitated for a moment. Once again, she did not hesitate. She chose without flinching the course for which on individualist principles, the principles of *Civil Government*, there was not a word to be said. Yet once again, the whole world flamed out in admiration of her loyalty. Her very tempter, for sheer shame, could not forbear from stammering that she was right.

The upshot of all this is that the only war, if war it can be called, admissible on Locke's system is the war *pro aris et focis*: the war waged by the individual against a savage invader in defence of bare life and personal liberty. All other forms of war demand the sacrifice of individual life and individual property to the welfare of the State. And that is a demand which no State framed on Locke's principles has the right to make; and which, if made, no individual in his senses would dream for a moment of accepting.

Thus, by reducing the State to a mere aggregate of individuals, Locke not only forbids it to take any care for the moral and spiritual welfare of its members. He even disallows the sacrifices without which the State is unable to protect itself against the armies of a foreign conqueror, without which its independence, its very existence as a separate and sovereign body, is impossible.

And what is the effect of this upon the life and conduct of the individual? How does the nakedness of his political outlook react upon his inner life, intellectual and moral? Let us grant, for the sake of argument, that the State, the organised life of the community, has had nothing to do with the formation of his moral standard. Let us grant that the individual brought with him into the civil state a full-fledged moral code, the 'law of nature'; that with this code the State, from first to last, has nothing to do but to respect it; and that, apart from the mere repression of fraud or violence, the only way to respect it is to leave both its maintenance and its interpretation to the sole discretion, and the sole conscience, of the individual. It is a large concession; but, large though it is, not large enough to cover the needs—not even the barest and most crying needs—of Locke and the individualists. Even with this start, they will still be unable to keep pace with the calls which the very most stinted ideal of the State is bound to make on them. This can easily be made plain.

The first result of demoralising the State is to demoralise the individual also. When the individual sees the State deliberately renouncing all thought for the welfare of its members, when he sees the ministers of the Law content to observe the mere outward forms of justice, while they grossly violate its spirit, what wonder that he should insensibly accustom himself to apply the same standard to his own personal dealings? that, when the State persistently refuses to level up the Law of the land to the 'law of nature,' he for his part should begin to level down the law of nature, the 'law written in his own heart and conscience,' to the Law of the land? In theory, the standard set up by the State, the standard of the Law Courts, may be no more than the *minimum* of social justice; in practice, it inevitably tends to become the *maximum*. The rank and file of the community are content if they do not sink below it. It is only the few who strive to rise above it.

It may be allowed at once that these consequences do not follow in the purely private relations of life: nor in the family, nor in the dealings of friend with friend. The reason is that this is the region strictly of the individual and is therefore little, if at all, affected by the standards which prevail in the wider world of economic, or purely civic, relations. But, directly we pass from the narrower to the wider circle, who will deny that under a full-blown individualism, or as near an approach to it as the happy inconsistency of human nature has ever been able to tolerate, such consequences have always tended to result? Who will deny that, in the hey-day of the individualist triumph, the employed was habitually treated as a mere chattel by his employer? that the bond between them was on principle reduced to a pure 'cash nexus,' from which all moral, all human considerations were relentlessly ruled out?

There may be a touch of exaggeration in the indictment of *Past and Present* and *Latter Day Pamphlets*. But when due allowance, and more, has been made for this, it remains true that the condition of England at that time was a scandal of which, even at this day, it is impossible to think without shame and indignation. And let it not be forgotten that this scandal was the direct fruit of an individualist theory, brutally conceived and shamelessly defended: a theory which, in the teeth of its manifest consequences, was upheld through thick and thin by economists and politicians and which, in the hands of the employers responsible for its working—there were happily not a few exceptions—became a mere cloak for the grossest selfishness and cruelty. Once more, it is impossible to banish morality from the life of the State without banishing it—and that, in some of the most vital matters—from the life of the individual also.

There are two tests by which any political theory—or indeed, any moral theory either—must stand or fall. The first, and the less important, is its inherent consistency. The second is the general tendency of its practical consequences: the preponderant effect, for good or for evil, that it is likely to have upon the life of any community, upon any party or group of men, that may adopt it. Each of these tests is fatal to the theory of Locke. It is not consistent with itself: for it can only be made plausible by the tacit acceptance of certain corporate instincts, of certain immemorial practices, which are wholly incompatible with its initial assumptions. Its practical consequences are, in the main, disastrous. It reduces the State to a mere aggregate of individuals, without cohesion and without any warrant of endurance. It robs the State of all sovereignty; and, with this, of all power to provide for the moral and intellectual welfare of its members within, or even for its own protection against any enemy from without. Lastly, by lowering the moral standard of the State, it inevitably tends—at least in regard to all economic and civic relations—to lower the moral standard of the individual also.

As a theory, therefore, the scheme of Locke and the individualists must unhesitatingly be rejected. So far from embracing all the elements which go to make the life of the State—and that is the least we can demand of any adequate theory—it leaves out precisely those which are most distinctive and most vital. So far from widening the civic interests of the individual, it contracts them beyond measure.

Nevertheless, to see nothing but evil in the individualist system—above all, as expounded in *Civil Government*—would be both idle and unjust. Taken at the worst, the individualist theory does at least lay hold of what is and must always remain one of the two chief elements in the life of the State: the element of individual will, energy and initiative. And thanks to its very one-sidedness, it does so with incomparable force. What is more, at the time when Locke wrote, in the lassitude that followed the Reformation and the Puritan Revolution, this was perhaps the element which was in most danger of going under: the element therefore which, for the welfare of Europe, there was most need to foster and sustain.

At the end of the seventeenth century, the two torch-bearers of Europe — politically speaking, the only two countries which counted beyond their own borders—were France and England. In the one, absolute monarchy was triumphant; in the other, it had twice bid for the mastery and twice—the first time after a desperate struggle — been defeated by armed force alone. The second attempt, as is well known, gave the occasion for Locke's treatise; and scorning mere palliatives, such as the 'recovery of the ancient liberties of England,' he boldly assails the evil at its root. The only alternative to despotic government, he urges in effect, is self-government: the only antidote to the sovereignty of the monarch is the sovereignty of the people. And to him, as we have seen, the sovereignty of the people—a term which he never uses[1]—means the sovereignty of the individual. The rights of Society are, in fact, merely the rights of the individuals who compose it. And it is only by preserving those rights intact that Society can be made endurable: that it can be saved from hardening into the most intolerable tyranny. Stripped of all accretions, all concessions to established fact, that is the principle which lies at the root of *Civil Government*. And whatever the dangers which lurk behind it, we must at least admit that it is a principle perfectly clear-cut and universally intelligible: a principle, moreover, which by its bold appeal to individual freedom and individual enterprise did in fact give an impulse to political self-reliance, to industrial—indirectly, even to intellectual and imaginative—activity for which Europe would otherwise have looked in vain. Hence the astonishing influence which it wielded both upon thinkers and upon practical reformers, alike in France, England and America, for at least a century after its publication.

In England, for the greater part of that century, its influence was rather negative than positive. It went rather to restrain the community from interfering with what were regarded as individual rights and interests than to give the State a new form, or to pour new life into the old one. That was because the old forms, with all their faults, were not immoderately oppressive: because the nation at large still believed—more firmly, in fact, than it had any right to believe—in their efficacy and vitality. In France, however, for the converse reason, the effect was exactly the reverse. There, naturally enough, the theory of Locke became the gospel of the opposition; and the institutions which he had heedlessly associated

[1] It was Jurieu who first brought the phrase, if not into use, at least into currency.

with it—the mixed monarchy, the elaborate checks and counter-checks, of England—became the ideal which many, though by no means all, of them desired to transplant bodily into their own country. It is enough to recall Montesquieu's enthusiasm for the constitution of England. It is enough to remember that even Rousseau, at the very moment when he was overthrowing the doctrine of *Civil Government*, conceived himself to be working 'exactly upon the principles of Locke': a belief which seems still to be shared by the majority of his English readers.

Thus the theory of Locke, in this country the bulwark of existing institutions, was a revolutionary force in France. For the institutions, which the one country was rapidly outgrowing, would have been a boon almost past praying for to the other. The individualism, which to the one nation was a cloak for the selfish tyranny of the rich, was the strongest lever against that tyranny in the other. But go on to the end of the century, and the positions are reversed. When the revolutionary spirit was at last let loose, when the old order, even the monarchy itself, was overthrown in France, then the insufficiency of individualism for constructive purposes, or even for the elementary duty of national defence, stood revealed to all who had eyes to see. And it was not in the name of Locke, but in the name of Rousseau—not on the strength of individual rights, but by the energy of a 'general will' acting, and often acting ruthlessly enough, with a single eye to the 'public welfare'—that the Revolution was carried through. The reaction upon the civic life of this country was what might have been expected. The Government took fright, not altogether without reason, at the excesses committed across the Channel. Monstrously repressive measures were put in force against the friends of the Revolution on this side of the water. And the weapon with which these measures were resisted was a sterner appeal to individual rights, a more passionate rally to the individualist standard, than this country had ever seen. In the heat of the conflict, the true meaning of Locke's argument was at last flashed upon men's minds. After a full century of misinterpretation, the author at length came by his own. And it was in *Civil Government*, as expounded to them by their leaders, that the revolutionaries of Sheffield found the authentic gospel of their aspirations and the surest warrant for their claims.

The revolutionaries of 1792 were the direct ancestors of the radical Reformers and the Chartists. Until the rise of the Trades Unions, the principles for which they strove were the chief force that made for political progress in this country. But, powerful to destroy, they were of no might to build again. And when the need of doing so was at last recognised, then the theory of Locke, the creed of the individualist, was of necessity thrown aside. A sounder conception of the State—a conception which found room not only for the rights, but also for the duties, of man—inevitably and justly took its place. And it was none too soon. In its application to the sphere of industry, to the rights of labour, to the relation between labour and capital, individualism had done more harm in a century than could be undone in generations. Locke and the economists were responsible for the mischief. It was reserved for teachers of a wider and more humane vision—for Rousseau and the Saint-Simonians, for Carlyle and Ruskin—to repair it.

CHAPTER V

THE ECLIPSE OF CONTRACT: VICO, MONTESQUIEU

THE theories of Hobbes and Locke were essentially abstract. They bore little relation to the political life of man, as it has shaped itself in actual fact. In particular, they had opened a false scent by reducing their problem, so far as human ingenuity could do so, to a question of origins; by assuming for the State an origin, Contract, for which, apart from all other objections, there is no historical basis; by their persistence in viewing the whole subsequent history of the State in the light of this imaginary beginning. The inevitable effect of this had been to spread an air of unreality, of fiction, over the whole of their argument.

From that atmosphere of fiction Spinoza, no doubt, made desperate efforts to escape. Even in his earlier treatise, the Contract plays no dominant part; from his later treatise, except by mere implication, it vanishes altogether. What fills the stage in both writings is the doctrine of expediency; and, with the doctrine of expediency, the world of Contract and fiction promises at last to fade into the background; the world of actual needs and interests seems about to spread itself before us. The promise, however, is very imperfectly fulfilled. For Spinoza also is still haunted by the ghost of that Contract which, with so much else, he had inherited from Hobbes. And the very idea of expediency is so handled by him—so rigidly conceived, so austerely interpreted—as to sacrifice more than half of the harvest which it might have been expected to yield. It ought to have peopled his world with men of flesh and blood. The beings it actually sets before us are little more than skeletons of men: calculating to a nicety, but as little like the men of experience and history as anything in human shape can readily be. Thus, with all his efforts, Spinoza also was unable to win his way into the world of realities. He too, though in a less degree than Hobbes or Locke, was still a victim to the abstractions with which an imperfect analysis is always ready to punish those who make it.

For these abstractions there was no remedy save in a more

accurate analysis. And that analysis might be one either of ideas or of facts. It might take the form of sifting out, more completely than had yet been done, all the elements which constitute the life of the State, as it is in actual experience and to thought. Or it might take the form of retracing the process by which the State has gradually been built up through the successive stages recorded in history and tradition. The former method—the more philosophical and, for that reason, the more fundamental—does not concern us for the moment. It was the task reserved for the brooding genius of Rousseau. The latter, the way of historical analysis, is the subject of the present chapter. It was the discovery, or rather the creation, of the age immediately preceding Rousseau; and, as we shall see in the sequel, it had the deepest influence upon certain aspects of his work. Of the two methods it was the less searching; but it was also the more novel; and, so far as the needs of the moment were concerned, it was likely to be the more effective and the more fruitful. Indeed, without a fuller presentment of the outward facts, a stricter analysis of the ideas which lie behind them was almost an impossibility. If worthily handled, the new method could hardly fail to bring men back to the concrete realities which had been banished by the philosophers, to redeem political theory from the barrenness which threatened it, to get rid of some at least of the errors in which a too abstract method had entangled it.

To have seen this and acted upon it was the immense service rendered by the two men whose work is now to be considered: both of them jurists by bent and training; both of them pioneers in the philosophy of history; both of them furnished with vast stores of historical learning, but of learning resolutely harnessed to the service of ideas. These are Vico and Montesquieu: the one an obscure Italian; the other a Frenchman, sole rival in his generation to the most brilliant of all Frenchmen, Voltaire. The work of both, all that is crucial in it, belongs to the second quarter of the eighteenth century: the *Scienza nuova* being first published in 1725, *Esprit des lois* in 1748.

The debt which political theory owes to these two men, and not least on those sides of it which touch most closely upon political practice, is hardly to be overrated. If we now believe that to find the origin of the State in Contract—that is, in the spontaneous consent of isolated individuals—is a historical impossibility, and therefore that the question of origins must be held strictly apart from that of Right; if we now hold that the birth of the State was due not to conscious—least of all, to material—self-interest, but to the blind working of a whole network of moral and religious beliefs—beliefs not necessarily, nor perhaps often, shared by the whole body, but rather, in many cases at least, imposed on the many by the few who, for one reason or another, were recognised as their 'betters'; if—passing to more recent times—we have come to see that the life of the community—political, social, moral, religious and intellectual—is not a matter of water-tight compartments, each with its own independent and separate existence, but rather an organic whole, no one activity of which can be altered without profoundly modifying the rest; if men have now commonly accepted the twofold inference, on the one hand that, as the inner life of the community gradually changes, so its outward forms and institutions must be reshaped accordingly, on the other hand, that unless it reflects some inner change, no outward revolution can by any possibility be either durable or fruitful: if this view of things, essentially concrete and historical, has dethroned the purely abstract conceptions which it has so far been our task to examine, that is largely due to the ideas which Vico and Montesquieu were the first to throw upon the world: to the vein of thought which they opened and which, in one direction after another, has been still further extended, deepened and widened by their successors.

It is with the later phases of the growth of the State that Montesquieu primarily concerns himself; though it must be remembered that he too, like Vico, had made a profound study of Roman history and that one of the most notable sections of his masterpiece, nearly a quarter of the whole book, is devoted to an investigation, perhaps the earliest of its kind, into the laws of the Franks and other 'barbarian' tribes, mainly with a view to explaining the subsequent working of the feudal system in France: a task which, it is significant to notice, exposed him to the facile sarcasms of Voltaire. The sphere of Vico, on the other hand, is primitive history and legend: a 'new science,' which he justly claims to have created; as, incidentally, he was also the founder of comparative mythology, of anthropology and even of what it is now the fashion to call the 'higher criticism' of literature.

Thus, between them, the two writers covered the whole circle of historical enquiry demanded by the needs of their time and necessary to the purpose which, perhaps half unconsciously, they had in view. Both writers—Vico for the earlier period, Montesquieu for the later—joined hands to lay the foundations of the philosophy of history. Both therefore must justly be credited with preparing—if we ought not rather to say, creating—material which has proved of inestimable value to political philosophy: with opening out a new horizon, which has poured an entirely fresh light not only upon the theory, but even upon the practical problems, of the State. Their results in detail may often have been revised, or even overthrown, by subsequent knowledge; but their glory, as pioneers and founders, remains untouched.

(A) Vico

Of the two men, Vico is at once the deeper and the more adventurous. He opened out more vistas; he was more keenly alive to the infinite reach, the inexhaustible implications, of his main theme—the needs, motives and aims of man as revealed in history, and above all in the dawn of history—than his great successor. There is one point, however, and it would be idle to make light of it, in which he is woefully deficient: that is, in power of expression. The thread of his argument may have been perfectly clear to his own mind—the contrary opinion seems to me quite unwarranted—but he was perfectly incapable of making it clear to others. And the fault grew upon him with years. The longer he brooded over his thoughts, the less easy he found it to explain them. He lingered so long over the details that, when the end was reached, he had not succeeded in laying out the argument which they should have illustrated, as a consecutive and intelligible whole.

Thus, of the three forms in which his theory has come down to us—the Latin treatise, *Jus universum*, of 1720–21, and the two successive drafts of the *Scienza nuova* in Italian (1725, 1730)[1]—the Latin version is the least fruitful, but the most intelligible; while, of the two Italian versions, the second is by far the deeper and the more suggestive, but it is also that which is by far the more difficult to follow. Despite the richness of its matter, despite the poetic phrases which condense whole pages of argument as in a flash of lightning, the book remains a jungle: resembling nothing so much as the 'vast forest of the earth' in which he conceives primitive man to have roamed, when he was yet only a step above the beasts, before the first dawn of awe and shame had given him the rude beginnings of a settled home, of family affections and of worship.

It is the common fault of the lonely thinker; and in Vico's

[1] The final edition, published immediately after his death in 1744, is throughout based on that of 1730, but with many additions and omissions, a table of which will be found in Ferrari's edition, *Opere*, vol. v. pp. xxv-xxxv. The edition of 1730, which (as compared with the first draft of 1725) is an entirely new work, was written in feverish haste, between Christmas Day, 1729, and Easter Day, 1730, as the author informs us in his preface (*Opere*, iv. p. 11). For a book of over 500 pages, this must be hard to parallel.

case, it was intensified by the exploring zeal of the antiquarian and the scholar. As each new illustration of his main thesis crowded into his mind, he could not refrain from laying bare its minutest details, from probing into its inmost recesses, from displaying it in every light that learning or ingenuity—often, misplaced learning and perverted ingenuity—could suggest. The result is that the task of the reader is made not lighter, but heavier: that the wood is not to be seen for the trees.

Under these conditions, what wonder if our first impression of the *Scienza nuova* is nothing short of bewildering? what wonder if we are tempted to doubt whether the author had any clear notion of the direction in which his enquiries were tending, any clear insight into the speculative principles which lie behind them? Such doubts have no justification. Further study will convince us that few writers have known better where they were going: that few have realised more exactly where and why they differ from those who have gone before them. And this applies to the speculative ideas which form the foundation of his theory no less than to the historical and critical conclusions to which they guided him. It is with the former that we are mainly concerned. The latter enter only by way of illustration.

What is it, Vico asks, that has made the political philosophy of the moderns—and of the ancients too, with hardly an exception—so barren as speculation and, in its practical consequences, so dangerous and subversive? It is that the method adopted has almost always been not concrete, but abstract; not historical, but dogmatic: a barefaced transference of the ideas and conditions of the present into the utterly alien world, the wholly different conditions of a remote, but still not irrecoverable, past. In such an enquiry, our first need is to throw ourselves into the mind, to take upon ourselves the nature, of man as he was when he first began to have dealings with his fellows [1]: a being, from the nature of the case, untamed, uncivilised, the creature not of intellectual abstractions, but of impulse, passion, imagination; not of cold reason, but of poetry. What the philosophers have done is exactly the reverse. Each of them in turn has striven to impose his own system—

[1] 'Come que' primi uomini, onde poi sursero esse gentili nazioni . . . andarono tratto tratto nelle loro posterità a disimparare la lingua di Adamo; e senza lingua, e non con altre idee che di soddisfare alla fame, alla sete, e al fomento della libidine, giunsero a stordire ogni senso di umanità: così noi, in meditando i principj di questa Scienza, dobbiamo vestire per alquanto, non senza una violentissima forza, una si fatta natura; e in consequenza ridurci in uno stato di una somma ignoranza di tutta l' umana e divina erudizione, come se per questa ricerca non vi fussero mai stati per noi nè Filosofi nè Filologi' (*S.N.* i. 32-3; compare *ib.* pp. 63-4).

abstract, arbitrary, one-sided—upon the flesh and blood of history and reality: to clip down the 'wild nature' of primitive man—so diverse, so 'ferocious,' so incalculable—to the single type which, by a long process of abstraction, he has chosen for his own academical ideal. To one, the moving principle is pleasure; to another, self-mortification; to another, blind force; to another, utility or self-interest. And this principle is asserted to the exclusion of all others; nay, in those remote ages it is assumed to have operated after precisely the same fashion as we have persuaded ourselves that it does in ours. What is more, all these principles are alike in ignoring what is, in fact, the most important principle of all: the impulse of religious awe, which is at once the deepest and most human impulse in the heart of man, and without which there could be no such thing as human society at all. All alike therefore have flouted the most vital elements of man's nature; all alike have trampled the roots of humanity under foot. And this is as true of the Stoics as it is of Epicurus: as true of Spinoza or Grotius as it is of Hobbes or Bayle.[1]

Plato, 'the divine Plato,'[2] had the wisdom to see that a vast complex of motives went to the making of even the simplest forms of human fellowship; and that, among these, the religious impulse—the sense of awe and shame in presence of a higher power—was the most deep-reaching and the strongest. Yet even Plato, at moments, falls into the same error as the rest: reading his own 'divine' philosophy, *sapienza riposta*, into the essentially human and popular creations, *sapienza volgare e poetica*, of Homer; and then, with fatal consistency, adopting for his own ideal commonwealth certain primitive usages, such as the community of wives, which belong to the almost 'bestial' beginnings of man's history and which, if he is ever to raise himself above the beasts, it is the first necessity of man to do away. In both cases the cause of the lapse is that he had failed to measure the vast space which separates the dawn from the full day of history, the deep gulf which parts primitive man from man as he becomes after long ages of civic discipline and reflection: in other words, that he too is liable to fall back into the abstract, dogmatic method, that even his faith in the principle of historical development is wavering and uncertain. It

[1] *S.N.* i. 14-15, 57, 129; compare *S.N.* ii. 48-49, 96, 106, 130, 137, 148, 176, 572-4; and *J.U. Proloquium*, 12; i. 30; ii. 211-21. This, so far as I know, is the one instance in which the first draft of *S.N.* is more explicit than the second.

[2] 'Il bene del gener umano si conserva sopra questo senso universale, che sia la Divinità provedente: ondi forze Platone, che la dimostra, meritò il titolo di *Divino*' (*S.N.* ii. 154).

is to be feared, the critic may add, that even this is too favourable an estimate of Plato's position in this matter.[1]

Yet Plato's lapses, so Vico continues, are as nothing in comparison with those of other theorists: above all, of Epicurus, Spinoza, and their hedonist or utilitarian disciples. The former had at least grasped the necessity of basing society upon religion; the principles of the latter are such—and here Spinoza is especially singled out for rebuke—as to render all civil life, all human fellowship in any form, impossible from the beginning.[2]

There is one point to which Vico returns again and again; and it is a sure proof of his speculative insight that he should have realised its importance. That is the idea of natural law, as expounded by Grotius and Pufendorf: above all, as he might have added but does not add, by Locke. That there is a law of nature, *Diritto natural delle Genti*, is, he holds, absolutely certain. It is, however, a law entirely different from that assumed by the philosophers. Like all laws which apply to living creatures, above all to their spiritual being, it is not stationary, but progressive: a law

[1] See references to preceding paragraph. It may seem strange that Vico does not turn rather to Aristotle, who can hardly be denied to have come nearer to accepting the idea of progress, and who had certainly a firmer grasp both of historical fact and of the historical method than his master Plato. The reason, no doubt, is to be found in his reverence for the essentially religious character of Plato's philosophy, which, from the days of the Renaissance onwards, had nowhere been so clearly recognised as in Italy. It is only fair to say that his references to Aristotle are frequent: *e.g.* *S.N.* ii. 121, 303, 342, 361, 368 (aristocratic oath of eternal hostility to Plebeians); *ib.* 114, 180, 210 (Aristotle's criticism of Plato's theory of language); *ib.* 381, 438 (Aristotle's theory of heroic character); *ib.* 168, 435, 441 (Aristotle's respect for the 'poetic lie' *l' impossibile credibile*); *ib.* 152 (the maxim, *nihil in intellectu quod non prius in sensu*, employed to illustrate Vico's doctrine of *sapienza volgare*). Yet, by way of general verdict, all he can bring himself to say is: 'La vera filosofia, ch' è la nostra Cristiana, dalle più sublimi filosofie, cioè dalla Platonica e *dalla Peripatetica*, *in quanto con la Platonica si conforma*, anco umanamente ci è confermata' (*S.N.* ii. 48).

[2] 'E finalmente Pufendorfio, che l' incomincia con un' ipotesi Epicurea, che pone l' uomo gittato in questo mondo senza niun ajuto e cura di Dio; di che essendone stato ripreso, quantunque con una particolar Dissertazione se ne giustifichi, però senza il primo principio della Provedenza non può affatto aprir bocca a ragionare di diritto, come l' udimmo da Cicerone dirsi ad Attico, il qual era epicureo' (*S.N.* ii. p. 176; compare p. 138). 'Benedetto Spinosa, il quale, perchè Ebreo, non aveva niuna republica, trovò una metafisica da rovinare tutte le republiche del mondo' (*ib.* p. 49; compare, 'Spinosa parla di Republica come d' una società che fusse di mercadanti,' p. 138; compare *S.N.* i. 159-60, 170-1).

varying with the stage of growth reached by a given community or nation, not a law the same always, everywhere and for all. To assume, as Grotius and the rest assume, that primitive man is at once a waif and stray, cast upon the world as a helpless, solitary 'simpleton' and, at the same moment, a being capable of abstracting for himself a 'natural law' valid for all men at all times and under all circumstances, is a sheer contradiction: the being so conjured up, a pure monstrosity. And to those who recognise that such an assumption is the very corner-stone of the systems reared by Locke and others—Hobbes himself not excepted—it will at once be apparent how deadly was the wound inflicted by the counterstroke of Vico. Vico, in his turn, lays his denial of natural law, in the absolute sense, at the foundation of his whole argument. Indeed, this denial was implicit in his very adoption of the historical method; as, conversely, any resort to the historical method would have been impossible without it.[1]

So much for the more speculative, which is also the more critical, side of Vico's theory. Alike in methods and results, it is manifest that he stands at the opposite pole from the writers of his own day and of the century before him. Where they are abstract, he is concrete. Where they deal in fictions, he appeals to history. Where they draw an impassable line between politics and morals, he conceives of man's nature as one organic growth in which politics and morals, reason and imagination, law and poetry, are all inseparably intertwined, all blended in one indissoluble whole.

[1] *S.N.* ii. 131-4. ('Questa [Degnità] stabilisce la differenza . . . del Diritto Natural delle Genti e il Diritto Natural de' Filosofi; perchè . . . i Filosofi il ragionano più perfetto di quello che 'l costuman le Genti; i quali non vennero che da un due mila anni dopo essersi fondate le Genti. Per [queste] differenze non osservate debbon cadere li tre sistemi di Grozio, di Seldeno, di Pufendorfio. Le dottrine debbono cominciare da quando cominciano le materie che trattano, p. 131. Per queste . . . li tre sistemi di Grozio [etc.] mancano nei loro Principj; ch' incominciano dalle Nazioni guardate tra loro nella Società di tutto il Gener Umano: il quale appo tutte le prime nazioni . . . cominciò dal tempo delle Famiglie sotto gli Dei delle Genti dette Maggiori; p. 132. . . . ch' essi tutti e tre errassero di concerto . . .; perc' an creduto che l' Equità Naturale nella sua idea ottima fusse stata intesa dalle Nazioni Gentili fin da' loro primi incominciamenti;' p. 134.) Compare *ib.* 140, 434-5, 469-70, 481-9: also *S.N.* i. 45, 47-8, 216-22; and *J.U.* i. 58-9, 83-8; ii. 239. As for Locke, it seems to me more doubtful whether Vico was acquainted with *Civil Government*. His references are so vague as to be, in my opinion, no more than inferences from the *Essay on the Human Understanding*: see *S.N.* ii. 49; i. 40. It is, I think, significant that in the list of Vico's chief opponents (*J.U.* pp. 12, 30) the name of Locke does not occur.

Finally, where they are materialist and utilitarian, he is defiantly religious and idealist. Here, therefore, if anywhere, we have a new departure. The contrast between him and his predecessors could hardly have been greater.

The same contrast, as was to be expected, is repeated and deepened in the more constructive side of his work. At the first step, no doubt, we might imagine ourselves back in the shadowy world of Grotius and the rest. In the centuries immediately following the Flood, Vico assures us, man roamed—a lawless, friendless, homeless wanderer—through the 'vast forest of the earth': obeying no law but his own will, bound by no tie except that of his own appetites, given up to his own fleeting caprices in the 'bestial community of women,' which served to keep the race from extinction, and for nothing else. It was only after the lapse of long time—one century for the descendants of Shem, two for the more degraded offspring of Ham and Japheth[1]—that the earliest thunderclaps, caused by exhalations from the slowly drying earth, awakened in him the first sense of religious terror, the first feeling of awe and shame in face of a higher power, and drove the more sensitive, who were also the fittest and strongest, members of the race to take refuge, each of them with one woman, the future mother of his lawful family, in the caves of the earth, where he henceforth lived apart, like the giants of Homer, 'giving the law to his own wife and children without heed of others,' and laying the foundation for all the future progress, the slowly advancing civilisation, of mankind.[2]

In the first stage of this process, it is manifest that we are for the moment carried backwards to the 'state of nature,' so dear to Grotius and Pufendorf, or forwards to the primeval forest, the home of unchartered freedom, the vision of which, painted by a passionate hand, was destined thirty years later to shake Europe

[1] *S.N.* ii. 66, 157-8, 399; *S.N.* i. 42. The 'descendants of Shem,' excluding the line of Terah-Abram, which kept the true faith.

[2] *S.N.* ii. 66, 109, 117, 126, 141, 157-61, 163-5, 168, 170, 242-5, 257, 334; *S.N.* i. 45-7, 80, 86, 92; *J.U.* i. 63, ii. 257-61. The classical references are to *Odyssey*, ix. 106-15, 526-36; to Plato, *Laws*, iii. p. 681, and to Aristotle, *Politics*, i. 2. It may be objected that the reference to the Cyclopes is, for Vico's purpose, a two-edged weapon; seeing that Polyphemus has 'no fear or heed of Zeus, nor of the blessed Gods' (*Od.* ix. 272-7). But he has faith in magic, and when Odysseus is about to escape him, he offers fervent prayers to Poseidon, who claims 'to be his father'; and his prayers are heard. What more could be desired? For Vico's explanation of the 'one-eyed' beings, see *S.N.* ii. 289; and for another explanation (justly rejected by Vico, upon reflection), *J.U.* ii. 261.

to its foundations. And this impression is not weakened, but strengthened, by the pathetic efforts of the author to square his fancies with the records of Scripture, to fortify them with touches drawn from the severer sciences. His picture, however, is inspired neither by the fiery zeal of Rousseau, nor by the phlegmatic complacency of the earlier writers. It is marked throughout by loathing and impatience: loathing for the 'bestial community of goods and women,' which he regards as the indelible brand of this lawless condition; impatience to escape from it into something better.

Accordingly, the first step once over, Vico never once looks behind him. With the second step, the age of the 'monastic' Family [1]—which, as he never ceases to remind us, is for man the *true* state of nature [2]—he stands already on the firm ground, if not of history, at least of widespread tradition, or probable inference from history. And with increasing assurance, with an ever-deepening reliance upon history, he remains there to the end. Even his first step, with all its vagaries, with all its parade of false science, must not be reckoned too harshly against him. Once raise the question of origins, and these are penalties which are hardly to be avoided. That which exists before the State must, by the very force of the term, be something which is not the State; and the temptation to go back behind the Tribe, behind the Family, to the irreducible unit, the naked, isolated individual—conceived as the absolute antithesis, the direct negative, of the State—is almost irresistible. To that temptation all the philosophers, with scarcely an exception, had given way. It is easy to blame Vico too heavily for following in their wake.

The significant thing is that this is the one concession he makes to the prevailing fashion; [3] and that, having made it, he hurries on with unconcealed satisfaction to the next stage: the first stage in the long 'education of the human race,' the birth of the religious instinct and, with it, of the Family. Here it is evident that he parts company with the system-mongers; and the parting is for good. From this moment the individual—the naked, abstract individual—of Locke and the others vanishes for ever from his canvas. Henceforth it is with the 'social, civil relations' of man—

[1] *S.N.* i. 47-8.

[2] *S.N.* ii. 103, 277, 367 ('lo stato di Natura, o sia quello delle Famiglie'), 335, 337.

[3] Vico repeatedly insists on his agreement with his predecessors in this particular: *e.g.* 'Or cominciando questa scienza—in ciò di concerto con Grozio e con Pufendorfio—dall' uomo solo, l' idee della Divinità non si può affatto intendere essersi destate . . . che con quest' ordine naturale'—*i.e.* that specified in the text (*S.N.* i. 49).

with man as a member of the Family, the Order, the State—and with these alone, that we have to deal. Even these terms, in fact, are too abstract for his purpose. For it is not with the generalised ideas of these things, but with the things themselves as presented in the concrete facts of Greek legend and, still more, of Roman history—in other words, with a highly particularised form of them—that he is concerned. That is the true originality of Vico: that is the barrier which parts him from the writers of the century before him.

What, then, is the primitive Family, the 'natural' unit, as conceived by Vico? and what are the further stages in the growth of mankind to which it eventually leads? As the Family is founded upon religion, by religion it is maintained.[1] The first care of the new-born household is to preserve the favour of the Gods who gave it life; and this is to be done only by obeying their will, as revealed in auspices and other forms of divination. Thus, from the first dawn of his new existence, the Gods are the ever-present guide of man in the daily concerns of life; their will, the law by which every action of moment is sanctioned and controlled. This applies to the ceremonies with which, in this new phase of his being, man begins to surround the chief events of his personal history: his marriage, the birth of his children, the burial of his dead. It applies also, and no less, to the recurring acts of his outward existence: in particular, to the rearing of his flocks and herds, to the yearly sowing and reaping of his crops. These are things in themselves probably altogether new to his experience; certainly so, in the sense that now for the first time is there anything that he can properly call his.[2]

Still deeper is the working of religion upon the inner life of the Family itself. From the first the head of the household is regarded as the sole channel of communication between Heaven and earth, between the Gods and man: in other words, as the sole representative of the Gods to his whole household. It is he who offers sacrifice to win their favour; he who takes the auguries which declare their will; he who determines what is right and what is wrong; he who rewards the good and punishes the wrongdoer. How unlimited his power must have been is proved by its survival in the *patria potestas* of the Romans; by the legend of Theseus and Hippolytus among the Greeks; by the story of Reuben and

[1] 'I Padri di famiglia apparecchiarono la sussistenza alle loro Famiglie eroiche con la Religione, la qual esse con la Religione si dovessero conservare' (*S.N.* ii. 277).

[2] *S.N.* ii. 108, 118, 137-40, 160-1, 166-9, 172-3, 259-61; *S.N.* i. 47-51, 80, 91-2; *J.U.* ii. 259-61, 302.

his sons, of Judah and Tamar, among the Hebrews.[1] Indeed, as record and legend conspire to show, the father was entitled to slay his children not merely when they had done what was recognised as wrong, but also when, for some reason the grounds of which are now half lost to us, he held their death a necessity to appease the wrath of Heaven. Hence the sacrifice of Isaac and of Jephthah's daughter in the records of the Old Testament; of Iphigenia, in Greek legend. Hence, again, the barbarity of those Eastern races who 'made their sons and daughters pass through the fire to Moloch': *Et Poinei solitei sos sacrificare puellos*, in the indignant words of Ennius.[2]

This, then, was the turning-point in man's destiny. The one act of planting himself in a fixed home carried with it a long line of further changes: changes which, even from the first, were enough to revolutionise his whole cast of thought, his whole bearing towards life. His sense of religion, of dependence upon a higher power, which lay at the root of all, was gradually deepened. His sense of Right in its double meaning of right as opposed to wrong, of his own rights or claims against the rights or claims of others, was slowly awakened. And this, in its turn, went hand in hand with a new-born sense of ownership, of property, of that which is not another's but his own, which has left what is perhaps the deepest of all marks upon the outward history of the race. In a word, religion, property, the moral sense, the sense of Right—none of these things would have been possible, had not man exchanged his wandering, solitary existence for the Family and the home. Every one of these things was contained—the first both as cause and effect, the rest as a linked chain of effects—in that one momentous act. To Vico, indeed, the foundation of the Family is the real escape from chaos; and the very idea of chaos was, in its origin, no physical conception, but a symbol of the 'confusion of human seeds,' of the 'bestial communism of women,' from which mankind was delivered once and for all by the Family and by that ideal of order, Right and religion which the Family brought with it.[3]

All these things, however—the whole argument of Vico is framed to prove it—were not so much diffused throughout the whole household as centred rigorously in its chief. Thanks to the 'natural right' of those days, he kept the rule jealously in his own hands. His word was law; he celebrated the sacrifices; he was sole arbiter of right and wrong. In short, within his own narrow

[1] Gen. xlii. 37, xxxviii. 24.

[2] *S.N.* ii. 118, 137, 251, 256-7, 297-8; *S.N.* i. 45, 48-51, 58-9, 84-91; *J.U.* i. 60-61; ii. 338-42.

[3] See *S.N.* i. 78, ii. 369.

boundaries he was at once prophet, priest and king.[1] Thus there is a certain sense—a sense, moreover, of the deepest significance—in which the primitive Family must be described not as a monarchy, but a theocracy: or rather, as at once a monarchy and a theocracy; and it was the one just because it was the other.[2]

How long this 'cyclopean' existence may have lasted there is no need to enquire; the variations from region to region were probably considerable. Nor, whatever the poets may have fabled, can it be supposed for a moment that this, the 'state of nature,' was in any sense a state of stagnation. On the contrary, both within and without, there was everything not only to confirm the advance already made, but to carry it yet further. On the one hand, as experience widened and fresh needs arose, the sense of dependence upon a higher power, so far from weakening, must have grown constantly stronger. We may even say that the Age of the Family, like the Heroic Age which followed, falls into a number of 'minute epochs,' each marked by the recognition of a new God, whose function it was to furnish his worshippers with the aid most needed at the moment. Thus to Jupiter, the God of the sky whose thunder had awed the primitive wanderers into their first attempt at settled life, were successively added Juno the Goddess of lawful marriage, Apollo and Diana the deities of the lawful family, Vesta the Goddess who kindled and kept alive the family hearth, and Ceres, possibly also Cybele and Saturn, the divinities who brought the seeds to birth and ripened the fruits of the earth against the harvest. The names of the Roman Gods are taken for convenience: the beings they stand for, the human needs they answer to, were the same everywhere and for all.[3]

On the other hand, there were constant dangers to be guarded against from without. The 'lawless vagrants,' as will appear directly, were ceaselessly active in assailing the homesteads of the settlers and burning, or carrying off, their crops. And whatever

[1] 'Et sic natura factum ut una res principio fuerit Sapientia—*i.e.* Scientia divinationis—Sacerdotium et Regnum' (*J.U.* ii. p. 302).

[2] *S.N.* ii. 20, 39, 117-18, 137-43, 234-6, 243-5, 254-71, 275-6; *S.N.* i. 23, 47-51, 57-9, 82-91, 245, 255; *J.U.* ii. 249, 302, 326-31, 362.

[3] *S.N.* ii. 241-4, 246-9, 261-5, 274-5. All the twelve *Di majorum gentium* are traced back by Vico in the first instance to the age of the Family, though he seems to regard their functions as having been more clearly defined, and their worship to have had a kind of second birth, after the foundation of the State; the most significant only are mentioned in the text. 'I dodici dei maggiori incominciando da Giove, dentro questa scorsa a' loro tempi fantasticati, si pongano per dodici minute Epoche, da ridurvi a certezza de' tempi la storia poetica' (*ib.* p. 396). Compare *S.N.* i. 169-70; *J.U.* ii. 325-414 (especially pp. 338-9, 389).

the cruelties of this warfare, it served at least to discipline the settlers, to foster their courage, to train their powers of endurance and, what was no less important, to deepen their sense of superiority, to make them cling more resolutely than ever to the way of life, the faith, the customs—to all, in short, which marked them off from their 'impious' assailants.[1]

With each generation, moreover, the numbers of every family, the size of every settlement, inevitably increased; and the increase was further swollen from causes to be mentioned directly. Hence the family insensibly grew into the clan, and the clan into the tribe; and this growth, even if none but natural causes had been at work, must have called out powers of organisation—of direction on the part of the head, of subordination and discipline on that of the tribesmen—for which, in the infancy of the settlement, there had been comparatively little need.[2] And if, as we shall see to have been the case, the Family contained within itself any body of alien members, it is obvious that the call for such organisation must have become infinitely more urgent. The general result of all this was that, before many generations had passed, the face of the land—at least round the springs and watercourses, whither the settlers had now descended from their original fastnesses—was sprinkled with innumerable 'minute republics,' each of them 'sovereign' within its own borders and each of them, so far as its ruling 'order' was concerned, bound together by common customs, by a common ancestry, by the worship of the same Gods.[3]

Such was the progress accomplished during the single period which Vico roughly distinguishes as the Age of the Family, the state of nature: a progress from the 'monastic household,' the solitary man and wife, of the opening stage to the 'tribe,' the ever-widening 'ramifications'[4] of that same household, still further enlarged by various accretions from without, which he sets before us at the close. This is not the State; but it contains the seeds of the State. And little beside time, the steadying, harmonising discipline of time, is needed to give them life and growth.[5]

[1] 'Gli empj dell' infame comunione; i violenti di Obbes; i licenziose violenti di Obbes' (*S.N.* ii. 279; i. 83, 85, 192).

[2] *S.N.* ii. 263; i. 48.

[3] *S.N.* ii. 126, 257, 399. 'Le Famiglie innanzi le città erano tante minute republichetti libere et sovrane, come pur l' udimmo teste narrare da Polifemo ad Ulisse' (*ib.* i. 86; compare *J.U.* ii. 340).

[4] *S.N.* ii. 173, 230; *ib.* i. 52. 'Il Diritto delle Genti [era] un diritto uscito coi costumi di certi Ceppi, da' primi padri del mondo diramate in molte famiglie, innanzi di comporsene le città.'

[5] 'Le Famiglie che sono il seminario delle Republiche' (*S.N.* ii. 334). 'Dalle [Famiglie] nacquero le prime Genti, o vero Attenenze o Casati, sopra le quali poi sursero le Città' (*ib.* i. 35).

But what of the accretions to which reference has just been made and which play so crucial a part in Vico's theory of the primitive Family and, through it, of the State? Among the customs which distinguish the primitive Family, not the least significant was the traditional character of the Family itself: an unit based not only on blood, but also on ascendancy; a whole composed not merely of those who claimed descent from a common ancestor, but also of a large and ever-growing body of inferiors and dependants. That this was the nature of the Family as it first appears in history, and as it must be inferred to have existed long before history begins, is proved not only by the records of Greece and still more of Rome, where the word *famulus* (slave) remains a standing witness to it, but also, in a yet more primitive state of things, by the whole story of the Hebrew Patriarchs: by the strife between the herdsmen of Lot and Abraham; by the part that Abraham took in the war of the nine kings; above all, by the pregnant words of Jacob: 'With my staff I passed over this Jordan, and now I am become two bands.' Until this truth is grasped, the whole of Greek history, with its Helots and other serfs, the whole of Roman history, with its Clients and Plebeïans, remain an unintelligible riddle.[1]

What we must start from, therefore, is the undoubted fact that, at least in the races referred to, the Family included a large alien element and that, in the case of Rome at any rate, that element has scarred a deep mark upon the subsequent history of the State. How, so Vico asks himself, is this alien element to be accounted for? and from what sources was it drawn?

As to the first step in his answer, he is in no manner of doubt. It came from the ranks of the 'lawless vagrants'; and it can have come from nowhere else. For the next step there are, in theory, two possible alternatives. The new recruits to the settled order may either have been prisoners of war, or they may have come in by way of voluntary surrender. The first alternative must be rejected at once. The feud between the two parties was an inexpiable feud; it was to be ended only by the extermination of one side or the other. If, therefore, any prisoners were taken by the settlers, we may be very sure that they were at once slaughtered in cold blood; sacrificed on the spot to the avenging wrath of Heaven: *Saturni hostiae*, victims to appease the God of tillage, as the tell-tale phrase of Plautus still remains to prove.[2]

[1] *S.N.* ii. 31-2. 'Le Città . . . sursero sopra le Famiglie non sol de' figlioli, ma anco de' Famoli . . .; sopra le Famiglie sol di Figlioli si dimostra che non potevano nè tali nè di niuna sorta affatto nascer nel mondo.' Compare *ib.* 117-18; *S.N.* i. 96; *J.U.* i. 61-6; ii. 378-80.

[2] *S.N.* ii. 26, 251-3, 275; *ib.* i. 97; *J.U.* ii. 369.

We are left with voluntary surrender. This explanation is both probable in itself; and it can be supported by more than one significant indication. The marauding 'outlaws' of Vico's theory, the 'wild men' of *Leviathan*, were the sworn enemies not only of the civilised settlers, but also, and in a yet more deadly fashion, of the weak and helpless—that is, the majority—of those who, like themselves, still wandered aimlessly upon the face of the earth. It would have been strange indeed if some at any rate of these weaklings had not from time to time thrown themselves upon the mercy of those whom they must instinctively have felt to be morally, as well as physically, their betters, and who, in any case, offered the only chance of escape from the cruelty of their oppressors and the misery of their present lot. In so desperate an extremity, it is manifest that they would have had no choice but to accept such terms as they could get. They could not look for equality: to be admitted as dependants, as 'clients,' as serfs, was all they could reasonably expect.[1]

To judge from the scanty evidence which has come down to us, it was all that they received. So much at least may be gathered from the records of the three primitive races of whom our knowledge is the least imperfect: from the surrender of the Gibeonites to be 'hewers of wood and drawers of water' to the children of Israel; from the 'altar of mercy' set up—and for what purpose but this?—by the hero-founder of Athens; from the asylum traditionally asserted to have been opened by Romulus expressly with this intention: *vetus urbes condentium consilium*, in the illuminating phrase of Livy. It is true that these examples are drawn from a somewhat later stage of man's development; but the analogy is none the less legitimate.[2]

That such dependants, as time went on, should learn much from their protectors, was in the course of nature. They could hardly live beside men, in many ways so obviously their betters, without acquiring many of the beliefs and usages to which that superiority was originally due: without taking over something of that respect for Right, something of that devotion to the Family, something of that reverence for the Gods and the memory of the dead, which the predominant caste itself had learned only under the discipline of a settled home. To the members of that caste, no doubt, all this may have seemed little better than a mockery: a contemptible parody of the civilisation on which they prided themselves, and prided themselves all the more because of the barrier it fixed between them and others. But, though the contempt may

[1] *S.N.* ii. 117, 280-3, 290, 309; *ib.* i. 99-100, 121-2; *J.U.* ii. 373.

[2] *S.N.* ii. 264-5, 285, 417-18; *ib.* i. 99-100, 249; *J.U.* ii. 374, 434-5.

have remained, the superiority which had once justified it must have insensibly diminished. Nor, however strong their contempt, could the original settlers have had any wish, even if they had the power, to drive out the newcomers. To banish their 'hewers of wood and drawers of water' might have gratified their pride; but it would have been the deadliest blow to their material interest.[1]

Thus, when the time was at last ripe for the formation of what is definitely to be called the State, it was no isolated individuals, it was whole families—and, what is more, families already built on a half-civic, it would hardly be too much to say a political, basis—that came together for the purpose. Each of these was itself a 'minute republic,' sovereign within its own borders and organised to deal effectively with the ordinary affairs of life; each of them, again, was composed of two distinct, not to say discordant, elements: the one, confident of its right to rule, strong in its long habit of command, proud of its birth, its ancestral Gods, its hallowed customs, its inherited traditions; the other, ill organised, downtrodden, half conscious of its own inferiority and half resolved never to admit it, half disheartened by the oppressions of ages and half in mute rebellion against them. There was here plenty of material for strife. But there was also plenty of material for discipline, for natural forbearance and concessions, for all that kindles and fosters the civic spirit. And in the end the latter proved to be of more moment than the former, the loss to be more than balanced by the gain. The typical instance of this, it need hardly be said, is furnished by the early history of Rome. But there is abundant evidence, obscured though it is by the mystical form in which it has come down to us, that the same thing is true of Greece.[2]

From all this it follows on the one hand that the connection between the primitive State and the Family is far closer, on the other hand that the analogy between them is far less complete, than is commonly supposed. There is a sense in which it is perfectly true to say that the State grew out of the Family. The only fault to find with the statement is that it does not go far enough. It would be nearer the truth to say that the early State *is* the Family:

[1] *S.N.* ii. 26-28, 118-19, 290-1, 295-6, 298-9, 313, 319, 342, 349-350; *ib.* i. 121-3; *J.U.* 332-40.

[2] 'Solamente ora sia lecito qui di riflettere, quanto vi volle, acciocchè gli uomini . . . dalla ferina loro natia libertà per lunga stagione di Ciclopica famigliar Disciplina si ritrovassero addimesticati negli Stati, ch' avevano da venir appresso, Civili ad ubbidire naturalmente alle Leggi' (*S.N.* ii. 256). 'I Polifemi . . . abbisognarono per ubbidire l' uomo all' uomo nello stato delle Famiglie e disporlo ad ubbidir alle leggi nello stato ch' avea a venire delle Città' (*ib.* 116). Compare *ib.* pp. 97, 362; and *ib.* i. 86.

or rather the union of all the Families—by which, to speak strictly, we must understand the ruling Order among all the Families—of which the community is built up. The Family organisation, the Family customs, the Family forms of worship were transported bodily into the larger whole which the original 'tiny republics' now united to create. Indeed, for certain purposes—of which the *patria potestas* is the standing, but by no means the only, example—each Family may be said to have reserved to itself powers or rights which later ages have come to recognise as the indefeasible province of the State. In this sense, therefore, the State *was* the Family.

On the other hand, it was from the nature of the case impossible that the essential mark of the Family, its monarchical character, should be reproduced in that union of Families which gives birth to the State. If the Family was to find any place in the State, it could only be on condition that every Family, through its head, should share equally with all the others in the government of the State. In other words, the Monarchy of the old order must inevitably give place to an Aristocracy in the new. 'So necessarily does it follow that, if the Tribes—that is, the incipient associations of Families—were from the first composed of Nobles, the State must from the first have consisted of Nobles, and of Nobles alone.' And those who maintain the primitive State to have been monarchical are purely the slaves of words. They have allowed themselves to be misled by the use of the word *king* in Homer and other early writers (*e.g.* Genesis xxxvi. 15-43—the 'dukes of Edom'): forgetting that, whenever such words occur, the context shows to demonstration that nothing more is meant than *noble* or *lord*.[1]

From all this it is plain that the primitive State, half like and half unlike the Family before it, rested upon two pillars: aristocracy and religion. Aristocracy: the rule not of the 'best,' but of the more highly organised and the stronger: in other words, of the heads of Families now firmly united, thanks to the discipline of the transitional period, into one ruling 'order,' that of ten 'fathers' or patricians. Religion: the forms of worship inherited from the primitive Family and now, with other family usages, transplanted bodily into that new unit which is, at bottom, nothing

[1] *S.N.* ii. 117-19, 235-6, 245, 255-6, 263, 281, 299-300, 331. 'E perchè i Padri crano Sovrani Re delle lor Famiglie nell' ugualità di si fatto stato, e, per la feroce natura de' Polifemi, niuno di tutti naturalmente dovendo cedere all' altro, uscirono da se medisimi i *senati regnanti*, o sia di tanti Re delle lor Famiglie . . . e i Nobili se ne dissero Patricj: onde dovettero i soli nobili esser i Cittadini delle prime patrie' (p. 299). Compare *S.N.* i. 94-96, 106-10; *J.U.* ii. 391-404.

more nor less than the pre-existing households henceforth blended, at least for most purposes, into one organic whole. Hence the name given by the Romans to the Gods traditionally recognised as the most powerful and therefore the highest: *Di majorum Gentium*, the Gods of the families who formed the primitive association; Gods therefore brought into the State at the moment of its formation; as opposed to the *Di minorum Gentium*, the Gods subsequently recognised as such—for instance, Quirinus—by the public authority of the State. Few things could illustrate more aptly the rooted belief of primitive ages that the Family is something yet higher, yet more sacred, than the State.[1]

Such was the general character, as of the Family, so also of the State to which the Family gave birth. It was the rule of the strongest, the right of might, qualified only by fear of the Gods to whom that might was due and by whose favour it was perpetuated and confirmed.[2] The qualification may, at first sight, seem of little worth. A moment's reflection will show that it is of the first importance. It makes all the difference in the world whether appeal is made to force as such, or to a Right which in its outward effects may appear to be hardly distinguishable from force and which, for its ultimate sanction, trusts avowedly to force and to little else. For the principle of Right, once admitted, is bound to work itself out with more and more fullness and consistency; it is the leaven which ultimately leavens the whole mass. The first step, in such matters, is therefore that which counts beyond all others. And that first step had been taken when the life of lawless vagrancy had been exchanged for the settled life of the Family and the home. Once taken, it could never be retraced. Insensibly, it led on first to the aggregation of Families, known to Vico as the Tribe; then to the more highly organised unification, distinguished as the City or State. With each stage in the advance, the idea of Right became more distinct and more articulate; until, with the formation of the State, however rude its early beginnings,

[1] 'Le Genti cominciarono prima delle Città, e sono quelle che da' Latini si dissero *Gentes majores*, o sia Case nobili antiche; come quelle de' Padri, de' quali Romolo compose il Senato, e col senato la Romana città: come al contrario si dissero *Gentes minores* le case nobili nuove fondate dopo le Città . . . Tale fu la divisione degli Dei, tra quelli delle Genti maggiori, o vero Dei consagrati delle Famiglie innanzi delle città . . . e gli Dei delle Genti minori, o vero Dei consegrati appresso dai popoli, come Romolo' (*S.N.* ii. 132). Compare *J.U.* i. 58-9; and contrast *S.N.* i. 53, where *Di minorum Gentium* are taken to be the Gods of the Plebeians.

[2] 'Il Diritto Eroico, o vero della forza, ma però prevenuta già dalla Religione, che solo può tener in dovere la forza' (*S.N.* ii. 465).

the outward framework of Government, the first condition of all Right, was more than half completed. The chief task that remained—a task, as all history proves, of enormous difficulty—was to work out the idea so embodied with greater fullness and greater consistency: above all, to extend step by step to the whole community the principles of justice, equity and equality which, in the first instance, were jealously confined to the ruling Order. 'Heroic justice,' which to later ages seems but another name for injustice, was, after long and bitter strife, to be replaced by 'humane justice': the justice of the privileged caste, by the justice which starts from the fixed faith that, in the eyes of God, all men are free and equal. The road is long to travel. But once more, it was the first step that cost. Without it, all the rest would have been impossible.[1]

So far we are on solid ground; for the rest, we are left mainly to conjecture. It has often been asked, for instance: What was the immediate occasion which precipitated the actual birth of the State? and what the exact manner of its formation? Both popular tradition and learning are ready with their answers. The former—we need only to recall the legends of Orpheus, Amphion and other shadowy figures of Greek story—is apt to give the credit to the poets; the latter, to the philosophers.

In this matter, as in so many others, the learned are in the wrong. To suppose that the philosophers, the men of 'abstruse wisdom,' can have had any hand in so rough a work, in one so manifestly the product of rude times and archaic prejudices, is to misunderstand the whole working of the human mind, to misread the whole course of history, to misconstrue the whole problem from the very beginning. Such men would have roundly denounced the work had they been there to witness it. And they could not have witnessed it, seeing that ages of civic life must have passed before philosophy, which is essentially a task of reflection, abstraction, speculation, could by any possibility have arisen. It is only after centuries of settled society, of the practical labour by which

[1] 'Ma gli uomini per la loro corrutta natura essendo tiranneggiati dall' amor propio, per lo quale non sieguono principalmente che la propia utilità; . . . quindi stabiliamo che l' uomo nello stato bestiale ama solamente la sua salvezza; presa moglie, e fatti figlioli, ama la sua salvezza con la salvezza delle Famiglie; venuto a vita civile, ama la sua salvezza con la salvezza delle città; . . . unite le Nazioni in guerre, paci, allianze, commerzj, ama la sua salvezza con la salvezza di tutto il Genere Umano: l' uomo in tutte queste circostanze ama principalmente l' utilità propia: adunque non da altri che dalla Provedenza Divina deve esser tenuto dentro tali ordini a celebrare con giustizia la famigliare, la civile e finalmente l' Umana Società; per li quali ordini, non potendo l' uomo conseguire ciò che *vuole*, almeno voglia conseguire ciò che dee dell' utilità, ch' è quel che dicesi giusto' (*S.N.* ii. 143).

settled society is created, that the very raw material of the philosophers is laid ready to their hands. Hence the absurdity of the tales, for the most part late inventions, which connect Numa with Pythagoras, the Law of the Twelve Tables with the refinements of Greek philosophy, the founding of Athens with the alleged wisdom of the Egyptians.[1]

For the popular version of the matter, the apotheosis of the poet, there is much more to be said. Its form is open to objection; but in substance it is probably true enough. Miracles apart, it may be impossible to credit any single poet with the achievements of Orpheus and the rest. But who can deny that poetry—still more, the imaginative impulse on which poetry is founded and to which poetry appeals—is a binding, as well as a civilising, force? or that, in an age when reason is of small account and imagination well-nigh all in all, the imaginative impulse—an impulse in those days amounting to a passion—of whole bodies or groups of men is likely to have played a large, very probably a decisive, part in the process of fusion which was to end in the foundation of Cities, of communities which are justly to be called civic? We have only to suppose, and the supposition follows almost of itself, that such an impulse was first awakened, or finally crystallised, by the inspired voice of the few, more gifted than the rest; that subsequently, by one of those personifications in which such times abound, the work of the few—the few who, let it not be forgotten, were but the spokesmen of the many—was dramatically transferred to one; and that the 'heroic character' thus created came down in popular memory as the sole representative, the typical embodiment, of the whole race. The marvels—the tigers' hearts softened, the 'bowing of the trees and mountain tops,' the moving of the stones each to his own place within the wall—are embroideries that popular fancy, stirred by the splendour of the achievement, added of itself. So it was that the 'theological poets' were the true founders of the State. Only, such poets were no mystics, but men who shared and moulded the

[1] *S.N.* ii. 16, 59, 96-8, 148, 155, 171, 238, 336-7, 532-5, 568. 'Il Diritto Natural delle Genti è uscito coi costumi delle Nazioni tra loro conformi in un senso comune umano, senza alcuna riflessione e senza prender esemplo l' una dall' altra' (*S.N.* ii. 131). Compare *S.N.* i. 24-5, 33, 41-3, 156, 190-3, 291; *J.U.* i. 113-15, 192-3; ii. 442-459. Yet this idea, the creative power of *Sapienza volgare*, though it lies at the very root of Vico's theory is, as an idea, realised no more than faintly in the *Jus Universum*: it is brought out more clearly in the first draft of the *Scienza Nuova*; but it is only in the second draft that Vico rises to a full sense of its importance. For Vico's criticism of the tales about Numa and Pythagoras, see *S.N.* ii. 78-9; i. 295; of the XII. Tables, *S.N.* ii. 124, 321-2, 327; *S.N.* i. 63-71; of the wisdom of the Egyptians, *S.N.* ii. 59, 67, 111, 113.

popular faith of their own day. They were no isolated individuals, but, like Homer in after days, the inspired mouthpiece, possibly the mere personification, of the race.[1] So that the 'popular wisdom' which is the creative force at the back of all human society, may with equal justice be called 'poetic wisdom'; and *sapienza poetica*, on Vico's lips, is interchangeable with *sapienza volgare*.[2]

The same principle must be applied to that other 'heroic character,' the Lawgiver, who appears in place of the poet, or side by side with the poet, in the legendary history of many States. It may be doubted whether the traditional legislators—Minos and Cadmus, Draco and Numa—ever existed in flesh and blood: whether they are not rather the giants by whom popular imagination has replaced a whole host of forgotten dwarfs. It is certain that another familiar figure, the warrior hero, Theseus for example, or Hercules, who reappears in the primitive story of more than one community, is a legendary creation. It is certain that he too, as originally imagined, was a 'political character,' the tamer not of beasts but of men: the idealised type of a hundred lesser champions whose very memory has perished, but who once played their part in the secular struggle between the few and the many, between the God-fearing and the impious, between Patrician and Plebeian. And with the necessary modifications, particularly in regard to the political reference, Vico is more than half disposed to apply the same measure to Homer.[3]

[1] *S.N.* ii. 16-18, 72-3 (Orpheus), 180-82 ('la poesia fondò l' Umanità gentilesche'), 152-7, 163-4, 166-9, 222-7, 238 ('I primi popoli, i quali furon i fanciulli del gener umano, fondarono prima il mondo dell' Arti; poscia i filosofi, che vennero lunga età appresso, e 'n consequenza i vecchi delle nazioni, fondarono quel delle scienze'); 256, 323, 387-8 (Orpheus); 423-7, 450 (Homer: 'a tante difficoltà si direbbe che Omero fusse stato un Poeta d' Idea, il quale non fu particolar uomo in natura'), 454. Compare *S.N.* i. 163-6, 185-7, 189 ('Omero meritò l' elogio di Fundatore della Greca Umanità'), 197-201; and *J.U.* ii. 254, 265-7, 277-9, 301-2, 332, 410. 'I primi popoli della Gentilità per una dimostrata necessità di natura furon *Poeti*, i quali parlarono per Caratteri poetici; la qual discoverta è la chiave maestra di questa scienza'; *S.N.* ii. 42.

[2] The title of his central *Book* (II.) is accordingly *Sapienza poetica*.

[3] *S.N.* ii. 187-92 ('Se non pure tal Solone furon essi plebei Ateniesi per questo aspetto considerati,' p. 188). For Hercules as founder of nations see *S.N.* ii. 56, 75, 109, 245, 248, 286; he also appears as tamer of the earth for the service of men, *ib*. pp. 268-70. Compare *S.N.* i. 167, 184, 213; *J.U.* i. 58; ii. 313. For Vico's conclusions as to Homer, which, in detail as well as in general scope, anticipate those of Wolf, see *S.N.* ii. 422-61; *S.N.* i. 187-93; and *J.U.* ii. 279-93. In the two earlier treatises, he is merely feeling his way; it is only in *S.N.* ii. that he works out his thoughts to their logical conclusion.

It has been said that the primitive State was essentially aristocratic; that its ruling principle was therefore force: physical force in the first instance, with a sanction, however, of moral and religious force behind. It was not only that the united Fathers, the Patrician order which alone formed the State, were better organised and therefore stronger than their despised and scattered subjects. It was also that they claimed, and to a large extent justly claimed, to have a higher moral and religious standard, a more assured moral and religious tradition: that they alone could point to the possession of inherited forms of worship, of recognised means for ascertaining the will and winning the favour of the gods, of a settled order for hallowing their marriages and honouring the sepulchres of their dead. The social bearing of all these things, the certainty that they would fix a deep gulf of inequality between the two classes, or rather nations, of men is obvious at a glance.[1]

Accordingly, we may well believe that the early history of the State in general is typified by that of Rome. Elsewhere, as well as on the banks of the Tiber, it is probable that the whole life of those early days centred round the conflict between Patricians and Plebeians. And if that be so, it is certain that, elsewhere no less than at Rome, that struggle must have raged round three points beyond all others: on the material side, round the possession of the land; on the moral side, round the exclusive claim of the Patricians to lawful marriage and lawfully born children; on the political side finally, round the consequent exclusion of all but Patricians from offices of State.[2]

As their numbers grew, as their intelligence quickened, the despised Plebeians must everywhere have felt a deepening sense of wrong. The resolution with which they pressed their claims must everywhere, as at Rome, have stiffened with every step forward that they won. And everywhere the stages of their advance must have been very much the same. Materially speaking, it was a progress from pure serfdom, first to precarious tenancy, then to fixity of tenure, and finally to 'quiritarian' ownership, qualified only by the supreme sovereignty, the *dominium eminens*, of the State. Morally, a gradual admission, extorted only at the point

[1] 'Il diritto Eroico, o vero della forza, ma però provenuta già dalla Religione che sola può tener in dovere la forza' (*S.N.* ii. 465; compare p. 35).

[2] 'Questo Principio della nobiltà . . . scoverto ad evidenza dentro la storia Romana antica . . . ne spiega la favolosa de' Greci, . . . e scopre le affatto nascoste di tutte le altre antiche nazioni' (*S.N.* i. 89; compare *ib.* 69). But the idea that Roman History is the type of all primitive history is implicit in the whole of Vico's theory. For the material, moral and political conflict between Patricians and Plebeians, see *S.N.* ii. 66-9, 72-5, 81, 85-92, 117-25, 133-4, 137-40, 278-337, 349-54, 359-65, 471-9, 491-8; *ib.* i. 82-137; *J.U.* ii. 363-404, 435-48.

of the sword, to the same rites of marriage and sepulture—and consequently to the same family status, legal and moral—as had been the Patricians' from the first. Politically, an equally grudging admission to one after another of the offices once jealously guarded as the sacred privilege, the divine right, of an oligarchy, the essence of whose pretensions was that 'the auspices were its own.'[1]

Such, as the records prove to demonstration, was the course of things at Rome. A hundred indications, drawn partly from history, partly from fragments of half-obliterated legend, show that so it was in Greece. A like picture, at least in its broad outlines, is offered by the feudal order indigenous to the Germanic tribes which overthrew the Roman Empire: 'primitive barbarism come again,'[2] in the recurrent phrase of Vico. How can we fail to infer that it was the same with many, perhaps with all, primitive communities? in short, that we have here an universal law of that 'ideal, eternal history which runs its course in time'?[3]

For our purposes, there is no need to follow Vico into further detail. It only remains to ask: What is the method by which he establishes these results? and what the general principles which lie behind them?

His method, described in the broadest possible way, is the comparative method; and the matter to which he applies it is the laws, the customs, the legends, the literature, the history of the ancient world; to which, as occasion serves, he adds some pregnant illustrations from the life and literature of modern Europe.[4] The

[1] See, in particular, *S.N.* ii. 190-91, 309-10, 325-8, 491-4; *ib.* i. 100-104, 110-15, 122-6; *J.U.* ii. 363-79, 468-9 ('Vides igitur Auspiciorum jus influere tanquam per duos rivos; altero in Jus Quiritium publicum; . . . et utrumque jus Quiritium, et privatum et publicum, jure divino et religione fundatum et conspersum').

[2] 'I tempi barbari ricorsi (ritornati)'; *e.g. S.N.* ii. 196, 352, 536.

[3] 'La storia ideale eterna che corre in tempo'; an oft-repeated phrase—*e.g. S.N.* ii. 17, 44, 147, 175. 'Si avrà la Storia ideale delle Leggi eterne, sopra le quali corron i Fatti di tutte le Nazioni, ne' loro sorgimenti, progressi, stati, decadenze e fini, se ben fusse, lo che è certamente falso, che dall' eternità di tempo in tempo nascessero mondi infiniti' (*ib.* 562). 'Un diritto eterno che corre in tempo' (*ib.* i. 43).

[4] *E.g.* his illustration of the sacredness attached by the Romans to fire and water from the Neapolitan practice, noticed also by Boccaccio as prevalent at Florence, of throwing incense on the fire on Christmas Eve (*S.N.* ii. 260); or his illustration of the Roman *patria potestas* from the customs of Tartary and Muscovy (*ib.* 298). See also *ib.* 550 (judicial combats in the kingdom of Naples) and 229 (the survival of sacred groves in Lapland and Livonia). His references to feudal customs may also be

few references he throws in to the Red Indians and Patagonians, to Japan and China, are too trite to deserve more than a passing mention.[1]

This is the one weak link in Vico's armour. And the weakness, for which he has no one but himself to blame, is difficult to account for. It is hardly credible that, among the large number of travellers' records accessible to him—records abundantly utilised by Montesquieu a score of years later—he could not have found a good deal of material suitable for his purpose.[2] But if his failure to turn this remote matter to account is hard to excuse, still more surprising is his neglect, or comparative neglect, of the Old Testament. Here he had spread before him an unrivalled harvest, springing from the very depth of the past and only waiting for the hand of the reaper. If there was any field which the explorer might be expected to work, any store richer even than that of classical antiquity, it was surely this. And if there was any man who might have been expected to work that field resolutely, it was surely Vico. Unfortunately piety forbade. And in the name of the Church—he was of the straitest sect of the orthodox—he steadily refused to make use of his opportunities: steadily insisted that the history of the Chosen People was entirely exceptional; that between Jew and Gentile, between a supernatural and a purely natural development, there could not, from the nature of the case, be any common measure.[3] Yet, obdurate as he was, there are

fairly reckoned under this head: see *S.N.* ii. 284, 311-17, 352, 537-62; and for references to Tacitus *Germania*, *ib.* 163, 225, 244, 246, 252, 267, 281, 283, 300, 307, 341, 365, 495.

[1] *E.g.* *S.N.* ii. 137, 140-41, 232, 269, 270, 286, 324, 559.

[2] In one passage he refers to Linschoten (for Guinea), to Acosta (for Mexico and Peru), to 'Aviot'—possibly a perversion of Hariot—(for Virginia); in another to Fracastorius (for the Red Indians). See *S.N.* ii. 140, 269. But that is nearly all. On the other hand he makes no use, so far as I have observed, of the *Recueil des voyages qui ont servi à l'établissement . . . de la Compagnie des Indes*, which yielded such rich stores to Montesquieu. This was first published, in Dutch, by Commelin in 1646: a French translation appeared in 1702, and a new edition of this, greatly enlarged, in 1725. This last was the edition used by Montesquieu; it surely might have yielded much to the second draft of the *Scienza nuova* (1730). The *Lettres édifiantes* again (published 1707–17 by Le Gobien and Duhalde) seem to have been entirely neglected by Vico; they were used to excellent purpose by Montesquieu. Prévost's *Histoire générale des voyages*, so largely used by Montesquieu and Rousseau, did not begin to be issued until 1746, two years after Vico's death. But most of its contents had been published separately long before.

[3] 'Questa Degnità (cv.) stabilisce la differenza del Diritto natural degli Ebrei del Diritto natural delle Genti . . . perchè le Genti n' ebbero i soli

moments when the scholar's instinct will have its way: when, in spite of Pope and Cardinal, he cannot refrain from breaking into the forbidden preserve—just enough to show what he might have done, had his lot been cast in kindlier circumstances; but, unhappily, no more. We must be grateful for these occasional lapses, and only regret that his vigilance did not allow them to be more frequent.[1]

With these reservations, Vico may fairly claim to have drawn upon all the sources then open to the explorer. And he uses them with an insight differing not only in degree, but in kind, from anything that had been known before him. Previous scholars—a partial exception must be made in favour of Gerard Vossius[2]—so far as they had concerned themselves at all with such matters, had treated them as questions of pure erudition, as things necessary to the understanding of certain classical allusions, and nothing more. Vico was the first to recognise that in old legends, old laws, old customs, are embalmed the primitive history, the primitive philosophy, the primitive psychology of the race: in his own words, that, 'if we had the primitive Laws of peoples we should also have the history of their deeds'; that 'the civil history of the earliest peoples is enshrined in their mythology'; and conversely, that 'the history of ancient Rome,' for example, 'is one unbroken mythology of the heroic history of the Greeks.'[3]

But, if this be true, it is clear that Vico combined within himself two gifts which have seldom been united: the gift of the scholar and the gift of the philosopher. On the one hand, he was an eager explorer, with an infinite zest for discovering new facts, for discerning new links between them and for placing them in an entirely new light. On this side, he must be regarded as the founder of Comparative Law, of Comparative Mythology: in one word, and in the widest meaning which can be given to the term, of primitive Folk-lore: the forerunner, therefore, of such men as Herder and Savigny and Jacob Grimm. On the other hand—and this, for our

---

ordinarj ajuti dalla Provedenza, gli Ebrei n' ebbero anco ajuti estraordinarj dal vero Dio' (*S.N.* ii. 131; compare *ib.* 54-9, 60-61, 68, 103-4, 112, 131, 147-8, 161, 176; *S.N.* i. 51; *J.U.* ii. 262-5).

[1] It should be noticed that the references to the Old Testament given above (pp. 218, 221) are by no means all to be found in Vico. And it is clear that, on any strict interpretation of his principles, not one of them has any right to be there. On this point, thanks to the author's unfortunate scruples, the *Scienza nuova* compares unfavourably with the *Tractatus theologico-politicus*.

[2] See his *De Theologia Gentili*, originally published in 1641. An enlarged edition was published (by Isaac Vossius) in 1668.

[3] *S.N.* i. 138; compare p. 74; ii. 102, 148; *J.U.* ii. 265.

purposes, is far more important—he was the first to employ the new knowledge so acquired, the new lights so opened out, the new method so discovered—the comparative method—to political philosophy: the first, therefore, to free that study from the abstractions which, for three generations, had made it so barren and so unmeaning; the first, in modern times, to base the theory of the State upon the ideas and 'deeds' through which the State, as we know it, has actually been built up; the first to allow the State to explain itself as a living growth through its own history and development, instead of explaining it away by fine-spun reasonings which take no account either of man's nature, as we know it from experience and history, or of the course which events have historically followed. Thus, in his hands, the comparative method becomes, what it always ought to be, the historical method also: the ideal life of the State, reconstructed from scattered hints and fragments, reveals itself as one connected whole.

At once scholar and philosopher—even now it is difficult to realise all that is implied in this unwonted combination. It is not only that, single-handed, Vico laid the foundations for what, a century later, was to be the life's work of three or four men—Niebuhr also and Wolf must be added to the list—each one of whom stands in the front rank of creative scholarship. It is also, and much more, that with infinite patience he made all these scattered lines converge upon one point, the end and aim of all his labours: the endeavour to breathe new life into political philosophy by recalling it to the actual conditions of the times in which men first began to weave social bonds with one another, and where, if anywhere, the first rude beginnings of the State must be discovered.

'The theory of natural Right, like all other theories, must start from the point where the matter of which it treats first began to take shape.'[1] It was because he had grasped this elementary principle so firmly that the work of Vico is so fruitful and the landmark set up in the *Scienza nuova* so enduring. But without the 'matter' of which his 'axiom' speaks, that work would have been impossible. And as no one else had been at the pains to collect it, there was nothing for it but that Vico should turn to and do so himself. In other words, before he could apply his principle to political philosophy, he had to create the very material upon which he was to work. As scholar, he had to discover the facts which he was to interpret as philosopher.

There had been nothing like it since Aristotle. And even Aristotle's task was much lighter than Vico's. The facts with

[1] 'Le dottrine debbono cominciare da quando cominciano le materie che trattono' (Degnità cvi.) (*S.N.* ii. 131; compare *ib.* pp. 22, 140, 162, 175 etc.; *S.N.* i. 18).

which he had to deal were, for the most part, widely known throughout the Greek-speaking world; and where they were not, a man of his standing and opportunities, to say nothing of his intelligence, could have found little difficulty in ascertaining them. Vico's facts, on the other hand, were to be amassed only by hard study, by long delving in the whole field of classical literature. To most men, it would have been the task of a lifetime. To him it was only one, and that not the worst, of 'the crushing difficulties encountered in the researches of at least twenty years.' [1]

Such is the comparative, such the historical, method as conceived by Vico; and such the material to which he applied it. As to the originality of the conception, there can be no manner of doubt. That he was always as happy in applying it in detail, can hardly be maintained. It would have been a miracle if he were. In fact, it is easy enough to lay the finger upon two points in which his procedure is, to say the least, open to criticism; perhaps even, altogether mistaken. These are his persistent resolve to interpret every mythological story in a political sense; and his equally persistent tendency to treat Roman history as the type to which the history of all other peoples must necessarily conform.

The first point can be made clear most readily by a few examples. It has often been the practice to assume that, in the absence of any special reason to the contrary, all mythological figures are to be taken as standing for one or other of the forces of nature; and consequently that all stories related of them should be interpreted in a physical sense. It will hardly be disputed that this is the prevalent tendency of such a work as Grimm's *Deutsche Mythologie* and of many later works in the same field. Vico will have none of it. To him 'all popular traditions must have some public ground of truth before they could spring to birth and for long ages be kept alive among whole peoples.' [2] And from the whole tenor of his work it is clear that by 'public' grounds he meant—mainly, if not solely—political or civic grounds: that the whole mythology of Greece or Rome, for example, was in his eyes one unbroken allegory of their civil history.[3]

Thus the Jupiter of the Romans who, in the first instance, was the god of the sky, or rather of the thunder which drove their forefathers from the 'bestial communism of goods and women' and forced them to take refuge in the 'monastic' life of cave or mountain-top—who offers therefore the nearest approach to a deified force of nature to be found in classical mythology—speedily becomes Jupiter *Stator*: the god who laid the first rude founda-

[1] *S.N.* ii. 141. [2] *S.N.* ii. 99, 414; *S.N.* i. 74, 169.

[3] 'Le nostre Mitologie, non isforzate e contorte, ma diritte, facili e naturali, si vedranno essere Istorie civili de' primi Popoli' (*S.N.* ii. 148).

tions of the Family and, through it, of settled society, or the State: the physical significance of the figure gradually fading into the background, its political significance thrusting itself more and more openly to the front.[1] Again, the legend of Athene springing fully armed from the head of Zeus is a purely political legend. It is the symbol not of any physical upheaval, but of the revolution which enthroned an armed aristocracy in place of the 'cyclopean' monarchies that covered the earth in the 'state of nature.'[2]

Take, lastly, the story of Cadmus. The slaying of the serpent symbolises the clearing of the 'vast forest of the earth,' a feat so often associated with the name of Hercules. The teeth of the monster, sown in the virgin soil, stand for the teeth of the plough with which the land was broken. The stones cast by the hero typify the hardened clods which his serfs would fain have seized and ploughed for their own behoof. The armed men who sprang from the furrows are the heroes, or nobles, who band together to defend their own against the robbers; fighting not, as the legend vainly declares, against each other, but against their revolted serfs. The furrows are the 'Orders,' the disciplined ranks of the nobles, the foundation on which the whole fabric of aristocratic, or 'feudal,' authority was based. Finally, the serpent into which Cadmus is transformed is an image—the recognised image in primitive ages, as it still is in China and Japan—of that rightful authority, whose outward sign is the ownership of the soil: *Cadmus fundus factus est*, as the Latin phrase, in the most archaic form of the language, must assuredly have run.[3] Thus 'the whole legend is seen to embalm within it many ages of poetic history': to be an imaginative summary of a contest, the most fateful of all contests, which, in truth of literal fact, lasted for generation after generation.[4]

These three examples, the last of them purposely given in full detail, will suffice to illustrate both the strong and the weak side of Vico's method. What modern votaries of the Great Dragon

[1] *S.N.* ii. 165-7, 243, 301-2. [2] *S.N.* ii. 295, 304.

[3] He is thinking of such phrases as *fundus est mihi pater*, equivalent to *auctor est mihi* (Plautus, *Trinummus*, 1123).

[4] *S.N.* ii. 365; compare 143-5, 209, 269, 270, 324. See also *S.N.* i. 173-4; *J.U.* i. 133-4; ii. 404. In the same way, the Sirens, the Sphinx, Marsyas, Circe, Ixion, Tantalus, Midas, Phaëthon, Antaeus, the suitors of Penelope are all symbols of the Plebeian revolt against the Patricians. So is Vulcan in the legend which tells how he was thrown from heaven by Zeus, and Venus in her conflict with Hera and Athene. So again is the tearing in pieces of Orpheus by the Maenads; *S.N.* ii. 348-353. It is in the same spirit that Ganymede is taken to stand for the Priests who read the will of Zeus from the flight of his eagles; *ib.* 249-50, 289.

and other primitive symbols may say of these interpretations, it might be rash to enquire. Some of Vico's guesses may seem far-fetched—in his own word, 'contorted'—enough. But the same might perhaps be said of those offered by later labourers in the field. And in a subject where guess-work is, from the nature of the case, not to be excluded, it is idle to complain because the guesses occasionally miss fire. We may regret that he should have shut his eyes to the physical meaning which must have lain behind some at least of the classical legends. We may regret that he should have made no allowance for what Grote, with a touch of pedantry, was wont to call the 'mythopoeic faculty': the delight in weaving a story purely for the story's sake, which we may well believe to have played some part in the shaping of them. But the really significant thing is that, being first on the field, he should on the whole have picked his way so surely: above all that, where many theorists have seen nothing but a reflection of the world outside man, he should have recognised a record of the struggle by which, on the one hand, man slowly tamed that outside world to his own uses and, on the other, slowly disciplined himself to the service of moral and civic ideals. That, in working out this intuition, he should have fallen into many errors and exaggerations was only to be expected. The wonder is that, with the means at his command, he should have won results so solid and so fruitful.

The second point on which Vico lays himself open to attack is his idolatry of the Latins, his inveterate practice of reading the history of all nations in the light of the Law and history of Rome. He would not have admitted this himself. But it is impossible to read any one of the three forms in which he expounds his theory without being forced to the conclusion that it is so.[1] He avows that the history of Rome is to him 'one unbroken mythology of the heroic history of the Greeks': in other words, that the latter is to be interpreted, or rather reconstructed, upon the model furnished by the former. He avows that 'the history of all nations alike' is a reflection of that 'ideal, eternal history' of which Rome is the most shining and the purest example. And if we put these two things together, it is hardly unfair to say that, in his eyes, the history of Rome is the type to which all other histories must adapt themselves; that the history of Rome is itself the 'pattern laid up in the heavens'; itself, so far as any thing in the world not of ideas but of facts can be, that 'ideal, eternal history which runs its course in time.'

The more general issues involved in this assumption will be

[1] His earliest work on the subject was avowedly inspired by his study of Roman Law, which, as speedily appears, is convertible, in his eyes, with *universal* Law. Hence its title, *Jus universum*.

best considered when we come to speak of the ideas which lie behind his method: in particular, the idea of progress and the whole range of ideas, so closely allied to it, which are summed up in the term, the 'philosophy of history.' For the moment we confine ourselves to narrower ground and ask: What is the degree of truth contained in this obvious exaggeration? how far was Vico justified in demanding for Roman history, if not an exclusive, at least a dominant place in the study of primitive institutions? how far was he right in treating Rome as the typical example of the manner in which the primitive States of Europe were first founded and then gradually built up?

Even in this form—a form, it will be observed, decidedly more modest than that adopted by Vico—the question hardly admits of a favourable answer. The truth is that, even now, our knowledge is too scanty. We know much about Rome; not so much about the Greeks; less about the Teutons; still less about the Celts; least of all about the Slavonic tribes, and those of Finnish kinship, which covered most of the rest of Europe; while of the few remaining races we know just nothing at all.

So much is virtually admitted by Vico himself. Saving for a few scattered references to the Celts—whom, so far as the inhabitants of Britain are concerned, he ominously calls 'the English'—his materials are drawn solely from the history of the first three races mentioned. And to extend his conclusions to any of the others—between them, they account for much more than half of the whole surface of Europe—was manifestly inadmissible. It was to defy the most elementary laws of historical evidence.

It follows that the claim to exalt Rome as the typical example of all Europe—not to say, of the whole world—must be summarily disallowed. It may be true, or it may not. The one thing certain is that Vico makes no attempt whatever to prove it; and that, for the very good reason that, on the evidence before him, no proof was so much as conceivable. All he did, all he could do, was to throw out a bald hypothesis, a conclusion without any premisses to support it. As a hypothesis, no doubt, it may yet have a very real value. It may serve to provoke enquiry; it may open the eyes of historians and antiquarians to the significance of facts which otherwise they would have allowed to pass unnoticed and unchallenged. It is even conceivable that, as knowledge widens, the hypothesis of Vico may become the established fact, the reasoned conclusion, of his successors. In his own day, however, and in the reckless extension which he gave to it, it was a hypothesis and nothing more.

Yet this is by no means the last word upon the matter. Within the narrower bounds just indicated, severely tied down to the Greeks, the Romans and the Teutons, Vico may fairly claim to have proved his point: to have established beyond reasonable doubt that, in these three cases at any rate, the primitive order of things was essentially aristocratic: more than this, that in all three cases alike, that aristocracy had a markedly religious, or sacerdotal, character. It was the study of Roman history which, in the first instance, led him to this conclusion. But he was able to show that it was true also of the Greeks and the Teutons.

It may be objected, no doubt, that the points of resemblance between these various races are very general; that, both as aristocracies and as religious organisations, they differed very materially among each other; and that the differences were, in fact, more important than the resemblances. He would have replied that this was not his concern; that he was the historian not of Rome, nor of Greece, nor of Germany, but of primitive civilisation as a whole; or rather, that he was not so much a historian as a philosopher: a philosopher who went to history for his materials but, having got them, used them for ends more general than the historian cares to seek. It was the generalisation which interested him, not the particulars, however much he had laboured over them, from which it is ultimately drawn. This will hardly perhaps excuse him for not deigning so much as to notice that the particulars did often differ, and differ substantially, as between one nation and another. Still less will it excuse him for invoking analogies which, when sifted, display discrepancies so marked as to make them no analogies at all. Was it fair, for instance, to press Egypt into the service of his priestly aristocracies, when it is evident that a sacerdotal caste, existing entirely apart from the other orders of the State, is not merely not the same thing as an aristocracy endowed with certain priestly functions, such as formed the governing order of Rome, but that the two things are about as sharply opposed to each other as it is possible to conceive?

These, however, are comparatively small matters. It remains true that, in recognising the aristocratic character of these primitive races, the *Scienza nuova* made a revolution in the study of their history. And this is true, above all, of the history of Rome. Previous writers, deceived by the words 'king' and 'kingdom,' had for the most part persisted in treating the early history of Rome as a pure monarchy: a monarchy only converted into an aristocracy by the expulsion of the Tarquins. Vico, if not the first to see, was at least the first to see with any distinctness, with any sense of the far-reaching consequences which follow, that this is an entire perversion of the truth: that, if this were so, the early history of Rome would be a thousand times more unintelligible than the fabulous history of the Greeks. When, a century later, Niebuhr and Arnold worked out this theme in detail, they were but following in the track that the Italian jurist had laid down.[1]

Nor did his services stop there. As little content with the abstract term *aristocracy* as he had been with the abstract term *monarchy*, he never rested until he had made a clear picture to himself of all it implied in the individual case of Rome: an aristocracy of birth in a stricter sense than anything known to modern, or even to medieval Europe: an aristocracy of birth, resting not merely upon ancestry, real or supposed, but upon a definite claim to religious, and therefore also to moral, superiority. And, proofs in hand, he is ready to show how that claim lay at the root not only of the historic conflict between Patricians and Plebeians, but also of the whole ordering of society which preceded that conflict, which is presupposed in it, and without which no such conflict could ever have arisen.

This alone is enough to give Vico a place by himself among those who have rebuilt the study of ancient history from its foundations; and he had the start of all the rest by nearly a century. With this to his credit, he might well be pardoned for exaggerations and distortions more serious than any that can be laid at his door. Indeed, it is only fair to acknowledge that whatever errors he falls into are nearly always to be corrected from the vital principles of his own teaching. As we have seen, it was his mission to recall political theory to the concrete facts of history; and whenever he goes wrong, it is owing to a momentary lapse into abstractions: those very abstractions against which it was his main purpose to protest.

Thus, when he reads a political meaning into every Greek myth, he is in effect forgetting his own cherished 'discovery,' the 'master-key' of his whole system, that 'to the first men, the children of the human race, the whole world was full of marvels'; forgetting that, if true at all, this must be true not only in one field, but in all: as true of the world of nature, or of man's inner experience, as it is of the world of politics. To credit primitive man with an 'imagination, robust, full-bodied, immersed in the senses,'

[1] The first edition of Niebuhr's *History* was published in 1811; the second, and revised, edition in 1827 and the following years—almost exactly a century after the *Scienza nuova*. The first two volumes of Arnold's *History* were published in 1838. His work is, of course, based on that of Niebuhr; but he had a genius for historical narrative—that is, a vivid and concrete imagination—which was altogether denied to Niebuhr. I cannot find a single reference to Vico in either of them. It is strange if neither of them knew of him: stranger still if, knowing, they made no acknowledgement of their indebtedness. Arnold certainly cannot be suspected of such ingratitude.

and then turn round upon him with the command: You shall use this imagination, you shall give the rein to these senses in one direction and for one purpose only, to give form and body to your political needs and aspirations—this is to deny the very freedom and spontaneity which he had begun by claiming for his children. It is to take away with one hand what he had given them with the other.[1]

In the same way, with his idolatry of Rome. If there is one principle for which he stands more than any other, it is that, in each case, the facts must be allowed to speak for themselves: that 'every theory must start from the point where the matter of which it treats first began to take shape.' And this principle is flatly defied when what is true of one nation—or at most, of two or three, and those, as we now know, all members of one group, the Indo-European—is assumed, without further enquiry, to be true of all. Once more, his own theory should have taught him that the conclusions which it had taken him 'twenty years of intense thought and study' to draw as to the Greeks and Romans, could not be transferred off-hand to races superficially at least so different from these, both in blood and in outward conditions, as the Red Indians or the Japanese. This is a curious way of letting the facts speak for themselves: a curious way of observing that inductive method which he admired so much in Bacon. *Cogitata et visa*—to record the facts as they stand and to interpret them by reflection—that, in a memorable page of his crowning work, is declared to be the guiding principle of the 'new science.' And, so far as the Greeks and Romans are concerned, he may fairly claim to have put the principle into practice. With regard to other races, the facts are conspicuously absent; and the interpretation offered is taken over wholesale from a body of facts to which, for all he knew or cared to enquire, they might stand in no relation whatever. His professed method was perfectly sound; but, in these instances, he failed lamentably to apply it.[2]

We pass now to the second branch of our enquiry, and ask: What is the driving force of Vico's theory? what are the vital principles which lie behind his method and results?

The first of them is very general, but it is none the less important for that. Trained in the abstract methods of the Cartesian philosophy, Vico was among the first to raise the standard of revolt against them. Locke had done so in the name of the senses; but, thanks to a one-sided interpretation of their working, his results were hardly less abstract than those of his opponents. Vico,

[1] *S.N.* ii. 42, 112, 163-4.

[2] *S.N.* ii. 22, 131, 140, 162, 175; for Bacon, *ib.* 103, 149; compare 44, 146.

bolder and more clear-sighted, went to the root of the matter and made his assault in the name of reason herself. And his two earliest writings—*De nostri temporis studiorum ratione* (1708) and *De antiquissima Italorum sapientia* (1710)—prove conclusively that he set about his task with the clearest consciousness of the issues he was raising.

The very symmetry of the Cartesian system, he urges in effect, is, in truth, its strongest condemnation. Human experience is not simple, but complex; not harmonious, but full of discords and contradictions. And the same is true of the reason which moulds it and which, in turn, is moulded by it: so that the one is inseparable from the other, and each is what it is only through and by the other. Hence it is not true to say that the 'distinctness of ideas is the surest evidence of their truth.' On the contrary, it is rather evidence of their incompleteness, or even of their falseness. At best, such distinctness is possible only with those ideas—those fields of knowledge, such as Physics and Chemistry—which are comparatively abstract; still more with those, such as Mathematics, where man starts from abstractions which he himself has deliberately made and to which, from beginning to end, he deliberately adheres. In all other fields of experience—above all, in those relating to the moral, political, imaginative and religious life of man—such distinctness is a pure delusion: 'it is the vice rather than the virtue of man's reason.' It is to be attained only by forcing within finite limits what, by its very nature, is illimitable and infinite. The ideas so arrived at may be distinct; but, for that very reason, they are radically false. 'When I suffer, for instance, I cannot recognise any form in my sufferings, nor set any limit to them. My perception of them is infinite and, because infinite, a proof of the greatness of man's nature. It is a vivid perception and bright beyond all others: so bright indeed that, like the sun, it can be observed only through darkened glasses': [1]

> Suffering is permanent, obscure and dark,
> And hath the nature of infinity.[2]

It was from a faint perception of this truth that Des Cartes habitually disparaged all but physical studies, dimly recognising that they alone could offer the distinctness, the demonstrative certitude, of which he was in quest. But here again he stands condemned. To decry the study of man's inner activities, to lay the ban upon history, upon philosophy, moral and political, upon all attempts to comprehend the imaginative and religious life of man, is to cut off more than half of the whole field of experience

[1] *Opere*, vol. ii. pp. 14, 20, 85.
[2] Wordsworth, *The Borderers*, Act III.

and knowledge. What is worse, it is to cut off precisely that part of it which concerns man the most deeply, where he is most himself, just because he is most spontaneous and most creative.[1]

Vico, indeed, is prepared to go a step further yet: to maintain that, when all is said and done, this side of his experience is more intelligible to man than the other: the world that he has created for himself more comprehensible than that which is given to him ready-made from without. Among the many doubts which this plea raises, there is no need to mention more than two: Does not such an assumption overlook that creative part which, as Kant was to prove, is played by the mind of man in the constitution of external objects and which, in proportion as it goes to determine them, must, on Vico's own showing, also go to make them more intelligible? and how is it to be reconciled with his own earlier plea that the world of inward experience, just because it is a higher world than that of outward nature, can never allow of that 'distinctness' which, with all its countervailing drawbacks, is the undeniable privilege belonging to the study of nature?

But, however it may be with this last argument, there can be no question as to the general drift of Vico's philosophy, nor as to the place it holds in the general movement of European thought and, what is no less important, of that prevailing opinion which is ultimately determined by thought. If on the one hand he offers the first sign of revolt against the abstractions of Des Cartes, on the other hand he marks the beginning of the reaction against that materialism which was the natural, though not the intended, outcome of the avowedly empirical philosophy of Locke. On both counts, therefore, he stands at the fountain-head of that movement which admitted the obscurer instincts of man—his moral and religious impulses, his imagination, all that gives voice to the 'blank misgivings of a creature moving about in worlds not realised'—to equal rights with that purely logical and analytic intellect which, alike by Cartesian and materialist, was recognised as the sole arbiter of truth, the sole judge of such knowledge as man can hope to attain. And, as we shall see directly, he applies this fundamental principle with unflinching consistency: to poetry no less than to Law and Government; to language no less than to the mythology in which primitive man finds the symbol not only of his convictions concerning God and nature, but even of his moral and political ideals.

From Vico the torch was passed on to Rousseau; from Rousseau not only to Kant and the philosophers who immediately followed Kant, but also, what is perhaps yet more significant, to the teachers, moral and political, and to the poets of the next hundred years:

[1] *S.N.* ii. pp. 13, 14.

to Burke and Joseph de Maistre, to Coleridge and Carlyle among the former; among the latter, to Goethe in Germany; to Blake, Wordsworth and Shelley in England; to Chateaubriand and the 'romantic' poets who derived from Chateaubriand, in France.

Widely as these men differ from each other, they are all at one in rejecting that abstract conception of reason which, at bottom, was common to the Cartesians and the materialists. Consciously or unconsciously, they all start from the assumption that the senses are not the only source of man's experience—there, at any rate, they are at one with the Cartesians—and that the logical intellect of man is not the only, nor indeed the most important or the highest, test of its truth. All are agreed in the conviction that, in every experience which does not come directly and solely through the senses, the faculty which 'creates the materials'—call it reason, creative power, intuition, or what we will—must have an equal voice with the logical intellect, or rather must become one with the logical intellect, in judging of their worth, in weighing the speculative consequences which they seem to carry in their train.

And if this is the conclusion which we reach on purely general grounds, never do we feel its force so strongly as when we are brought face to face with any of the creative periods of man's history: above all, perhaps, with that period the secret of which was so strangely anticipated by Vico. And the reason is plain. Never has there been a revolution that has revealed more clearly the creative power which lies at the root of man's nature or that has wrought deeper changes in his religious and moral life, in his imaginative outlook, in his political ideals and achievements than that which, doubtless with many halts and checks, has been going forward in Europe for the last century and a half. And never have the champions fought with so clear a consciousness of the goal that lay before them.

Of this revolution—in all that concerns imaginative creation and political theory, though assuredly not in matters of political action—Vico was the prophet and precursor. He was so, as we have seen in his conception of the birth and growth of man's civic relations. He was so no less in the part he assigns to the imaginative element in man's nature and in the canons by which he tests the worth of all imaginative creations. In an age when 'correctness' was loudly proclaimed to be the one thing needful for the poet, when a network of rules, the 'legislation of Parnassus,' was gravely laid down for securing it, when poetry tended more and more to sink into mere 'reasoning in verse,' a voice was suddenly raised to denounce this whole order of ideas as false and pedantic, the whole body of poetry produced by it as spurious and degenerate: abstract, when it should have been concrete; intellectual, when it should have been imaginative and impassioned. The true poetry, it was defiantly asserted, is not subtle and sophisticated, but 'sublime, full of marvels, immersed in the senses,' addressing itself not to the 'good sense' of the few, but to the heart, the 'popular wisdom,' the fantasy of the many. It is the poetry not of Pope, but of Homer; not of Boileau, but of Dante, 'the Homer of Tuscany.'[1] Well might Michelet say that Vico wrote not for his own age, but for that which was to dawn half a century after his death; not for the eighteenth century, but for the nineteenth.[2]

Even from the first, however, some at least of his countrymen seem to have had a dim monition of his greatness. Within three years of its appearance, his book was recommended to Montesquieu during his sojourn at Venice. On the eve of the conflagration in France, his manuscripts were shown to Goethe, in his native city, Naples. And the poet was quick to notice that Filangieri, who acted as guide on the occasion, handled them with a kind of religious awe—as though they had been 'Sibylline oracles,' is his comment.[3] Sibylline oracles they were in truth: and that, in a sense both wider and deeper than either Goethe or his host can be supposed to have divined. He had changed the whole face of political theory. He had anticipated much of what is most fruitful in the intellectual life, especially in the evolutionary thought, of our own day. He had pointed the way to that revolution in imaginative feeling which offers no monument more perfect than the earlier poetry of Goethe. The first of these was, after all, his main achievement; and we now turn to consider the wider ideas which lie behind it, the general principles which inspire the work of Vico, as political philosopher.

In the forefront must be set the use he makes of the idea of evolution: of the gradual process by which, when once he has been drawn into any sort of fellowship with his kind, man advances from the less to the more conscious apprehension of the goal towards which he is moving, from the less to the greater success of his endeavours to attain it. The latter conception is inherent in the very idea of progress; and, except that he was the earliest writer to work it out in any detail, there is little to distinguish him from others in the use of it. The former is entirely his own; and for nearly a century it was destined to remain so. Even when, at the end of that period, it was taken up by Fichte and Hegel, the form they gave to it was so negative as to rob it of the significance, so abstract as to strip it of the concrete body and substance, which it

[1] *S.N.* ii. 162-6, 425-6, 435-6, 439, 441.

[2] Michelet, *Œuvres choisies de Vico.*

[3] Goethe, *Italienische Reise* (March 5, 1787), ed. Weimar, vol. ii. pp. 27-8, 'Sie ziehen ihn (Vico) dem Montesquieu vor'—he remarks of Filangieri and his friends.

bears in the hands of Vico. The only writer, in fact, who can be said to have caught anything of the spirit of Vico in this matter—and that but very imperfectly—is Herder.

What, then, is the distinctive form which Vico gives to this conception? and what its bearing upon the general tenor of his theory? The answer to this question is closely bound up with that doctrine of 'popular wisdom,' with that contrast between it and the 'abstruse wisdom' of the philosophers which plays so large a part in Vico's theory and of which something was said earlier in this chapter.[1] Briefly it is that the truths which it most concerns man to know are first summarily, and therefore imperfectly, apprehended by the imagination; and that, as man slowly awakens to a consciousness of himself and of his place in the world, these imperfect perceptions are subsequently completed and, where need is, corrected by reason and reflection. But the whole course of the argument is so typical of Vico's method that it is worth while to explore it in greater detail.

Philosophers and moralists, he observes, have loved to persuade themselves that the world was never so good and wise as it was in the beginning: that every discovery of later ages is no more than a rediscovery of truths known, of virtues habitually practised, in the dawn of settled society, but subsequently forgotten or fallen out of use. This is the dream of a golden age; the pathetic effort of men, by glorifying the past, to console themselves for the miseries and shortcomings of the present.

In reality, it is a gross illusion. The 'golden age,' as revealed by the 'new science,' is seen to have been in truth an age of iron. The temper of man, even towards his own family, is shown to have been not mild and merciful, but relentless and cruel; the 'cyclopean discipline' of Sparta, the *patria potestas* of Rome, the inhuman sacrifices to Moloch and other deities—we find traces of them even in the Old Testament—are sufficient proofs of this. His wars, the wars of the heroic age, but, 'springing as they did from religious pride and religious hatred, more bloodthirsty than any upon record.' His religion, so far from embodying the pure truths of philosophy, was in fact a 'very fanaticism of superstition.' And the reason for all these things is plain. It lies in the utter inability of primitive man to grasp general truths, to guide himself by the reason which alone discovers general truths, in his consequent enslavement to the senses and to the imagination which works in and through the senses.[2]

[1] See above, pp. 209-10, 223-5.

[2] *S.N.* ii. 112-14, 162-4, 251-3, 361-5, 'Le virtù della prima Età furono . . virtù mescolate di religione e immanità, . . una inumanissima Umanità' (*ib.* 250, 252).

Was man then, in this state, utterly incapable of perceiving truth? was he nothing more than the slave of his own blind passions and equally blind imaginations? Or, to put the same thing otherwise, is it true that his passions were entirely blind and his imagination irredeemably and wholly vain? To assume this would, in its turn, be a gross delusion. And it is just because this has been the general assumption that many moderns have gone so wildly wrong in their judgement of the primitive world and, consequently, in their knowledge of the manner in which the mind of man actually works, of the course which human progress has actually followed.

If the 'new science' proves anything, it proves that, from the moment when man formed the first crude beginnings of fellowship with his kind, his passions were not wholly blind, nor his imaginations the vain thing they had been when he roamed, a lawless vagrant, through 'the vast forest of the earth.' In that moment, and by that act, two truths of the last importance had been borne in upon his mind: the sense of a divine power above him and around him; the sense of duties which bound him alike to that power and to his neighbour.

It is quite true that both these discoveries came to him not through the reason, but the imagination: the one through the impulse of awe which made him fly in terror before a God of wrath; the other through the sexual appetite—doubtless acting on and acted on by the imagination—which made him cling to one woman and afterwards, for her sake, to the children she bore him. It is quite true that for that very reason each of them was apprehended by him but very imperfectly and was rigorously limited in its application. The image of God, as a bigger and stronger man, is an image which belongs to the childhood of the race, not to its full growth, nor even to its youth. The fear of God may be the beginning of wisdom, but it is not the end, nor anywhere near the end. In the same way, the love of wife and children is not the love of mankind, nor even of our neighbour in any sense which would seem tolerable to an enlightened pagan, much less to a Christian. At best, it is the more or less disinterested love of one or two, to the utter exclusion of the rest. At worst, it is the pride of ownership, hardly distinguishable from the pride a man takes in his home, or horse, or sword. But it is of the essence of the imagination to see only the particular; to disengage the general from the particular, to discern the general through the particular, is the subsequent work of reason. And to complain that the imagination has not done what, by its very nature, it is incapable of doing is the idlest thing conceivable.

Nevertheless, it remains true that in these intuitions—unreasoning, imperfect though they were—lay the whole future of the race. They may have come without reason; but on that very account they were held with all the more obstinacy and passion. They sank into man's inmost self, they became part of the very fibre and tissue of his being. Nothing henceforth could tear them from him. Indeed, the real danger lay in the opposite direction: it was that he would cling with unyielding stubbornness to the highly specialised, and consequently imperfect, form under which they had first come to him; that he would never throw off the 'fanaticism of superstition,' the 'inhuman humanity,' with which his first acceptance of them was bound up. And a thousand indications are there to show how slow man has in fact been to wean himself either from the cyclopean discipline of the Family, or from the purely material conception of God, from which he originally started. There, if anywhere, lies the tragedy of his early history: indeed, so far as his conception of God is concerned, of a great part of his later history also.

Progress, however, there has certainly been: even the blindest must admit it. And if we ask, How has that progress come about? and what is the instrument by which it has been accomplished? the only possible answer is that which the *Scienza nuova* offers. It is the work of reason which, step by step, has risen to a fuller consciousness of itself, step by step has reformed the errors in which man had been entangled by his unguarded imagination; and step by step has rebuilt the world of inward belief, both religious and moral, by the new lights which from time to time have dawned upon him: with the world of inward belief, remodelling also that of the outward institutions in which it is embodied. In the first making of those worlds reason, in the sense of conscious deliberation, had no part nor lot; imagination was all in all. It is only as reason comes to life, as reason slowly grows in strength, that little by little they are recast and, in recasting, purged of the defects inseparable from the manner of their first making.[1]

How great these defects are, Vico makes no attempt to conceal. On the contrary, he is never weary of returning on them and enforcing them. Barbarism, savagery, a very fanaticism of superstition—such are the terms with which he brands the beliefs and customs that man first shaped for himself under the spell of an overmastering imagination. Yet the other side of the picture is no less present to his mind: the mildness and clemency—comparative at least—which is the ideal, if not always the practice, of the modern world. And if he heightens the colours of the one, it is in order to give relief and vividness to the other. More than that: if his

[1] 'Gli uomini prima sentono senz' avvertire; da poi avvertiscono con animo perturbato e commosso; finalmente riflettono con mente pura' (*S.N.* ii. 112; compare *ib.* 162-9).

first task is to insist upon the contrast between the one and the other, his second and more cherished concern is to prove how inseparably they are united. It is to prove that the later stage would have been impossible without the earlier: that the earlier contains—and contains in the only shape that could have come home to primitive man—the germs which slowly ripened into the full fruit of the later. In this very barbarism and fanaticism, he argues, lay the whole promise of the future. Harsh, crude and cruel as they now seem, they yet enshrined ideas and beliefs without which man is no better than the brutes; but, with which, he has already planted his feet upon the rock, has already established the certainty of becoming, and becoming in ever fuller and fuller measure, 'a reasonable being and a man.'

The first step of man's advance may seem, at first sight, unpromising enough: brute force the sole claim which the Gods have upon his reverence; brute force the apparent basis of the bond which binds him to his fellow-men. But there are two new elements which have now entered into his experience: two things which irrevocably alter the whole character of his being. Beneath the appearance of brute force, a moral relation has for the first time been set up between him and his fellows; and that moral relation, hidden beneath the semblance of brute force, has its source and sanction in religion. The inevitable result is that force, which in his unregenerate state had the first and last word in the matter, is now thrust down into the second place; that, so far from being the ruling principle of his dealings with others, it is henceforth no more than an external support, an outer shell to protect the growth of another principle which is higher and more vital. As that growth advances, as the higher principle slowly gathers strength, the external support is doomed to fall away, the outer shell to burst asunder; until in the fulness of time, the plant stands in its own strength, the fruit casts aside its withered husk and offers to man its nourishment in the present, its seed of promise for the future. Everywhere death gives place to life: the dead weight of force to the vital play of self-sacrifice and love.

And this leads us to another idea that lies at the root of the whole theory. If the primitive history of man shows this continuous advance, this unbroken progress, from the less to the more conscious, from the less to the more complete, apprehension of truth and justice, that can only be because there is an unseen force by which—at first unconsciously, then with ever-increasing consciousness—he is impelled along the path that, on looking back, we can see that he has prevalently followed. In other words, it can only be because, through all his errors, through all his apparent failures, he has never ceased to be guided by Providence, has always, consciously or unconsciously, been an instrument in the hands of God. And the same thing, though in a different form, holds good of his later history also. If it is true of those early days in which the advance is from an imaginative intuition to a reasoned conception, it is no less true of the succeeding ages, in which it is from a less to a more fully awakened reason. The mental process is slightly different; but the guiding principle, the overruling Providence, is the same.

Divina providentia, tanquam muro, circumagitur mundus. So runs the sentence with which Augustine's disciple opens his History of the World. Such also, but with a difference, is the faith of Vico. The difference is this. To Orosius, as his simile implies, the action of Providence is mechanical and from without. To Vico, it is the vital force which shapes man's destiny from within. God orders the course of history; but he orders it through purely human instruments, through the natural needs and impulses which he has implanted in man from the beginning. Of special interventions, of 'chosen peoples,' Vico will have nothing: or rather, when his orthodoxy compels him to admit them, it is to the doubtful glory of unaccountable exceptions—almost, of freaks—which lie wholly apart from the main stream of progress, which have nothing to teach us of man's nature, nor indeed, for aught that concerns any but the Jewish race, of God's either. Thus in his Providence there is nothing of the supernatural: nothing that is not entirely natural and human. His God works solely through the agency of man. More than that: not so much through the few picked men who stand out above their fellows, as through whole communities and nations; not so much through the special qualities which mark out one man from another, as through the humbler faculties which are common to all: through the common impulses, the common aspirations which bind all men together; through the 'common sense' which guides all men along a common path and which—just because it works instinctively, without any need to analyse, or even consciously to realise, the manner of its working—is the common property of all.

Once again, therefore, Vico throws himself back upon the 'popular wisdom' which, for practical purposes, is a far surer guide than the 'abstruse wisdom' of the philosophers and without which that abstruse wisdom could never have come to fruit. The hand of God is visible in both of them; in the former, however, more directly and more clearly than the latter. More directly, because the matter on which the philosophers work is itself laid ready to their hand by the common sense of the whole race; because it is the function of abstruse wisdom not to create in its own strength, but to interpret, to lay bare, the inner mind, the hidden purpose, of that which popular wisdom has long ago created and put in practice. More clearly, because the common sense of the whole race, if taken in sufficiently large masses and over sufficiently long periods, is incapable of error—to us, at any rate, it is the ultimate authority, the court of final appeal, which cannot be questioned without presumption—while the work of the philosophers, being the work of individuals, is always open to the intrusion of personal bias, always liable to be vitiated, in whole or in part, by individual short-sightedness, by individual caprice.

Thus, for the fulfilment of the divine purpose, nothing more is needed than the natural instincts of man, acting on and, in turn, acted on by the purely natural operation of circumstance and physical condition. In the history of man, everything is mysterious, but nothing is either arbitrary or supernatural. From the first step to the last, everything is at the same time natural and providential. It was a divine—but, none the less, a strictly human—necessity which in the first instance drove him into the rude fellowship of the 'monastic' Family. It is a divine—but, none the less, a strictly human—necessity which has prompted every further step on his road towards ever closer and higher forms of union with his kind, towards an ever fuller and clearer knowledge of God. *Ipsis rebus dictantibus*, as the Roman jurist asserted, *regna condita*. And to the same dictation—that of circumstances from without, that of his own nature from within—are due all the subsequent advances that man's history records. On this crucial matter, let Vico speak for himself:

'The will of man, by its very nature wavering and uncertain, finds assurance and determination in the common sense which in all matters of man's necessity or convenience—and these are the only two sources of natural Right—is the guide of the whole race. This common sense is a judgement formed entirely without reflection and shared in common by a whole Order, a whole Nation, the whole Race. . . . This common sense of the whole race is the organ of judgement which divine Providence has granted to all nations, so as to make them capable of arriving at certitude in all that concerns the natural Rights of men. And such certitude is attained when men discern the substantial points of agreement in which, despite variations of detail, all nations are at one.' [1]

[1] 'L' umano arbitrio, di sua natura incertissimo, egli si accerta e determina col senso comune degli uomini d' intorno alle umane necessità o utilità: che son i due fonti del Diritto natural delle Genti. Il senso comune è un giudizio senz' alcuna riflessione, comunemente *sentito* di tutto un ordine, da tutto un popolo, da tutta una nazione, o da tutto il gener umano. . . . Il senso comune del gener umano è il criterio insegnato alle nazioni dal Provedenza divina, per diffinire il certo d' intorno al Diritto

Here, in brief, we have Vico's whole theory of Right; and with it—for, in his view, the two things are inseparable—his whole theory of progress and of Providence. To him, as to Burke, 'the rights of men are their advantages.' Only, as their advantages, their interests, are perpetually changing with time and circumstance, so their rights also are constantly expanding, constantly demanding and receiving a wider and ever widening interpretation. At first confined to the individual, they are then at the height of intensity, but at the height also of exclusiveness. With the formation of the Family, however, the horizon of man necessarily begins to widen; and as it spreads from the individual to the Family, from the Family to the Order, from the Order to the Nation, so his interpretation of his rights little by little loses its primitive intensity: and, at the same time, its primitive narrowness and exclusiveness. He no longer thinks only of his personal interests, but of those which belong to his whole Family, to his whole Order, to his whole Nation. Eventually, the rights of the Nation itself are seen to be imperfect, to carry with them a contradiction which, until the horizon is still further opened, it is impossible to do away. And this brings man, at least in theory, to the final stage of his progress: to the acknowledgement that nothing short of mankind, as a whole, will meet his requirements; that nothing less than man, as man, can offer any satisfaction to his inborn, yet constantly broadening sense of justice. That is the history of Roman jurisprudence; and in this, as in other matters, the history of Rome is, on a small scale, the history of the whole world.

And what does this mean but that the conception of rights—a conception, by its very nature, partial and imperfect—is gradually merged in that of Right? the sense of individual claims and interests, of justice to the self—it may be the narrower, or the wider self—slowly replaced by the sense of justice to all: of the duty which lies on every man to take thought for the whole race? Only, let it never be forgotten that the wider conception would have been impossible without the narrower; that the last stage could never have been reached except through those that went before it. Justice to all is doubtless the final goal of man's endeavours. But the Family, the Order, the State are the successive 'schoolmasters to bring him' thither: or even to give him that distant vision of it which is all he has hitherto attained.

In all this there is the closest analogy with that doctrine of

---

natural delle Genti: del quale le nazioni si accertano, con intendere l' unità sostanziali di cotal Diritto, nelle quali, con diverse modificazioni, tutte convengono' (*S.N.* ii. 98-9; compare *ib.* 143-8).

progress which has found wide acceptance in our own day: with the theory which lies at the root of the whole system of Hegel; still more, with the far purer and more fruitful teaching of Vico's own countryman, Mazzini. Are we then entitled to claim Vico as a precursor of these later thinkers? Can it be justly said that he forestalled the modern belief in progress as the vital principle which underlies the whole course of human history, and without which that history would be a mere assemblage of brute facts, with no connection and no rational explanation? That would be to lose sight of one crucial consideration: of the limits which Vico himself is careful to set to the scope and range of progress. Within those limits, the idea of unbroken progress is as valid to him as it is to Hegel or Mazzini. But beyond them it has no claim to acceptance whatever. It is valid, that is, only for detached periods of history. As each of those periods comes to an end, the world sinks back into barbarism; the whole fabric of progress is violently cast down and needs to be built again from the very ground.

It is manifest that we have here Aristotle's theory of 'cataclysms,' furbished up for the use of the 'new science' and supported by a certain array of evidence—or rather, by a highly questionable interpretation of certain evidence—which lay beyond the range of Aristotle's experience. It is true that within the limits of each period—and, in the last resort, there are no more than two to reckon with, the ancient and the modern—Vico works out the idea of progress with a fulness and richness to which neither Aristotle, nor any writer between his own day and Aristotle's, makes even the most distant approach. So much will be evident from what has been said already. But it is also true that, by denying the uninterrupted flow of progress, by reducing it to a merely circular movement—the ebb and flow, the *corso* and *ricorso*, of his closing chapters—he does his best to darken the light which he had thrown up in his main argument, to ruin the force of a plea, which had promised to revolutionise the whole study of history, by tacking to it a gratuitously lame and impotent conclusion.

Such is the glaring defect in Vico's theory of progress. We should do ill to make light of it. We should do still worse to be blinded by it to the incalculable advance which he made upon any previous theory of the kind; to the immense inferiority of anything that was added by subsequent writers for at least two generations after his death. And if we ask how it was that, having accomplished so much, he should not have accomplished even more, the answer is once more to be found in his idolatry of Rome: in his inability to see that the fall of Rome, which marks the turn between his flow and his ebb, did not also mean the fall of the whole world. Thanks to this initial error, he was unable to recognise that the barbarian invaders not only poured new blood into the dying frame of Europe, but that they also brought two entirely new springs of thought and action to the service of her spiritual life: a sense of individual freedom such as was unknown to the ancient world; and a sense of nationality which for many centuries doubtless remained in little more than germ, but which was eventually destined to change the whole face of man's civic activities and

> To cast the kingdoms old
> Into another mould

—a mould at once freer and stronger than anything offered by the past.

For this failure there was a further reason which cuts even deeper than that already given. It is that Vico's grasp of the idea of humanity was manifestly still very imperfect; that his horizon was, for all vital purposes, still bounded by the vision of the State, or of the Empire as the State which embraces the whole world; that he had not risen to the conception of humanity as an equal partnership of free nations: a partnership in which each contributes of its best to the common good and in which each in turn takes up the standard of progress as it drops from the hand of another—

> Et quasi cursores vitai lampada tradunt.

Hence the end of ancient civilisation inevitably presents itself to him as the end of all things. He is unable to discern the fresh elements which were brought into play by the birth of the new order, or even to detect the continued working of such elements as, doubtless under an altered form, were taken over from the old.

Yet, imperfect as was his grasp of some sides of the problem and unfortunate his enslavement to the classical tradition, Vico must be allowed to have seen both further and deeper, in this matter, than any of those who went before him, than any of those who immediately followed; to have laid the foundations on which any rational theory of progress must be built; and, so far as concerns the more primitive stages of the process, to have left little of vital importance for his successors either to alter or to add. As a work of historical research, it is astonishing enough. As a landmark in the history of ideas, it is more memorable still.

In his own mind the two strains, the ideal and the historical, were inseparable. The facts were to be interpreted in the light of the idea, and had no value apart from the idea; the idea had no reality except as embodied in the facts and discoverable through the facts. This was at once the foundation and the coping-stone of his whole theory, at once the deepest and the most fruitful thought by which it was inspired. That, however, is not to say that he held, or even attempted to hold, the balance absolutely equal. The very nature of the relation between the two elements—between the idea and the fact, between the principle and its outward expression—made it impossible that he should. Accordingly, when at the end of his Introduction he pauses to tell us in what spirit he would wish his work to be read, it is not upon the historical, but upon the speculative, side of it that he deliberately lays stress.

It is true, he admits, that it is a work of erudition; and, as such, 'it has made great and varied calls upon the learning' of the author, as it will upon that of the reader also. Yet, in the last resort, these things are no more than the mere 'furniture of the mind'; the mere brute matter from which vital truths are drawn; the mere terms, assumed to be already familiar and, as such, employed by the reason in the framing and proof of propositions which, at bottom, are 'essentially metaphysical and ideal.' It is the mind, the vital truths, the metaphysical propositions which have the first word and the last. Indeed, still under the spell of the Cartesian philosophy, as Spinoza had been before him, he even goes the length of describing his method as 'strictly geometrical': the method which 'passes, by immediate intuition, from one truth to another.' In this last point he was manifestly mistaken; or rather perhaps, in his zeal for the enforcement of what was really true, he suffered himself to be seduced into a metaphor which, if taken literally, could not fail to give an impression wholly false. Another of his metaphors—this time obviously intended for no more than a metaphor—is more happily chosen; though even here, it must be owned, there is some trace of exaggeration. 'The reader,' he says, 'must put off his whole bodily nature (*corpolenza*) and all that pure reason draws from his bodily nature. He must for the time being lay imagination to rest and put memory to sleep; because, if these faculties are awake, the mind can never bring itself to that state of pure intelligence, uncumbered with any definite form, without which this Science can never be understood.' [1]

Here we have the inner mind of the writer concerning the scope and method of his book: his conviction that the historical element in his work was subordinate to the philosophical; that he was throughout concerned rather with ideas than with facts; that it was as philosopher, rather than as historian or antiquarian, that he had a right to be judged. The longer the time that passes, the more strongly is it likely that this claim will be confirmed.

What, then, are the chief ideas which Vico cast upon the world?

[1] *S.N.* ii. 50-51.

What the services which give him an abiding place, and a place with the foremost, in the history of political philosophy?

He was the first to revolt against the individualism which, from the Reformation onwards, had swept everything before it; the first to brush aside that initial error, to re-establish the elementary truth that man is by his very nature a civic being and that, for that reason, his beginnings are to be sought not in the isolated individual, but in the Family and in its necessary outgrowth, the State.[1] Hence the idea of Rights, which was the watchword of the individualists, is in the *Scienza nuova* replaced by that of Right: the idea which isolates each individual from all the others, by the idea which conceives each of them as living only in the common life of all, as finding his true interest, his true individuality, only in the common good.

But, if Vico is sworn foe to the individualists, he is so no less to the utilitarians, as already represented by Spinoza, as soon to be reinforced by Hume with his French and English disciples. ' A society of hucksters ' is his verdict on the State as conceived by Spinoza. It would have been his verdict upon the State as painted by the later utilitarians also; and with the Platonic modification, ' a city of pigs,' upon the hedonist variety also.

It is against the individualists, however, that his main assault is directed. And starting, as we have seen, from the principle that Society is the ' natural state ' of man—that ' art,' as Burke said, ' is man's nature '—he was inevitably led on to insist that the problem of political philosophy is to be solved not by deductions from unreal abstractions, such as the ' individual ' and his ' rights,' but by a faithful study of Society, as it is presented to us in experience, and of the changes through which history, checked by vigilant reason, shows it to have passed. And this, in its turn, means that the method to be employed is not that of analysis—not the dissection of a matter assumed to be stationary and invariable—but the historical method which starts from the conception of development, of organic and continuous growth. Hence the stress he lays on the idea of progress: of progress, through ideals which perpetually expand and purify themselves, to a divinely ordered end: of progress which begins with the few, but gradually widens its movement until it encompasses the whole race.

[1] ' Le cose fuori del loro stato naturale nè vi si adagiano, nè vi durano. Questa Degnità sola, poichè 'l gener umano, da che si ha memoria del mondo, ha vivuto e vive comportevolmente in società, ella determina la gran disputa, della quale i migliori Filosofi e i Morali Teologi ancora contendono con Carneade, scettico, e con Epicuro—nè Grozio l' ha pur inchiodata—se vi sia diritto in natura, o se l' umana natura sia socievole, che suonano la medesima cosa ' (*S.N.* ii. 97; compare *ib.* 129-30).

Thus the story of man's civic life ends, as it began, with God. His first step from the outer darkness was prompted by the sudden intuition which revealed to him God's wrath and, by way of propitiation, drove him into his first union with his kind. And at every subsequent stage of his advance the same twofold process—at once divine and human, at once religious and moral—has been repeated. If every forward step has brought him a clearer and fuller knowledge of God, it has also brought him a wider and deeper sense of his duties towards his fellow-men. The latter would have been impossible without the former: the outward sign of progress without the inner spirit which alone can give it permanence and strength. It is not enough that man's destiny should be guided by Providence; he must consciously recognise it to be so, or the guidance will lose more than half of its effect. So it is that the deepening sense of brotherhood between man and man goes hand in hand with a deepening reverence for God. Inseparably intertwined, they form together the golden thread round which is woven that 'ideal, eternal history which runs its course in time.'

In this recognition of religion as the essential basis of man's civic, no less than of his moral, life Vico goes back to his master, Plato; he reaches forward to such later thinkers as Burke on the one side and Mazzini or Rousseau on the other. Contrast his ardent conviction on this matter with the conventional lip-service of Locke or Grotius—still more with the silence of Hume and Bentham, with the open hostility of Holbach and Helvétius—and we have the measure of the gulf which parted Vico from the prevailing fashion of political thought, as it was in his own century and in the century before him.

(B) Montesquieu

Montesquieu can hardly lay claim to the same degree of originality. But his principles are, to a large extent, analogous to those of Vico. He reached them, it would seem, in entire independence of Vico.[1] And he was gifted by nature with a power of exposition

[1] We learn from Montesquieu's Journal that the *Scienza nuova* was recommended to him during his sojourn in Venice (1728); and a copy of the first draft (1725) is still preserved in the Library at la Brède (see Croce, *Filosofia di Giambattista Vico*, Eng. transl., p. 269). But it may be doubted whether he ever read it; and it is certain that, if he did, it made little or no impression upon him. Thus, to take a crucial instance, his view of early Roman History is entirely unaffected by Vico's 'discoveries' in this field. To him, as to all other writers before Niebuhr (Vico alone excepted), the primitive government of Rome was not an Aristocracy, but a limited form of Monarchy, at once 'monarchical, aristo-

and a mastery of style which were wholly beyond Vico's reach. His aims, moreover, were far more practical than Vico's. He was less of an antiquarian; and if he was also less of a philosopher, he had a far keener sense of the forces at work in his own day and he was far more of a reformer.

Accordingly, while Vico remained wholly unknown for at least a century and has even yet hardly come by his just dues, the fame of Montesquieu was assured from the first moment; it stands, and justly stands, unshaken to the present day. If any gathering of educated men were asked who it was that first applied the historical method to political philosophy, it is probable that nine out of ten of them would answer without hesitation: it was Montesquieu. With even more of justice—for, as we have seen, in this matter Vico was before him in the path—all would agree that, of the four chief writers who prepared the way for the Revolution in France, Montesquieu was certainly not the least; and that, of all the political works produced in Europe during the half century before the Revolution, the only one which can stand comparison with the *Contrat social* is *Esprit des lois*. Where indeed, in the whole range of political literature, shall we find a book more solidly argued? the materials of which are gathered from a wider field, or more firmly welded together? Are there many books, we may even ask, whose ultimate principles are at once so simple and so fruitful, or whose influence upon those who form public opinion in these matters has been wider and more salutary?

With all this in his favour, it is idle to wonder why the fate of Montesquieu should have differed so widely from that of Vico. The mere fact that his chief concern was not with the remote past but with questions which bore directly upon the needs and interests of the present is enough, even if there had been no other reasons, to account for the difference. The fundamental distinction between the chief possible types of Government—republican, monarchical and despotic—and the causes from which they flow; the close connection between the outward circumstances and the inward character of nations; the inevitable influence of both these things upon the constitutional form of their Government and on their historical development; the essential unity of a nation's life, and the consequent folly of attempting to divorce any one side of it—religious, moral, constitutional, commercial and so forth—from the rest: these and kindred matters form the staple of Montesquieu's argument. And they are matters which, at the first appeal,

---

cratic and popular.' So far as he was concerned, that is, Vico might just as well never have written. See *Grandeur et décadence des Romains* (1734), chaps. i., viii., and *Esprit des lois*, xi. 12-14.

were bound to come home to the generation for which he wrote: a generation which was still groaning under the burden laid on France by the ruinous policy of Louis XIV.; which was fertile in schemes, some wise and some foolish, for lightening it; and which —so far, at least, as the more educated classes were concerned— was rapidly becoming more and more hostile to the religious creed, more and more critical even of the political institutions, which had been handed down from the past.

Thus, even apart from his style and his genius for exposition, there was an actuality about his application of the historical method which was wanting to that of Vico: a cut and thrust in the dexterous rapier of *Esprit des lois* which was not to be looked for in the 'disembodied ideas' of the *Scienza nuova*. Not that Montesquieu parades his mastery of the weapon. Good taste and prudence alike forbade. What he said of his Reply to an egregious reviewer may be applied, though in a less degree, to the treatise itself: 'The charm of my *Défense* to the reader is not that he sees the venerable theologians thrown roughly to the ground, but that he watches them slide gently down.'[1] It is plain that the charm was felt by the writer also; and it may be suspected that there were moments when he allowed it to draw him a trifle further than, in his heart of hearts, he had intended to go.

Within the soul of Montesquieu there were, in fact, two men struggling for the mastery: the political philosopher and the practical reformer. The one, as Voltaire and Helvétius were not slow to detect, essentially conservative: reverent of the past; keenly alive to the organic unity of national life in all its varied expressions; averse from innovation, if only because he was aware that a change in one direction commonly brings with it, and ought to bring with it, a thousand changes more; firm in the conviction, the fruit of long study and reflection, that without religion there can be no healthy national existence, and that the established form of religion is not more, but less, easily altered than that of any other object to which men have given their loyalty and devotion.[2] The other, a true

[1] Lettre à Mme. du Deffand, Sept. 13, 1754: 'Ce qui plaît dans ma *Défense*, ce n'est pas de voir les vénérables théologiens mis à terme; c'est de les y voir couler doucement' (*Correspondance de Montesquieu*, ii. 536; and *Œuvres de Montesquieu*, 6 vols., Paris, 1816, vol. i. p. xxxiii.). The attack to which the *Défense* was a reply had appeared in the *Nouvelles ecclésiastiques*, a Jansenist organ, of October 1749. There was also an attack in the Jesuit organ, *Journal de Trévoux*, in the April of the same year.

[2] See *Esprit des lois*, xxiv. 1-3. See also his letter to Warburton of May 1754 (*Correspondance*, ii. 528: ed. Paris, 1914): 'Il n'est pas impossible d'attaquer une religion révélée, parce qu'elle existe par des

child of his age and country, eager for reform; impatient of abuses, especially when they cut athwart his instincts of humanity; and in matters of religious observance, critical, sceptical and, at moments, not a little contemptuous and satirical. The two strains are not easy to reconcile. But the one is no less characteristic than the other; the one needs to be no less carefully reckoned with than the other.

There is one point, however, in which the two strains meet and mingle. If any case should present itself in which the abuse, so far from being of old growth, was a recent innovation—still more, if it should appear that the innovation was one of those which strike root rapidly and threaten to spread swiftly and widely—it is evident that then both the conservative and the reforming instincts of the author would be enlisted under the same banner; that his whole nature would at once rise in rebellion; that he would put forth all his powers to warn his countrymen of the danger and to combat it with every weapon at his command.

Such a case was presented by the recent history of the French Monarchy: by its increasing tendency to draw the whole life of the nation into its own grasp, to stifle all the independent sources of energy, especially of organised energy, that still survived from the middle ages and from the period of civil strife which followed. The champions of the Gallican liberties, the Huguenots, the Jansenists, the Parlements—and each of these, in their own way, stood for freedom as against the overweening claims of Royal or Papal absolutism—felt the heavy hand of the King or his ministers. And though the hardest blows against the Parlements were not dealt until after his death, Montesquieu—who, as ex-*Président à Mortier*, was acutely sensitive on the point—clearly foresaw the dead set that was to be made against their rights and bitterly resented it. Together with the obvious hostility of the Crown to all forms of religious independence, he took this, and justly took it, to betray a settled design on the part of the King and his ministers to destroy all such forces as still barred the way to absolute power; to convert a more or less limited Monarchy—for such he labours to prove that the French Monarchy was—into a pure despotism; in a word,

---

faits particuliers, et que les faits, par leur nature, peuvent être une matière de dispute. Mais il n'est pas de même de la religion naturelle: elle est tirée de la nature de l'homme, dont on ne peut disputer, et du sentiment intérieur de l'homme, dont on ne peut pas disputer encore.' What follows is curious: 'J'ajoute à ceci: Quel peut être le motif d'attaquer la religion révélée en Angleterre? On l'y a tellement purgée de tout préjugé distracteur qu'elle n'y peut faire de mal et qu'elle y peut faire, au contraire, une infinité de biens.' It is quite true that he was writing to a future Bishop. But it is not to be supposed that, for complaisance' sake, he was capable of feigning opinions which he did not hold.

to carry on and complete the work of Richelieu and Louis XIV. And—if we may take Louvois to stand for his august master—we know that, in his judgement, these were 'the two worst citizens' that recent French history had produced.[1]

Hence the deep undertone of uneasiness which marks all that he writes about Monarchy and Despotism. It is the exasperation of the thinker who sees his most cherished distinctions trampled under foot; the anguish of the patriot who watches his country driven to ruin by a dissolute monarch and a gang of placemen who sacrificed everything to the alleged convenience of the moment, content, like their master, with the coward's maxim: After us, the deluge. Unless this be borne in mind, some of the most striking pages of *Esprit des lois* will remain an undecipherable riddle.[2]

What, then, are the leading ideas of this memorable treatise? and what their bearing upon the history of political philosophy? In his opening chapter Montesquieu himself is careful to mark the order of ideas to which he has given his allegiance; the vital principle which gives unity to his necessarily scattered details; the torch, in the light of which every detail is seen to take its place as part of an ordered and intelligible whole. As was to be expected, there is no part of the treatise which has met with criticism so bitter and, in the main, so unintelligent and wrong-headed.

What is the first impression, he asks, of any man who looks out upon the innumerable laws and institutions which present themselves in experience and history? Is it not that the whole thing is a labyrinth without a clue, an inextricable confusion in which it is impossible to find any principle of reason or order? in which everything is the prey of blind chance and arbitrary caprice? The same, however, must have been the first impression of man as he looked out upon the face of Nature. It was only by long observation and reflection that he was able to draw order out of chaos, to disentangle the laws, now universally recognised, which lie behind the apparent haphazard and confusion. Is it not probable, we must ask ourselves, that the same thing will be found to hold good of man's civic history also? that here too the seeming chaos will, with patient reflection, gradually reduce itself to order? the apparent

[1] 'Les plus méchants citoyens de France furent Richelieu et Louvois': *Pensées diverses* (*Œuvres*, vi. p. 523). As Louis was the political heir of Richelieu and the accomplice of Louvois, it is hard to believe that Montesquieu did not equally condemn him. Only, unlike the Abbé de Saint-Pierre, he was too prudent to say so. His defensive *Reflections* on Louis (*Esprit des lois*, ix. 7) are a very half-hearted performance. A more hostile, and probably a more candid, estimate is to be found in *Lettres persanes*, xxiv. and xxxviii.

[2] See, in particular, *Esprit des lois*, viii. 6-9; ix. 6-7; x. 9.

lawlessness give place to general laws? blind chance and wilful caprice to the operation of principles at once well-grounded, reasonable and simple? After all, man is a rational being; and to suppose that such a being should suffer itself to be the sport of blind chance or fate is 'a great absurdity': one of the greatest that it is possible to conceive.[1]

The first of these principles—that, indeed, from which all the others must be held to flow—is involved in the very conception of Law. All law—in the sense of the principles underlying any matter of man's knowledge or experience—is relation: everything is what it is in virtue of its relation to the rest of our experience, by reason of the place it holds in the whole universe of being. In that sense, even God has His laws: the laws which man discovers by studying the relations He has established between one object and another in the world of nature, between one man and another in the world of action; between Himself and the world of nature on the one hand, or the heart of man upon the other.[2]

This principle once firmly grasped, it follows that, if there are any laws which the political life of man follows, any generalisations to be drawn from his actions as a civic being, they are to be discovered solely by a study of the relations in which he stands to his outward surroundings and to his fellow-men: including, and including above all, those relations which, just because they are the most intimate and deep-reaching, we roughly describe as constituting his intrinsic nature: on the one hand, that relation to his fellows which we have in mind when we say that he is an essentially moral being, with a sense of duty and responsibility both to other men and to God; on the other, those evident relations, both to other men and to the world without, which spring from his primary instinct of self-preservation, his innate desire to secure his own welfare and happiness.

Each of these two main kinds of relation—alike that of duty and that of interest—carries with it far-reaching consequences. On the one hand, if man is by nature a moral being, a being bound to his kind by ties from which there is no escape and no release, and if those ties of duty are further strengthened by innumerable promptings of self-interest, then there is no need to ask when and how civil society had its origin, no need to look for that origin in any 'covenant' such as been supposed to constitute the obligation which binds men to civil society, in any 'contract' such as is sometimes alleged to have drawn him from a previous 'state of nature.' The real state of nature, for man, *is* civil society; and there was no need of any contract or covenant to draw him thither.[3] For this

[1] *Esprit des lois*, i. 1. [2] *Ib.*

[3] 'Je n'ai jamais ouï parler du droit public qu'on n'ait commencé par

reason, if for no other, the individualist theory of the State must be rejected without ceremony. Man is what he is by relation to his fellows. The naked, isolated individual is an abstraction, and a false abstraction, if there ever was one.[1]

No less sweeping are the consequences upon the other side: that of self-interest, expediency, utility—whether individual or collective. And these, let it not be forgotten, are considerations which enter not only into those matters where their presence is admitted by all, but even, and no less inevitably, into those which, at first sight, we are apt to regard as questions of pure duty. I may know perfectly well that I have a duty in a given matter of conduct. But what that duty is, how precisely I ought to act with a view to fulfilling it, can only be known when I have asked myself, What course of action is most for the advantage of the community at large? how will the interest of the men, or body of men, to whom I acknowledge my obligation be most effectually furthered? It is quite true that in nine cases out of ten, at least in regard to my conduct as an individual, the answer to that question is given ready to my hand by previous experience, whether my own or taken on trust by me from others. But in the tenth case it may well happen that I have to work out the problem for myself. And if in the nine remaining cases I am spared the trouble of doing so, that is only because I suppose, rightly or wrongly, that it has already been worked out, beyond possibility of mistake, by others.

So far as to matters of purely individual conduct. When we turn to matters of 'civil government'—still more perhaps, to the questions which arise between State and State—it is obvious that the calculations required will be even more complicated, that the part played by considerations of expediency, in the broader sense of the term, will consequently be even greater. Here, therefore, still more manifestly than in matters of personal conduct, we are brought face to face with the study of relations: those relations, or 'circumstances,' which, in Burke's language, 'give to every political principle'—he might have added, to every moral principle also—'its distinguishing colour and discriminating effect.'[2] On

---

rechercher soigneusement quelle est l'origine des sociétés: ce qui me paraît ridicule. Si les hommes n'en formaient point, s'ils se quittaient et se fuyaient les uns les autres, il faudrait en demander la raison et chercher pourquoi ils se tiennent séparés. Mais ils naissent tous liés les uns aux autres; un fils est né auprès de son père, et il s'y tient: voilà la société et la cause de la société' (*Lettres persanes*, xciv.).

[1] Compare Burke, *Appeal from the New to the Old Whigs: Works*, i. pp. 522-25.

[2] Compare Burke, *Reflections: Works*, i. p. 324.

this side, no less than on those of the primary duties which are the most fundamental of all relations, we are driven back on the idea of relation as the key to all political, as well as to all moral, decisions.

'All knowledge is knowledge of relations.' To our ears this may sound little better than a truism. It would be accepted—doubtless in different senses and with widely different implications—by all schools of thinkers: by materialist as well as idealist; by disciples of Bentham, as well as by disciples of Rousseau or disciples of Mazzini. To the eighteenth century, however, it was a dangerous heresy. And Montesquieu, if not the first to proclaim it, was at least the first to give it currency in the field of politics. What is yet more to the purpose, he was the first to grasp it as a general truth; the first to apply it to the whole range of political discussion. What Vico had been dimly groping after is set in the clearest light by Montesquieu. What is implied throughout the *Scienza nuova* is explicitly asserted and worked out in *Esprit des lois*.

That is why the idea of relation is placed in the very forefront of his treatise; that is why his opening sentence defines *Law* as 'the sum of relations which necessarily flow from the nature of a given object.' This was no vain parade of 'metaphysical subtlety,' as Voltaire was pleased to suppose.[1] Still less was it a blundering confusion of issues which 'enlightened philosophy had set asunder for all time,' as Helvétius roundly declared.[2] On the contrary, it was the pressing need of the explorer to make his intended course plain from the first step, to give warning of the gulf which parted him from the prevailing fashion of his time at the very start.

The warning was timely, and it was needed in two different quarters. The two theories which divided the world at the time when Montesquieu wrote were the theory of abstract Rights and the theory of expediency: the theory of Locke, and the theory which had been Spinoza's and which, in a watered form, was soon to become the theory of Helvétius and of Bentham. That the

[1] 'Ne nous jouons point dans les subtilités de cette métaphysique. Gardons-nous d'entrer dans ce labyrinthe,' is his comment on Montesquieu's first chapter: *Idées républicaines*, *Œuvres* (ed. 1785), vol. xxix. p. 354 (ed. 1877, xxiv. 424).

[2] 'Je finirai par vous avouer que je n'ai jamais compris les subtiles distinctions sans cesse répétées sur les différentes formes de gouvernement. Je n'en connais que deux espèces: les bons, qui sont encore à faire; les mauvais, dont tout l'art est, par différents moyens, de faire passer l'argent de la partie gouvernée dans la bourse de la partie gouvernante.' This was Helvétius' honourably candid avowal, in returning the MS. of *Esprit des lois*, which Montesquieu had sent to him for criticism (1747): *Correspondance de Montesquieu*, ii. 21. It is only fair to say that in his later works, *De l'esprit* (1758), *De l'homme* (posthumous) 1772, Helvétius shows a much more open mind. See below, Chapter VI.

former of these theories was at variance with that of Montesquieu is evident at a glance. That the latter was hardly less so, and that the grounds of opposition were almost identical, will not perhaps be so readily admitted. Yet it is the case. The truth is that, whatever their apparent hostility, the two theories had much in common. What is the first, and most obvious, objection to the theory of Rights? It is that such a theory makes no allowance for the infinite diversity of man's political conditions: that it assumes an abstract man, the same at all times, in all places, under all circumstances whatever. From this objection, if not from others, the theory of expediency is commonly held to be absolutely and necessarily free. And so, in the form with which recent writers have made us familiar, it may reasonably claim to be.

With the form which it took in the eighteenth century, however, this is very far from being the case. To Helvétius, Bentham and others, expediency, so far from being a flexible principle, is in effect hardly less stark and rigid than the rival principle of Rights. The 'man,' by whose interests, or 'utility,' all things are to be tested, is not the infinitely variable being—the creature of time, place and circumstance—revealed to us by history. He is essentially an abstract being: the same always, everywhere and in all conceivable surroundings.

It is obvious that this carries with it a corresponding change in the nature of the expediency, or 'utility,' which man has to consult. If man is the same at all times and under all circumstances, it follows that what is for his interest, what is expedient for him, at one time or under one set of conditions, will be the same for him in all: in other words, that circumstances, so far from being the dominant factor in his life, are of no account whatever. At that rate, it should be possible, and even easy, to draw up a code of interests, of 'utility,' which shall be the same always, everywhere and for all. And the natural inference would be that a 'felicific calculus' can be framed of a certainty as infallible as any mathematical calculus that the genius of Newton or Leibnitz could discover. As all the world knows, this is the inference which Bentham actually draws. And if Helvétius does not push his logic to that extremity, at least we are left with the haunting sense that he ought to have done so: that he could hardly have written as he does, had not some such assumption been hovering before his mind. The whole sting of his protest against Montesquieu's argument lies in his assertion that 'there are only two kinds of Government, the good and the bad'; that the former is still unknown to the world; and that any attempt to account for the latter is no better than an insidious way of justifying its abuses. If this be true, all we can say is that the case is still more desperate than Helvétius supposed. The 'felicific calculus,' so far from being the easiest thing to discover, is the hardest in the world: man has been in quest of it for fifty centuries, and he has not found it yet.

Of the utilitarian theory, so conceived and applied to politics, there can be no serious defence. It is of the essence of that theory, on any intelligible interpretation of it, to take expediency as the sole guide in political discussion. It is of the essence of expediency, on any rational construction of the term, to vary with varying circumstances. To frame a code, therefore, which, while claiming to base itself upon circumstances, yet deliberately refuses to consider those very circumstances which are manifestly the most important, the circumstances of the given time and the given place, is to deny in detail the very principle which has been asserted in gross. It is to lay down a truth of universal application, and then run violently athwart it the first time it is put to the test of practice. For all practical purposes, as we shall see in the next chapter, the expediencies so arrived at are as rigid, as intolerant of individual circumstances and peculiarities, as a code of absolute Rights. They are, in fact, only another name, and a highly misleading name, for Rights.

That Montesquieu was aware of the hostility with which both these schools—both the champions of abstract Rights and the champions of abstract expediency—were bound to regard his doctrine of relativity, is certain; and it might have been expected that he would openly forestall their attack. That, however, was not his way. He had a natural distaste for the more boisterous methods of controversy, for 'throwing his adversaries roughly to the ground'; his real delight was to 'watch them sliding gently down.' It was so with the 'venerable theologians'; it is so equally with the far more formidable champions of absolute expediency and of absolute Rights.

But, however veiled his assault, the enemy was at no loss to understand its bearing and importance. Both Voltaire and Helvétius felt the necessity of repelling it. Each of them composed a running commentary—Voltaire's largely composed of sneers and sarcasms—upon the offending document; and Voltaire returned to the charge a few years before his death.[1] Even Rousseau,

[1] The commentary of Helvétius is to be found in many editions of Montesquieu's works; several further criticisms appear in his *Réflexions morales* (cxlix.-clx.): *Œuvres* (ed. 1795, 14 vols. 12mo: vol. xiv.). Voltaire's two attacks are embodied in his *Commentaire* (1777) and the *Idées républicaines*, which in ed. 1877 is attributed, on what appear to be very flimsy grounds, to 1762; but in ed. 1785 (Kehl) to 1765. If, as it seems to me, there is a reference in it to Rousseau's *Lettres de la Montagne*, which

despite his undisguised veneration for the author, could not repress an occasional grumble at the more speculative consequences of his doctrine: a smothered lament that, after all, Montesquieu, like Grotius, was too apt to 'establish the right by the fact,' and so to confound two things which it is the first business of the philosopher to keep apart.[1]

Undismayed by the fear of these and other criticisms, Montesquieu goes steadily on his way, working out in detail the general principle thus laid down from the beginning. And it is with this practical application of his doctrine that by far the greater part of his book is taken up. Strictly speaking, it is perhaps beyond the scope of our enquiry to follow him in such a task. But, even apart from the intrinsic interest of the subject, it is impossible to understand the full meaning of the doctrine, until we have grasped at least the main lines of its application: still more impossible to estimate the greatness of the man, unless we have watched his mind at work, calling order out of chaos, moulding his rebel material, the harvest of long study and deep reflection, to his will.

Starting, then, from the general principle that everything is what it is in virtue of its relations, What, he asks, are the relations which have counted the most in moulding the political and social life of man? There is, in the first place, the relation of man to his outward surroundings: the influence of soil and climate upon the character of a given community,[2] upon its social and economic

---

appeared in December 1764, the latter is the correct date. The original edition was undated; but the Kehl editors, writing within a few years of Voltaire's death, are likely to have been well informed (see ed. 1877, vol. xxiv. pp. 413, 424). The reference to the *Lettres de la Montagne*, which I believe myself to find is: 'Ce sont les livres d'injures qu'il faut brûler . . parce qu'une injure est un délit'—while the *Contrat social*, being 'un œuvre de raisonnement,' however illogical, ought to have been refuted, but otherwise left alone (ed. 1877, xxiv. 424). The earliest mention of Montesquieu in Voltaire's *Correspondance* is in a letter to the Duc d'Uzès of September 14, 1751: 'Mme. du Deffand a eu raison d'appeller son livre *de l'esprit sur les lois*: on ne peut mieux, ce me semble, le définir' (*Corr.*, ed. 1785, vol. iii. p. 359). Mme. du Deffand's epigram is repeated again in the *Commentaire* (ed. 1785, vol. xxix. p. 381.)

[1] See *Émile*, livre v. (*Political Writings of Rousseau*, ii. p. 147). In *C.S.* II. vi. he attacks Montesquieu for drawing an analogy between a political law and a law of nature; he really ought to have known better. In general, the references to Montesquieu, which are more frequent than to any other author, are in the last degree respectful. And the same, it is pleasant to note, is true of Helvétius' references—that is, in his later works, *De l'esprit* (1758), and *De l'homme* (1772)—however much of disagreement they may embody.

[2] *Esprit des lois*, livres xiv., xvii.

existence,[1] upon the whole tissue of morals and manners which is inseparably bound up with these,[2] upon the form of government best adapted to its character and way of life,[3] upon its bearing towards the fundamental problems of man's being—above all, towards those religious problems which lie at the root of all.[4] All these things are so closely interwoven with each other—soil and climate, for instance, acting largely through national character and forms of government, national character and forms of government reacting readily upon soil and climate—that it is often impossible, and seldom necessary, to disentangle the one from the other. But directly or indirectly, mediately or immediately, it cannot be doubted that the outward conditions of man are of the deepest importance to his political and moral existence: that there is a sense, and a very real sense, in which 'the first of all empires is the empire of climate.' [5]

This, however, by no means exhausts the fertility of Montesquieu. Besides the mutual action and reaction between man's outward conditions and the inward life — moral, political and religious — which he gradually builds up for himself, there is another kind of relation which meets us at every turn of *Esprit des lois*: which, in fact, is deliberately singled out by the author to set in the forefront of the consequences which flow from the acceptance of his central principle. That is the relation between the outward form of a given Government—republican, monarchical, or despotic—and the secondary laws and institutions which each of them carries in its train: between the constitutional, or fundamental, laws of a given community and the civil laws, the social order, the administrative machinery which each of these types severally demands.[6]

This is the more distinctively political part of the treatise; and, with the exception of those chapters which deal with religion and which were thought, justly enough, to deny that Christianity could ever be the universal religion—to assert that it too, like all other things in this world, is subject to every kind of physical and social condition [7]—it is the part which, among the author's contemporaries, aroused more interest and more controversy than any other. To lay bare the distinctive nature of the different types of Government, to trace the manner in which each of them works itself out and articulates itself in practice, modifying, as it does so, the whole structure of the national life down to the minutest detail; to prove that the whole social and civil life of every community depends,

[1] *Esprit des lois*, livres xv., xviii., xx., xxi., xxii.

[2] *Ib.* livres xvi., xvii., xix., xxiii.

[3] *Ib.* livres xiv., xvii., xviii.

[4] *Ib.* livres xxiv., xxv.

[5] *Ib.* xix., 14.

[6] *Ib.* livres i.-viii.

[7] *Ib.* xix. 18; compare xxiv. 24, 25.

in the last resort, largely upon the particular form of Government established in it: this was to touch a responsive chord in the minds of men, to come home very 'close to their business and bosoms.' Much of *Esprit des lois* is a far-reaching philosophy of history. Much of it is concerned, by implication at least, with the questions which lie at the root of political philosophy. But here, at any rate, we are brought face to face with the problems which confront the practical statesman. And it was for this reason, doubtless, that Montesquieu chose to devote the opening books of his treatise to this discussion.

The moving principle, the 'spirit' of the republican form of government, is found by Montesquieu, as is well known, to lie in 'virtue': by which it is evident that he understood an exalted form of public spirit, of devotion to the common weal.[1] This virtue is demanded in the highest degree by a Democracy; in a less, but still a marked, degree by an Aristocracy.[2] The spirit of Monarchy—above all, of Monarchy as it had grown up in such a country as France—is, after the same fashion, found to consist in 'honour'; [3] and that of Despotism—on this point there is no room for dispute — in brute force on the part of the ruler, in terror on that of the ruled.[4] The one and only check on the caprice of the despot is religion: the impossibility of running counter to precepts, or even to prejudices, which are supposed to be sanctioned by a higher power, and therefore to be 'given over the head not only of the subject, but of the ruler also.' [5] And as 'the prejudices of superstition are the strongest of all prejudices,' such a check may not seldom serve to punish, if not to prevent, the extreme of wrong-doing and oppression.[6] The check is often belated, and always capricious, in its working. What can be said for an abuse which has no better remedy than this?

From these verdicts, it is manifest that Montesquieu draws the hardest possible line between Despotism and all other forms of Government. The despot is not to be tolerated except in backward countries, or in countries where the nature of the climate inclines, or even compels, men to accept him; [7] and even so, he is treated as no more than an odious necessity.[8] As for the other three types of polity—Monarchy, Aristocracy and Democracy—all of them are capable—in many passages he seems to imply, equally capable—of being made good instruments of Government; and the causes which have determined the establishment of one,

[1] *Esprit des lois*, livres iii. 2, v. 2. [2] *Ib.* iii. 4.
[3] *Ib.* iii. 7. [4] *Ib.* iii. 9. [5] *Ib.* iv. 10.
[6] *Ib.* xviii. 19. [7] *Ib.* ii. 15.
[8] 'Le principe du gouvernement despotique se corrompt sans cesse, parce qu'il est corrompu par sa nature' (*ib.* viii. 10).

rather than another, of them in a given community must be sought among those which have already been indicated—variations of soil and climate, of national character, of historical tradition—or rather, in all of them together.

With the exception of Despotism, then, there is no form of Government which may not be made to serve the good of the community which has adopted it. Two conditions, however, must be jealously observed. Care must be taken from the first to guard against the abuses incident to each of them: against the danger that Democracy will degenerate into anarchy; Aristocracy or Monarchy into despotism, or something hardly to be distinguished from Despotism.[1] And in devising the checks necessary for this purpose, equal care must be taken to keep the original constitution true to the type from which it started: to avoid anything that is incompatible with the vital principle which it embodies.[2]

The latter condition, no doubt, is less absolute than the former. It holds good only so long as those concerned take for granted—as, in fact, they seldom fail to do—that at all costs revolution is to be avoided. In the absence of this assumption, it manifestly falls to the ground. To introduce changes radically at variance with the spirit of the constitution may, indeed, be an excellent method of paving the way for a revolution. And if on other grounds a revolution is desirable, there is nothing to be said against this way of invoking it.[3] Only, those who do so must be prepared to pay the price; and the price may easily prove to be heavier than they reckoned on.

Having thus established the relations which concern the internal life of the State, Montesquieu goes on to investigate those which concern its dealings with neighbouring communities. This brings him straight across the canons so ruthlessly laid down a century earlier by Grotius, so lightly accepted by a long line of intervening writers: the chain of assumptions summed up in the fateful phrase, the 'rights of war.'

[1] *Esprit des lois*, viii. 2, 3, 5, 6.

[2] 'Chaque gouvernement a sa nature et son principe. Il ne faut donc pas que l'aristocratie prenne la nature et la principe de la monarchie' (*ib.* v. 8; compare v. 9). This principle, indeed, is involved in the very title of livre v.: 'Les lois que le législateur donne doivent être relatives au principe du gouvernement.' Compare xix. 5.

[3] Even so, however, Montesquieu has his doubts: doubts based upon grounds of public policy—in particular of public morality. 'Il y a beaucoup à gagner, en fait de mœurs, à garder les coutumes anciennes. . . . Rappeller les hommes aux maximes anciennes, c'est ordinairement les rappeller à la vertu' (v. 7). This is said with special reference to Democracy; but it must apply—in some measure, at any rate—to Monarchy and Aristocracy also.

To Grotius, the rights of war are laid in the indefeasible right of the conqueror to annihilate the whole nation whose hosts he has defeated in battle: a right which, if mercifully disposed, he may commute into that of eternal enslavement.[1] This alleged right of wholesale slaughter, replies Montesquieu, is a pure invention. It is directly contrary to every one of the principles, or sanctions, which have been invoked in its favour. The 'law of nature'—that is, the law which regulates the inanimate world and the world of purely natural agents—is dead against it; for that law tends not to the destruction, but to the preservation, of every created species. So is the 'natural light' of conscience; for that commands us to do by others as we would be done by ourselves. So is the 'political law,' the principle upon which the whole life of every civil community is manifestly based; for that assumes that any community, once formed, has the right to maintain itself for ever. So, lastly, is the law of expediency, or self-interest; for that commands every man, the conqueror included, to make the best of what he has acquired; and how can he do so, if his first act is to destroy it? [2]

Thus the whole argument of Grotius is seen to rest upon a rotten foundation; and, with the foundations, the superstructure—the right of enslavement, still more of perpetual enslavement—falls hopelessly in ruins. The supposed 'right of war,' in truth, has not even the poor justification of fact; for 'no conqueror with a particle of common sense' has ever availed himself of its pretensions. The only conquerors who have attempted to do so are those who have wielded a pure despotism over all their subjects; and for that very reason their conquests have commonly been as short-lived as they were violent and oppressive. The only permanent conquests are those built upon the precisely opposite principle: moderation, clemency and conciliation. In other words, 'the wars of despotism are no more than invasions.' It is only a temperate Government—only a Monarchy, therefore, as Montesquieu understood the term, or a Republic [3]—that can hold what it has conquered. And the greater the moderation of the conqueror,

[1] Grotius, *De jure Belli et Pacis*, lib. iii. capp. iv.-viii.

[2] *Esprit des lois*, x. 3.

[3] And, for very good reasons, Montesquieu is very much less sure about the latter than the former. It will always, he says, excite resentment that those who claim 'freedom' for themselves should refuse it to others. And the consciousness of this is likely to make their rule harsher than it would otherwise have been. Their action, therefore, will be a violation not only of Right but of the higher expediency. Both his examples are taken from the history of *aristocratic* Republics, Carthage and Genoa. A memorable instance of the same thing might have been found in that of the Democracy of Athens (*ib.* x. 6-8).

the more pains he takes to conciliate and 'enfranchise' his new subjects, the more lasting, the more profitable, his conquests are likely to be. And that is only as it should be. For 'the right of conquest, however necessary and legitimate, is at best an invidious and unhappy right. It leaves the conqueror with an immense debt to human nature, which he is bound in honour to make good.'[1] And there is no way of doing this but by admitting the vanquished, sooner or later, to equal rights with the victor. This was, at least in theory, the policy of Rome. It must be the policy of every nation which seeks to emulate either the wisdom or the prosperity of Rome.[2]

Of relations between States, other than those of war and the conditions arising out of war, Montesquieu has little to say. The one point—but it is a point of the first importance—at which he touches on this group of questions is the matter of Federation; and the main service of his rapid discussion is to have furnished the hint for the ideas which, a few years later, took shape in the brooding mind of Rousseau.[3]

It would be impossible to end this sketch of Montesquieu's argument without some reference to his conception of liberty and of the means by which liberty may be most effectually secured. 'Liberty,' he justly reminds us, is one of the vaguest words known to speech. It has been confined to Monarchies; it has been confined to Republics. It has been interpreted as the right to bear arms, as the right to wear a long beard, or a short kilt. It has been used, in short, by a thousand peoples to describe the form of Government—tribal, monarchical, aristocratic, democratic, theocratic—which best sorted with their daily way of life: which long use, or a new-born enthusiasm, had most endeared to their imagination.[4]

Such perversions of the term are mere popular abuses. Its legitimate uses, so Montesquieu urges in effect, may be fairly reduced to two—the absolute and the relative: the unrestrained

[1] *Esprit des lois*, x. 3-4.

[2] *Ib.* x. 6-9. With all her tolerance of local self-government, it must be remembered that the practice of Rome fell far behind her theory. It was not until far on in the last century of the Republic that she extended the full rights of citizenship even to the whole of Italy; and Italy then meant something much smaller than it does to us. It was not until the reign of Caracalla (*circ.* A.D. 200) that she admitted the whole adult male population of the empire to the title of citizen. And long before that time it had become a mere title. It had ceased to have any political meaning; it conferred no more than equality of civil rights—and an increased burden of taxation.

[3] *Ib.* ix. 1-3. See *Political Writings of J. J. Rousseau*, i. 95.

[4] *Ib.* xi. 2. The climax is reached when Hegel, followed by a select band of English writers, identifies 'liberty' with the Prussian Constitution.

liberty of the individual to do anything he may desire; and the equal liberty of all to do all that is not forbidden by a rational code of Law.[1] Unqualified liberty, or liberty qualified by a sense of obligation to others, of duties accepted by the whole community and clearly defined by the Law which speaks for the whole community: these are the only alternatives which it is worth while to consider.[2] The former sense of the word is the ideal of the more extreme forms of Democracy; it is the ideal also of any Government, democratic or aristocratic, in which, formally or virtually, the liberum veto is enthroned.[3] The latter sense—and it is the only sense in which liberty can be an object of rational desire—is that which alone Montesquieu deigns to follow up. What, he asks, are the surest guarantees for liberty, so understood? and in what forms of Government are they most likely to be found? [4]

As all the world knows, his answer to the first question is that the best and surest guarantee for such liberty is that the three main functions of the State—legislative, executive and judicial—should be kept entirely separate: that is, that they should be lodged in three separate and independent organs. And his answer to the second is that, in theory, such a separation may be attained in any of the three legitimate forms of Government—Monarchy, Aristocracy, or Democracy; but that, in practice, there are few Governments, to whichever of these types they may belong, that have attained it. France, for instance, while keeping the Judicature more or less independent, has allowed the legislative and executive powers to be united in the hands of the monarch.[5] Many democratic Republics—Athens, for example, and, as later observers might be inclined to add, the first French Republic—have permitted

[1] *Esprit des lois*, xi. 3-5.

[2] 'Il est vrai que dans la démocratie le peuple paraît faire ce qu'il veut; mais la liberté publique ne consiste point à faire ce que l'on veut. Dans un État, *i.e.* dans une société où il y a des lois, la liberté ne peut consister qu'à pouvoir faire ce que l'on doit vouloir, et à n'être point contraint de faire ce que l'on ne doit pas vouloir. Il faut se mettre dans l'esprit ce que c'est que l'indépendance et ce que c'est que la liberté. La liberté est le droit de faire tout ce que les lois permettent; et si un citoyen pouvait faire ce qu'elles défendent, il n'aurait plus de liberté, parce que les autres auraient tout de même ce pouvoir' (*ib.* xi. 3; compare viii. 3).

[3] 'L'indépendance de chaque particulier est l'objet des lois de Pologne: et ce qui en résulte, l'oppression de tous' (*ib.* xi. 5).

[4] *Ib.* vi. 5-6; viii. 6-7; livre xi. *passim*.

[5] 'Les trois pouvoirs n'y sont point [*i.e.* in France] distribués sur le modèle de la constitution d'Angleterre. Ils ont chacun une distribution particulière, selon laquelle ils approchent plus ou moins de la liberté; et s'ils n'en approchaient pas, la monarchie dégénérait en despotisme' (*ib.* xi. 7).

all three powers to fall, in name or in deed, into the grip of the popular Assembly.[1] And, when all concealments are stripped off, the same is true of the Aristocracy of Venice; even perhaps of the later days of republican Rome.[2] It is the special distinction of England, so Montesquieu delights to insist, to have kept the three powers wholly separate and independent.[3] This, in his view, is the surest sign of her wisdom and the true secret of her strength. It is her example, more than anything else, which inclines him to regard a limited Monarchy as, on the whole, more favourable than any other form of Polity to the 'separation of powers' and therefore, in words that he would gladly have taken for his own, to 'a manly, moral and regulated liberty': the only liberty which man is justified in seeking.[4]

In view of subsequent controversies, it is well to add that Montesquieu accepts the representative system, as established in England, with a whole heart; in particular, that he will not hear of reducing the representatives to mere delegates: that to him, as to the National Assembly, the *mandat impératif* is a mischievous delusion. Among the motives which drew him to this conclusion, we can hardly doubt that a leading, perhaps the dominant, motive was a conviction that this was the only method of making the legislative Power a reality: above all, the only method of guarding it from the usurpations of the Executive.

This must suffice for a sketch of Montesquieu's main argu-

[1] It is curious that, with the history of Athens ready to his hands, Montesqueiu should have given no instance of this abuse in a Democracy.

[2] *Esprit des lois*, xi. 6, 16-18. [3] *Ib.* xi. 6; xix. 27.

[4] One of the reasons that he gives for this conclusion is highly disputable. It is that an Executive appointed by, and drawn from, the Legislative Body—and this he seems to have regarded as the only possible alternative to a Monarchy—will always have interests and feelings in common with that Body. A President elected by the whole nation, as in the United States, would manifestly satisfy the conditions he lays down. But, naturally enough, this solution had not occurred to him. Had he written a generation later, it would have been otherwise. Moreover, to any one who knows how uncommonly easy Cabinet Ministers find it to separate their cause from that of the Legislative, to which they owe their authority, his suspicions will seem gratuitous enough. The conclusion of Montesquieu is further weakened by the fact that, on his own admission, it is doubtful whether England was to be reckoned a monarchy at all: 'cette nation où la République se cache sous la forme de la monarchie' (*ib.* v. 19). With this estimate it is curious to come upon that of Vico: 'La Svezia e la Danimarca, come oggi tuttevia la Polonia e ancor l'*Inghilterra*, quantumque sieno di stato monarchiche, però aristocratemente sembrano governarsi' (*S.N.* ii. p. 560). But Montesquieu seems to have considered England a democratic rather than an aristocratic republic.

ment. Let us now turn to consider how far it is itself valid, and what is its bearing upon the general course of political speculation.

The central doctrine of *Esprit des lois*, as we have already seen, is the doctrine of relativity: the plea that every action of man, collective if not individual, is determined by his relations. The various kinds of relation which the writer has in view—physical, moral, religious, or those merely of convenience—have already been sufficiently indicated. It remains to ask: What is the precise sense in which the conception of Law—that other, but closely allied, conception which dominates the whole treatise—is applicable to each of them? what is the degree, as well as the kind of necessity, which, in each case, it entails?

The highest degree of necessity, Montesquieu evidently holds, belongs to the relation in which man stands to his physical surroundings: 'the first of all empires is the empire of climate.'[1] Many critics, from Voltaire and Helvétius downwards, have regarded this as the most vulnerable point of his argument. But it may well be doubted whether they have understood his meaning. The root of the misunderstanding lies in the assumption that the 'laws' of Montesquieu are absolute laws: that he conceives each of them as working in entire independence of all the rest. In the letter of the text there is nothing, so far as I know, to warrant this assumption; and the spirit of the whole argument is dead against it. The idea of relativity is, in fact, no less applicable to the laws themselves than to the men whom they affect. In other words, each of them works, not independently of the others, but in the closest interaction with them; each of them is liable to modify, and be modified by, the others.

Thus, when Voltaire points out in triumph that, between the fall of the Roman Republic and his own day, the character of the Italian people had admittedly changed, while the climate presumably remained the same, Montesquieu might fairly reply that a political cause, misgovernment and the social corruption bred by misgovernment, had been at work for generations and that, among other evil consequences, the folly of man, especially in the Papal dominions and those of the Spanish Bourbons, had succeeded in changing the very climate for the worse. This is, doubtless, an exception—or rather, an apparent exception—to the empire of climate But, for that very reason, it is a startling confirmation

[1] *Esprit des lois*, xix. 14. Curiously enough, this very passage clearly indicates the relativity of the very law whose 'empire' it asserts: 'Ce qui rendit le changement—*i.e.* les réformes de Pierre Ier—plus aisé, c'est que les mœurs d'alors étaient étrangères au climat et y avaient été approchées par le mélange des nations et par les conquêtes.' If this means anything, it means that political causes are capable of overriding the influence of climate.

of the still more general principle that all the laws which control the destiny of man are themselves relative in their working: that each of them is liable to be counterworked and deflected by any of the others.

Yet, when all allowance has been made for such deflections and counteractions, it remains true that they are possible only within certain limits. In particular, it remains true that, the more extreme the effects of climate, whether for heat or cold, for barrenness or fertility, the less easily are they to be modified or counteracted by the energy and intelligence, the negligence or folly, of man.[1] As the earliest and greatest of Montesquieu's disciples said: 'Let us never forget to distinguish between the general law and the special causes which are capable of modifying its effects. Even if all the South were covered with Republics and all the North with despotic Governments, it would still be true that, so far as climate goes, despotism is the Government suitable to a hot country, barbarism to a cold, and a reasonable Polity to the regions which lie between the two. . . . Liberty is not a fruit for all climates; it is therefore not within the reach of all peoples. The more we reflect on this principle established by Montesquieu, the more deeply do we realise its truth: the more it is questioned, the larger the opportunity for confirming it by new proofs.'[2] Montesquieu may have been too sweeping in his assertion of the principle; he may not have been guarded enough in its detailed application.[3] But his contention is sound at bottom; and of modern writers, he was the earliest to see its importance.

So far, then, we have arrived at two facts about the 'relations' with which Montesquieu is concerned. The first and the most important, that in these matters there is no such thing as absolute necessity: that every one of these laws, even the most cogent, is subject to modification by the others. The second, that the most cogent of all laws in his view—and, with the limitation just indicated, it is a perfectly sound view—is the law imposed on man by soil, climate and other physical conditions: that 'the first of all empires'—first in order both of time and of intensity—'is the empire of climate.'

Between this 'first law' and all the others there is one broad and obvious distinction. The one springs from the relations which are, in the first instance at any rate, purely external to man;

[1] *Esprit des lois*, xiv. 2. [2] Rousseau, *Contrat social*, III. viii.

[3] Yet see *Esprit des lois*, xiv. 5: 'Que les mauvais législateurs sont ceux qui ont favorisé les vices du climat, et les bons sont ceux qui s'y ont opposés. Plus les causes *physiques* portent les hommes au repos, plus les causes *morales* les en doivent éloigner.'

the latter from such as belong to the workings of his own nature: which are, as we say, of his own making. These are the relations which prompt him, on the one hand to seek his own welfare and convenience; and on the other, often at the price of his own convenience, to strive after what he believes to be the welfare of the community at large. On the one hand, the relation of expediency; on the other, the relation arising from his moral and religious instincts. From the nature of the case, it is obvious that these self-made relations are much more liable to modification, much less undeviating in their operation, than those with which we have been dealing hitherto. And that, for two reasons. On the one hand, being the offspring of man's own nature—and that, a nature infinitely variable, 'diverse and fluctuating'—they are themselves bound to vary, and to vary within very wide limits, as time, place, circumstance and character may dictate. On the other hand, being all of a piece, each of them inextricably bound up and interwoven with all the others, they offer a far wider field for that interaction of each with the others, that liability of each to be complicated and deflected by the others, which we have already noticed, though on a far smaller scale and to a far lower degree, in the relations which arise between man and his outward surroundings.

Of all this Montesquieu was keenly aware. As he passed to the field of purely human motive and causation, he knew, no man better, that the difficulties were bound to thicken on his path. And it is among his capital merits that he steadily refused to shut his eyes to any one of them: to conceal or evade them by any one of the thousand expedients which the fashion of his time laid ready to his hand. To reduce everything to a question of abstract Rights, to reduce everything to a matter of pure expediency—these were methods which would have infinitely simplified his enquiry. They were methods loudly pressed upon him now by one, now by the other, of the two hostile camps into which the political thought of his own day was divided. Montesquieu, however, would have none of them. Widely as they differed among themselves, both methods in his eyes were equally vicious. Both alike suffered from the incurable fault of ignoring the facts: the facts, not only as they may happen to be in a particular age, not only as they may appear to the votaries of a 'vain world that Kings and Priests are plotting in,' but as they are and are bound to be 'so long as man's nature remains the same'; so long as he is swayed neither solely by motives of abstract Right, nor solely by motives of expediency, even if that expediency were more liberally interpreted than it was by Helvétius and his confederates, but also, and no less, by those moral and religious motives, the sense of man's brotherhood with his fellow-men and of his dependence upon God, which meet and blend in the idea of duty.

All these various springs of action are lightly indicated in the opening pages of *Esprit des lois*. From the nature of the case, it was inevitable that considerations of expediency should bulk more largely than any others in the subsequent discussion. What law was ever passed except because men believed it to be expedient? But, from the first page to the last, Montesquieu never loses sight of the generous design which he had chalked out at the beginning. Throughout, motives of Right, of duty, of religion, of equity take their place side by side with calculations of expediency. Throughout, the State is conceived as existing not merely to satisfy the 'gross, animal needs of man'; not merely to meet his intellectual sense of fitness, order, convenience, utility; but also, and still more, to provide security for the free play of his spiritual and moral nature; to protect him against 'his own ignorance, his own passions, his own liability to error'; to 'recall him to the sense of that moral law which at every moment he is tempted to forget'; to prevent him from 'using that society, which is necessary to his own safety and welfare, as an instrument for the oppression of others.' [1]

And this brings us to the final difficulty which besets both the practical statesman and the observer who is in search of a clue to guide him through the labyrinth of political motives and political institutions. Among the things against which man requires to be guarded, it will be observed that Montesquieu places 'his own ignorance, his own passions, his own liability to error.' He is here speaking, no doubt, primarily of personal conduct. But he was well aware that what he says applies equally to collective action; that, if it is true of the individual, it is no less true of the State. And when he says 'the State,' he is careful to warn us that he is thinking by no means only of the Government, of 'the magistrate.' On the contrary, if the Government goes wrong, it is commonly because the community has gone wrong before it: 'the prejudices of the magistrate have generally begun by being the prejudices of the people.' [2]

Here we have a sufficiently explicit avowal that, however much all these things have their cause, yet that cause is by no means always one that can be justified by reason. Ignorance, passion, prejudice—nay, pure miscalculation—have played their part in the life of the State as they have, and do, in the life of the individual. Because a given course of action has been followed by the State, because a given institution exists in the State, we can no more infer that it is reasonable than we could infer the same

[1] *Esprit des lois*, i. 2. [2] *Préface*.

thing of a theft or murder committed by an individual. It is true that, the course of action once taken, the particular institution once founded, the community is no longer entirely a free agent: that more harm may be done by a sudden reversal of the past than by accepting it and making the best of it. That, however, is a wholly different question: a question which, for each case as it arises, must be decided on its own merits. What we are here concerned with is to clear Montesquieu from the charge of worshipping the accomplished fact, of accepting the doctrine, so dear to many who invoke his authority, that 'whatever is, is right.' On the contrary: there are few writers who make more explicit allowance for the presence of folly and perversity in human action, collective as well as individual; few thinkers who have been less apt to confound the maxim, 'all things are to be accounted for,' with the very different maxim, 'all things are to be justified.' His unceasing denunciations of despotism—dénunciations which barely conceal a deep anxiety for the future of his own country—are, in themselves, enough to prove this.[1] Other proofs, perhaps yet more significant, will offer themselves before the end of our enquiry.

The fact is that, from end to end of *Esprit des lois*, there run two strains which need to be held carefully apart: the strain of the pure historian, whose one care is to ascertain the facts and to explain how and why each of them arise; and the strain of the practical statesman, whose main concern is not with facts but with values, whose aim is not merely to understand the facts, but to discover how they may best be handled for the lasting good of the community or of mankind. Montesquieu himself was at little pains to disentangle the one strand from the other; his readers, to judge from their criticisms of him, have too often been at less. But until we have learned to recognise the presence of each, until we have schooled ourselves to follow, page by page and chapter by chapter, the seemingly capricious manner in which each sometimes blends and sometimes conflicts with the other, the real meaning of the book will remain as dark to us as it was to Mme. du Deffand and Voltaire.

Of the historical vein, unbending and unalloyed, it is easy enough to find examples. The last five books of *Esprit des lois*[2] —in strictness, however, the twenty-ninth book ought to be excepted[3]—are one long case in point. They are the work not of a political philosopher, but of an historian—doubtless, a highly philosophical historian—pure and simple. Their avowed object

[1] E.g. *Esprit des lois*, viii. 6-8; x. 9.

[2] *Ib.* livres xxvii.-xxxi.

[3] *Ib.* livre xxix.: *De la manière de composer les lois.*

is to give a reasoned account, in the first place, of the Roman Law of Succession; and in the second, of ' those Laws which at a given moment sprang to life over the whole of Europe, establishing a general system with a bias towards anarchy, and anarchy with a tendency to order and harmony ': in one word, of that fabric of Law and social order which we roughly describe as *feudal*.[1] Yet even here Montesquieu is at pains to bring his discussion into some kind of connection with the main thread of his argument: in the former case, by insisting that the successive variations in the Roman Law of Succession exactly correspond with the fluctuations which can be traced in the political ideals prevalent at various periods of Roman history; in the latter case, by an accumulation of proofs that the Laws of the Germanic Tribes which overran the western Provinces of the Roman Empire have left an indelible mark upon the laws and customs still in force in each of those Provinces; and upon none more than those of France.

It is true that, even so, this large section of his work, nearly a quarter of the whole book, has little bearing upon the problems of the practical statesman; that its interest still remains mainly of the theoretical or historical kind. This, however, was implicit in his scheme from the first. If it was part of that scheme to lay stress upon the closeness of the bond which exists between the political framework of every community and the laws, the social order, the manners, the morals, the religion which constitute its inner life, it was equally within its scope to insist upon the obstinate hold which the past lays upon the present, the impossibility that any nation should ever wholly escape from its former self. The two ideas spring from a common root; the continuity of history, the essential unity of past and present, inevitably follows from the unity of national life.

Indeed, if any complaint is to be raised against Montesquieu, it is that he has made too little, rather than too much, of this side of his theme. He was so much engrossed in proving the unity of a nation's life at any one period of its history that he had scant attention to spare for the parallel truth of the unity which binds one period to another. And it may well be doubted whether, as a speculative principle, he had grasped the latter truth at all as firmly as the former. It is all the more welcome, as it is all the more surprising, that in this closing section of his work he should have given so masterly an example of the manner in which History may trace the roots of the present as stretching far back into the past, the beggarly elements of the past as containing in germ the full growth of the present. If the continuity of history is not explicitly proclaimed in the elaborate investigation, it is unquestion-

[1] *Esprit des lois*, xxx. i.

ably implied. And with so splendid a model of the idea in its practical application, who would be churlish enough to complain that, as an idea, it is never stated, perhaps was never realised by the author, with sufficient clearness?

To Voltaire, however, all this is anathema. In spite of the *Essai sur les Mœurs*, the idea itself, the continuity of history, had never taken firm root in his mind. And this particular application of it, the debt of modern Europe to the Feudal System and the 'barbarians' who fathered it, was an unfailing mark for his scorn and derision. Thus, when Montesquieu justly commends the comparative equity of the laws which compelled the victors to live in some approach to equality with the vanquished, 'the barbarians to behave themselves as fellow-citizens of the Romans,' Voltaire gives way to a frenzied outbreak against 'these strange legislators,' these 'monsters, wretches and Arians'; and when reminded that 'the Germans are our fathers,' violently repudiates the paternity and will hear of nothing but the Institute and Decretals.[1] Tell me, he answers in effect, tell me of the Civil Law, that undying monument of human reason and enlightenment. Tell me of the Canon Law which, 'audacious usurpation' as it was, has at least left its mark upon the history of Europe 'by crushing the civil Power beneath the ring of the Fisherman.' But do not speak to

[1] 'Les lois d'Euric, de Gondebaud, de Rotharis firent des barbares et des Romains des concitoyens': *Esprit des lois*, x. iii. To this Voltaire replies: 'Euric était un Goth que les vieilles chroniques peignent comme un monstre. Gondebaud fut un Bourguignon barbare vaincu par un Franc barbare. Rotharis le Lombard, autre scélérat de ces temps-là, était un bon Arien. . . . Voilà d'étranges législateurs à citer. Et Montesquieu appelle ces gens-là *nos* pères' (*Commentaire: Œuvres*, xxix. p. 392 (*Œuvres*, 1785)). 'Je m'attendais à voir dans *l'Esprit des lois* comment les Décrétales changèrent toute la jurisprudence de l'ancien code romain; par quelles lois Charlemagne gouverna son empire, et par quelle anarchie le régime féodal le bouleversa; par quel art et par quelle audace Grégoire VII et ses successeurs écrasèrent les lois des royaumes et des grands fiefs sous l'anneau du Pêcheur, et par quelles secousses on est parvenu à détruire la législation papale. . . . Je cherchais un fil dans le labyrinthe; le fil est cassé presqu'à chaque article. J'ai été trompé; j'ai trouvé l'esprit de l'auteur, qui en a beaucoup, et rarement l'esprit des lois. Il sautille plus qu'il ne marche; il amuse plus qu'il n'éclaire; il satirise quelquefois plus qu'il ne juge; et il faut souhaiter qu'un si beau génie eût toujours plus cherché à instruire qu'à étonner' (*Idées républicaines*, § 61: *Œuvres*, xxiv. pp. 206-7 (ed. 1877)). The same perverse blindness to Montesquieu's meaning is shown in Voltaire's remark on *Esprit des lois*, vi. 16: '*Soixante-dix personnes conspirèrent contre Basile*. Qu'a de commun l'inepte cruauté de Basile avec l'esprit des lois?' The answer is plain; it offers one more proof of the 'inept' caprices of despotism. See Voltaire, *Œuvres*, xxix. p. 355.

me of the laws of those stupid and ignorant Barbarians; and above all do not call them 'our fathers.' It is all very human; but it is neither very candid nor very philosophical. And what strange inconsistency to accept the doctrine of historical continuity in the case of the Civil and the Canon Law, but to reject it in that of the feudal customs, the action of which, for good or for evil, met his eye at every turn.

Of the historical interest pure and simple, which plays so large a part in *Esprit des lois*, the closing Books are, no doubt, the standing example. But in many of the earlier Books it enters as an important factor: sometimes by itself; more often perhaps in combination with the practical interest—the interest of the statesman, occasionally of the ardent reformer—which made equal, if not higher, claims upon the allegiance of Montesquieu. Thus, on the one hand, much of the long sections which he devotes to Commerce—the destination of Solomon's fleets, the various attempts at the circumnavigation of Africa—is of a purely historical, not to say antiquarian, character.[1] And on the other hand, even when he is dealing with such themes as the influence of the soil upon national manners and of these, in turn, upon social and political institutions—both of them subjects which evidently fall within the province of the political philosopher—he is apt to stray off into matters, such as the nature of the Salic Law or the long hair of the Frankish Kings, which have only the remotest connection with the general question which he had set out to discuss.[2] These things had interested him as an historian; he knew that his researches had enabled him to explain them; and he could not resist the temptation of offering his explanation, even at the risk of some irrelevance, to the world.

Yet, when the largest allowance has been made for the purely historical vein in *Esprit des lois*, it remains true that the essence of the book is to be found neither here nor in the wide scope which the author assigns to the accidents of time and place, or to the ignorance and stupidity, the infinite capacity for miscalculation, of his human agents. As all the world has seen, it lies in his exposition of the intelligible and therefore calculable laws which regulate the actions of men: the laws imposed by their outward surroundings and, still more, the laws which flow from their own inner nature—their sense of expediency on the one hand, their sense of duty, their sense of Right, their sense of religion, upon the other.

None of these laws, as we have already seen, is conceived by Montesquieu as an absolute law. On the contrary, every one of them is liable to be met and countered by any of the others; and in the last resort, the decision rests with the human agents—the

[1] *Esprit des lois*, xxi. 6, 10. [2] *Ib.* xviii. 22, 24.

Government, or the community behind the Government—who are immediately concerned. Thus, even the most 'imperious' of these laws, the law of climate, can within certain limits be modified—that is to say, corrected by the wisdom and courage of man. And it is the duty of every Government to see that this is actually done; 'the bad legislators being those who encourage the vices due to the given climate, and the good those who strive to correct them.' [1]

As for the other laws, it is still more obviously true that they habitually interact with and counteract each other. And the general character of every nation is determined by the proportionate stress which it lays upon each of them. 'Men are controlled by many different things: by climate, by religion, by laws, by general maxims of government, by the precedents of the past, by moral ideas, by manners and customs. The total result gives us the general character—the "spirit"—of the nation. The greater the influence that any one of these things—or "causes"—has upon any nation, the less the room left for the action of the others. Among savage peoples, nature and climate reign almost unchallenged; the Chinese are governed by manners and customs; in Japan we have the tyranny of the Law; ancient Sparta took its tone from moral ideas; Rome from the union of traditional morality and traditional maxims of Government.' [2]

From this list—and the examples given by the author might easily be multiplied—more than one inference may be drawn. In the first place, it is well to observe his blunt statement that to yield blindly to climate is the mark of a savage race; though how far the savagery is the result of such submission, and how far it is the cause, he makes no attempt to determine: the question of racial character, original or acquired, not having dawned upon the men of his day, as, when all is said or done, it has not moved many steps towards solution even in ours. In the second place, the 'causes' of Montesquieu, when fairly sifted, will be found to coincide closely enough with the 'laws' indicated on an earlier page and in the opening chapters of the treatise. With 'climate' we have already dealt. 'Maxims of government'—and, to some extent perhaps, 'manners and customs' also—correspond with sufficient accuracy to the maxims of expediency, in the lower sense; as, with one exception, those higher motives, which taken together go to make up expediency in the wider and nobler sense, are explicitly mentioned in both places. For the 'moral ideas' of Sparta, the 'traditional morality' of Rome, are the 'sense of duty,' the 'moral law,' of the author's opening chapters; while religion—it is strange that he should have shrunk from naming the Jewish Commonwealth

[1] *Esprit des lois*, xiv. 5. [2] *Ib.* xix. 4.

as the shining example of a State devoted to this object [1]—finds a place to itself in both passages.

The one exception is curiously significant. It is his exclusion of Right. With the idea itself he cannot but have been familiar. Handed down from Locke and his disciples, it had enlisted more champions than any other political watchword of the time. It was about to receive new currency—a currency which itself testifies to the existing prevalence of the doctrine—from the hands of Rousseau. If therefore it does not appear in Montesquieu's list of ' laws ' or ' causes,' we can only conclude that the omission was deliberate. And the explanation manifestly is that in the absolute form which it assumed on the lips of Locke and his followers—that of abstract Right, valid for all times and under all circumstances—such a doctrine was utterly alien to his whole cast of thought: more than this, that it was flagrantly at variance with that belief in the relativity of all things which it was his chief object to expound and to drive home.

Yet to suppose that the idea of Right, under any and every form, is rejected by Montesquieu, would be a great mistake. With many qualifications, doubtless, and with severe restrictions, it enters, as we shall see directly, into the ' moral law,' the ' relations of justice,' of which he speaks in his opening chapter. It enters, perhaps still more evidently, into that ideal of individual liberty which he found embodied in the English character and the English constitution, and which he made no secret of regarding as the highest ideal that any community could seek.[2] Are we then to say that Montesquieu holds up the constitution of England as the model which other nations would do well to follow? That, in his weaker moments, is the conclusion which Burke at any rate would seem to have drawn. ' You might have profited of our example,' he tells the French Constituents, and vehemently reproaches them for having failed to do so. But it is certainly not the conclusion drawn by Montesquieu himself. The whole of *Esprit des lois* might be described as one long sermon on the impossibility of transplanting a particular constitution, a particular political temper, from one nation to another. Such a change, he insists, even if possible, would still be full of danger, if not of demonstrable mischief. All the strands of a nation's life—social, moral, religious and intellectual—are so closely interwoven that it is impossible to change or shift any one of them without opening the way to an infinite number of further changes, the nature and extent of which even the wisest can hardly be trusted to foresee. And he is careful to point the moral by taking his own country for his example. ' Leave us as

[1] This omission is made good elsewhere: *Esprit des lois*, xi. 5. Compare *Contrat social*, II. vii. and xi. [2] *Esprit des lois*, xi. 6; xix. 27.

we are,' says the French nobleman who acts as his mouthpiece for the occasion; 'leave us as we are'—for fear of worse.[1]

Thus the Right admitted by Montesquieu is essentially a guarded and a qualified Right. It is a Right which has been able to embody itself in a given constitution, to transfuse itself into the life-blood of a given nation: not a Right which is of universal validity; not that which is the same always, everywhere and for all. It is a Right therefore which would have been repudiated with scorn by the disciples of Locke in Montesquieu's own day; with yet greater scorn by those who claimed Rousseau for their master in the generation which was to follow. So much for the limitations which Montesquieu imposed on the idea of Right, in its political sense: the sense it bore to the generation which proclaimed the Rights of the Man and the Citizen.

There is however another, a more strictly personal, sense in which the term is habitually used: the sense in which we speak of a man's right to his life, to his personal freedom, to his freedom of conscience, to his liberty to worship God as he thinks fit. Such rights as these are universally felt to stand on a different level from those mentioned in the last paragraph. They are admitted as 'rights' even by those who deny the name to the other kind of benefits; and by those who claim both kinds as rights, they are regarded as something higher, something even more fundamental, than the political rights of which we have just spoken.

No man could have felt this distinction more keenly than Montesquieu. If political rights are to him little more than a mere matter of convenience, of historical accident—if, that is, they are to him, in the strict sense, no rights at all—the same could never be said of those human and personal rights which are now in question. Here, if anywhere, he takes his stand upon those 'relations of justice which exist before all positive Law' and which it is the duty of all positive codes to recognise and to safeguard by all means in their power. In such matters as these he will hear nothing either of national convenience or of historical tradition. These are the fundamental rights of man, which no community can disregard save at its own peril. 'They are anterior to all Law. And to say that there is no such thing as justice or injustice except what is commanded or forbidden by positive Law is to say that, before we have drawn the circle, all the radii were not of equal length.'[2]

This declaration is the more significant, because it is manifestly aimed against two distinct schools of opponents: against the

[1] *Esprit des lois*, xix. 5-6. Compare viii. 14: '*Comment le plus petit changement dans la constitution entraîne la ruine des principes*.' See also the close of xi. 6.

[2] *Ib.* i. 1.

extreme champions of expediency on the one hand and against the extreme champions of the State upon the other. The former, as now and again happens to Helvétius, were prone to argue that the interest of the community, or rather of the governing class, is always and everywhere the sole test of justice;[1] the latter—Rousseau, for instance, in a suppressed passage of the *Contrat social*—that whatever the Law determines must of necessity be just, 'seeing that the Law is anterior to justice, not justice to the Law.'[2] It is true that neither Helvétius nor Rousseau had written at the time when Montesquieu made his protest. But such doctrines were as old as the days of Greek Philosophy, and we may well believe that they were once more in the air.

So much for the general principle which Montesquieu rightly saw to be at stake. No man, however, was less likely to content himself with generalities. And when the moment comes, he lets us know beyond possibility of mistake what was the depth of his feeling against the most flagrant violations of such rights: against the iniquity of slavery and the iniquity of religious persecution. The chapters in which he speaks his mind on these matters are the most striking, as they are the most passionate, of the whole treatise.

His indictment of slavery is cast in the form of a mock apology, and the indignant irony of the pleader scorches everything before it. 'The nations of Europe, having exterminated the natives of America, have been compelled to enslave those of Africa, lest all those vast lands should go untilled.—Sugar would be too dear, if slave labour were not employed to grow the canes.—The African slaves are black from head to foot, and they are so flat-

[1] *E.g.* 'Si M. de Montesquieu eût médité profondement ces faits il eût senti qu'en tous ces pays les hommes sont unis par l'amour du pouvoir; mais que ce pouvoir s'obtient par des moyens divers selon que la puissance suprême ou se réunit . . dans les mains d'un seul, ou se divise . . dans le corps des grands, ou se partage, comme à Rome et à Sparte, dans les divers ordres de l'État; que c'est à la manière différente dont le pouvoir s'acquiert que les hommes doivent leurs vices et leurs vertus, et qu'ils n'aiment point la justice pour la justice même' (*De l'esprit*, iv. 11).

[2] In justice to Rousseau, it must be said that the context sets the argument in a rather more favourable light: 'C'est ainsi—*i.e.* de la protection de cette société dont nous sommes membres—que se forment en nous les premières notions distinctes du juste et de l'injuste. Car la loi est antérieure à la justice, et non pas la justice à la loi. Et si la loi ne peut être injuste, ce n'est pas que la justice en soit la base, ce qui pourrait n'être pas toujours vrai; mais parce qu'il est contre la nature qu'on veuille nuire à soi-même, ce qui est sans exception' (*Contrat social* (première version), II. iv.: *Political Writings of J. J. R.*, i. p. 494). It is hard to believe that Rousseau had not the above passage of *Esprit des lois* in view when he wrote this.

nosed that it is hardly possible to feel pity for them. Who could bring himself to believe that God, who is all-wise, can have put a soul, above all a good soul, in a body utterly black?—It is impossible to suppose that such creatures are men; because, could we do so, we should begin seriously to doubt whether we, on our side, are Christians.' [1] All this is the more remarkable, in that Montesquieu was the first man, in the front rank of reputation, to denounce the wickedness of the whole business: the first to open the struggle which was not carried to final triumph until more than a century after his death.

Even more fiery is his assault on religious persecution. Dropping the thin veil of irony which had served him against slavery, he now challenges the enemy face to face in a white heat of scorn and passion. Speaking in the name of a Portuguese Jew, he pleads with the Inquisitors as follows: 'We conjure you, not by the God whom we both serve, but by the Christ who, as you say, took upon him the nature of man in order to leave you an ensample—we conjure you to do by us even as, were he still upon the earth, he would himself. You wish to make us Christians, and you will not be Christians yourselves. But if you will not be Christians, at least consent to be men. Treat us as you would do if, left to the light of natural justice, you had no religion to guide you and no revelation to enlighten you. . . . One warning we are bound to give you. It is that, if in future ages any man should dare to call this century civilised, you will be cited as proof that it was barbarous. The records of history will cast shame on your century and hold up all the men of your day to the hatred of mankind.' [2] Voltaire did yeoman's service to the cause of religious freedom; but this breathes a purer spirit than all the quips and cranks of *Candide*.

Between the Inquisition and slavery, even in the aggravated form it assumed in the American Colonies and the West Indies, it is obvious that Montesquieu drew a sharp distinction. The latter was a violation of liberty; the former of life itself—and that under the most odious of all pretexts, the honour of God and of 'the truth.' The former, therefore, can at no period have been other than execrable.[3] The latter, even at the worst, might claim

[1] *Esprit des lois*, xv. 5. [2] *Ib.* xxv. 13.

[3] As Rousseau was to point out (*Contrat social*, IV. viii.), religious persecution, strictly understood, can hardly be said to have begun until the advent of Christianity: firstly, with the persecution of Christians by the pagan Government; then, with the persecution of one Christian sect by another. In the former case, persecution was largely determined by political motives; and the same is true of the persecution which broke out with the Reformation. It is to the Albigensian 'crusade' and other like events, both earlier and later, that we must look for examples of purely religious persecution.

to be one degree less deep in villainy; at certain times and under certain conditions it may even claim to have had a qualified justification. And the justifications suggested by Montesquieu throw a significant light on both the strength and the weakness of his whole theory.

Dismissing then, as we have already seen, any claims which have been built upon the supposed ' rights of war ';[1] dismissing also —though less decisively, and with a back-handed compliment to Aristotle—all claims that rest upon the alleged ' natural superiority of one race to another,'[2] Montesquieu admits one ground, and one ground only, as a justification of slavery: that is, the direct and unforced consent of the slave himself, ' a reciprocal agreement between the one party and the other.'[3] And when he asks himself, Under what circumstances, if any, is this consent likely to be forthcoming? his answer is, They can hardly arise except under a despotic Government—Muscovy and the Far East are the instances he brings forward—when the protection of a master affords some refuge, however slight, against the tyranny of the despot. It must be observed, he adds, that the slavery resulting from such an agreement, or contract, is necessarily an ' extremely mild ' form of slavery. Who indeed would voluntarily accept slavery except on terms which he expected to find lenient in the working?[4]

Yet even the mildest form of slavery still remains slavery; and, as such, Montesquieu is clear that it is ' against nature,' against the natural law which declares that ' all men are born equal '—perhaps the nearest approach which he allows himself to

[1] See above, pp. 267-8.

[2] ' Aristote veut prouver qu'il y a des esclaves par nature; et ce qu'il dit ne le prouve guère. Je crois que, s'il y en a de tels, ce sont ceux dont je viens de parler: *i.e.* il y a des pays où la chaleur énerve le corps et affaiblit si fort le courage que les hommes ne sont portés à un devoir pénible que par la crainte du châtiment; l'esclavage y choque donc moins la raison; et le maître y étant aussi lâche à l'égard de son prince que son esclave est à son égard, l'esclavage civil y est encore accompagné de l'esclavage politique' (*Esprit des lois*, xv. 7). It is clear from the last sentence that Montesquieu cannot have been thinking of slavery as it existed in Greece, or in republican Rome. It is equally clear for other reasons (*ib.* xv. 5) that he was not thinking of negro slavery, as it existed in the West Indies and the American Colonies. He would probably have found it hard to say what precise countries he had in mind.

[3] *Esprit des lois*, xv. 6.

[4] *Ib.* Montesquieu is careful to insist that even the mildest form of slavery is useless, and worse than useless, in Europe. He enforces his argument by contrasting the output of the German and Hungarian mines, worked by free labour, with those of Turkey, worked by slaves (*ib.* xv. 8).

the doctrine of abstract rights.[1] It follows that even the mildest form of slavery, even that which rests on the natural causes above mentioned, is not to be justified by reason or equity; that it is a thing to be tolerated only for fear of worse: one of the thousand evils that spring from a form of Government which, in itself, is no more than a hateful necessity, to be swept away at the first chance. As for all other forms of slavery, they are absolutely illegitimate: a violation of the fundamental rights, the 'eternal relations of justice,' such as no sophistry can excuse.[2]

In this sweeping condemnation, it may perhaps be objected that Montesquieu pays less heed than might have been expected to the historical causes which have led in the past to the wide prevalence of slavery. It may even be suggested that, had he paid more regard to such considerations, his verdict on the whole matter might have been very different from what it is. The latter suggestion must be at once rejected. It is abundantly plain that nothing could have shaken his rooted abhorrence of slavery and all its works. And it is just because that hatred is so intense that he virtually refuses to consider the historical causes which, in the past, made the adoption of slavery almost everywhere inevitable. If he should once admit this of the past, he seems to have feared that he might be held to justify its continuance in the present. And that, rightly enough, he was resolved at all costs to avoid.

The truth is that, here as elsewhere, the argument of Montesquieu suffers from his imperfect grasp of the idea of progress. The difficulty he had to meet was, in reality, extremely simple. It was to account for the fact that what to one age, to one stage of civilisation, seems perfectly just and natural, should by another age, another stage of civilisation, be condemned as utterly contrary to all justice, to the most elementary principles of equity, or Right. So long as we start from the assumption that the moral standard of men has never varied, that it is the same at all times and in all circumstances, the difficulty is insuperable. It is to be explained, if at all, solely on the assumption of a moral obliquity, a 'fond election of evil,' which, being itself quite inexplicable, serves only to thrust the difficulty one stage further back: that is, under the thinnest of disguises, to leave it as insoluble as before. On the other hand, directly we admit that, like all other things, the moral standards of men are liable to change; that in every age they are the outcome of a whole tissue of convictions—moral, religious, intellectual—which themselves are demonstrably subject to incessant modification; that in no matter is this so obvious as in those things where questions of humanity, of mercy, of the extension

[1] *Esprit des lois*, xv. 7.

[2] *Ib.* xv. 1-7.

which is to be given to the idea of brotherhood, are at stake: from that moment the difficulty vanishes, and we are able to accept, with as little reserve as Montesquieu himself, the new lights of the present, without condemning, as ruthlessly as he seems to do, the comparative darkness of the past.

If there is any man who might have been expected to grasp this truth, it is the author of *Esprit des lois*. No man had known how to make fuller allowance for differences of soil, of climate, of social circumstances, of political tradition, of historical accident. In the face of such difference, no man had shown himself more tolerant or impartial. That circumstances, and therefore maxims of conduct and policy, differ among different nations in the same age, in the same stage of civilisation, he had been the first to see clearly; and he had driven home his conviction with every variety of argument and example. That they differ also, and are bound to differ, as between different stages in the growth of the same nation, of the same group of nations, he had a much less vivid perception. As we have already seen, it is more than doubtful whether, as a general truth, he had ever brought himself to recognise this at all. The result is that, when he is confronted with problems of this character—in particular, with problems involving the growth of moral ideas, which of all such problems are the most important—his heart seems to fail him: he shrinks from applying to the relation of past to present the very same order of ideas, the relativity or contingency of all human laws, customs, institutions, which had served him so well in his treatment of past and present, taken separately. The idea of growth, of development, of progress presents itself no more than fitfully to his mind. To use terms which have often been employed in this connection, his conception of history, of man's political and social life is, in the main, static; it is only at rare moments that it becomes dynamic.

Aptly enough, one of those rare moments occurs in the course of his discussion of slavery: 'Plutarch tells us that, in the age of Saturn, there was neither master nor slave. In our own part of the world, Christianity has brought back the age of Saturn.'[1] Had he only consented to work out this flash of insight to its logical consequences, he would have found the clue of which he was in search. And this clue would not only have shown him the way out of the difficulties with which he was struggling at the moment. It would also have enabled him to reach a more general truth, in the light of which his whole theory might have been completed and enlarged. He would then have understood how it came that an institution which seems so hateful to the modern reformer should have been viewed with complacency by the ancients: that

[1] *Esprit des lois*, xv. 7.

it should have been tacitly accepted by one of the two masters of Greek thought and loftily defended by the other. He would have understood also how all the other revolutions which have silently changed both the outward and the inner spirit of Europe have inevitably come about. He would have recognised that the very teaching of Christianity has unfolded itself step by step, like all the rest. He would have seen that the moral standard of Christendom itself, at any rate on the social and political side, was something very different in his own day from what it had been to the Apostles: how it was that customs which to him seemed abominable were accepted as natural and inevitable by them. In the light of the last instance, he would have been forced to admit that to have accepted the old order is not necessarily a mark of moral obliquity; that it is often, perhaps more often than not, the result of an intellectual blindness which, given the frailty of human nature, is a thing hardly to be avoided. He might even have begun to suspect that not a few of the institutions for which he himself took up the cudgels—for instance, the venality of judicial offices—were certain to be condemned, as they have in fact been emphatically condemned, by posterity.

But the question returns: Is it possible to excuse the injustice of the past without giving a licence to the same injustice in the present? is it possible to pardon the slave-holders of Rome and Athens without justifying the Asiento? The answer, according to the spirit (if not the letter) of *Esprit des lois* is perfectly plain. Between slavery as exercised by the Greeks and the Romans and slavery as exercised in the colonies of the New World there is one vital difference. That is the moral revolution which has brought Europe to recognise that, within her own borders at any rate, slavery is a flat defiance of the first rudiments of Right. And that principle once granted, how is it possible that what is wrong in one hemisphere should become right in the other? that what would excite abhorrence, if done in Spain or England, should be permitted and even commended, when done by Spaniards and Englishmen on the other side of the Atlantic? It is vain to argue that such treatment is only what the negroes themselves expect; that it is only what they would, and do, inflict upon their enemies, whenever they get the chance. That may be; though, even so, it may be doubted whether they would stoop to such refinements of cruelty as the middle passage. But that a Gold Coast native should enslave enemies of a kindred tribe is one thing; that he should suffer the same fate from an Englishman or a Spaniard is quite another. Such a practice is not against the negro code of conduct; it is against the code of men who profess to be Christians and are undoubtedly Europeans. It is the 'right' of a backward race;

for a race which claims to be civilised, it is an intolerable wrong. Rights may, and do, differ as between race and race. Among members of the same race they are, at a given moment, everywhere the same. A morality which varies according to latitude and longitude—what Burke brands as 'geographical morality'—is the negation of all morality,[1] the violation of all Right. It is true that 'all things are relative.' But the relations which are paramount to all others—even, in the last resort, to those of soil and climate, which it is often the business of the legislator to control and counteract—are the moral relations; and it is by the moral code, not of the backward, but of the more civilised race that these must be read.

We have now traced the main lines of Montesquieu's theory and are in a position to judge what are the main avenues which he opens out, and what the chief issues raised by his enquiry. That in man's political life all things are relative, that 'all law consists in relations'—this, as has been urged from the first, is the central idea of the whole treatise. And, as we have seen, it was an idea equally fatal to both schools between which the political thought of France, and of England also, was at that time divided: to the school of abstract expediency represented by Helvétius, no less than to the school of abstract Rights which found its gospel in the *Civil Government* of Locke.

From this central idea radiates a whole web of consequences, the chief of which have been set forth in the foregoing pages. That the whole life of a nation is woven of one piece, and therefore that it is impossible to make sweeping changes in one direction without laying the train for a thousand changes, unforeseen and perhaps undesired, in other directions also; that in this vast tissue of relations—relations of physical surrounding, of material needs, of historical antecedent, of national character original or acquired, of expediency, of Right, of justice, of religion natural or positive—one strand is perpetually liable to run athwart the others, one relation to find itself in conflict, more or less deadly, with the others, and therefore that there is constant need for adjusting the one to the others:—these are perhaps the most significant of the inferences which Montesquieu draws from his fundamental principle, and which he drives home with an abounding wealth of historical illustration. To these must be added one further inference which, though nowhere distinctly stated, is yet, as we have seen, implied in the whole tenor of his argument: the inference that the present is the child of the past, that the life of a nation at any one moment is a growth determined by all that has gone before.

It is manifest that the first and third of these inferences follow

[1] See Burke's Introductory Speech on the Impeachment of Hastings.

a line of thought very different from that of the second. The two former belong to the contemplative and conservative strain of Montesquieu's nature; the latter to that which he had in common with the practical statesman, perhaps even with the reformer. And it is in the conflict between these two strains that the main difficulty of interpreting him has always been found to consist.

Up to a certain point, no doubt, the two strains may be said to run parallel, certainly not counter, to each other. And that is particularly the case when it is the problems of the statesman, rather than the historian, that Montesquieu has in view. 'Wisdom,' said Burke, and it is the wisdom of the statesman he is speaking of, 'wisdom does not create materials; her pride is in their use.' And Montesquieu would heartily have echoed the assertion. The relations with which the statesman has to deal, he urges in effect, are given ready to his hands: given either in the inherent nature of man, or in his physical surroundings, or in the traditions and bias which he has inherited from the past. And it is the business of the statesman to make the best of them: to discern which of them at the moment is the most important for his purpose; which of them must, for the moment, be subordinated to the others; to which of them, in his final choice, he ought to give the greatest weight. To adjust the balance between the diverse elements of a nation's life, to distinguish how far it is necessary to bow to the 'empire of climate,' how much must be given to the material needs of the community, how much to the traditions which have come down from the past, how much to the claims of expediency, how much to those demands of justice which, just because they are the least ponderable, are the most apt to be thrust into the background: to judge of the relative worth of each of these—and that, not only in the abstract, but as they are under the particular circumstances in which he is called upon to act—that, to Montesquieu as to Burke, is the chief, if not the only, task of the statesman; the chief, if not the only, test of his wisdom and capacity.

With the necessary changes, that is true also of the historian: of the historian, that is, such as Montesquieu conceived him; such as he was himself in that part of *Esprit des lois*—and it is by far the greater part—in which he is not first and foremost a political philosopher. What the statesman does for the present and the near future, that the historian who accepts the ideal of Montesquieu strives to do for the past. Looking back upon the past, he sets himself to discover what have been the 'relations' at work in the formation of a given institution, a given national character, a given tradition, a given law, a given course of conduct. Among the various relations which have contributed to any such result, he will endeavour to pick out those which have played the leading part, which have given to the whole its 'distinguishing colour and discriminating effect.' In proportion as he does so, he will have watched national life and character in the making; by dint of intense study and imaginative insight, he will have witnessed the shaping of laws, customs and policies; he will have divined the motives by which the human agents who took part in the process were in the main determined; even when he conceives mistakes to have been made, he will yet be able to account for them, to lay his finger upon the reasons, plausible or otherwise, which have led to their commission.

This is what Montesquieu himself attempted, and in great measure achieved, in *Esprit des lois*; and in so doing, he revolutionised not only the methods, but also the ideals, both of political philosophy and of history. He redeemed history from the mere record of facts to the study of causes and of motives. He warned the political philosopher that the life of the community depends at least as much upon historical causes as on the working of abstract ideas; and that, until those ideas have taken flesh in a given national will and bowed themselves to the concrete conditions of a given national life—that is, until they have submitted to qualification by all the other 'relations' which combine to form that life—he can neither say that they wield any effective influence upon the affairs of men nor expect the historian, whose task it is to interpret the actual facts and struggles of the past, very seriously to reckon with them. Thus, by the same stroke, he made history rational and the historical method a vital necessity to political philosophy. Thanks to his teaching—as, more indirectly, to that of Vico before him—both studies were henceforth to be dominated by the idea of growth, of organic development. For, whether fully realised or no, this is among the conceptions which lie at the root of his whole theory. All that he left to his successors was to lift that conception into clearer consciousness, to work it out with ever-increasing fullness.

It is the chief blot on Montesquieu's achievement that he never thought out this question to its final issue: that, believing the present to be determined by the past, he never clearly recognised that, the present being different from the past, such determination necessarily carries with it the idea of growth; still less, that in such matters, growth is only another name for development or progress. This means that his conception of 'law' was coloured rather by physical than by biological associations: that it was mechanical rather than organic. And what is the result of this upon his handling of human action? It is obvious that the more mechanical a law is, the less is the freedom it leaves to the human agents it controls. And those who have been the most ready to bring the life of the community under such laws have seldom wholly escaped from the danger of treating men as machines. In their zeal for general tendencies, they have too often forgotten that it is the men who make the tendencies, at least as much as the tendencies the men. So far as regards the past, Montesquieu is saved by his keen perception that the relations in which man finds himself are infinitely various and that his first duty has always been to discriminate and to judge between them. But when he comes to the problems of his own day, can it be said that he shows the same even-handed justice? Like many of those whose studies are concerned mainly with the past, he is hardly to be cleared of allowing the past to tyrannise over the present: of denying to his own generation that spontaneity, that freedom of action, which he had conceded to its forerunners. And this discrepancy, latent in Montesquieu himself, becomes glaring in some of his successors. What in him is no more than a markedly, but not immoderately, conservative bias—a ' disposition to preserve,' so far as may be, the order inherited from the past—is in them, above all in Burke, little better than a gospel of stagnation.

That Montesquieu himself, like the majority of those who have heartily welcomed the historical method, was strongly, if not consistently, conservative in temper, is evident at a glance. He was so in matters of politics; witness his oft-repeated insistence that, all the elements of national life combining to form one integral whole, it is impossible to tamper with any one of them without endangering all the rest; witness also his disposition—sometimes severely checked, however—to accept the accomplished fact as necessarily rational and to build upon it a general principle of wide, if not universal, application accordingly: in other words, as Rousseau complains, to 'establish the right by the fact.' He was so, which was less to be expected, even in matters of religion; witness the letter in which he complains of Bolingbroke for 'discharging his blunderbuss against Christianity,' especially the significant question with which it closes: ' What motive can there be for attacking revealed religion in England, where it has been so completely purged of all hateful prejudices that it cannot do any harm and, on the contrary, may do an infinite amount of good? '[1] At first sight, this may seem to sit strangely on the author of *Lettres persanes*; it shows, however—what, after all, was to be looked for—that, with him, the preoccupations of the statesman counted for more than the disinterested search for truth.

That, like many of his disciples, he turned the organic wholeness of the communal life into something of a fetish, that he

[1] Lettre à Warburton, May 1754 (*Correspondance*, ii. p. 528. Ed. Paris, 1914).

exaggerated the importance of doing nothing to destroy the 'general spirit,' the traditional character, of a nation, unless where there is some flagrant injustice to be remedied, is not to be denied. And this means that he would always have been opposed to sweeping changes: in particular, that he would have had nothing to say to the French Revolution, at any rate from the moment when the royal authority, as tempered by that of the Estates, and the independence, as distinguished from the 'hateful prejudices,' of the Church became avowed objects of attack. It is hard to believe that he would not have joined, from the very bottom of his heart, in Burke's fervid lament that 'the age of chivalry was gone,' that the spirit of honour—that honour which, in his view, was the 'vital principle' of the French nation, the fine flower of French breeding—had received its death-blow from the Revolution. And however little we may share in such regrets, it is only fair to remember that there is this side to the account: that, over against the abundant gains brought by the Revolution, must be set the unquestionable loss; that the 'great renewal' of the whole nation was only won, and was only to be won, by the sacrifice of an intensely beautiful, if too exotic, ideal—an ideal which, though neither Burke nor Montesquieu would have acknowledged it, was confined to a small caste. The mischief is that both writers were constitutionally blind to the other side of the question. And in the eighteenth century, above all at the stormy close of it, that other side was, on a balance, the more important.

Constitutional blindness, the bias of a naturally conservative temperament, was one cause of Montesquieu's distaste for sweeping change. But, as we have seen, there was another cause which lay more in his own power. He had never worked out his principles to what, in the light of subsequent speculation and subsequent experience, we can now see to be their logical result. The idea of progress had therefore hardly more weight with him than it had with most of his contemporaries; and change, so far from being the rule in his scheme of national life, was the rare, perhaps the lamentable, exception.

Yet, if he failed to pursue to the end the line of thought which he had opened out, that must not be reckoned seriously against him. It is the fate of almost all those who have thrown new and fruitful ideas upon the world. And who can deny that he had, in the fullest measure, the quality which goes hand in hand with this defect? the power of spontaneous intuition which bids defiance to all rules and prescriptions, the flashes of insight which, in an instant, forestall the toilsome reasoning of years? And, as there seems to be much misapprehension on this point—he has been praised for strict adherence to a particular method, he has been blamed for a significant lack of all method—we shall do well to ask ourselves where exactly the truth is to be found.

The method attributed to him by some zealous admirers is the inductive method.[1] That, however, to say the least of it, is altogether too high-sounding a term to describe the method of *Esprit des lois.* The mass of materials from which the author distilled, or with which he illustrated, his conclusions was far too vast, the conclusions themselves are far too tentative, to justify any claim so formidable as this. And Montesquieu himself, we may be very sure, would have been the last man in the world to make it. The truth is that any such claim, if it does more than justice to his scientific precision, does infinitely less than justice to his sagacity and his genius for divination.

It does more than justice to his precision: since with all history, ancient and modern, for his field of enquiry, how was it possible that he should apply the tests—the successive processes of exclusion and the like—demanded by even the loosest forms of induction? How was it possible that he should use that field as more than a storehouse of illustration for truths which he had reached by quite other—and, if we choose to say so, less scientific—methods: by deduction from his central principles or, more often perhaps, by pure introspection, lit up by his own inimitable sagacity and power of divination? Is it not evident that, judged by the inductive standard, his method, so far from satisfying the demands of Bacon, or indeed any other advocate of the art, hardly gets beyond the way of 'simple enumeration' which all alike agree in despising? The only part of his work in which he can be said even remotely to approach the way of induction is that in which, confining his view to a carefully limited field, he sets himself to consider the vicissitudes of the law of succession among the Romans and the Salic Franks, or the customs which regulated the fines for homicide and the whole framework of feudal society, among the Franks, the Burgundians and the Lombards. And this, as we have already seen, is an excrescence, and an excrescence which, however admirable in itself, has little relation, either in manner or in method, to the main body of his work.

That Montesquieu himself would have repudiated the claim put forward by these unwary disciples is tolerably clear. 'I have laid down principles,' he says in his Preface, 'and have seen the details conform to them, as of their own accord. I have satisfied myself that the history of every nation follows naturally from these general principles; that each particular law is closely bound up with other laws, or depends upon a higher law more general

[1] 'Montesquieu's method was essentially inductive.' *Encyclopædia Britannica*, xxv. p. 256 (article on Adam Smith).

yet.' Is this, it may be asked, the language of one who believed himself to be working by the inductive method? Does it not rather suggest a conclusion exactly the reverse? How else could a man express himself, if he wished to say that his conclusions, though freely checked by the facts of experience and history, were in their origin rather of reason than of 'experiment': in other words, that they were reached, in the main, not by induction, but by deduction? [1]

It is, of course, true that his 'general principles' themselves owed much to a historical learning which, for his own time at any rate, was exceptionally wide and deep. It is probable, however, that, so far from being built up methodically—and if terms are to have any meaning, induction must mean that—they had formed themselves by a process of half-unconscious reflection, and 'of their own accord,' in his mind; and that the conscious process only began when, having formulated them provisionally, he hastily reviewed the vast stores of his knowledge in the light of them; modifying and even rejecting them, in case of need; but far more often, we may well believe, maintaining them and enforcing them with the illustrations which 'of their own accord' thronged into his memory. It is in this sense, and not in any alleged adherence to the inductive rigours, that he may be rightly said to have followed —indeed, with due allowance for the claims of Vico, to have introduced—the historical method into political philosophy.

But, if some critics have claimed too much method for *Esprit*

[1] This seems to have been the opinion of the most clear-sighted of his contemporaries. See an illuminating article in the *Mercure de France* (April 6, 1784), which was clearly written, if not by one who had known him personally, at least by one who was familiar with those who had: 'Montesquieu, qui méditait pendant vingt ans les sujets de ses ouvrages, avait pourtant une extrême promptitude d'esprit, des *saillies de réflexion*, suivant l'expression de Vauvenargues, et ses pensées les plus profondes le saisissaient quelquefois comme une impression rapide. C'est alors qu'il s'écrie: " Je découvre ce que j'ai longtemps inutilement cherché. . . . Je vois la raison de ceci. . . . Je vois beaucoup de choses à la fois; il faut me laisser le temps de les dire." . . . Il était surtout extrêmement distrait; il n'était jamais sûr ni d'écrire ni d'avoir écrit ce qu'il avait trouvé de plus beau dans la méditation. De là ces formules si fréquentes: " J'allais oublier de dire . . . j'ai oublié de dire . . . ai-je dit? " Et ces choses qu'il va oublier, qu'il a oubliées, qu'il n'est pas sûr d'avoir dites, sont très souvent des pensées, des vues sublimes. Avec la douceur et la facilité d'un enfant dans le caractère, il en avait souvent l'impatience, et le législateur des nations laisse percer quelquefois cette humeur impatiente: " Je suis embarrassé de tout ce que mon sujet me présente dans ce livre; . . . j'écarte à droite et à gauche; je perce et je me fais jour." ' This article is quoted in Firmin-Didot's edition (1 vol.) in a note to xix. 1.

des lois, there is no doubt that others have credited it with too little. To contrast the stately order of the seventeenth-century writers —Bossuet, for example—with the more popular appeal, the more discursive manner, of their successors in the next century, is sound enough. Between the *Variations du Protestantisme* and the 'six thousand pamphlets of Voltaire,' or the rapid improvisations of Diderot, the contrast holds good, and it is significant. But there are exceptions to the rule; Rousseau is one of them, and Montesquieu is another. And to range the latter with Voltaire and Diderot, to assert that his methods, like theirs, were those of the pamphleteer, to describe him as writing a chapter or two on one subject and then darting off to write one or two more on quite another, is surely something of a libel. That, in style as in other things, Montesquieu was the child of his century, that he has much of the lightness, the point, the epigram of Voltaire himself, is perfectly true; though even here there are many qualifications. It is true, again, that his immediate theme is constantly changing, that he is seldom minded to pursue any one theme to its minutest details. How should it not be so, when the subject he had chosen was so wide and the issues it raised so many-sided and so various? But apart from the purely historical chapters—and even those are, at bottom, entirely relevant—who can say that any one of the themes he discusses was not essential to his purpose? who can deny that, through the inevitable diversity of his divisions and subdivisions, there runs a thread of the most orderly connection? Bossuet himself, had he ever been moved to preach from so pregnant a text, could hardly have acquitted himself in more logical fashion. Indeed, in the nearest approach he allowed himself to an enterprise of this sort—his far more abstract, and therefore more manageable, *Politique tirée de l'Écriture sainte*—it may well be doubted whether he did so.

Before leaving Montesquieu, we cannot avoid asking ourselves: What was his influence upon his contemporaries? and what has it been upon succeeding generations, above all upon the generation immediately following his own: the age of the great upheaval?

The men of his own day, with one exception, remained singularly cold to him. In the name of abstract Right, in the name of an Expediency hardly less abstract, they looked with barely disguised suspicion on his doctrine of 'relations'; they broke out into open protest against the weakness for established creeds and established institutions with which they credited him and which they not unnaturally took to justify their worst suspicions. A committee of his friends—Helvétius, Hénault, Silhouette and Saurin—unanimously dissuaded him from publishing his masterpiece; and when this well-meant advice was discreetly disregarded, Helvétius

—to say nothing of Voltaire—composed a hostile commentary upon it. Voltaire indeed, to the end of his days, never ceased to gibe at his alleged patronage of the Jesuits, his *gasconnades* and other miscellaneous delinquencies. Helvétius, it is pleasant to record, had the wisdom to recognise the injustice he had originally done the author, and the frankness virtually to acknowledge it.[1]

The one exception to this chorus of disapproval is to be found where few would have thought to look for it: in the man who is still too often regarded as the fanatical champion of the Gospel of Rights, the sworn foe to all the mitigations of expediency. From the moment that *Esprit des lois* was published, Rousseau seems to have recognised its importance; and from the first of his political writings to the last—from the *Économie politique*, published in 1755, the year of Montesquieu's death, to the *Gouvernement de Pologne*, written in 1772—we can watch the influence of Montesquieu deepening and strengthening its hold upon his mind: until the abstract strain which he had inherited from Locke, and which was obviously congenial to his native temper, is modified beyond all recognition by that respect for concrete circumstance, that reverence for historical tradition, that 'horror of revolution' which he—and he almost alone among the leading spirits of his time—had in the first instance learned from Montesquieu. In his very criticisms there is a deference which is conspicuously wanting to the laboured protests of Helvétius; much more, to the captious sarcasms of Voltaire. 'The illustrious Montesquieu, the only modern writer capable of creating the great, but useless, science of political Right'—that is his final verdict on the man to whom he owed more than to any thinker except Plato. And though edged with a lament that he had not chosen to execute the task of which 'he alone was capable,' the tribute is none the less sincere and none the less impressive.[2]

[1] Perhaps the coolness with which Hume, and still more Gibbon, both of whom had intimate relations with the French 'philosophers,' regarded him, may be referred to the same source. See Hume, Essay xi. (the influence of despotism on population, *Esprit des lois*, xxiii. 19), and *Enquiry concerning the Principles of Morals*, § ii. (the doctrine of 'relations'); and Gibbon (ed. Smith and Milman, 8 vols.), i. pp. 256, 362, 383; ii. pp. 229, 333; iii. pp. 97, 129, 242, 299, 302, 305. There is hardly one of these passages which is not tinged with more or less pronounced irony. It must be remembered, of course, that such references are, from the nature of the case, largely controversial. But I do not think that this wholly accounts for their tone. Gibbon seems to have reckoned Montesquieu more 'ingenious' than solid.

[2] For early references see *Discours sur l'inégalité* (ed. Hachette, i. p. 86: 'un philosophe illustre'), and *Éc. pol.* (*ib.* iii. p. 301: 'les Platons

With the next generation came a turn in Montesquieu's favour. But here again it is important to distinguish. He has been claimed as one of the standard-bearers of the Revolution. It has been seriously maintained that in the National Assembly his was no less the dominant influence than that of Rousseau in the Convention. This, however, is entirely misleading; indeed, for all practical purposes, it must be dismissed as false. That there was a reforming —and therefore, things being what they were, a revolutionary— side to Montesquieu's genius is, no doubt, perfectly true, it has been pointed out again and again in the foregoing pages. On that side, however, it is evident that his star paled before that of Voltaire and Diderot, of Helvétius and Holbach, of Mably and Raynal: above all, before that of Rousseau. And as for his influence on the National Assembly, the smallest acquaintance with its debates is enough to show that, on the revolutionary side, he counted for little or nothing. It is in the conservative interest, and in that almost alone, that his name is invoked.[1] Those who think otherwise have been misled by the seeming enthusiasm with which the majority declared itself for the English ideal—the ideal acclaimed by Montesquieu—of Constitutional Monarchy. Such enthusiasm, however, was manifestly the work not of conviction, but of circumstance; not of choice, but of necessity. So deeply had

---

et les Montesquieux'). For later references, see *C.S.* II. vii.-x.; III. iii.-viii.; *Lettres de la Montagne* and *Gouvernement de Pologne*, passim. For his final verdict, *Émile*, livre v. (*ib.* ii. p. 430).

[1] With the history of the United States it is a very different story. There, as has often been pointed out, the influence of Montesquieu was probably the strongest influence at work. Yet even there it was the reverse of a revolutionary influence; and, as was natural, it went rather to matters of practical application than to speculative ideas. For instance, in *The Federalist*, which represents more completely than any other writing the principles which guided the fathers of the Federal Constitution, as drawn up in 1787, there are three crucial references to Montesquieu. Two of these are in support of the general principle of Federation, as against the looser Confederacy, hitherto in force; the remaining one urges the authority of Montesquieu in favour of that 'separation of the three Powers,' which is so marked a feature of the American Constitution: with the warning, however, that the doctrine of Montesquieu has often been too rigidly, and therefore erroneously, interpreted. See *Federalist*, Nos. 9, 43, 47 (ed. London, 1888, pp. 47-51, 270-74, 300-302). So far as I have observed, *The Federalist* contains not a single reference to Rousseau, although, both in *Émile* (livre v.) and in *La Paix perpétuelle*, he had written on Federation in much the same spirit as Montesquieu and in far greater detail. Considering the conservatism of Hamilton and Madison, this is only natural. It was otherwise with the Declaration of Independence (1776), drawn by Jefferson.

Monarchy struck root in France that even the stoutest reformers never once thought of deposing a king whom yet, in their heart of hearts, they deeply distrusted. It was only after a bitter experience, only after the king had repeatedly proved his hostility to the new system, that the age-long prejudice was at last uprooted; that the elaborate scheme of checks and counterchecks devised by the Constituents was swept away and the Republic, which from the first had been latent in the revolutionary movement, was set up in its place. The doctrine of Montesquieu had, at bottom, as little to do with the one policy as with the other. It was the spirit of Rousseau—it was, still more, the force of circumstance—which inspired all that was vital in the work both of the Constituent and the Convention: which, on the one hand, swept away the absolute Monarchy and the tottering fabric of Feudalism; which, on the other, dictated both the Declaration of Rights and the enthronement of the Republic.

It is in quite another direction that the influence of Montesquieu must be sought. It was not with the champions, but with the opponents, of the Revolution that his word was a power. And, though it found echoes on the lips of conservative orators, it was not so much with the politicians as with the thinkers that it bore fruit. If his wise speech slept in the ears of the Maurys and the Cazalès, it was received as an oracle by Burke and Joseph de Maistre. How much either of these men was actually swayed by Montesquieu, it is, of course, impossible to say. That both of them profoundly admired him, it needs no argument to prove. With de Maistre it is a pervasive admiration, which seldom finds utterance in words.[1] To Burke he seemed the counterpart of 'the universal patriarch in Milton,' looking forth not with prophetic, but reverted, vision upon the whole history of the race: 'bringing together from the east and west, the north and the south, all the schemes of Government which have ever prevailed among mankind; weighing, measuring, collecting and comparing them; joining fact with theory and calling into council all the speculations which have fatigued the understandings of profound

[1] After recording the tribute which Montesquieu and Rousseau joined in paying to the Senate of Bern (*Grandeur et décadence*, chap. ix.; *C.S.* III. v.) de Maistre significantly adds: 'Il me semble qu'on doit un compliment au Gouvernement assez sage pour se faire louer tout à la fois par la sagesse et la folie': *Étude sur la souveraineté*, ii. 3 (*Œuvres*, ed. Lyon, 1884, etc., i. p. 458). There are other references to Montesquieu: *e.g. ib.* i. 4 (p. 329), ii. 4 (p. 465); and *Du Pape*, chap. iii. (vol. ii. p. 364). But, especially in his earlier writings—*Considération sur la France*, *Le Principe générateur* and *Étude sur la souveraineté*—the author's general affinity of thought with Montesquieu is unmistakable.

reasoners in all time.' It is one of the most splendid panegyrics ever uttered.[1]

Unfortunately, the praise is not altogether disinterested. It serves, as any skilful guesser might have predicted that it would, to enhance the value of Montesquieu's preference for the English Constitution: to point the contrast between the 'sense' of the Patriarch and the nonsense of his countrymen who, in the teeth of his precepts, had chosen to ransack 'Knaves' Acre for the rotten stuff of outworn delusion and sedition,' rather than profit by 'the collected wisdom of mankind' which he had spread before them. Here we have the secret of Burke's admiration. It was the conservative strain in *Esprit des lois*, the conservative moral naturally suggested by his method and the general tenor of his argument, that drew him to Montesquieu; and—at any rate, in his later years, the years of the anti-Jacobin crusade—it was little else. And that conservative moral he was willing—or rather, eager—to accept in its extremest form: preservation of the existing order—in the spirit, if not in the letter—at all costs; absolute stagnation, sooner than any material change either in the inward balance, or in the outward direction, of the Constitution which had come down from the past. 'Let the whole movement stand still, rather than that any part should proceed beyond its boundary,' and by so doing alter the general character of the whole.[2]

That Montesquieu himself would ever have gone to such lengths is hardly to be believed. With all his conservatism, there was too much of the reformer in him for that. Indeed, in his famous eulogy of the English Constitution, he touches on this very point, but handles it in a spirit which is clearly distinguishable from that of Burke. 'The balance between these three Powers'—King, Lords and Commons—'might be expected to end in rest or inaction. But the inevitable march of things compels them to move; and for the reasons stated, they are forced to move in concert.'[3] That, it may be objected, is pretty much Burke's theory, as it stood before his nerves had been upset by the Revolution. It may be so; but it would be hard to bring any passage, even from his earlier writings, in which the Holy of Holies is represented as capable of 'march' or 'movement'; in which the Ark of the Covenant is conceived as anything but 'standing still.' The metaphors he delights to use are of 'repairs' to be executed, of 'restorations' to be effected, of 'balance' or 'equipoise' to be preserved. In other words, they are all drawn from the statics of the subject, not from its dynamics. The stationary was his

[1] Close of *Appeal from the New to the Old Whigs*: *Works*, i. p. 535.

[2] *Appeal*, *Works*, i. pp. 534-5.

[3] *Esprit des lois*, xi. 6; compare xix. 27.

ideal. Can the same thing be fairly said of Montesquieu? Not, surely, to the same extent; not, surely, without some sweeping qualifications.

That the influence of Montesquieu has, in the main, been a conservative influence, it would be idle to deny. The admiration of Burke, the hostility of Voltaire and the Encyclopedists, would alone be enough to prove it. And the reason is plain. The mere fact that he employs the historical method, the mere fact that he insists upon the inseparable connection of the political with the social, the moral, the religious life of every community, of the present with the past, inevitably points the way to caution; inevitably disposes men to be wary how they touch the life of this 'mysterious incorporation' in one member, lest, without meaning it, they do violence to the rest.[1] The warning was salutary; and it is the enduring service of Montesquieu to have given it: or rather, to have laid the train of speculative argument from which it inevitably results. If no wise man now thinks that it is possible to make sweeping changes in one direction without opening the door to changes of incalculable extent in many others, that is largely due to his teaching; and, it must in fairness be added, to the deepening and strengthening which that teaching received at the hands of Burke.

The warning was salutary. But has its full bearing been always, or even commonly, understood? The truth is that to the argument of Montesquieu, and of Burke also, there is another side which has too often been forgotten. If the conservative moral is that which suggests itself to our first thoughts, our second thoughts will warn us that a precisely contrary moral lies behind. If all parts of a nation's life are inseparably interwoven, the more necessary is it jealously to guard against the corruption which must inevitably spread from one part to the rest. If the present has its roots deep down in the past, by the same principle the future must draw its life from the present. And when one generation allows abuses to go unchecked and uncorrected, the next generation, or those that come after, must look to pay the penalty. That penalty may take one of two forms. It may either lie in the increased difficulty of rooting out an abuse which has been suffered to grow and spread beyond all knowledge, or it may lie in the blind fury of a revolution which will sweep away the good with the bad, the wheat with the tares, in a whirlwind of indiscriminating vengeance.

Thus the reformer's inference is as valid as the conservative's. Once grant that the life of the community, its history past and present, forms one organic whole—a whole of which each part is conditioned by all the others, each moment by all that has gone

[1] Burke, *Reflections*: *Works*, i. p. 394.

before—and the one consequence is as inevitable as the other. If it be true that nothing can be changed without change, or risk of change, to all that surrounds it and all that comes after it, it is equally true that nothing can be left standing without incalculable consequence, for evil as well as for good, to all succeeding generations. To suppose that all the risks lie on one side, is to fly in the face of all experience and all reason. There is a risk in standing still, just as there is a risk in moving forward; and true wisdom lies in the capacity for judging rightly when to move, no less than when to stand.

Of the one danger we hear much from Montesquieu, still more from Burke; of the other, little or nothing. In the earlier writer, to whom revolutions were no more than a dim memory of the past, that may readily be forgiven. The later writer, the sworn denouncer of the French Revolution, can plead no such justification. And we, with the warning of at least three such earthquakes before us, deserve no pity if we refuse to take the lesson to heart. The historical method, the historical argument, in politics knows no distinction of side or party. When rightly interpreted, it is essentially double-edged: as favourable to the conservative cause as to the liberal; as favourable to the liberal as to the conservative. And it is not the least of Montesquieu's merits that, with all his conservative leanings, he should have held the scales so comparatively even between the one side and the other: that he should, on the whole, have employed both method and argument in a spirit so equitable, so different from the reckless partisanship of Burke—much more, of Joseph de Maistre.

With the generation which followed the Revolution, the curtain may be said to fall upon the figure of Montesquieu. His direct and recognised influence upon those who have themselves moulded public opinion was virtually at an end. Hegel indeed, with a liberality which he seldom showed to foreign thinkers, makes more than one acknowledgement of the services he rendered to political thought; and always on the same ground, that he was the first to assert the organic wholeness of national life.[1] Other tributes, generally less intelligent, might easily be cited from the secondary writers of that period: all of whom, however, had lived through the revolutionary storm and framed their systems in conscious hostility, or conscious devotion, to its principles.

In later times such references have been rare. This, no doubt, is largely because his teaching has now passed into the common

[1] *Rechtsphilosophie*, §§ 3, 261 (pp. 25, 316); *Geschichte der Philosophie*, iii. p. 475; *Philosophie der Geschichte*, pp. 10, 79. In the last passage, Montesquieu's name is not mentioned, but the reference to him is plain.

stock of educated opinion. But it is also due to a less creditable reason: to the sectarian taint which clings to some of the more recent schools of political thought: to many of the socialist sects, on the one hand; to belated individualists, such as Herbert Spencer, upon the other. Pure individualism, a purely industrial socialism —each of these, for different reasons, is wholly incompatible with that integrity of the national life which, alike as historian and philosopher, it was the mission of Montesquieu to drive home. To the extreme individualist, the nation is either a trivial fiction or a gross usurpation. In the more fanatical forms of socialism, one element of the national life, the industrial element, annihilates all the others; one class of the community, that engaged in manual labour, claims to ride rough-shod over the rest. What has either of these schools in common with the principle which maintains that the individual exists, and can only exist, as member of a community? that the very idea of a community carries with it a tissue of relations, each of which claims a fair field for its own activities, but each in turn qualifies and is qualified by the rest? It was the purpose of Montesquieu to insist upon the significance of the past to a true judgement of the present. Consciously or unconsciously, it is the work both of individualist and of extreme socialist to deny it.

CHAPTER VI

THE ASSAULT ON CONTRACT: HUME

THE main movement of political controversy from the time of Hobbes onward centres, as we have seen, round the individualist theory of Government: centres, that is, essentially round the question, What is the source and nature of Right? Even within the lifetime of Hobbes, however, Spinoza had attempted to change the issue of Right for that of Expediency or Utility; and two generations later, the same attempt was renewed by Hume. For the second time, therefore, we find ourselves compelled to break the main thread of our enquiry, in order to follow the course of a movement which, whatever may be thought of its fruitfulness, yet won a strong backing both in England and in France: in France, during the generation which preceded the Revolution; in England—it must be added, in America also—for at least a century and a half.

It was a new issue. But there is a sense in which it is not altogether out of connection with the old. So far as theory goes, there is nothing to prevent the utilitarian from being an individualist in practice; neither is there anything to prevent him from being a strong supporter of State action and State control. The course he takes on these matters will be determined solely by what he considers to be the expediency of the case. The one thing certain is that his decision will not be rested on the grounds which determine either the individualist or his opposite: that it will have nothing whatever to do with considerations of Right. In this country, no doubt, as well as in America, the utilitarians have shown a strong tendency to range themselves, for practical purposes, side by side with the individualists. That is true, in the main, of Bentham; it is equally, perhaps still more markedly, true of the 'philosophical radicals' who inherited his tradition. But it is emphatically not true of Helvétius, nor of other French utilitarians. It is not even true, without reserve, of Bentham, nor of the Mills, father and son.

The truth is that, in each country, the practical policy of the utilitarians was determined largely by the needs and prejudices of those around them. In England, the main task of reformers was to sweep aside an antiquated system of State control and State interference. This the utilitarians realised; and they saw at the same time that their only possible allies in such a task were those who held the pure faith of individual Rights. Accordingly, being compelled to act with the individualists, they naturally learned to tolerate their principles and even to fall, on occasion, into their characteristic forms of speech. In France, on the other hand, where there was no tradition of individual freedom, the very reformers were tempted to look for help to the strong arm of the State. This was true before the Revolution; and after the first fervour of the Rights of man had been quenched in fire and blood—that is, after a brief space of three years—it became true again. It was only after a bitter experience of the evils which go hand in hand with the benefits of a strong Government, that there was some reversion—Benjamin Constant and Joseph Chénier are its most representative figures—to the individualist faith; so that in the group that gathered round both men we find—as in England, by whose example, in fact, both men were deeply influenced—a strange blend of the individualist with the utilitarian stock of ideas.

One further warning must be given. Knowing the stirring part which Utilitarianism has played alike in the moral and in the political thought of this country, an Englishman is apt to assume that the same must be true of Europe as a whole. Few mistakes could be greater. Save for the brief reign of the Encyclopedists in France, the utilitarian scheme of things has been a food for English consumption only. Strongly entrenched in this island, it has never, with that exception, made good the passage of the Channel. Forming, for at least three generations, the main stream of English speculation, on the Continent it has never been more than a backwater. And as our concern is with the flow not of English but of European theory, its history—however interesting, however instructive—is, for us, no more than a side-issue.

Of all the forms taken by the utilitarian theory, whether in morals or politics, that given to it by Hume is beyond question the most original and the least open to attack. He drew something from Locke; much more from Hobbes. But he added so much that was entirely new; he forestalled and guarded against so many of the objections which lie against the utilitarian system, as commonly professed and understood—against all, in fact, save that which constitutes its inmost essence and without which it would lose its very reason of being—that, in his hands, it became something which it has never been before or since: a theory which honestly recognises most, if not all, of the facts which dominate the political and moral life of man; which accounts for the seeming contradictions with amazing ingenuity; and which, with one fatal exception already indicated—the failure to give any satisfactory account of that idea of obligation which he yet admits to be a necessity—weaves all the strands of explanation into one intelligible and apparently consistent whole.

No doubt, the admissions which honesty impelled him to make greatly multiplied the difficulties in his path; and it may be questioned whether he ever completely realised either the extent of his concessions, or the full bearing of the consequences which they carried in their train. Yet, even if this be the case, homage is still due to the honesty which dictated them, as well as to the resourcefulness which never failed him and which, again with one exception, enabled him to turn every fresh difficulty into occasion for a fresh triumph.

His theory, as is well known, appeared in two distinct shapes: in the *Treatise of Human Nature*, published in 1739–40; and in the *Enquiry concerning Human Understanding and the Principles of Morals*, published in 1748–51, and eventually (1753–4) incorporated with the *Essays*.[1] The latter, as Hume himself desired, is the form more generally known. But if we would understand the full scope of his argument or do full justice to his genius, it is necessary to turn to the former. It is from the former accordingly that most of our references will be drawn.

The earlier writing was 'projected before the author left College'; it was written before he was five-and-twenty, published before he had turned thirty, and on its appearance, it was universally neglected; in his own words, it 'fell dead-born from the press.' Such readers as it found were apparently unable to grasp the significance of the new system; they had no eyes for the originality of the new writer. Hume, there can be no doubt, was bitterly mortified. He had produced the most profound work in philosophy which had yet appeared in the English language. At one stroke he had distanced Locke and thrown even Hobbes into the shade. Yet all this was to go for nothing; he was not to receive even the poor compliment of abuse. He did well to be angry; but whether he took the best way of showing his resentment is another matter.[2]

[1] See Hume's *Works*, ed. Green and Grose (4 vols. 1875), vol. iii. pp. 49-52 and 59.

[2] See *ib.*, advertisement to vol. iv., and *My Own Life*, vol. iii. p. 2: 'Without receiving such distinction as even to excite a murmur among the zealots' (of the *Treatise*); and 'henceforth, the author desires that the following pieces (*i.e.* the *Enquiry*) may alone be regarded as containing his philosophical sentiments and principles' (*Advertisement*).

What he deliberately set himself to do was to re-cast his system in a more palatable—and, for that reason, a less philosophical —shape. With that object in view, he abbreviated, transposed, omitted; much after the fashion of a distressed lecturer, who strives to adapt a complicated subject to the needs of a modestly trained, but highly critical, audience. In all this there is no ground for supposing that he was minded to withdraw by a hair's-breadth from any one of the crucial positions which he had taken up in his original statement. Such sacrifices as he made were made, it would seem, purely with a view to literary effect: for the sake of gaining a fair hearing and for nothing else. Yet the inevitable result of all these changes—they are more drastic, however, in the metaphysical than in the moral part of the *Enquiry* —was to blur the outlines so sharply drawn in the earlier *Treatise*: in particular, to take the stress, in some measure, off the primary principle of the theory and to lay it upon what, after all, are secondary applications. So far as the moral part of the *Enquiry* is concerned, the most marked result of the abbreviations which Hume thought fit to make is to cut down the psychology—the Book devoted to the Passions—which had formed not the least original element of the *Treatise*; and by an inevitable consequence, considerably to obscure the extent of the adulteration which the pure gospel of Hedonism had suffered at the hands of its latest exponent.[1]

It remains true, none the less, that the *Enquiry* is, and was meant to be, in all essentials a reproduction, though a popular reproduction, of the *Treatise*; and that an alert reader, if at the same time he were perfectly candid, would draw the same conclusions from the later, as he would have done from the earlier, version. Thus, in all probability, it was not the *Treatise*, but the *Enquiry*, which first roused Kant 'from his dogmatic slumbers' and started him on the train of thought which was to revolutionise the whole course of subsequent speculation.[2]

Not all readers, however, were as sharp-sighted as Kant. And the general effect of the *Enquiry*, as supplemented by the *Essays*, was to persuade the world that the author was only one, if among

[1] The Dissertation on the Passions, which in the *Treatise* had taken over 150 pages, is reduced to 27 in the *Enquiry*. The corresponding numbers of the distinctively ethical part of the two surveys are 140 and 117.

[2] It is significant that all Hegel's references are to the *Enquiry* and the *Essays* (*Geschichte der Philosophie*, iii. pp. 446-52); and that, although a German translation of the *Treatise*, by Jacob, had appeared in 1790. The Lectures, on which this book of Hegel's was founded, were first delivered at Jena in 1805-6; then at Heidelberg, 1816-18; finally during the whole of his time at Berlin, 1819-31.

the most distinguished, of the vast army of 'philosophers'—'the mob of gentlemen who wrote with ease'—moving, here and in France, to the destruction of the old order in metaphysics, morals, politics and religion, and pledged to the erection of a purely materialist structure in its stead. To the more sceptical side of his argument—much more, to the concessions which he had made in favour of the more spiritual, the more creative, side of man's nature—the 'age of reason' was constitutionally blind. For the men of his own generation, Kant alone perhaps excepted, all this —and it is this which constitutes the truly original and vital strain in his philosophy—was a sealed book. So far as this side of his teaching was concerned, he might just as well never have written. It is hard to believe that the same result would have followed, had it been not the *Enquiry*, but the *Treatise*, by which his system became generally known.

In any case, he had his reward. For every reader found by the *Treatise*, the *Enquiry* and *Essays* must, at a modest computation, have secured a thousand. They were widely circulated in the home country; they were translated into French, and so passed into the currency of Western Europe.[1] They established the fame of Hume as a philosopher. They won him the friendship of the best wits of Edinburgh and London and, much to the amusement of his friends, made him the idol of the Paris salons. He has been charged with an inordinate share of vanity; but, except in so far as this caused him to repudiate the first and best 'heir of his invention,' and eventually to desert Philosophy for History, it would be idle to reckon this seriously against him. The provocation he had suffered was great; and on a just view, he must be allowed to have met it with unfailing dignity, if not with the highest form of courage.

What are the main lines of Hume's political theory? what his specific contribution to European thought in this matter?

The first thing to strike us is that his political theory is firmly embedded in his moral theory; that, unlike Locke and other champions of individual rights, he makes no attempt to separate

[1] The *Enquiry concerning Human Understanding* was translated into French by Mérian (Amst., 1759; 2nd ed., Berlin, 1761). The *Enquiry concerning the Principles of Morals* was translated by Robinet (Amst., 1760). An Italian translation, by Griggi, was published long afterwards (1818). Of this translation, vol. i. contains Hume's Autobiography and Sections i.-viii. of the *Enquiry concerning Human Understanding*; vol. ii. contains the rest of the *Enquiry concerning Human Understanding*, and the *Dissertation on the Passions*. Whether there was a third volume, containing the *Enquiry concerning the Principles of Morals*, I cannot say; the copy in the British Museum has no more than two volumes.

the one thing from the other. This marks a reversion to the sound practice of Plato; in a less degree, of Spinoza also. It is an initial warning that, in the enquiry which follows, we are not to look for that de-moralisation of politics, that endeavour to empty the State of all moral significance, which has been the besetting sin of every form of individualism. That there are distinctions between the two fields of action, Hume is well aware. As will appear in the sequel, he makes too much allowance for them, rather than too little. But that must not blind us to the service he rendered in breaking down the absolute barrier which Locke—and, to a less degree, Hobbes—had set up; in admitting that, whatever their differences, the political and the moral life of man spring, in the last resort, from the same root.

It follows from this that it is impossible to understand the political theory of Hume without considering his moral theory also: that it will be necessary to open our survey of the former with a brief account of the latter. And if, in the course of this examination, it shall be found that, in passing from metaphysics to ethics and from ethics to politics, he insensibly shifts his ground, that with each step he takes he departs more and more widely from the cardinal principles with which he started, then we shall be forced to conclude that he stands self-condemned; that the system so carefully pieced together will not hold water.

The starting-point of Hume's moral system is that 'reason is a perfectly inert principle': incapable of originating action; incapable of determining the ends of action; capable solely of suggesting the means by which those ends, supplied from quite other sources, may most conveniently be attained. The function of reason, therefore, is a purely subordinate function; she is the obedient handmaid of some other faculty, some other principle of man's nature; she has no rights, no independent powers, of her own. Once grant him this position, and, thanks to his amazing ingenuity, the rest of his argument follows almost of itself.[1]

The particular form of the opposite doctrine which Hume here has in view—the only form of it, in fact, which he deigns to notice—is the peculiarly abstract and untenable form which it had lately assumed in the hands of Clarke: the theory of 'the eternal fitness of things' which was to be satirised a few years later in one of the most telling figures of *Tom Jones*.[2] But it is evident

[1] *Treatise*, Book II. (*of the Passions*), Part iii. § 3 (vol. ii. pp. 193-197); Book III. (*of Morals*), Part i. § 1 (vol. ii. pp. 233-8).

[2] Clarke's theory is embodied in his Boyle Lectures delivered 1704-5, and republished in 1738, a year or two before the publication of Hume's *Treatise*. See also Clarke's *Sermons*, xli., cxi. (*Works*, 1738, vols. i. and ii.).

that his hostility to any other form of the doctrine—that given to it by Kant, for instance, half a century later—would have been equally unflinching. How, indeed, could he have accepted any possible variety of it, without surrendering his whole system and being false to his whole nature?

His rejection of reason in the field of morals, it need hardly be said, is a direct consequence of the narrow functions which he had assigned to it in the field of 'understanding.' In the one sphere, as in the other, it is an 'inert, inactive, impotent' faculty: confined, in the one case, to arranging the materials it has received from 'impressions,' as a man might arrange books in his library, subject only to the 'law of association'; and in the other, to acquainting the passions with the means by which their ends may most readily be attained. It is true that, in popular language, we are apt to talk of a conflict between passion and reason. That, however, is an abuse of language. What we really mean, or ought to mean, by it is a conflict between a violent passion and a calm passion: between an intense passion of the moment and a 'sedate' passion which persists for a lifetime and which, being persistent, may in many cases prevail over its more turbulent, but possibly fleeting, rival. 'Reason,' he concludes, is 'wholly inactive, and can never be the source of so active a principle as conscience, or a sense of morals.'[1] In fact, to say that Hume's doctrine is represented by the familiar line of Pope—

Reason the card, but passion is the gale—

is to say much less than the truth. So far from being, even in the humblest sense, a guide or 'card' to the passions, reason is, to him, no more than their obedient slave.[2]

Having thus swept away reason, as a possible claimant for the function of determining the ends of action, Hume is left with the question: What, then, is to take its place? As to the answer, he is in no manner of doubt. It is the 'passions' alone which determine man to action, or yield the state of mind which may ultimately result in action. And as the exercise of the passions is inseparably bound up with pleasure and pain, it may be truly said that, so far as man acts deliberately and with a conscious end of any kind before him, the desire to obtain pleasure and to avoid pain is the sole motive to all his action.

Hume's words are: 'Those eternal immutable fitnesses and unfitnesses of things cannot be defended by sound philosophy' (*Treatise*, vol. ii. p. 240).

[1] *Treatise*, vol. ii. pp. 193-7, 233-8.

[2] 'Reason is, and ought only to be, the slave of the passions, and can never pretend to any other office than to serve and obey them' (*ib.* p. 195).

So far, the theory of Hume has, in the main, followed the beaten track of hedonism. It is in his handling of the qualification just indicated—in his insistence that not all acts are prompted by a conscious desire for an end of any sort or kind—that his originality, the vital force of his system, first makes itself felt. Unfortunately, it is also just here that his argument is most confused and most contradictory.

The confusion lies in the fact that under the term 'passions' he includes things so different as mere emotions, animal appetites and conscious desires, without any serious effort to distinguish between them. The contradiction—and this is a still more serious blemish—is this: Having begun with the sweeping assertion that 'the passions, both direct and indirect, are founded on pain and pleasure and that, in order to produce an affection of any kind, 'tis only requisite to present some good or evil,' on the very next page he allows himself the admission—'the curiously cool admission,' as it has justly been called—that 'besides good and evil—or in other words, pain and pleasure—the direct passions frequently arise from a natural impulse, or instinct, which is perfectly unaccountable. . . . These passions, properly speaking, produce good and evil, and proceed not from them, like the other affections.'[1] As among these refractory passions he explicitly reckons 'the desire of punishment to our enemies and of happiness to our friends'—that is, the passions which he elsewhere describes as 'anger' and 'benevolence,' the former of which insensibly leads on to malice and envy, while the latter is inseparably bound up with love, sympathy and pity[2]—and as, under that name, they have previously (and rightly) been ranked with the *indirect* passions, it is manifest that the scope of the admission is considerably wider than Hume himself would have us believe.[3] 'Hunger, lust and a few other bodily appetites,' among the direct passions; anger and benevolence, with the attendant passions which belong to each, among the indirect: all these are explicitly mentioned as forming exceptions to the general principle that 'the passions are founded on pain and pleasure.'[4] Indeed, once the question is raised, it becomes clear that *all* the emotions, as distinguished from the desires and appetites, fall under this description; that of *all* the emotions it is just as true as it is of anger and benevolence that they 'arise from a natural impulse which is perfectly unaccountable'; that, though they produce pain and pleasure, they proceed not from them, like the

[1] *Treatise*, vol. ii. pp. 214-15 (Book II. Part iii. § 9).
[2] *Ib.* pp. 76-7, 153-73 (Book II. Part i. § 1; Part ii. §§ 6-9).
[3] *Of the Passions*, I. § i.; *Treatise*, vol. ii. p. 77.
[4] *Of the Passions*, III. § ix.; *Treatise*, ii. p. 215.

other affections.[1] And we are left to wonder what is the use of a rule which, as soon as laid down, is thus whittled relentlessly away.

The most damaging thing about this admission is that it is absolutely demanded by the facts. And it is much to the credit of Hume that, in face of the huge scar which it left on his theory, he should have had the candour to make it. In this, as in so many other of his reservations, he was not followed by his utilitarian disciples. With one consent, they continued to confound the actions which are done for the sake of the pleasure they are expected to bring—in Hume's phrase, the actions 'which are founded on pain and pleasure'—with the actions which, though they give pleasure, are not done for the sake of that pleasure, but from some irrepressible impulse, whether 'bodily' or mental. Their theory may gain in consistency; but for that very reason it falls hopelessly out of relation to the facts.

The inconveniences of the admission are obvious enough. On the one hand, it destroys at one stroke that unity and simplicity which have always been the chief attraction of the hedonist system. On the other hand, it carries with it the danger lest these refractory passions may, on further reflection, be found to contain elements which are not merely extraneous to the principle of pain and pleasure—so much is frankly admitted by Hume himself—but absolutely at variance with it. The former evil was irremediable; and Hume's subsequent efforts to show that his 'cool admission' is after all not incompatible with some form of hedonism only serves still further to complicate his theory. The latter danger was more insidious; and when the time comes it will be our object to show that, with all his ingenuity, he was unable entirely to escape from it. For the moment, it is our business to take up the thread of his theory, as given in the *Treatise*.

Having made this candid admission, Hume, with his usual adroitness, at once finds means of turning it to good account. After all, he urges in effect, what else was to be expected? 'Unless Nature had given some original qualities to the mind'—he writes of the 'original impulse' which, by compelling man to refer certain things, pleasant or unpleasant, to self as their 'object,' gives rise to the emotions of pride or shame—'it would never have any secondary ones; because in that case it would have no foundation for action, nor could ever begin to exert itself.'[2] The matter could not have been put more clearly. The only thing to regret is that he confines this observation to the particular emotions of

[1] So also of Pride and Humility: 'The peculiar object of pride and humility'—*i.e.* the reference to self—'is determined by an original and natural instinct' (*Passions*, I. § v.; *Treatise*, vol. ii. p. 84).

[2] *Passions*, I. § iii.; *Treatise*, vol. ii. p. 80.

pride and humility, instead of extending it to all emotions and bodily appetites without exception. The truth is that these 'passions,' so far from forming an exceptional case, are, almost by his own admission, examples of the general rule which governs all the emotions; and if there are any exceptions to that rule, which it would be hard to prove, it was his business to produce them.

It is needless to pursue the matter further; the more so, as Hume himself, strangely enough, does not seem to have realised its importance. Throughout the bulk of the *Treatise*, he writes as though the damaging admission had never been made; as though it were universally true, as indeed his argument required it to be, that 'the passions, both direct and indirect, arise immediately or by the conjunction of other qualities, from good or evil, from pain or pleasure'; as though there were no exception to the rule that 'the chief spring, or actuating principle, of the human mind is pleasure or pain.'[1]

At first sight, this may seem as complete an acceptance of the hedonist principle as it is easy to imagine. And, as a rough description of his theory, there is no objection to such a label. Utilitarian, or largely so, on its political side, on its moral side Hume's system is, in truth, essentially that of hedonism. Further inspection will show, however, that it is a highly specialised form of hedonism: hedonism after a pattern very different from that adopted by the common herd of hedonists and, what is more, far less open to objection.

The rock upon which hedonism, in any of its familiar forms, has always split is its manifest incapacity to distinguish between different kinds of pleasure. Once reduce all action to desire for pleasure, and we have deprived ourselves of every test which can enable us to discriminate between good and evil pleasures: in other words, between right and wrong. To plead, as the Cyrenaics and others have done, that we are still entitled to distinguish between refined pleasures and gross pleasures, between those which are worthy of the wise man and those which are not, is in effect to surrender the whole theory. It is either to smuggle back 'good' and 'evil' under the thin disguise of 'gross' and 'refined'; or it is to introduce an ideal of character which has no relation whatever to the pursuit of pleasure and which, alike in conception and attainment, must be the work of reason and of reason alone. In either case, the result is the same. It is to find our test of pleasures in a principle which has nothing to do with pleasure. In other words, it is to dethrone pleasure and exalt a rival principle in its stead.

To this objection it is clear that Hume was keenly alive. It would not be too much to say that his main purpose, throughout

[1] *Passions*, I. § i. p. 76; *Morals*, III. § i. p. 334.

the ethical part of the *Treatise*, was to guard himself against it: to discover some test, or standard, of pleasures which should not involve the surrender of pleasure, as 'the chief spring and actuating principle' of all man's moral activities. But how was this purpose to be attained?

To the men of the next generation, to those who claimed to be his disciples, there was no doubt about the answer. They found such a standard, such a means for distinguishing between good and evil pleasures, in the principle of utility. Such a principle, they urged, affords a plain test for distinguishing between good and evil, between desirable and undesirable pleasures; it being always possible for the agent to foresee what pleasures are likely to be for his ultimate advantage, and what are not. At the same time, no one can fairly object that it is a principle alien—still less, hostile—to that of pleasure. For what can afford more pleasure to the agent than the advancement of his own interest? and how can a principle, defined as that which assures the 'greatest happiness' of the agent, be said to cater for anything but his pleasure? Here therefore, if anywhere, we have found that which satisfies both the conditions of which we are in search. On the one hand, utility furnishes the requisite means of distinguishing between the good pleasures and the bad. On the other hand, the test thus furnished, so far from being incompatible, is exactly identical with the fundamental principle of pleasure. The test and the thing tested are of precisely the same nature. To test one species of pleasure by another species of pleasure, the fleeting pleasure of the moment by the enduring pleasure, the settled happiness, of a lifetime—what could be easier, what could be more natural?

Whether this answer was present to the mind of Hume, it is impossible to say for certain. What is certain is that his own answer is framed on entirely different principles; that, if his object had been to avoid all the fallacies of the utilitarian answer, he could hardly have achieved it more effectually. It is of the essence of the utilitarian theory to judge of actions by their consequences. It is the underlying principle of Hume's theory that they are to be judged only by their motives. Quite apart from all other objections which might be brought against 'the greatest happiness principle'—in particular, the objections attaching to the 'felicific calculus'—this alone is enough to set an impassable barrier between his theory and theirs.

That the motive is the essential thing in action, that all actions are to be judged by their motives and by nothing else, this is the principle which forms the starting-point of Hume's constructive reasoning. It is implied throughout the discourse on *The Passions*, which serves as introduction to his ethical argument. It is placed in the forefront of that ethical argument itself. The following passage is as explicit on this point as any one could wish: ''Tis evident that, when we praise any actions, we regard only the motives that produce them, and consider the actions as signs or indications of certain principles in the mind. . . . It appears, therefore, that all virtuous actions derive their merit only from virtuous motives and are considered merely as signs of those motives.' [1]

But if this be conceded—as Hume, entrenching himself in the common sense, the common conscience, of his day, is confident that it must be conceded—it follows that we cannot, at the same time, place any intrinsic merit in the action taken purely by itself. 'From this principle,' he continues, 'I conclude that the first virtuous motive which bestows a merit on any action can never be a regard to the virtue of that action, but must be some other motive or principle. . . . In short, it may be established as an undoubted maxim that no action can be virtuous, or morally good, unless there be in human nature some motive to produce it, distinct from the sense of its morality.' [2]

The latter part of the passage reveals a second reason which led Hume to dwell upon the importance of motives. A knowledge of the motive is necessary not only on moral grounds, as a means, and the only means, of distinguishing between virtuous and vicious actions; but also as a means, and the only means, of accounting for there being such a thing as action at all, for action as a purely natural phenomenon. If it is necessary for the purposes of the moralist, it is also, and no less, necessary for the purposes of the philosopher, of those who concern themselves with the natural history of the human mind. The significance of this, in both its aspects, will become apparent when we come on to consider Hume's doctrine of the 'moral sense.'

The first and chief purpose of Hume, in establishing these 'maxims,' was, no doubt, to bar the door against the doctrine that duty alone, duty pure and simple, can ever be a sufficient motive for the first performance of any action.[3] Even allowing the idea of duty to have validity, we are still confronted with the fact that some other motive, some 'motive in human nature,' must have disposed us to the action, before we are in a position to ask ourselves

[1] *Morals*, Part II. § i.; *Treatise*, vol. ii. p. 252.

[2] *Treatise*, ii. pp. 252-3.

[3] Hume is careful to confine this to 'the *first* virtuous motive.' He freely admits that when a certain type of action is once generally recognised as a matter of duty, a man who feels his heart devoid of 'the motive appropriate to it,' may yet perform the action without the motive, from a certain sense of duty, in order to acquire by practice that virtuous principle, or at least to disguise to himself as much as possible his want of it (*ib.* p. 253).

whether it is in accordance with that idea, or no. More than that: we should still have to admit that, before we can pronounce the motive of any action to be good, or 'virtuous,' there must, quite apart from the question of obligation, be some natural feeling, some instinctive 'sense,' which assures us that it is so. Or to put the same thing in other words, however much the idea of duty may have subsequently supervened, it can have played no part either in the first 'production' of the given act, or in our judgement that it is a good act: an act, that is, which springs from a 'virtuous motive.'

But, if the main object of this argument was to exclude the idea of duty, as an original principle of human nature, there can be little doubt that Hume intended it to serve another, and a more special, purpose also: to strike a parting blow at Clarke and his 'eternal fitnesses.' To maintain that the virtue of an act lies in its own intrinsic nature, and to maintain in the same breath that it lies in the motive of the agent, is evidently, as Hume points out, to 'reason in a circle.' [1] And what school of moralists is more flagrantly guilty of this inconsistency than those who, starting from the principle that the standard of goodness is to be found in the eternal fitness of certain acts, yet never weary of telling us that the outward act has no significance except in so far as it reveals the workings of the agent's heart? The Gospel, no doubt, teaches us that the motive is all-important; that out of the heart the mouth speaketh. But when a man has once persuaded himself that the cause of religion is bound up with the eternal fitnesses, that nothing short of them can satisfy our faith in an all-wise Providence, he must be content to part company with the Gospel.

But if the doctrine of motives is fatal to the system of Clarke, it is still more fatal to that of the utilitarians. If it debars us from judging a man by his outward acts, still more does it debar us from judging him by their consequences. Between the outward act and the motive, the relation is fairly uniform; how else should we be justified in taking—as, on Hume's showing, we habitually do take—the one for a 'sign,' or token, of the other? Between the motive and the consequence, however, there is no relation whatever. It is impossible to argue, either backwards or forwards, from the one to the other. The utilitarians themselves have been quick to perceive this; the first whisper of motive is enough to throw the most placid of them off his balance. It follows that any argument which denies the validity of judging by the act must, *a fortiori*, deny the validity of judging by its consequences. And as the validity, or rather the imperative necessity, of the latter judgement is the cardinal principle of the utilitarians, we must

[1] *Treatise*, p. 253. For Clarke's moral doctrine cf. p. 308, *n.* 2.

conclude that Hume's argument tells with yet greater force against their system than against that of Clarke.

That Hume foresaw and intended this application of his argument, there is no need to maintain. All we can say is that, consciously or unconsciously, his system is so framed as to avoid the dangers which beset all other forms not only of the hedonist, but also of the utilitarian, theory of morals: in particular, to elude the snares into which the utilitarians of the next century and more allowed themselves to fall without a struggle. Whether this was due to deliberate foresight or, as is perhaps more likely, to an uncanny instinct, it would be rash to pronounce. In either case, it would be hard to find stronger proof of his clear-sightedness or sagacity.

Having thus, consciously or unconsciously, disposed of rival theories, Hume is now free to proceed with laying the foundations of his own. The problem before him, as we have seen, was, while retaining pleasure as 'the chief spring and actuating principle of the human mind' in these matters, to find some test, some means of distinguishing between good and evil, between virtuous and vicious, pleasures which should not involve the admission of some other 'actuating principle' behind and above pleasure. The champions of reason, he held, had gone wrong because they rejected pleasure, root and branch. The Cyrenaics had lost the battle because, preferring to put pleasure in the first place, they had ended by degrading it into the second. And the utilitarians, though they might choose a different road to it, were destined to reach substantially the same result. With all these danger signals in front of him, was it possible to discover some principle of discrimination which should not be reason, either avowed or masquerading under the clumsy *alias* of 'refinement,' or 'utility'? Was it possible, in short, to find some test of pleasure which should itself be nothing more than a special modification of the primary sense of pleasure?

Hume, at any rate, was confident that he had found it: found it in that modification of the general sense of pleasure which, adroitly availing himself of a term first brought into currency by Shaftesbury, he described as the 'moral sense.'[1] To Shaftesbury this term had meant the rational conviction, intuitively arrived at, which leads men to sacrifice their own personal interests to those of the society, large or small, of which they are members; to postpone the 'private order' to the 'public'; to subordinate the self to the common good. In other words, it had been practically equivalent to the sense of duty. To Hume it bears an entirely different meaning. To him, as to Shaftesbury, it is no doubt

[1] *Morals*, I. § ii.; *Treatise*, vol. ii. pp. 246-51.

an intuitive perception. But there the resemblance ends. To Shaftesbury it is a rational principle; to Hume, one of pure sensibility. To Shaftesbury it is a sense of duty; to Hume, a sense of pleasure. Pleasure, no doubt, 'of a particular kind'; but, in principle, nowise different from the pleasure which comes to us through the senses, or from the satisfaction of such 'passions' as pride, benevolence, or love.

What then are the particular feelings involved, what the specific passions called into play, in the process which constitutes the moral sense? They are two: sympathy and, alternatively, either love or pride: love, if the action—or rather the qualities, the prevailing character, implied in the action—be contemplated in another; pride, if attributed to ourselves.[1] Sympathy is required; for it is only by sympathy that we can enter into the feelings of another; that we can become aware of the feelings which are passing in his breast, either when he performs a given action himself, or when he witnesses its performance by us. And love, or pride, are the passions naturally and inevitably called forth, according as we either witness the performance of that action by others, or conceive of it as performed, or about to be performed, by ourselves.[2]

In those cases where we ourselves are about to act, it must be observed that sympathy has a yet further operation: that it performs, in short, a double function. On the one hand, just as in the simpler case where we merely contemplate the acts and motives of others, it serves to inform the agent what are the feelings actually entertained by those around him. On the other hand, blending with pride, it supplies him with the strongest possible motive to frame his own course accordingly. Where it is a question, not of determining our own action, but merely of contemplating that of others, this further operation is of necessity excluded. Yet even here, sympathy is not without its practical value; even here, it serves to quicken the moral sense, to keep it alert and vigorous against all future calls to action.

[1] *Morals*, III. § i.; *Treatise*, vol. ii. pp. 334-8. It is significant that Hume does not come to close quarters with his analysis of the ***natural*** virtues and of the moral sense, which manifestly operates with the greatest purity in the natural virtues, until after he has disposed of the artificial virtues, those implied in the existence of organised society. This proves him to have clearly seen that even the 'private' virtues could never have arisen, or taken root, except in civil society: as he says himself, that 'our private duties are more dependent on our public duties, than our public on our private' (*Morals*, II. § viii.; *Treatise*, ii. p. 310).

[2] Hume's account of Sympathy is to be found in *The Passions*, I. § xi. and II. §§ v.-vii.; of Pride, *ib.* I. §§ i.-xii. (*Treatise*, ii. pp. 110-14; pp. 145-157; pp. 75-120.

From this account it results that the moral act is that which is done, the moral character that which habitually finds outward expression, in response to, or in conformity with, the demands of which we are instinctively conscious either in ourselves, or in those around us; the immoral or vicious character, that which habitually defies them. Or to put the matter yet more simply, morality, in Hume's sense of the term, consists in doing what is expected of us by the public opinion of our community, or of those with whom for the moment we are brought in contact. The 'moral sense' is the faculty which intuitively, and on 'the mere view and contemplation,'[1] informs us what those expectations actually are; and the passions through which the moral sense works, of which the moral sense is the joint expression, are sympathy and, alternatively, either pride or love.

This then is the theory by which Hume sought to account for the working of the moral consciousness; by which, in particular, he strove to provide a test, at once effective and natural, as between good and evil, between virtuous and vicious pleasures. It only remains to ask how far his venture prospered; how far he succeeded in satisfying the conditions which he accepted from the start.

These conditions, as we have seen, may be reduced to three: the first, that the thing to be considered is not the outward act, but the motive which produces it; the second, that this motive must either be desire for pleasure or, when put in operation, must at least result in pleasure; and the third, that the principle by which we distinguish between good and evil pleasures must itself be some form of pleasure: the determining motive which leads us to seek the one and reject the other must be itself the desire for 'a particular kind of pleasure.'

Allowance being made for the complication, not to say the inconsistency, involved in the qualification attached to the second of these conditions, Hume may fairly claim, at least on the surface of the matter, to have satisfied all three. He does consistently base his argument, not on the outward act, but on the motive which produces it. He does consistently find that motive power—or, failing that, its inevitable consequence — in pleasure. And he does consistently find his discriminating test between good and evil pleasures in a principle which is itself a particular form of pleasure: the pleasure resulting to the agent from the sense that he is feeling and acting in 'sympathy' with those around him. Finally—but this is virtually implied in the statement that the moral sense, like all the other practical faculties of man, is itself a sense of pleasure—his discriminating test is a test which works not by reason, but by

[1] *Morals*, I. § ii. (*Treatise*, ii. p. 251); 'from the survey,' *ib*. p. 247.

intuition: on a 'mere view and contemplation' of the motive, not by inference or elaborate calculation.

Whether this appearance of consistency will sustain a more searching scrutiny, is another question; but it is a question which must be reserved for future consideration. For the moment, it is our business to let Hume speak for himself.

There is, indeed, one objection to the theory which Hume himself is at pains to meet and answer. How, it may be asked, is this public opinion, this popular judgement which finds an echo in the heart of every individual, itself formed? Is it purely 'unaccountable'? or does it rest upon an intelligible foundation? If the former, how can we escape the conclusion that our moral code is a mere accident of circumstances? If the latter, how avoid the necessity of falling back, after all our efforts, upon either the rationalist, or the utilitarian, explanation? Either alternative has its risks. But, of the two, it is clear that Hume considered the less dangerous to be the second. The rationalist explanation, indeed, it was impossible for him to accept. It is therefore upon the utilitarian account of the matter—or rather, upon something which might easily be mistaken for it—that he ultimately settles down.

Accepting the common division of virtues into social and self-regarding, we readily recognise, he urges, that the former are valued on account of 'their tendency'—a tendency to be judged broadly and with many individual exceptions—'to the good of mankind':[1] in other words, on account of their public utility. In the case of those social virtues which are purely 'artificial'—the 'political' virtues of justice, fidelity to promises, and the like—this is evident at a glance.[2] But it is also true of those other virtues which we distinguish as 'social,' in the narrower and more distinctive sense of the term, and which, in Hume's vocabulary, are not artificial but natural: such virtues as 'meekness, beneficence, charity, generosity, clemency, equity,' and others of the same stock.[3] The very name 'social,' in fact, has been adopted in order to mark their 'tendency to the good of society.' Such virtues, unlike their political brethren, are purely 'natural'; and the 'passion' of our nature from which they ultimately spring is the passion of sympathy: a passion, it may be observed, which here plays a part quite distinct from that which it plays in moulding the 'moral sense,' and a part infinitely more active. The main point, however, is that what constitutes the value of all such qualities is our instinctive sense of their utility to society; that 'it is our concern for the interests of society which makes us approve them.'[4]

[1] *Morals*, III. § i.; *Treatise*, ii. p. 337.
[2] *Morals*, II. § ii.; pp. 268-73. [3] *Ib.* III. § i.; p. 338. [4] *Ib.*

With the self-regarding virtues the case is manifestly different. The name itself is enough to show that there can here be no question of the interests of society. Yet even here, though under another form, interest—or pleasure, which in this case is hardly to be distinguished from interest—is the principle at work: the interest not of society, but of the individual in whom such qualities are recognised. 'Prudence, temperance, frugality, dexterity'—however useful such qualities may indirectly be to society, no one will argue that this is the reason why, 'on the mere survey,' they give pleasure to the spectator. It is evident that they 'acquire their merit' in his eyes because they bring pleasure, and perhaps profit also, to their possessor.[1] Finally, there is yet another class of qualities—'wit,' for instance, 'and a certain easy, disengaged behaviour' in social intercourse—which, again 'on the mere survey,' are at once recognised as giving pleasure both to their possessor and to others. And this is enough to awaken a corresponding pleasure in the mind of the spectator. Of the self-regarding virtues, then, this must be our general conclusion: that, 'as some of them acquire their merit from their being *immediately agreeable* to others, without any tendency to public interest, so some are denominated virtuous from their being *immediately agreeable* to the person himself who possesses them.'[2]

Such, then, is the ultimate basis of our moral code in all its various divisions. The political virtues are virtues because they are recognised as essential to the interests, the very existence, of civil society; the social virtues, because they conduce to the welfare of mankind, of 'man, as he is man.' And of self-regarding virtues, some are such, because they give immediate pleasure to the agent himself; and the rest—that is, the greater number—because they give pleasure both to him and to others. It is, therefore, either interest or pleasure—the interest, the pleasure, of men with whom we are either immediately brought in contact or who, for some obvious reason, are vividly present to our imagination—which is the spring that opens our sympathies and, by so doing, gives rise to our moral judgements, supplies the rational justification of our moral sense. It is by no means necessary that every link in this chain of inferences should be present to the mind of the spectator or the agent. The essential point is that his sympathies are in fact so framed as to make him always instinctively judge after this fashion and not infrequently act in obedience to such judgements. That his judgements, however intuitive, have a rational foundation, and that it is of the nature here stated, is a matter of reflection. And this reflection is a process quite distinct from that of the moral judgement, which is intuitive. It is a

[1] *Treatise*, ii. pp. 345-7. [2] *Ib.* p. 348.

process which the spectator or agent—and it is with them alone that we are directly concerned—may, or may not, be minded to carry out.

But if this is a correct account of Hume's argument, it is clear that his position differs widely from that of the utilitarians, who are commonly reckoned as his disciples. To him, the moral judgement is dictated by the pleasure of the moment, the 'particular kind of pleasure' which springs from sympathy with those around us. To them, it depends on the pleasure, not of the moment, but of an imagined future: an unreal abstraction, if there ever was one. To him, it is an intuitive judgement; to them, a matter of laborious calculation. To him finally, the 'actuating principle,' from first to last, remains essentially pleasure. To them, however much they may strive to disguise the change, it insensibly passes into a very different principle: a principle which it is impossible to distinguish from reason—from reason, indeed, under what, on their principles, is the highly objectionable form of duty. All this will become more apparent when we come to treat of the theory subsequently elaborated by Bentham.

So far, we have been concerned with the distinctively ethical part of Hume's system. We are now in a position to turn to its political application. The guiding principle of this has already been indicated in his account of the 'artificial' virtues, as briefly sketched above. As will have been seen, it is of the essence of his theory to draw a sharp distinction between the artificial and the natural virtues; and that distinction lies in the fact that, whereas the natural virtues, even those which we define as 'social,' all appeal to our immediate sense of pleasure, the artificial virtues, being a matter of convention, are, at least in the first instance, based, not on pleasure, but self-interest. It is here, therefore, and here alone, that Hume becomes an utilitarian; and even here, as we shall soon see, he is an utilitarian with a difference.

Like most men of his day, Hume succumbed to the temptation of dabbling in origins; and by an inevitable Nemesis, he at once found himself brought face to face with the state of nature and the Contract. It was an awkward moment; and he can hardly be acquitted of coquetting with both of them. But if he comes near to accepting them, it is at least in a highly attenuated form. For, if mankind was born to something remotely resembling the state of nature, it was only incontinently to come out of it: *tantum ut exiret*, to transfer to the state of nature the phrase which Locke had used of certain imaginary forms of the civil state. And if some kind of agreement was involved in the passage from the natural to the civil state, such an agreement has at least none of the formalities of a contract; nor does it carry any of the binding force which Locke and others had given to the Contract, and in which they had found the sole source of political obligation. Nowhere, indeed, is he more happy than in his demonstration that such a doctrine is doubly untenable: that it is false historically, and that it involves a logical contradiction. His conclusion is perhaps not very easy to reconcile with the earlier stages of his argument; but it is sound in itself, and it makes a landmark in the history of eighteenth-century speculation.[1]

Starting, then, from the assumption that the first state of mankind was a state of individual isolation, Hume bestirs himself to prove it impossible that such a state should be of more than the most fleeting duration. The powers of the individual man are weaker, his needs are proportionally far greater, than those of any other animal. And the only remedy for this 'unnatural conjunction of infirmity and necessity' is that he should tear himself from his solitary existence, and join forces with others, who are as much in need of his aid as he of theirs. Society, in fact—as he felt dimly from the first, as he can now see with fuller reason—was an absolute necessity for man.[2]

'But, in order to form society, 'tis requisite not only that it be advantageous, but also that men be sensible of these advantages. And 'tis impossible, in their wild uncultivated state, that by study and reflection alone they should ever be able to attain this knowledge.' How then was the knowledge of this necessity borne in upon their minds? The answer is that another and still more imperious necessity—a necessity imposed not by circumstances, which may always be disputed, but by an overmastering instinct—had already, and from the first moment of his existence, driven man into a rudimentary form of society: the society of the Family. And this simple form of society serves not only to suggest to his mind the more complex form with which we are now familiar, but also to prepare him for it by a training which goes far to anticipate its often harsh discipline and dispose him to put up with its inevitable restraints: to 'make men sensible of the advantages they may reap from it, as well as fashion them by degrees for it, by rubbing off those rough corners and untoward affections which' would otherwise 'prevent their coalition.'[3]

The mere formation of society, however—the term is henceforth used in its larger, its more 'artificial,' sense—would mean nothing, unless it went hand in hand with some passable provision for that which is at once one of the chief motives to its original

[1] Hume's political theory is set forth in the *Treatise*: *Morals*, II. §§ ii.-xi. (vol. ii. pp. 258-330) and in the *Essay*, Part II., Essays xii. and xiii.: *Of the Original Contract* and of *Passive Obedience*.

[2] *Morals*, II. § ii. (vol. ii. p. 258).

[3] *Ib.* pp. 259-60.

acceptance and one of the chief obstacles to its endurance: that is, for the regulation of property, of all that we subsequently come to include under the term *justice*. Unless, or until, some rough rules are established for the sake of deciding the rival claims of its members in this all-important matter, society cannot be said, in any real sense, to exist at all.[1]

It has been argued, indeed, that the required security for property is furnished by man's natural sense of equity: in other words, that 'justice' is not an artificial, but a natural, virtue. That, however, is plainly not the case. The rules regarding Property can manifestly never be anything but arbitrary rules. More than that: they must, from the very nature of the case, be general rules; and general rules, so far from commending themselves to such natural sense of equity as man possesses, are often in the most flagrant contradiction with it. However harsh, however inequitable, their operation in a given case, they must in that case, as in all others, be relentlessly enforced. Otherwise they will afford no certainty, and without certainty we might just as well have no rules at all. Such rules, in fact, are adopted solely because they are felt to be necessary to the very existence of society; and except as part and parcel of the whole fabric of society, they would be the most absurd thing in the world. From all this we may conclude that, like society itself, they rest, in the last resort, upon the manifest interest of those who establish them: in other words, that Justice—in Hume's sense of the term—is not a natural, but an artificial, virtue; that it is as much a matter of convention as Society itself.[2]

'This convention, however, is not,' in either case, 'of the nature of a promise; for even promises themselves arise from human conventions. It is only a general sense of common interest; which sense all the members of the society'—or, in the alternative case, all the individuals who are in course of 'coalescing' into a society—'express to one another, and which induces them to regulate their conduct by certain rules' tacitly recognised as being for the common interest of all. 'When this common

[1] *Morals*, ii. pp. 261-2. It must be observed that Hume persistently uses the word *justice* in its narrower or juridical sense: *i.e.* as a general term to denote the principles which determine the nature and limits of Property. The most trenchant expression of this unfortunate, but characteristic, conception of Justice is to be found in the Essay *Of the Origin of Government*: 'We are to look upon all the vast apparatus of our government as having ultimately no other object or purpose but the distribution of justice; or, in other words, the support of the twelve judges' (*Essays*, vol. i.; Essay V. p. 113). His word for the *moral* quality, ordinarily called *justice*, is *equity*. See above, p. 319.

[2] *Morals*, II. § ii. pp. 263-70.

sense of interest is mutually expressed and known to both, it produces a suitable resolution and behaviour. And this may properly enough be called a convention or agreement betwixt us, tho' without the interposition of a promise; since the actions of each of us have a reference to those of the other and are performed upon the supposition that something is to be performed on the other part'; even as 'two men who pull the oars of a boat do it by an agreement or convention, tho' they have never given promises to each other.' [1]

It is, therefore, upon an informal convention, upon a 'tacit understanding,' that Hume ultimately settles down; and that, for the origin not only of Property, but even of Society itself. In one sense, no doubt, this is to say that the origin of both, if indeed it is possible to distinguish between them, is not natural, but artificial. For, being both founded upon interest, the manifest and pressing interest of all the individuals concerned, they both spring from the reasoning, rather than from the emotional or 'passionate' side of man's nature; and that, to Hume, is the essential ground of distinction between the artificial and the natural virtues. But in another, and a truer, sense they must both be accounted natural. For, when all is said and done, the understanding is just as much a part of man's nature as the passions. Both Society and Property are devised—or rather, both naturally suggest themselves—as a remedy, and the only possible remedy, for the 'incommodities' of man's primitive condition and for the follies into which he is too often hurried by his passions. It may be true that, in the sense above indicated, 'the remedy is derived not from nature, but from artifice.' But, 'more properly speaking, nature provides a remedy in the judgement and understanding, for what is irregular and incommodious in the affections.' [2]

If indeed it could be proved that the process by which man discovers his true interest in these matters is a 'very abstruse process,' and the remedy of very 'difficult invention,' then we should be forced to admit that 'society is, in a manner, accidental, and the effect of many ages. But if it be found that nothing can be more simple than the rule for establishing stability of property; that every parent, in order to preserve peace amongst his children, must establish it; and that these first rudiments of justice must every day be improved, as the society enlarges: if all this appears evident, as it certainly must, we may conclude that 'tis utterly impossible for men to remain any considerable time in that savage condition which precedes society, but that his very first state and situation may justly be esteemed social. . . . Philosophers, indeed, may, if they please, extend their reasoning to the supposed

[1] *Morals*, ii. p. 263. [2] *Ib.* II. § ii. p. 262.

state of nature.' But this is only on condition that 'they allow it to be a mere philosophical fiction, which never had, and never could have, any reality.'[1] A conclusion which, in the face of what he had said in the first stage of his argument, is surely a little hard upon the state of nature.

So much for the origin of Society and its necessary complement, the first rude beginnings of Justice. We have yet to account for the origin of Government, without which neither Society nor Justice can long maintain themselves or play their part in any but the most imperfect manner. What was it that led men to this further change? and how was it brought about?

The answer to the former question is not so simple as is sometimes supposed. It is quite true that subsequent experience has shown a settled Government to be greatly to the interest of man. It is quite true that, without a constituted authority to compel them, there is no warrant that men will abstain from violence, or observe even the plainest rules of justice. It might be thought therefore that, once society was founded, there was every reason why so simple an expedient as the appointment of officers specially charged with the duty of enforcing justice should promptly occur to its members, and with equal promptness be carried into effect. There were, however, two obstacles in the way. On the one hand, in the total absence of experience, the expedient was by no means so obvious as Hobbes and others have silently assumed. And on the other hand, even if this objection be waived, even if for the sake of argument we allow the remedy to have been plainer than it really was, there were too many apparent interests, too many undoubted passions, arrayed against it, to admit of its prompt adoption.

The conditions, in fact, are once more much the same as they were on the original formation of society: the passions of men are arrayed against their true interest. The conditions are the same, but with this serious difference: that the interest of men in making the step in advance is now perceptibly weaker; and that there is no cementing passion, such as was the sexual impulse at the earlier stage, to throw into the scale against those which tell for disruption. It is admitted by all that men have a 'violent propension' to prefer the passion, which for all practical purposes is also the interest, of the moment to their real, or permanent, interest: 'to prefer contiguous to remote.' And that being the case, it is possible, and even probable, that some time may pass before the members of the new-born society can bring themselves to complete their work, to perfect their half-built fabric by 'having recourse to the invention of Government.'[2]

[1] *Morals*, ii. p. 265.
[2] *Ib.* II. § vii.; *Treatise*, vol. ii. pp. 300-304.

So strong, indeed, is the 'propension' in question that, had the young Societies been left purely to themselves, it might not impossibly have never been overcome. Fortunately, outward forces were generally at work to drive them into some kind of settled Government, to compel them to the step from which, on purely domestic grounds, they might stubbornly have shrunk. It is to war with neighbouring communities, with its natural sequel of civil strife over the spoils of war within the community itself, that the new advance is commonly due. 'Camps are the true mothers of cities'; and from the sheer necessities of the case, men will submit to a leader in battle, when they would never have endured his control in the less urgent, though none the less serious, needs of civil life. Such leadership, however, is no more than a 'shadow of authority,' while it lasts; and when the immediate need is passed, it is speedily thrown off. But the same need constantly recurs; and the same remedy is as constantly invoked. Repeated experience at length convinces men of the advantage to be gained by submission to settled authority; they apply to peace the lessons they have learned from the bitter necessities of war. So it is that the slow work of social 'coalition' is at length completed by the establishment of settled Government. So it is also, adds Hume, but with questionable accuracy, that the form of control suitable to war repeats itself in time of peace: that 'all Governments are at first monarchical, without any mixture and variety.'[1]

What then is the essence of the change thus brought about? and how does it accord with the results which analysis of man's moral motives has already put into our hands? The evil to be remedied is that, so long as men are left to themselves, it is often their immediate interest to violate those rules of justice which it is yet their real and permanent, though remote, interest to observe and maintain. And the essence of the remedy is to make it the immediate interest of the few, those charged with the government of the community, to enforce the observance of those rules upon the many: that is, by rewards and punishments, to make it the immediate, as it was always the remote, interest of the many to obey that law of justice, without which Society must fall in pieces.[2]

It may be asked how the consent of the many to these restrictions is either wrung from them in the first instance, or subsequently maintained. The answer is that, unless when immediately under the spell of temptation, all men are perfectly aware of their frailty, and are both willing and anxious to take precautions against it. Just as a man who knows himself to be subject to mad fits may have himself put in a strait-waistcoat when he feels one of them coming

[1] *Morals*, II. § viii.; *Treatise*, ii. pp. 304-6.

[2] *Treatise*, ii. pp. 301-4.

on; just as Ulysses had himself lashed to the mast when he neared the island of the Sirens, lest he should yield to their seductions. Then, when the moment of trial comes, it is too late to draw back. The trial passes; reason returns; and the very man who the moment before would have given worlds not to have put himself under restraint, has now no feeling but one of relief that he was wise enough to do so.[1]

Such is the history, both inner and outer, of the change which brought man from Society without Government to Society with Government, and to those settled rules of justice which nothing but Government can uphold. And it is evidently in complete accordance with the theory of political motives, of the 'artificial virtues,' which Hume had previously laid down. The motive which originally draws man into Society is consistently represented as a motive of self-interest. So is the motive which leads him to the further step, the establishment of settled Government. Yet, in both cases, the need is so pressing, the means which offer themselves for its satisfaction so obvious, that there is no call for elaborate calculation. In both cases, the critical decision is rather not so much of choice as of necessity for those who make it: the necessity, to use Burke's phrase, 'which is not chosen, but chooses.' In both cases, the subsequent story of the process, the gradual tightening of the bond thus established, is the work rather of time than of deliberate intention on the part of those concerned in it; indeed, they may well be hardly conscious of the change which is slowly coming over them. This is Hume's way of avoiding the difficulties which have beset most forms of the utilitarian theory of politics: the excessive strain which they put upon men's powers of foresight and calculation. On this side of the account his record is perfectly clear. Whether he was equally successful in guarding against the dangers which threatened from the other side—the danger of admitting those distinctively moral motives which it was his first business to bar out—is another matter, but one that must be held over for the present.

Settled government once firmly established, Hume feels himself at liberty to let the motive of self-interest, the principle of utility, drop swiftly into the background. It remains, indeed, as the *ultima ratio*: an argument to fall back upon when all the ties that ordinarily bind man to man have for the moment been violently broken. It remains as a last hope of recalling men to their senses, when all else has failed. But in quiet times and happier circumstances, its place is taken by a motive of a very different stock: the motive of 'allegiance,' of loyalty to the order in which we find ourselves placed and which, except under pressure of

[1] *Treatise*, ii. pp. 301-2.

extreme necessity, we recognise that we have no right to disturb. It is replaced, that is, by a motive of obligation: by an unreasoned, intuitive sense of duty. We thus acquire an instinctive repugnance to any breach of the artificial virtues, to any course of action which leads to the overthrow of the existing order, comparable to that which we feel at any like breach of the natural virtues: an irrepressible 'uneasiness' at the 'mere survey and contemplation' of such actions, or of the state of mind from which they result. And in nine cases out of ten—nay, in ninety-nine out of a hundred—this is the motive, the actual and operative motive, which holds society together. No ruler bases his authority upon an appeal to the self-interest of his subjects. On the contrary, he demands their allegiance as a right on his part and a duty on theirs. In the same way, 'the far greater part of the nation' obey their king, or other constituted authority, not because it is their interest to do so, but 'because they were born to such an obedience': in other words, because habit has made them regard it as a duty, and the breach of it as a sign of vice and moral deformity.[1]

Thus the motive which holds Society together, when fully formed, is altogether different from that which gives birth to it in the first instance. The latter was a motive purely of self-interest, though of an interest so urgent as to allow of no dispute, to leave little room even for deliberation. The former, to the vast majority of men and in the vast majority of cases, is essentially a moral motive: a motive of duty, hardly to be distinguished from that which impels us to the natural virtues; a motive of the same order as that which, intuitively and 'on the mere survey,' disposes us to admire benevolence in others, to foster it in our own heart and outward acts.

If this were all, however, there would be no reason for distinguishing between the natural and the artificial virtues. Yet Hume, as we have seen, is deeply concerned to draw such a distinction; and it is a distinction which, in some sense or other, corresponds with the plain facts of the case. It is necessary, therefore, to follow Hume's argument in some further detail: the more so, as this is the only way of fixing his attitude towards other theorists of his time; in particular, towards the champions of Contract. His argument is as follows:

It has been the fashion—the fashion of Locke and his followers, as we speedily discover—to derive the civil obligation, the obligation on which Society is founded, from what is assumed to be the natural obligation of a promise or Contract. The object of this device is manifestly to provide a 'natural' sanction for what all admit to be an artificial institution: that of civil society, or the State. The truth is, however, that the two things are 'exactly on the same

[1] *Morals*, II. § viii.; *Treatise*, ii. pp. 308-10.

footing': the obligation to perform promises is just as much an artificial obligation, fidelity to the given word just as much an artificial virtue, as the obligation to maintain the Society of which I am a member is an artificial obligation, as the virtue of allegiance is an artificial virtue. In both cases, the proximate sanction is what, in process of time, has come to be a sense of duty. In both cases, the ultimate sanction is self-interest: the sense that for every one of us life would be intolerable without the given artificial convention: intolerable, that is, unless, in the one case, we could all count on the sanctity of promises; unless, in the other, we could all count on the maintenance of an ordered Society, of a settled Government, which undertakes, as one of its first duties, to enforce them.[1]

It is quite true, Hume admits, that, on the first formation of Government, the 'subject' may have made a promise of allegiance to his appointed Ruler; and consequently that, '*upon its first establishment*, Government would naturally be supposed to derive its obligation from the laws of nature'—laws which, in spite of their title, are still, in Hume's view, mere matters of convention and therefore, strictly speaking, not natural, but artificial, laws—'and, in particular, from that law concerning the performance of promises.' This, however, is no more than a passing phase; and as soon as the Government is firmly in the saddle, the obligation of promise is replaced by the far stronger and more enduring obligation of duty: an obligation itself resting, in the last resort, upon an ever deepening sense of interest, or utility. Indeed, if in earlier days and before the bond of duty has had time to weave itself, the sanction of interest is reinforced by that of promise, this is on exactly the same principle as that by which, in the ordinary affairs of life, men will often bind themselves by promises to the performance of that which it would have been their interest to perform, quite apart from those promises; so giving others a fuller security, 'by superadding a new obligation of interest'—for promises too rest upon interest 'general, avowed and of the last consequence in life'—'to that which they formerly lay under.' And we are no more entitled to draw any speculative inference, as to the nature of the obligation incurred, in the one case than in the other.[2]

The truth is that, though both things, the sanctity of promises no less than that of civil Society and Government, rest upon the same basis, utility or self-interest, each is yet entirely independent of the other. They arose at different times: promises, like Property, in the days when Society existed but was not yet organised under a settled Government; Government, as the sign and instrument of that subsequent organisation. They were devised for

[1] *Treatise*, ii. pp. 306-8.

[2] *Morals*, II. § viii.; *Treatise*, ii. pp. 306-9.

wholly different purposes: the one for the convenience of ordinary intercourse between man and man; the other for the far more complicated ends of distinctively civil Society: that is, a Society which exists not merely for the immediate convenience of its individual members, but also for those manifold purposes which belong to a body organised as a corporate whole.

Civil Society, no doubt, was instituted largely, perhaps chiefly, as a security for the observance of promises and of those other 'natural laws'—the rules of Property—which are binding as between man and man.[1] But that is no more reason for basing civil Society—and with it, Government—upon Promise than for basing it upon the rights and rules of Property. 'Our *civil* duties are, indeed, so far connected with our *natural* that the former are invented chiefly for the sake of the latter; and the principal object of Government is to constrain men to observe the laws of nature. In this respect, however, that law of nature concerning the performance of promises is only comprised along with the rest; and its exact observance is to be considered as an effect of the institution of Government, and not the obedience to Government as an effect of the obligation of a promise. Tho' the object of our civil duties be the enforcing of our natural, yet the *first* motive of the invention, as well as the performance of both, is nothing but self-interest. And since there is a separate interest in the obedience to Government from that in the performance of promises, we must also allow of a separate obligation. To obey the civil magistrate is requisite to preserve order and concord in society. To perform promises is requisite to beget mutual trust and confidence in the common offices of life. The ends, as well as the means, are perfectly distinct; nor is the one subordinate to the other. . . . In short, if the performance of promises be advantageous, so is obedience to Government. If the former interest be general, so is the latter. If the one interest be obvious and avowed, so is the other. And as these two rules are founded on the obligations of interest, each of them must have a peculiar authority, independent of the other.' [2]

Such are the speculative reasons against the attempt, so persistently made by Locke and others, to base Society upon a contract between its members; and by Hobbes and popular prejudice, to base Government upon a promise on the part of the governed, or upon a contract between them and their governors. In the subsequent part of his argument, as well as in two of the most

[1] According to Hume, 'the three fundamental laws of nature are the stability of possession, its transference by consent, and the performance of promise' (*Morals*, II. § vi. p. 293).

[2] *Morals*, II. § viii.; *Treatise*, ii. pp. 308-9.

notable of the *Essays*,[1] Hume comes down to the plainer ground of experience and history; and here again, he finds insuperable obstacles to the acceptance of any such explanation. It is true, he admits once more, that upon its first establishment, the authority of Government may have been buttressed by a promise of fidelity on the part of the subject. But it is clear that this does not carry us to the root of the matter. For a promise can never be more than a secondary and subordinate sanction; it always implies some other motive, behind and beyond it, for the performance of a given act: a motive either of interest or of duty, in this case manifestly one of interest. And even apart from this, which may be regarded rather as a speculative than a practical objection, the commonest experience will convince us that no such promise as is here supposed is ever considered to be absolutely binding on those who make it; that, in case of intolerable misgovernment, they will always throw this promise to the winds and transfer their allegiance to some other chieftain, who may be expected to use his power better: that is, more in accordance with the interest of his subjects. In these cases, the secondary sanction is at once swept aside, and the primary sanction is left to stand, without disguise, on its own merits.

A Government the authority of which is never seriously questioned by the governed, may justly be said to rest upon their consent: the two statements are practically convertible. But to say that such a Government rests upon a contract between the two parties is an abuse of terms. For a contract must either be, as it was to Hobbes, a promise of unconditional obedience on the part of the governed; and in that case, as we have seen, it is a pure fashion of speech which, as soon as occasion arises, is treated, in Hobbes' own phrase, as mere 'words and breath.' Or it must be, as it was to the Convention Parliament, a bargain on terms between the one party and the other; and that, as Hume justly observes, is a thing not to be thought of in those primitive times: it is 'an idea far beyond the comprehension of savages.' In the former case, therefore, it is an unreality; in the latter, an impossibility. In either case, it must be summarily dismissed.[2]

But if Promise or Contract thus fail to account even for the most primitive forms of Government—that is, even for those forms which, at first sight, seem to lend themselves the most readily to this explanation—much more do they fail to account for those forms of Government with which History presents us: those forms which confront us, and confront us without exception, in the experience of the present. It is notorious that all existing

[1] *Essays*, Part II. §§ xii. and xiii.: *Of an Original Contract*, and of *Passive Obedience*.

[2] *Essays*, vol. i. (ed. Green and Grose), p. 445.

Governments—and not least, that of the United Kingdom—sprang in the first instance from a happy usurpation: sprang, that is, from brute force. And brute force excludes not only Promise or Contract, but even that tacit consent which has sometimes been confounded with Contract, but which, as we have seen, needs to be carefully distinguished from it. To say that the English consented to the usurpation of the Conqueror, or the Romanised Gauls to the domination of the Franks, would be no better than a mockery. And though time, with other cases, may in some countries have brought about a temper which might more aptly be described as consent—the consent of use and wont—that leaves us still very far from the state of things represented by the word Contract.[1]

Even in England, which is justly reckoned to be 'freer' than most other countries, what ground is there for saying, as was roundly said at the time of the Revolution, that the existing Government is based upon Contract? The change made by the Revolution is, on close inspection, seen to have been extremely small. 'It touched not a single flower of the Crown. It gave not a single new right to the people.' All that it did was to make a slight deflection in the line of succession. It was planned entirely at the will of a few magnates. The people at large had no voice whatever in summoning the Prince of Orange to replace his uncle. And the same is true of all other political convulsions. The more revolutionary they are, the less the voice they allow to the will of the people as a whole. What is worse, the more the voice they do allow, the more conclusive is the proof that the voice of the people is not the voice of God. 'In reality, there is not a more terrible event than a total dissolution of Government, which gives liberty to the multitude and makes the determination or choice of a new establishment depend upon a number which nearly approaches to that of the body of the people; for it never comes entirely to the whole body of them. Every wise man, then, wishes to see, at the head of a powerful and obedient army, a General who may speedily seize the prize and give to the people a master whom they are so unfit to choose for themselves. So little correspondent is fact and reality to those philosophical notions.'[2] So utterly without warrant is that 'refined system' which theorists have built upon a supposed Contract between the governors and the governed.[3]

[1] *Essays*, i. pp. 446-8.

[2] *Ib*. p. 448. 'Were one to choose a period of time when the people's consent was least regarded in public transactions, it would be precisely on the establishment of a new Government' (*ib*. vol. i. p. 450).

[3] *Ib*. i. p. 446.

So much for those existing forms of Government which, allowing as they do some voice to the will and therefore to the consent of the governed, are clearly the most favourable to the theory of Contract. But cast our eyes over Europe—much more, over other quarters of the globe—and we recognise at once that very few communities offer even the semblance of such popular control. The United Kingdom, the Dutch Netherlands, a handful of Swiss Cantons—that almost exhausts the list of 'free' States. Nearly all the rest 'live under an absolute Government,' sometimes aristocratic, more often monarchical, in form; and are well content to do so. So that, to put the matter at the very lowest, absolute Government must be allowed to be 'as natural and as common as any' other. That being so, we have the choice between two alternatives. We must either maintain, with Locke, that the absolute Governor, though he abounds in fact, has no place at all in respect of right: in other words, that he has no claim on the allegiance of his subjects. Or we must once more admit that the theory of Contract is a pure delusion. The former is a desperate solution; it is a bid for that universal dissolution of Government which has been plainly shown to be against the interest of all. What is perhaps yet more fatal, it ignores the fundamental truth that, 'in all questions with regard to morals,' the final appeal lies not to theory, but to fact: not to what the philosopher thinks men ought to do, but to what they actually do—to 'the common sentiments of mankind, and to the practice and opinion of all nations and all ages.' We are, therefore, once more driven back upon the latter.[1]

Such is Hume's verdict on those who find in Contract a philosophical explanation of the origin of Government. Both on speculative and on practical grounds, they must be held to fail completely. Put the question on a lower level, however, and they have much, he admits, to plead in their defence. And the same is true of those who have pinned their faith to the rival and opposite theory: the theory of divine Right. Neither of these doctrines has any speculative value. Each of them has considerable merit, as a popular battle-cry: as a rhetorical statement of a half-truth, which no wise man will dream of taking for the whole. Thus the theory of Divine Right, absurd and pernicious when used as a cloak for 'legitimist' misgovernment, is true and wholesome when taken for a recognition of the fact that any Government which, on the whole, secures the good of the governed, may claim to be of divine origin and to rest under divine sanction. In the same way with the theory of Contract. Quite untenable as a

[1] *Morals*, II. §§ viii., ix.; *Treatise*, ii. pp. 313, 316.

[2] *Treatise*, ii. p. 311; *Essays*, II. § xii. (pp. 446, 451, 460).

theory, it has at any rate the merit of proclaiming that no Government which does not secure at least the tacit consent of the governed deserves to be maintained: further than this, that the more any Government throws itself upon the consent of the governed, the better, the more 'sacred' are its claims.[1] So it is that both Locke and Filmer have their justification: not, however, as masters of the whole truth, nor even as fully possessed even of the half-truth which each was striving vainly to express. The true theory will be that which, finding room for each of these rival elements, shall raise both of them to a higher level and unite them in some wider truth that retains the gold, but rejects the dross, of each.[2]

Such a theory, Hume believes, is offered by that expounded in the *Treatise* and *Essays*. Both the required elements are there represented: the human element, in the plea that the ultimate origin, and with it the ultimate sanction, of all Government is to be found in the felt interest of the governed; the divine element, or what may pass for such, in the admission that no Government can claim to have fairly established itself until the motive of self-interest has sunk into the background, and its place in the foreground, its place as immediate and effective motive, been taken by the very different sanction of obligation, or duty: of duty to the Government we happen to be born under; of obligation to the particular order in which we find ourselves placed.

In closing this sketch of Hume's political theory, it is well to gather up its main issues, whether as a constructive argument or as a weapon of offence. On the constructive side, it stands for by far the subtlest and most effective attempt ever made to establish the State on utilitarian principles: on the interest of the individual, in the first instance; on the interest of the community, as the sum of all its component members, in the second. In this respect, Hume is not only more logical than Bentham; but, thanks to the qualifications which he introduces, he also avoids the practical difficulties, the necessity of crediting man with incredible powers of foresight and wisdom, which are fatal to Bentham's system and, for that matter, to Spinoza's also. The crucial qualification consists in his bold transition from the principle of interest to that of duty: a transition which makes it possible for him to release the citizen from the hopeless task of measuring his steps, of cal-

[1] 'My intention here is not to exclude the consent of the people from being one just foundation of government, where it has place. It is surely the best and most sacred of any. I only pretend that it has very seldom had place in any degree, and never almost in its full extent.' This qualification was added in a later edition (1753-4).

[2] *Essays*, II. xii.; vol. i. pp. 444-5, 450; *Morals*, II. § ix.; *Treatise*, ii. pp. 313-14.

culating the pros and cons at every turn, and at the same time provides him with a stronger motive for loyalty, whether to his rulers or his fellow citizens, than can ever be yielded by the shifting sands of expediency or utility. It is in this qualification that we must look for his vital originality. The rest of his theory—as he himself would have admitted, the yet more fundamental part of his theory—is common to him with Spinoza, as well as with other modern champions of utility.

As for his assault on rival theories—in particular, that of Contract—he has the merit of distinguishing, as many have failed to distinguish, between the two different stages at which the idea of Contract has been applied: between the Original Contract[1]—and it is this alone that can rightly be called the Social Contract—which may be supposed to have united isolated individuals into one community in the first instance; and that secondary Contract, which some have believed to pass between the community so founded and its rulers, at a later date. In the former case, as he justly argues, the idea of Contract is utterly inadmissible. The whole range of ideas expressed by the terms *Contract*, *Promise*, *Covenant* is, of necessity, wholly unknown to man in anything that can be called the 'state of nature.' These ideas imply the previous existence of that very Society to which, according to Locke and others, they gave birth. They are 'artificial' ideas; the virtues corresponding to them—trustworthiness, fidelity to the plighted word, and so on—are 'artificial' virtues, which could never take rise until Society, itself a wholly artificial creation, was fully formed and its various conventions were already an established fact. The criticism is conclusive, and it would have been well if Rousseau and other later writers had laid it more seriously to heart.

Against the second application of the Contract theory—the supposed bargain between king and subject, between the governors and the governed—there is no objection so deadly in the speculative sense. Hume's own criticism of it is based, as we have seen, mainly, though not solely, on grounds of experience and history; and on such grounds it is evidently untenable. But it would be idle to repeat what has just been said on that matter.

One more point must be added: a point which has hardly perhaps received sufficient notice. What was Hume's bearing towards the historical method? The future historian of England might have been expected to make liberal use of this method in

[1] It is rather unfortunate that Hume, following in the steps of the Convention and of popular practice, should apply the term *Original Contract* to the supposed secondary covenant between king and subject. See his Essay of that title.

his political speculations. And in those parts of his argument which concern the origin of Society, and still more the origin of Government, he does in fact make considerable, and often very effective, play with it. Yet it is clear that these things lie merely on the fringe of the subject, as he conceived it: that the heart of his theory lay in the doctrine of utility and in the wise qualifications with which he guarded it. Some may suppose that it is among the merits of the utilitarian theory to lend itself to the free adoption of the historical method. And, as an abstract statement, this may be true enough. Unfortunately, the concrete utilitarian—Helvétius, for example, much more Bentham and his following—has been singularly slow to take advantage of this opening. It is the honourable distinction of Hume that, on occasion, he is ready to do so. Such occasions, however, are comparatively rare; and on the whole, his argument would seem to have been cast from the first in a purely speculative mould, to which the facts of history were subsequently fitted, by way of illustration. This is clearly not what is meant by the historical method.

There is, however, one passage of the *Essays* which leaves a strangely different impression: showing as it does an almost uncanny insight into some of the grounds on which the historical method is evidently rested, and which were to be still more clearly stated by one at least of those who have applied that method, and applied it with unrivalled mastery, to questions of political speculation. The passage is as follows:

'Did one generation of men go off the stage at once and another succeed, as is the case with silkworms and butterflies, the new race, if they had sense enough to choose their Government, which surely is never the case with men, might voluntarily and by general consent establish their own form of polity, without any regard to the laws or precedents which prevailed among their ancestors. But as human society is in a perpetual flux, one man every hour going out of the world, another coming into it, it is necessary, in order to preserve stability in government, that the new brood should conform themselves to the established constitution and clearly follow the path which their fathers, treading in the footsteps of theirs, had marked out to them.' [1]

As is usual with Hume, the argument is cast in a more or less speculative form, and he refrains from pressing it more closely home. But the consequences are obvious. If, for the reason stated, there can be no clean slate in politics, it follows that the true life of every community, the true springs of its action, are to

[1] *Of the Original Contract*: *Essays*, vol. i. p. 452. It is significant that this paragraph appears for the first time in the posthumous edition of the *Essays* (1777).

be discovered not by the application of any abstract formula—the Rights of Man, the Divine Right of Princes, the interest of the stronger, the 'rules of arithmetic,' or any other similar catch-word —but by a watchful study of all that it has inherited from the past, of all the modifications which have been brought about, or are in the way to be brought about, in response to the ever-changing needs of the present. It is substantially the same consequence that was to be subsequently drawn by Burke, and drawn in words which give a startling echo to those just quoted from Hume:

'One of the first and most leading principles on which the Commonwealth and the Laws are consecrated is lest the temporary possessors and life-renters in it, unmindful of what they have received from their ancestors or of what is due to their posterity, should act as if they were the entire masters; that they should not think it among their rights to cut off the entail or commit waste upon the inheritance, by destroying at their pleasure the whole original fabric of their Society; hazarding to leave to those who come after them a ruin instead of an habitation; and teaching their successors as little to respect their contrivances as they had themselves respected the institutions of their forefathers. By this unprincipled facility of changing the State as often and as much and in as many ways as there are fleeting fancies and fashions, the whole chain and continuity of the Commonwealth would be broken. No one generation could link with the other. Men would become little better than the flies of a summer.' [1]

What a resemblance, and what a curious contrast! The idea of the continuity of national life is, to Hume, little more than an intellectual perception; and one, moreover, which he never bestirred himself to work out in detail. To Burke, it is a passionate conviction, welcomed with all the ardour of a born conservative, and worked out with unflagging zest, in relation to each new question which came under his notice: to the life of each nation in turn—England, the American Colonies, India, France—that circumstances called upon him to study and make his own.

Such are the main outlines of Hume's political theory. How far, we now ask, is that theory consistent with itself and with the rest of the system of which it forms an inseparable part? How far, again, can it be said to offer a satisfactory account of the facts of that political life which it professes to explain? Both questions are necessary; but they need to be kept carefully apart.

Thanks to his extreme candour, it is easy to show that Hume sacrificed consistency at every turn. He begins by laying down sweeping principles. But as his enquiry goes forward, one after another of them is either explicitly or tacitly surrendered.

[1] Burke, *Reflections on the French Revolution: Works*, vol. i. pp. 416-17.

The main purpose of his metaphysical system had been to deny any creative faculty to the understanding. And the main principles on which he relied for the purpose are two. The first, that all knowledge consists solely in 'impressions,' which is his equivalent for sensations; what we take for 'ideas of the mind' being, in fact, no more than a fainter survival of such impressions in the memory of the man who has once received them. The second, that, just as we have no knowledge of outward objects, but only of the impressions which, without any valid ground for doing so, we assume to be caused by outward objects, so we have no knowledge of the impressionable self except in the fleeting moment of the impression and the equally fleeting moment of its recurrence to memory, or 'in idea.' The impression of the moment then, without any reference either to a permanent object on the one hand, or to a permanent self on the other—that is the sole constituent of our knowledge. All else is a mere illusion.

That such an account of the matter plays havoc with our ordinary conception of what is meant by knowledge, Hume readily admits. Take away the idea of identity in its double application: the conviction that the experience which we have at the present moment is identical with the experience which we remember to have had at some moment in the past, and the conviction that we who now have that experience are the same being that had it in the past; take away the idea of cause and effect, the conviction that between two given experiences there is a necessary connection, a connection depending not on the caprice of our own mind—for what else is the wonder-working 'law of association'?—but on something which our mind apprehends as given from without: sweep away these things, and our knowledge manifestly becomes something much more modest, something much less substantial, than we had vainly imagined it to be. All our knowledge, all our science as commonly understood, presupposes these convictions. Yet we are summoned by Hume to reject them as illusions.

Two serious difficulties at once present themselves to our mind. How can the understanding which is capable of forming such gigantic illusions be refused the credit of that creative faculty which it is Hume's first object to repudiate? And how, in the absence of such ideas as cause and identity, can even the beggarly rags of knowledge, which are all that Hume leaves to man, hold together for a moment? What man would be so foolish as to base even the most trivial action, the most indifferent conclusion, upon grounds so flimsy as that two sensations, so far as his memory served or his power of discerning resemblances and differences went, had always accompanied each other in the same order to his experience in the past and therefore may always be expected to do so in the future until, by whatever accident, the association shall be broken and all be to begin anew? Even allowing that there is here no illicit intrusion of the forbidden ideas—which is far from being the case—is this an adequate account of even our most obvious processes of reasoning? of even the most ordinary, but none the less necessary, actions which we base upon them? And if it fails to explain these simple matters, how much more does it fail to account for those complicated trains of reasoning which are involved in the processes of any experimental science, in any mathematical and physical demonstration, or in the philosophical arguments of such a work as Kant's *Kritik*, or the *Treatise of Human Nature*? Take the *Treatise*, for instance, and we shall find that, at every turn, Hume avails himself of the idea of cause and effect for the purpose of destroying our belief in it; that a permanent self in a world of permanent and causally related objects is presupposed at every step of the argument which is built up with the sole purpose of denying them. Hume was right in contending that the idea of cause and effect is not, and cannot be, given in sensation; so far, his argument is irrefutable. The proper inference, however, to draw from this is not that such an idea is illusory, but that it is contributed by the mind: the inference, that is, which was subsequently drawn by Kant.[1]

[1] It is strange to see how completely the real drift of Hume's argument has been misunderstood by some of his critics, even by those who claim to speak with authority on such matters. Huxley, for instance, writes throughout on the assumption that Hume accepted the idea of causation, and that his criticism was concerned solely with its application to particular cases, or, at most, with its extension from cases already verified up to the present moment to like cases liable to occur in the future. According to him, Hume's sole purpose was to utter a warning that any particular induction—or, for that matter, any particular deduction also—is liable to be upset by fresh experience, or by more rigorous reflection: in other words, merely to repeat the lesson of Bacon. It seems never to cross Huxley's mind that the real object of Hume was to assail the very idea of causation—that is, of a fixed dependence of one object or one experience upon another—root and branch. This is not the fault of Hume, who knew perfectly well what he wanted to say, and said it—at any rate in the *Treatise*—with all the clearness and force of which he was so great a master. The fault lies solely in the incomprehensible blindness of his critics. It is true that Huxley has chosen to take not the *Treatise*, but the *Enquiry*, for the text of his sermon. But, apart from the perversity of the choice—the watered after-brew, instead of the undiluted original—the real nature of Hume's argument as to cause and effect, though obscured, is still discernible even in the *Enquiry* (Part I. §§ iv. and v.). See Huxley's *Hume*, in English Men of Letters, chap. vi. pp. 120-5.

Such are the difficulties, and such the consequent inconsistencies, which beset Hume on the metaphysical side of his system. When we turn to the moral and political side of it, they become not less, but more, apparent. The moral philosopher has always found it a harder task to deny creative faculties to the human mind than the metaphysician or the man of science. And with all his subtlety, Hume is no exception to the rule. He had failed, as we have seen, to carry out this exclusion consistently in the easier field; what likelihood was there that he should succeed in the more difficult?

Before the end of his metaphysical argument, he had, consciously or unconsciously, been driven to surrender, in at least two cardinal matters, the principles with which he started. He had admitted that the idea of personal identity, unproved as it is and unprovable, is yet a necessary assumption which lies at the base of all man's experience. And he had conceded to the mind all and more than all that creative faculty which it was his chief purpose to repudiate. He had credited the understanding, that is, with the faculty of conceiving ideas, such as that of cause and effect, which, as he rightly saw, could never come to it as a mere passive recipient, could never enter it by way of sensation. He strives to parry this admission by the counterplea that, after all, such conceptions are a pure illusion. But he fails to see that this leaves the creative faculty of the mind precisely where it was before, or rather throws it into yet stronger relief. Nor, in spite of all his efforts, can he save himself from employing the illusion, throughout the whole course of his argument, just as if it had been a reality.

Turn to his moral argument, and we find him entangled in precisely the same difficulties. Once again, and in a manner yet more glaring, he has to admit the idea of personal identity: to lay it, in fact, at the very base of his theory of the 'moral sense.' Once again he has to make the largest allowance for the creative power of the mind: this time, not in the shape of cause and effect and other 'forms of thought' necessary to the constitution of knowledge, but in the no less formidable shape of duty, as the practical principle by which all desires and impulses are liable to be qualified and controlled. Leaving aside all other objections to his moral theory, let us briefly examine the grounds on which this criticism is based.

The former of these objections, which is also the less important, may be swiftly despatched. It is one of the chief merits of Hume's moral theory that, unlike his utilitarian disciples, he refuses to test acts by their consequences: that he persists in looking behind the consequences to the act itself; behind the act to the motive; behind the motive to the character, the whole tissue of motives, from which it springs.[1] So much is plainly demanded by the facts of the case. Nothing less than this will satisfy the moral consciousness of the world, as it has come to be after ages of discipline; as, among the more enlightened spirits, it had already come to be ages before the birth of Christianity.

The principle is unassailable. But, considering the arid atmosphere of his day, it is no small thing that Hume should so heartily have welcomed it. Had he clearly seen all that it involved, we may well doubt whether he would have had the courage to do so. For if the crucial thing in regard to conduct is neither the outward act, nor even the motive which lies behind it, but the character as a whole—the dominant tissue of motives which constitutes the moral being of the given agent—then we have the manifest admission that there is such a thing as a permanent self; a self which remains the same through all apparent changes; a self which is the true source of all action, the true object of all moral judgements. We have the manifest admission that it is by the dominant character of that self, and not by any single act or any single group of motives involved in it, that a man both habitually acts and is habitually judged; that it is this abiding character which alone calls out either the pride or shame of the agent, either the blame or admiration, of those who know him. And this admission is not thrown out by the way; it is inseparably bound up with doctrines which lie at the root of his whole theory. Yet, as we have seen, this involves the acceptance of the very thing which, in the metaphysical part of his argument, he had set himself to deny.

Exactly the same inconsistency appears again in his account of Pride: that is, of the emotion with which he chooses to open his account of *The Passions*, which forms the corner-stone of the whole of that part of the *Treatise*, and which reappears as an indispensable link in his doctrine of the 'moral sense.' It is of the essence of Pride, he argues, to carry with it a reference to the self of the man who feels it. We take pride in a thing or quality—riches, beauty; wit, wisdom, virtue and so forth — because it is *ours*. These

[1] *Of Morals*, Part II. § i.; Part III. § i. 'All virtuous actions derive their merit only from virtuous motives and are considered merely as signs of those motives. . . . A virtuous motive is required to render an action virtuous,' in the former chapter; and 'when any quality. or character, has a tendency to the good of mankind, we are pleased with it and approve of it'; ''tis from the influence of characters and qualities upon those who have an intercourse with any person that we blame or praise him,' in the latter chapter—these may be taken as typical sentences, embodying this side of Hume's moral theory.

matters are the 'subject' of Pride; and it is manifest that, in themselves, they excite a pleasurable feeling wherever they are found and to whomever they may belong. It is only when they belong to *us* or to some person who stands in close relation to *us*—from whom, therefore, we can claim a kind of reflected glory—that they excite pride; and of that pride we ourselves are necessarily the 'object.' Now every one will admit that the more permanent we regard such possessions as being—that is, the closer their relation to ourselves—the greater the pride we take in them. Hence the pride excited by the good things of the mind is greater than that aroused by such outward goods as riches, or even beauty; because we flatter ourselves they can never be taken from us. So that, here again, we are thrown back upon the idea—or, what is still more to the purpose, upon the instinctive sense of a permanent self, subsisting through all changes and chances: through all the several 'impressions' or 'ideas' which we are capable of receiving. In his own words, 'the idea of ourselves is always intimately present to us, and conveys a sensible degree of vivacity to the idea of any other object to which we are related.'[1] Once more a complete surrender of the doctrine on which Hume had insisted in the first part of the *Treatise*.

We pass now to the far more serious question: How does Hume deal with the idea of Duty?

At the outset, we have once more to acknowledge his extraordinary candour: his readiness to admit facts which, at first sight, might seem to run directly counter to the principles on which his whole system was built up. He was well aware that the idea of duty in the field of morals is, at least on the surface, as hard to square with the principle that all action is based on pain and pleasure as the idea of cause and effect is hard to square with the principle that all perceptions are based solely on sensation, in the field of knowledge. Yet, in the one case as in the other, he boldly admits the presence of the unwelcome idea, as an undeniable fact of consciousness. All he seeks to do is to prove that it is not incompatible with the principle from which he started.

In the case of morals, indeed, he carries his concessions a clear stage further than he had been willing to do in the case of knowledge. In the matter of cause and effect, he had argued that even the reduced value, which was all that on his system could be allowed to that idea, is sufficient for all practical purposes, whether of science or of every-day experience. In other words, he had whittled down the idea to suit his cherished principle. He had admitted just so much of the current conception as he supposed,

[1] *Of the Passions*, Part II. § iv. p. 142.

rightly or wrongly, to be consistent with his own fundamental assumptions, and had thrown away all the rest. He had retained the bare idea of succession; the belief in the necessity of that succession; the belief that it is a succession, not of sensations but of objects, he had branded as an illusion. In the matter of duty, on the other hand, he accepts, for practical purposes, all that is involved in the current conception.[1] He differs only as to its speculative justification. The popular belief is that the idea of duty is an ultimate idea, which it is impossible to resolve into simpler elements: least of all, into any form of pleasure. Hume endeavours to show that, in the last resort, it is identical with pleasure: with the 'particular kind of pleasure' which he analyses in his doctrine of the 'moral sense.'

It is just here, however, that his difficulties begin. The current conception does not stop short with the acceptance of duty as a fact. It includes the conviction that duty is an ultimate idea: an idea which is not merely distinguishable from the sense of pleasure, but even by its very nature in the sharpest possible hostility to it. To destroy this conviction is to change the whole character of the idea itself. But it is the sole purpose of Hume's argument to prove any such conviction to be false: to be an inference as illegitimate as that involved in the current conception of cause and effect. His position therefore is this. He retains the idea of duty, as a fact. He admits that it is an inseparable part of the moral consciousness, that it is indispensable to all sound moral action. But at the same time he cuts away the ground upon which it is universally rested: a ground which is just as much an integral part of the moral consciousness as that part which he retains. And he expects the idea, so shorn of all rational justification, still to influence men's minds and conduct; still to bear fruit in motive and action, although he has done everything in his power to kill it at the root.

This proceeding is, in itself, questionable enough. And it is evident that the only chance of maintaining such plausibility as it has was to keep the door rigorously barred against the intrusion of duty, or of ideas ultimately reducible to that of duty, into the explanation by which he proposes to replace the one commonly accepted. And the question we have now to ask ourselves is:

[1] The words *duty*, *obligation*, *moral obligation* are hardly less common in Hume than in any other moral philosopher. Thus on the second page of Part II. § i. (of Justice and Injustice) we have the significant sentence, 'But may not the *sense of morality or duty* produce an action without any other motive'? and the words 'duty' or 'moral obligation' occur no less than eight times more within the next page (pp. 253-4), each time, be it observed, by way not of criticism, but acceptance.

Does Hume's doctrine of the moral sense satisfy that condition? or does he allow the idea of duty to creep, openly or covertly, into what professes to be a reduction of all motives, duty included, to a mere desire for the attainment of pleasure and the avoidance of pain? If he does, then we shall be justified in concluding that his whole argument falls to the ground. It will be our object to show that there are at least three links in the chain of his argument which involve the admission—an admission, on his principles absolutely illegitimate—of the idea of duty.

The first of these links is to be found not in his account of the moral sense itself, but in the negative argument which serves as preface to it: the argument which refutes the attempt of Clarke and others to base morality upon reason. In that opening chapter, he scornfully rejects the possibility that our moral experience can have anything to do with reason; that our 'passions, volitions and actions can be either contrary or conformable to reason.' Some judgement or other, he admits, may—or rather, must—be passed upon them. It is not, however, that they are 'reasonable or unreasonable,' but that they are 'laudable or blameable,' that they have 'merit or demerit.'[1]

The negative side of this pronouncement—apart from its limited application to Clarke and his 'eternal fitnesses'—is sufficiently disputable. That, however, is not now the matter in question. The point to be urged is that the positive side of it contains precisely the admission which, for the sake of keeping his own principle watertight, he should have been most anxious to avoid: the admission of something 'laudable or blameable,' of something to which we attach 'merit or demerit,' in our motives and volitions. How is it possible, we ask, to praise or blame an act or motive, unless we have some standard by which to judge it? some idea of character to which we think that all men ought, more or less, to conform? some conception of duty—and that, not as an abstract idea, but as a code more or less fully articulated—by which we believe all men to be bound? How is it possible to speak of 'merit and demerit,' unless we consider the agent bound in duty so to act and think as to earn the one and not be chargeable with the other? Is it not evident that, unless such terms carry with them an acknowledgement of duty, they have no meaning whatsoever? Yet here they are planted down on the very threshold of Hume's moral theory; representing the very first elements of the truth on the matter of moral conduct and the moral judgement. What is more, such terms, or their equivalents, are absolutely unavoidable. If Hume was unable to keep clear of them, what master of thought or language can hope to succeed

[1] *Of Morals*, Part I. § i. p. 236.

better? It is one more proof, if proof were needed, that it is impossible either to think or speak of morals without at once speaking the speech, and thinking in terms, of duty.

To such an objection Hume, no doubt, would at once reply that this is precisely the difficulty which his doctrine of the moral sense was deliberately designed to meet; that the peculiar merit of that doctrine is, while amply providing for the practical claims of duty, yet to prove that, in the last resort, duty is identical with pleasure—' a particular kind of pleasure '—and that pleasure therefore is the ' actuating principle ' to which all our actions may ultimately be traced. Let us turn, therefore, to his account of the moral sense, and consider whether it does, in fact, fulfil this necessary condition; whether, on his own showing, the ultimate springs of action are so completely purged of the taint of duty as he supposed and intended them to be.

Broadly speaking, and quite apart from all argumentative details, there are two main objects which Hume's doctrine of the moral sense was intended to attain. On the one hand, it was to prove that the sense of duty is, at bottom, only a particular form of the sense of pleasure. On the other hand, it was to provide a test—a test itself reducible to a form of pleasure—by which we are at once enabled to distinguish between good and evil pleasures and furnished with a motive for preferring the former to the latter. On the one hand, therefore, like most other forms of hedonism, it had the merit of insisting that, whatever else it may be, ' morality ' cannot be *against* man's natural instincts; that, even if purely natural motives are not enough to account for it, they must at least play their part, and that a leading part, in its formation; that they must at least supply the foundation on which all the rest is built. He doubtless goes much further than this. But this much, at any rate, must be accepted as sound; as a necessary bulwark against all forms of the ascetic principle: that principle which, however necessary it may have been as a protest against certain kinds of corruption and at certain periods of man's history, can never be more than a blank negation, against which the healthy conscience of mankind has always risen in revolt. On the other hand, as we have already seen, he is careful to guard himself against the chief danger to which the hedonist theory has commonly lain open: the inability which it has laboured under of finding any logically defensible test between good pleasures and bad. That is the danger which his doctrine of the moral sense honestly, though it may be unsuccessfully, endeavours to avert.

The pivot upon which that doctrine avowedly turns is sympathy. And it is by a scrutiny of what he tells us about that quality that the answer to our question—How far does Hume succeed in excluding from his explanation all trace of the idea of duty?—is most readily to be found.

On the hedonist principles from which he started and which it was his main purpose to uphold and justify, sympathy can be nothing more than either a mere feeling, a feeling of pleasure at the sight of certain actions, motives, types of character, exhibited by others; or a desire for the pleasure arising from the consciousness that we are exciting the like feeling in the breast of others. In fact, however, it is neither. On the contrary, it is a feeling qualified either by a conception of what I wish to see in other men; or, on the alternative supposition, by a conception of what I am aware that others expect of me, and by a desire for the pleasure which will result from acting in such a way as to win their approval. In other words, it is a feeling dependent upon the acceptance of a certain standard of action, a certain ideal of character and motive. And that ideal, like all other ideals, can only be the work of reason. It is so, directly and obviously, in the former of the cases, that of the outside witness. It is so, indirectly but none the less truly, in the case of the agent whose action is determined by what he knows is expected of him on the part of others. He is aware of the standard, the ideal, existing in their mind. He finds a reflection, an echo, of it in his own; and he acts accordingly. More than that: this ideal, like all others, carries with it implicitly the idea of duty: of a standard which I ought to come up to, of a perfection after which I ought to strive. And the more Hume takes the stress off outward action, the more he lays it upon inward motive and character, the more obviously is this the case.

Thus, in the course of his argument, Hume insensibly shifts his ground. For the bare feelings with which he started he unconsciously substitutes feelings qualified by rational conceptions and ideals. But feelings so qualified have entirely changed their character. The significant thing about them is no longer what they were, or may have been, in the first instance; but what they have become.

That Hume was aware of the transition he was making, is not to be thought of for a moment. Nevertheless, the apparent success of his argument entirely depends on its being made. So long as the feelings in question remained feelings and nothing more, so long was it impossible to make them yield even that semblance of ' merit ' and ' duty ' which it was his task, alike as philosopher and as moralist, to wring from them. On the other hand, as soon as they allowed themselves to be qualified by conceptions of reason, of ' morality,' above all of duty, from that moment his fundamental principle was surrendered. The test by which he seeks to distinguish between good and evil pleasures is no longer itself a sense of pleasure: not even of a 'peculiar kind of pleasure.' However it may strive to disguise itself, it is a distinctively *moral* sense: a sense determined by ideas of reason and implicitly containing the idea of duty.

The truth is that, when it comes to the point, Hume finds himself in precisely the same difficulty which besets all other hedonists. Like all other hedonists, he has to secure two ends which no ingenuity can reconcile. On the one hand, he has to uphold the principle that man is capable of no motive but desire for pleasure. On the other hand, he has to provide some valid reason why some pleasures are to be avoided, and others, no less diligently, to be sought after and approved. On the one hand, he has to keep the sovereignty of pleasure watertight. On the other hand, he has to account for the semblance, even if it be no more than a semblance, of 'merit' and 'duty' which we attach to certain actions or motives, of 'demerit' and 'blameworthiness' which we attach to certain others. The two things are manifestly incompatible. The more faithful he was to the former end, the more impossible would he make it for himself to take even the first steps towards the accomplishment of the latter. The nearer he comes to embracing the latter purpose, the more complete must be his surrender of the former.

In the ground we have traversed so far, that surrender has already gone considerable lengths. He has explicitly admitted that the idea of merit and demerit, of what is laudable and what is blameable, lies on the very threshold of every moral judgement that we pass, of every moral idea that we are capable of forming. He has admitted—this time, not explicitly but by implication—that an ideal of character and conduct lies at the bottom both of our own actions, such at least of them as involve any moral conflict, and of our judgements upon others. And it is evident that neither of these admissions—neither that of merit and demerit, nor that of an ideal of character—has any meaning unless it is recognised as carrying with it the idea of duty. We have now to ask what light the remainder of his argument throws on the concessions already made; whether we may even find that they are followed by more.

In that argument, which expounds and defends his doctrine of the 'moral sense,' everything turns upon the place and function of sympathy. Yet it is just here that Hume betrays a fatal vacillation. Sympathy is, in fact, one thing in the opening stages of his account of the moral sense, and quite another thing at the close.

In the original version of his doctrine, sympathy appears as little more than a mere animal feeling, instinctively aroused by the consciousness that this or that passion is working in the mind of those around us, and by the irrepressible tendency—a tendency which experience shows to be common to all men—to be 'actuated with a like emotion.' The primary consciousness which forms the starting-point of the whole process is itself not a simple perception: it involves at least three mental acts. We first observe certain outward eccentricities, certain peculiarities of 'voice and gesture,' in our companions of the moment. We immediately infer that these are the outward signs of certain 'emotions,' or 'passions,' working within their breast. Finally, we look about for the probable causes of these emotions; for the incidents—whether in the way of purely outward circumstance, or in the way of some act performed, some word spoken, by ourselves or by others present at the moment—which may have excited them; and according to the conclusion we draw, we at last arrive at the specific nature of the passion which may be supposed to be at work. 'No passion of another discovers itself immediately to the mind. We are only sensible of its causes and effects. From *these* we infer the passion; and consequently *these* give rise to our sympathy.' All this is given as the first step in the 'discovery of the true origin of morals and of the love or hatred which arises from mental qualities.' In other words, it is sympathy, so interpreted, which lies at the base of Hume's doctrine of 'moral sense.' [1]

So understood, it will be admitted that, except towards those actually face to face with us, sympathy must be impossible. The reference to 'voice and gesture' would be unmeaning on any other supposition. By a stretch, the scope of the emotion might perhaps be extended to those with whose feelings and judgements on such matters, thanks to a like experience in the past, we are already familiar: that is, to our immediate friends and kinsfolk. That, however, is the utmost limit. Beyond that narrow circle sympathy, in Hume's sense of the term, cannot be conceived as reaching. The significance of this limitation will appear directly.

Meantime, Hume finds himself face to face with a difficulty which he is too candid not freely to acknowledge. The passions thus 'communicated' to us by sympathy with others, the passions which form 'the true origin of morals,' must, as we have seen, be the very passions actually felt, or inferred to be felt, by those around us. Why else should Hume have troubled himself with the above elaborate explanation? But, as he himself admits, the moral judgements we adopt for ourselves are not the moral judgements actually passed by those we are engaged in observing. The judgements of such persons, or indeed of any specified man or group of men under the influence of 'passion,' are always partial and biassed judgements. They vary with the varying interests, pre-

[1] *Of Morals*, Part III. § i. pp. 335-6.

judices, idiosyncracies of each individual, or each group. They are therefore incapable of yielding that ' generality ' which we look for, and to some extent actually find, in our moral judgements: that generality which is necessary to all rational thought and all rational speech upon such matters. ''Tis impossible we could ever converse together on any reasonable terms, were each of us to consider characters and persons only as they appear from his peculiar point of view.' [1]

How is the difficulty to be met? Hume is at once ready with his answer. It is to be met by striking an average: by framing for ourselves a purely ideal public opinion, a public opinion such as it would be if all the individuals who contribute to it, ourselves included, could be stripped of those disturbing passions and interests which, as things stand, come in to upset the balance. ' In order to prevent those continual *contradictions*, and arrive at a more *stable* judgement of things, we fix on some *steady* and *general* points of view; and always, in our thoughts, place ourselves in them, whatever may be our present situation.' [2]

This modification—for it is presented as no more than a modification—of his earlier statement is clearly a necessity; it is forced upon him by the plain facts of the case. Our moral judgements, as distinguished from the mere caprices of the moment, do not in fact vary as, if they depended upon the personal peculiarities and the fleeting moods of ourselves and those around us, they would be bound to vary. They do, in truth, have something of that ' steadiness and generality ' which, in his amended statement of the case, he boldly assigns to them. But then, what becomes of the doctrine of sympathy? of all that elaborate machinery for proving that our moral judgements are a reflection of the judgements expressed, in word or sign, by those around us, and cannot possibly be anything else? It is clearly thrown to the winds; and we are left with hints—they are unfortunately no more than hints—of a very different doctrine which is silently made to take its place.

The amended version is as follows. It is not the actual emotions felt by those around us, it is not the actual judgements resulting from them, that ' communicate ' themselves to us; but those emotions, those judgements, as ' corrected ' from other sources. What precisely those other sources may be, Hume can hardly be said to tell us. The process is loosely described as ' fixing on some steady and general points of view ': that is, we may suppose, as a process of comparing the judgements passed by different men, ourselves included, of different characters and in different circumstances; of striking off one eccentricity against another, and thus arriving at a common remainder. In other words, it is not a

[1] *Of Morals*, Part III. § i. p. 340.

[2] *Ib.* pp. 340-1.

process of feeling at all, of feeling communicated from one man to another by a kind of moral electricity; it is a process of conscious reflection. But this is to destroy the whole base upon which the original theory was built up.

The virtue of that theory, for Hume's purposes, was to base all our moral judgements upon 'impressions': and that, not simple impressions but, to make assurance doubly sure, impressions 'communicated' from one person to another; so repeating in the moral sphere that reference of all experience to sensation, which he had already worked out in the field of intellect and which is the corner-stone of his whole system, both intellectual and moral. Now, however, he suddenly replaces impressions by ideas: ideas, moreover, not at all in the sense in which alone he was entitled to use the term—that is, impressions grown faint [1]—but in the sense attached to it by common usage: that is, conceptions which can only be formed by the exertion of reason, as an active principle, and which include, among other things, the conception of a certain character, as an ideal to be striven after, and of duty, as a guiding principle of life.

If anything could increase our surprise at this sudden change of front, it is the manner in which Hume proceeds to explain and justify it. 'Experience,' he assures us, 'soon teaches us the method of correcting our sentiments.' But it was of the essence of his original theory to represent our 'sentiments' in the field of morals, like our sensations in the field of cognition, as an ultimate *datum*; as an experience from which there is no appeal; as a fixed point which neither reason, nor any other mental faculty, has the right, or indeed the power, to tamper with. Yet here he is, coolly tampering with it in the name of reason: calmly informing us that, unless it is so tampered with, it is of no use for the purpose which it professes to serve, of no value as a foundation for the 'moral sense.' Having begun by assuring us that all moral experience is reducible to feeling—either our own feeling, or the feeling of some other party, 'communicated' to us by sympathy—he now turns round and offers us a moral standard which may represent—and does, on his own showing, commonly represent—the feeling of

[1] 'All the perceptions of the human mind resolve themselves into two distinct kinds, which I shall call *Impressions* and *Ideas*. The difference between these consists in the degrees of force and liveliness with which they strike upon the mind, and make their way into our thought and consciousness. Those perceptions which enter with most force and violence we may name *impressions*; and under this name I comprehend all our sensations, passions and emotions as they make their first appearance in the soul. By *ideas* I mean the faint images of these in thinking and reasoning' (*Of the Understanding*, I. § i. (*Treatise*, vol. i. p. 311)).

no one in particular: the reasoned conclusions of a purely ideal personage, of a mere abstraction which is nothing more nor less than a personification of reason itself. A pretty complete surrender of the fundamental principle from which he started.

The lapse is made still more serious by the argument which Hume offers in its defence. Why should we wonder, he asks in effect, that such corrections are a necessity? We make them every day in our æsthetic perceptions,[1] whether of nature or of art. We make them in all matters of intellectual cognition. How should we expect not to make them in matters of morals? Once more, 'Such corrections are common with regard to all the senses; 'twere impossible we should ever make use of language, or communicate our sentiments to each other, did we not correct the momentary appearances of things and overlook our present situation.' Exactly: that is just what the opponents of 'impressionism' have always maintained. The only novelty is that, this time, the assertion comes from the lips of the arch-impressionist. And the more sweeping the form in which he casts it, the more fatal is it to the cause of which he had made himself the champion.

It is an astonishing confession; for, at one stroke, it knocks the bottom out of Hume's whole system: his theory of the Understanding, no less than his theory of Morals. It tells us, as plainly as words can tell, that there is no field of our experience in which 'impressions' alone have the last word: that it is only when sensations cease to be sensations that they become the raw material of knowledge; only when 'sentiments' and pleasures cease to be sentiments and pleasures that they become the source of moral judgements, the motive power of any action that is worthy of a man. In both fields alike, we need to compare, to contrast, the present experience with the past; to 'correct the momentary appearances of things' by their abiding reality, their formlessness, as a mere succession of feelings, by the moulding power of the mind; we need, in one word, to reason, to reflect.

[1] This assertion, if meant to be taken rigorously, is certainly mistaken. If there is any matter in the world where we rely upon our unadulterated impressions, it is the field of beauty, both natural and artistic. In a work of art—to take the easier illustration—everything depends upon the impression. If the artist is unable to make that speak, he has missed his mark. The form, the colour, the musical notes, the words *are* the work of art; and by them he must be judged. No doubt, if he *is* an artist, he will make them suggest the imaginative feeling which he is seeking to express. That feeling may perhaps fairly be called the soul of which they are the body. But it is no more the 'correction' of the outward form than the soul of the living organism is the correction of the body. Any talk of correction in this sphere is purely misleading.

Such is the unexpected conclusion of an argument which had begun with a defence of impressionism—and that, alike on the side of intellect and on the side of morals—as unflinching as any upon record. Starting, as we have seen, from the assumption that sympathy is a mere animal feeling, a sort of mental infection which cannot be caught except from those actually present and speaking to us, we discover before the end, and that on Hume's own admission, that it is a feeling qualified and 'corrected' by all kinds of rational conceptions: including the conception of judgements passed, or liable to be passed, by persons we have never seen, whom we are never likely to see, and who may have no existence save in our own thought or our own imagination. So transformed, the doctrine of sympathy ceases to have any meaning whatever. It would have been at once simpler and truer if Hume had said from the beginning what he is compelled to say at the end: that our moral judgements are from the first determined by rational conceptions: by the code of conduct which we find accepted in the world around us, qualified and 'corrected' by what we, as individual agents, conceive to be demanded of us by our duty to ourselves and our fellow-men.

That the doctrine of sympathy, in its original shape, had broken down Hume himself seems dimly to have suspected. Certainly in the closing stages of his argument it assumes a very different form and carries with it a wholly different meaning. On its first appearance, as we have seen, the part assigned to sympathy is no more than passive; the active share in the formation of the moral judgement, or the volition, falls exclusively upon one or other of the two complementary passions, love and pride. It is for sympathy to inform us what others are thinking: what is passing in their minds, as they either act themselves or are spectators of our action. It is for love or pride, on the other hand, either to award approval to others' actions, or so to frame our own conduct as to win their approval for ours. The work of the one passion, it may fairly be said, is with the intellect—or, to speak more truly, with the sensitive faculty. It is the others, love or pride, which alone directly determine either the practical judgement or the will.[1]

As the argument proceeds, however, we become aware that the part played by sympathy is something far more active, far less that of a mere register, than this. As the passion which makes us feel that the interest of all is bound up with the maintenance of Society and all its institutions, 'it is the source of the esteem which we pay to all the artificial virtues.' For a like reason, seeing that they 'acquire our approbation because of their tendency to the

[1] *Of the Passions*, Part I. § xi.; *Of Morals*, Part III. § i.

good of mankind, it gives rise to many '—or rather, as he immediately corrects himself, 'to most'—'of the natural virtues' also. So that, 'if we compare all these circumstances, we shall not doubt that sympathy is the chief source of all moral distinctions'; that it is the quality to which we must attribute most, if not all, that is good in our own actions; most, if not all, that is sound in our estimate of others.[1] From all this it is clear that sympathy has ceased to be a mere record of outward facts; that, as 'the chief source of moral distinctions,' it has become an active principle determining not only the judgement, but the will.

The net result of all this is to transform Hume's argument beyond all possibility of recognition. It is virtually to withdraw pleasure, as 'the chief spring and actuating principle of the human mind,' and to put sympathy in its place. His defence, doubtless, would be that he has from the beginning defined the moral sense—and therefore sympathy, its main constituent—as a 'peculiar kind of pleasure.' But we are entitled to ask: What is it that constitutes this peculiarity? what is it that makes the pleasure of sympathy differ from all other kinds of pleasure? Does not the difference lie just in this, that it is a pleasure qualified by elements which are not, and never can be, of the nature of pleasure? a pleasure determined by distinctively moral ends? a pleasure taken out of itself, and transformed by the sense of duty?

The truth is that, unless it is so qualified and transformed—unless, that is, it has ceased to be a mere feeling—it is impossible that sympathy should have either the force or the binding power with which, in the closing stages of his argument, Hume is constrained to credit it. Unless, or until, men come to feel that they are under an obligation, that it is their bounden duty, to seek the good of their fellow-men—and that, alike as individuals and as members of the same community—a mere 'natural' feeling of sympathy, even when reinforced by that active 'benevolence' which Hume ends by including under this elastic term, could never extend beyond the narrow circle of those who happen to come immediately under our own eye.[2] Even towards them, moreover,

[1] *Of Morals*, Part III. § i. p. 337; § v. p. 371.

[2] That the sympathy which is 'the source of all the artificial virtues and of most of the natural virtues' also and which is further defined as the chief source of moral distinctions (*Of Morals* III. §§ i. v.; pp. 337, 371), must include an active feeling of benevolence, can hardly be denied. But the artificial virtues at any rate are, by Hume's own admission, based not on our feelings towards individuals (which are often in flagrant opposition to them) but on 'general tendencies' (*ib.* II. i. ii.; pp. 252-70). And we are then met by the rather glaring contradiction that 'benevolence,' as Hume repeatedly assures us, is always directed towards individuals, that

it could never be more than a mere sentiment: a sentiment at once tepid, fitful and capricious in its operation; a sentiment which could never hold out against the self-sacrifice that sympathy, even in its more humdrum forms, demands of us; which assuredly could never have grown into the consuming passion to spend and be spent for others that we see in the noblest characters—the reformer, the saint, the martyr. The latter, the more exalted forms of sympathy, might have found little favour with Hume, or with other men of his day and temper. But the former, the less intense, manifestations of it are, as he well knew, an absolute necessity to man's every-day existence; without them, there could be no such thing as either civil society or the commonest charities of life. So much he freely admits. The misfortune is that the grounds on which he seeks to account for it are wholly insufficient. So far from explaining the results which sympathy produces, he in effect explains them away.

This is the practical objection which lies against the argument of Hume, as it lies against that of all other hedonists. It corresponds to the speculative objections which have been urged at length in the foregoing pages. On practical, no less than on speculative, grounds his argument, with all its ingenuity, must be held to have broken down.

If this estimate be doubted, we have only to ask ourselves one simple question: What light does Hume's theory throw upon the principles which govern human action, which determine the will of the individual agent? That must always be the main problem of moral philosophy. And by the manner in which it goes about to solve that problem any system may fairly be judged. It is just here, however, that Hume's theory is weakest. He has much to tell us about the formation of the moral judgement, as apart from action. He has little to say about the far more important question: After what manner is the will determined to action itself? One more glance at his doctrine of the moral sense—it shall be the last —and all doubt on the matter will be set at rest.

Both to earlier and to later writers—to Shaftesbury on the one hand, to current moralists on the other—the 'moral sense' is directly concerned with action. It is the faculty which enables the agent to distinguish between good and bad, between right and wrong, and to shape his own course accordingly. And this is the meaning in which it has passed into common speech. To Hume, on the other hand, it is an essentially contemplative faculty. Its

---

there is no such passion in human minds as the love of mankind merely as such, independent of personal qualities, of services, or of relation to ourself (*ib.* p. 255).

first and chief business is not to guide the individual's own action, but to pass judgement on the acts—or rather, on the motives and characters—of others. No doubt, he felt the need of so stating his theory as to cover both functions, if required: as to make the moral sense capable, at least in the abstract, of serving the former purpose as well as the latter. When he spoke of Pride as playing the same part in the formation of our own motives as is played by Love, when we contemplate those of others, it is clear that this, and nothing else, was the object he had in view. Formally, therefore, he must be allowed to have satisfied this, the first demand that every moral philosopher may justly be called upon to meet. It is equally clear, however, that this is not the main purpose for which his theory is built up; that his chief stress is throughout deliberately thrown upon the other side of the argument; that 'the pleasure of moral sentiment, as he thinks of it, is essentially a pleasure experienced by a spectator of an act who is other than the doer of it'; [1] a pleasure felt not by the agent who is determining his own course of action, but by a disinterested witness who is watching him from without. In other words, it is not a theory of action that Hume offers us, nor even a theory of the motives which bear directly upon action; but a theory of friendship and enmity, of admiration and repulsion. It tells us little of that which affects, still less of that which may serve as a guide for, our own conduct; what Hume was really concerned that we should learn from it is the manner in which we are affected by the conduct of others. He invites us, in short, to leave the main road of moral philosophy and turn our steps into a by-path.

What was his motive for adopting this curious course? How did he come to reconcile himself to this lame and impotent conclusion? Was he dimly aware that the motives which may be amply sufficient to determine our judgement, as mere spectators, can have little power to determine our will in the storm of desires and appetites that beats upon us, as agents? that what may be strong enough to arouse a 'sedate' pleasure, when we 'contemplate' other men's acts and motives, will be the flimsiest of bulwarks against the opposing force of passions so headstrong as lust, or greed, or the thirst for revenge, when they assail us from within? And was it an uneasy consciousness of this glaring difference which led him to thrust into full light the subordinate issue, where his argument, so far as it went, was comparatively strong; and to keep the main issue, where it had little or no force, resolutely in the shade? It would be unfair to dogmatise; but it is hard to resist the sus-

[1] These words are quoted from the most searching criticism ever made of Hume's theory: that of T. H. Green. See his Introduction to vol. ii. of the *Treatise*, p. 67.

picion that this is the real course which his discussion of moral motives, his theory of the moral sense, actually takes.

For all we learn from that discussion, there might be no such thing as moral conflict—there would be little exaggeration in saying, no such thing as evil passions—in the world. There would be no exaggeration at all in saying that he spares no pains to keep this side of our moral experience, the very side which in practice is the most insistent, so far as may be out of sight. Yet, in spite of all his efforts, there these passions remain; and the only barrier he can devise against them is that reflected repulsion, that distaste at second hand, which he is pleased to call the moral sense. It is this, more than anything else, that gives to his system that air of unreality, which is the common nemesis of all fine-spun ingenuity.

We are left, then, face to face with this dilemma. Either the doctrine of the moral sense is concerned not with the agent himself, but with those who watch his 'qualities and character' from without. Or it is to be applied, as Hume himself manifestly shrinks from applying it, to the agent also. In the former case, it has little or no bearing on the main problem of moral philosophy. In the latter case, the 'moral sense' is, strictly speaking, the sense not of the agent himself, but of those in whose presence he happens to find himself at the moment when he is called upon to act. His real self is to be found *not* in the 'calm and sedate' passions which are, or may be, 'infused' into him by sympathy with the company that surrounds him;[1] but in the 'intense and violent' passions which his adventitious self—the self that merely reflects the feelings or judgements of others—holds, or ought to hold, in check. Under such circumstances, what chance is there that the calm and sedate passions—commonly called the voice of reason—will ever make themselves heard above the tumult? More than that: can we offer, does Hume offer, any just cause why they should? He insists that this, and no other, is the way by which the idea of duty creeps into men's minds. But, when all is said and done, he signally fails to explain how it does so. He furnishes no reason why men should consider it their duty to obey the one voice rather than the other; nor even, why they should take a greater pleasure in following the judgements of others rather than their own natural impulse, in listening to their fictitious, rather than their real, self. After all his cunningly devised premisses, we wait in vain for his conclusion. After all his accumulation of fuel, his argument ends

[1] When any affection is infused by sympathy, it is at first known only by its effects and by those external signs in the countenance and conversation, which convey an idea of it: *Of the Passions*, I. xi. (vol. ii. p. 111). 'Diffused' is used in the same manner; *Of Morals*, III. ii. (vol. ii. p. 350).

in smoke. At the end, as at the beginning, the moral sense remains no more than a particular form of 'taste.'[1] Like the æsthetic sense, with which he is never weary of comparing it, its sole motive power is to be found in pleasure:[2] 'a peculiar kind of pleasure'—and no very cogent kind, at that.

So far, then, from owning himself defeated, Hume gallantly keeps his colours flying to the end. In spite of all his concessions, avowed and unavowed, he still remains an unrepentant hedonist. In spite of repeated surrenders in detail, he still maintains that 'the chief spring and actuating principle' of man's moral life is pleasure or pain. Yet to those who have followed his argument closely, these concessions may well seem formidable enough. The admission of a permanent self, on the one hand; the admission of duty as a potent, if not altogether legitimate, spring of action, on the other: these are perhaps the chief inroads which, as moralist, he is compelled to make on the pure gospel of naturalism which he had delivered as metaphysician and which he had reasserted in the forefront of his moral system. The former appears in his insistence upon character, distinct from outward act and even motive, as at once the source of all moral activity and the object of all moral judgements. It appears still more plainly in his treatment of Pride, one of the corner-stones of his whole moral argument. The latter, the idea of duty, is from the first recognised as a practical necessity, as a principle which, for purposes of action, is acknowledged by all men. But it makes its way, though in a veiled form, into his speculative theory also: in his acceptance of merit and demerit, as the idea which underlies all moral judgements; in his admission that there is such a thing as an ideal of character; in his endeavour, however ill sustained, to prove that it flows naturally from the working of the moral sense; in his revised version of sympathy, as 'the chief source of moral distinctions'; as well as in

[1] There are instances . . . wherein this immediate *taste* or sentiment produces our approbation: *Of Morals*, III. § i. (vol. ii. p. 348).

[2] This identification of the moral with the æsthetic sense, which is the inevitable consequence of his whole argument, is a perpetual source of embarrassment to Hume, who at times betrays unmistakable uneasiness at the lengths to which it leads him; for instance, when it constrains him to reckon Wit among the moral virtues (*Of Morals*, III. § i.; vol. ii. p. 348. See also *ib.* I. § i. pp. 247-8; III. § i. pp. 336-7, 347-49; III. §§ v. vi. pp. 371-2). 'Sentiments must touch the heart, to make them control our passions; but they need not extend beyond the imagination to make that influence our taste,' he says truly enough (*ib.* III. § i. p. 344). But when we ask wherein lies the distinction between *heart* and *imagination* he maintains a discreet silence. His whole argument has gone to prove that there is none.

other ways indicated during the course of our discussion. And behind both is the implied admission that Reason, so far from being bound down to the homely task of registering impressions, or, in the moral sphere, of adapting means to such ends as are given to it from without, is, on the contrary, under the name of the 'calm passions' (above all, of sympathy), capable of determining its own ends, of creating the ideal which the permanent self knows itself to be under the obligation of pursuing.

It is true that, like a good son of his time, Hume is little disposed to recognise as legitimate any ends or ideals but such as commend themselves to the plainest common sense: a life of reasonable moderation and self-control, of refined intellectual and moral pleasures. All the rest—the aims of the moral and social reformer, the temper of the saint or the martyr—all these are dismissed as the dream of the 'enthusiast,' as delusions unworthy of an age which has replaced Cromwell by Sir Robert Walpole and banished the *Pilgrim's Progress* for the *Essays of Addison*.[1]

This, however, only enhances the significance of the surrender. If the humbler task, that of the man who makes no pretension to heroic virtue, is to be accomplished only through a sense of duty and in the light of an ideal more or less consciously accepted for our own, much more must the same be true of the higher task: that which draws out the deepest and noblest qualities of which man is capable: that of the reformer who sacrifices everything, even to life itself, for the good of his fellow-men; that of the thinker, or poet, who deliberately rejects all worldly advancement, for the sake of accomplishing the work to which he has appointed himself. Had Hume desired to disprove the text from which he started, had it been his avowed purpose to convince us that Reason is *not* a 'perfectly inert principle,' that the pleasure which moves the world is a pleasure which presupposes an ideal of achievement, a pleasure inspired and transformed by a sense of duty, he could hardly have gone about it in a better way.

Hume had made so many concessions in the course of expounding his moral theory that few, if any, were left to make when he came on to its distinctly political application. It is true that the cardinal principle of the latter is not the same as that of the former;

[1] 'Whoever would assert an equality of genius and elegance between Ogilvie and Milton, between Bunyan and Addison, would be thought to defend no less an extravagance than if he had maintained a molehill to be as high as Teneriffe, or a pond as extensive as the ocean. Though there may be found persons who give the preference to the former authors, no one pays attention to such a taste; and we pronounce without scruple the sentiments of these pretended critics to be absurd and ridiculous.' Essay xxiii. 'Of the Standard of Taste' (*Essays*, vol. i. p. 269).

that what was pleasure in the one has become self-interest, or utility, in the other; in one word, that he has passed from the hedonist camp into that of the utilitarians. But this makes little or no difference to the concessions which, in his candour, he feels called upon to make. In the one field, as in the other, he is constrained to admit the idea of duty. In the one field, as in the other, he is compelled, however little he may realise it, to allow the existence of a permanent self.

The latter concession, as we have seen, is by far the less important; and it may be despatched as swiftly as it was in connection with his moral theory. Indeed, but for the remarkable argument by which Hume supports his position, there would have been little need to dwell upon it at all.

On any rigorous interpretation, no doubt, it might fairly be contended that the mere establishment of permanent institutions—in other words, the bare existence of the State—implies the existence of a permanent self, capable of looking before and after, in the individuals who create them. So far as Hume is concerned, however, no such rigour is required. In face of his own arguments, it would be sheer labour lost. For what is the motive which he assigns for the establishment of Government and to attendant institutions? Briefly, it is that, after some experience of unorganised Society, men find that the security, which is the chief end of Society, is still grievously lacking. They discover without much difficulty that the cause of the evil is their own lack of self-control: their own deplorable habit of sacrificing their permanent interests to the passion of the moment, of 'preferring contiguous to remote.' They foresee that the only remedy for this evil is to make it the business of some person or persons to uphold those permanent interests on their behalf; and without fear or favour to punish any one, themselves included, who under stress of passion shall be perverse enough to resist. And they act accordingly.[1]

On this showing, the sole purpose for which Government is instituted is to save men from themselves. And they themselves are all the time acutely aware of it, or they would never have put themselves to all this trouble. In other words, every one concerned in the establishment of Government thinks of himself as a permanent subject, liable to incessant conflicts between passion and interest: or rather between the calm and sedate passions on the one hand and the violent, but fleeting, passions on the other. And it is in this permanent subject, not in that which receives passing impressions or is swept away by momentary passions, that he deliberately chooses to find his true self. Such is Hume's

[1] *Of Morals*, II. § vii. pp. 300-304.

argument; and as an admission of the reality of the permanent self, it must be allowed to be conclusive.

The other concession is a much more serious matter. While maintaining that the ultimate motive for obedience to Government is self-interest or 'utility,' Hume is equally ready to admit—or rather, to insist—that the proximate motive, in the vast majority of cases, is a very different one: the sense of duty. He applies this argument impartially to both sides of the relation. On the one hand, he pleads, 'it is certain, as a plain matter of fact, that every one thinks he is under an obligation to submit to Government'; and for that very reason, if we accept the doctrine of the moral sense, it must at once be admitted that he is so. On the other hand, it is equally certain that no Government which ever existed has been willing to base its claims upon the interest, as represented by the voluntary consent, of the subject; that all of them have claimed his obedience as a matter not of choice, but of obligation; and the more nearly their title has approached to one of pure consent on the part of their subjects, the more eager have they shown themselves to veil the unwelcome truth under a fiction of 'legitimacy,' or even of 'divine right.' Hence the politic prevarications of Henry IV. and Henry VII., neither of whom was in fact anything more than a fortunate usurper, white-washed by Parliament after the event.[1] Hence, he might have added, the like prevarications of Somers and others, when the crown was transferred from James to William at the Revolution.[2]

Thus, on both sides, Government is admitted to rest, for all practical purposes, not on the felt interest of the governed, but on their sense of duty to their appointed ruler. Or, to use Hume's technical terms, Allegiance, which took its rise as an artificial virtue, becomes in process of time hardly less of a natural virtue than clemency or benevolence. Like the natural virtues, it awakens, 'on the mere survey and contemplation,' an intuitive sense of pleasure; while the breach of it, whether by ourselves or others, arouses an equally instinctive feeling of uneasiness and displeasure. Like the natural virtues, therefore, it falls under the operation of the moral sense.[3]

It is quite true that the ultimate justification of such allegiance

[1] *Of Morals*, II. § viii. (*Of the Source of Allegiance*); vol. ii. pp. 306-16; *Essays*, Part II. xii. (*Of the Original Contract*); *Essays*, vol. i. pp. 444-54.

[2] See Macaulay's *History of England*, chap. x. (People's Edition, vol. i. pp. 634-50); and Burke, *Reflections* and *Appeal from the New to the Old Whigs*.

[3] The way for this assimilation between the natural and the artificial virtues had been paved by the plea that sympathy is, with some trifling qualifications, the source of both. See above, p. 352.

is to be found in the general sense of its advantage or utility; and that the reasoning which convinces us of this is so simple that almost any man is capable of understanding it. But, at bottom, much the same is true of the distinctively 'natural' virtues also. Even benevolence, for example, has come to be valued because it is demonstrably for the advantage of Society and all its members. And if the same cannot be said of the more exclusive qualities, such as wit and beauty—on Hume's showing, it would hardly be too much to call them virtues—at any rate the main source of the pleasure they give is to be found in the sense of the advantage which they bring to their possessors.[1] Hence also, it may be added, the possibility and rightfulness of renouncing allegiance, when it is manifestly for the advantage of the community to do so; or the like possibility and rightfulness of refusing to perform a given act of benevolence when its performance would manifestly be against the general interest.

From all this it results that the difference between the natural and the artificial virtues is not so great as the opening stages of Hume's argument might have led us to suppose. In both, the immediate motive is furnished by the pleasure felt on the mere survey and contemplation. In both, this intuitive pleasure eventually translates itself into an equally intuitive sense of duty And in both, the ultimate cause—whether of the pleasure, or the sense of duty which springs from it—is to be found in the belief that a given course of action, or rather the motive which habitually gives rise to it, is to the advantage of Society as a whole: is to be found, that is, in its expediency or utility. No doubt, the centre of gravity is not quite the same in the one virtue as in the other. With the natural virtues, the stress lies on the element of pleasure; with the artificial virtues, on the element of utility. But though differently mixed, the elements are the same. And, what mainly concerns us, the idea of duty follows, however mysteriously, in the one case as in the other. It plays a part only a shade less important in Hume's political, than it does in his moral, theory.

Some surprise may perhaps be felt that, when he allows so much to duty in respect of the relation between the Government and the governed, he should make no such allowance—none, at least, that he himself can be supposed to have intended—in respect of the yet more fundamental relation between one member of the community and the rest, between the individual members and the community as a whole. Yet, if the bond of duty is essential in the one case, it may well be thought to be still more essential in the other. The reason for this omission is, no doubt, to be found partly in the general temper of his time. Alike in theory and in

[1] *Of Morals*, II. §§ ix. x. (*Of the Measures*, *Of the Objects*, of allegiance.)

practice, the community had long counted for little or nothing; the State, perversely identified with the Government, was virtually all in all. A wider and truer view of the matter came only with Rousseau in the field of theory, with the French Revolution in that of practice.

The real cause of Hume's silence, however, clearly goes deeper than this. It was a necessity of his whole argument to assume that the idea of duty was a purely secondary idea, an idea arrived at only by a slow process of development: an idea, moreover, of more than doubtful legitimacy, however widely it may be accepted in fact. That being the case, it was possible for him, as a matter of origins, to admit that it was one of the motives which first drew men together in civil society. It was not easy, though it was not wholly impossible, for him to admit it to be one of the motives which come to hold the individual members together, when the community is once fully formed. For that would have been to admit a moral bond between man and man, a moral element in the life of the community, of a sort alien, if not to his intellectual principle, at least to his whole temperament and habits of mind. The nearest he comes to the former admission on the subject of origins is his plea that, on the first formation of society, it is not the individual, but the family, which is the unit; and that the process of 'co-alescence' is made the easier because the members of those families have already had their 'rough corners and untoward affections rubbed off'—in other words, because they have already passed under a moral discipline, inseparably bound up with a sense of duty—while they were still in the state of nature. The nearest he comes to the latter admission is in his amended doctrine of sympathy, which, as we have seen, is not to be sustained unless, which Hume himself would steadfastly deny, it be held to contain a sense of obligation as between man and man, purely on the ground of their common humanity. Hume, however, makes no attempt to apply this doctrine to the community as distinguished from the individual, to the realm of politics as distinguished from that of morals. What is yet more decisive, neither in one case nor in the other, neither in what he says of the Family nor in what he says of Sympathy, does he ever admit the further implications which seem to lie behind the concessions he actually avows.

All this must be borne in mind when we speak of the part which Hume assigns to duty, alike in his political and his moral theory. Yet, when all deductions have been made, that part still remains a very considerable and, in view of the thesis which he was out to maintain, a very strange one. For it must never be forgotten that, in both theories alike, the idea of duty is a pure intruder; and that in neither theory does he make any effort to account for, still less to justify, the intrusion. In dealing with the parallel idea of cause and effect, he had at least made a feint of invoking the 'law of association' as the channel through which the illicit inference had insinuated itself into men's minds; though even here the explanation misses fire, seeing that, unless the idea of causation were already in the mind, no coincidence of two experiences in the same order, however often repeated, could avail to suggest it. But in the case of duty, no explanation whatever, good or bad, of the mystery is offered. All we are told is that, when 'a particular kind of pleasure' has been experienced sufficiently often, the mind does, as a matter of fact, begin to attach to it the idea of duty. No attempt is made to reduce the latter to the former. No attempt is therefore made to prove that the former expresses the real truth of the matter, while the latter is no more than an illicit inference. On the contrary, no Christian moralist could insist more forcibly than Hume either on the necessity of duty or on the vast influence which it wields upon motive and action. The idea is abruptly thrown upon us. Its effects are duly expounded. But how, or why, it arose; how it sprang out of an idea so utterly opposed to it as that of pleasure, or interest—all this is left a blank.[1]

And this from the man who plumed himself upon maintaining the principle of naturalism more rigorously than any of his predecessors; who at the beginning of his ethical discussion pledged himself, if not to exclude the idea of duty, at least to explain and account for its supervention: to 'give a reason for what seems altogether inconceivable, how this new relation'—that of duty—'can be a deduction from others, which are entirely different from it.' But let the great writer speak for himself:

'I cannot forbear adding an observation which may perhaps be found of some importance. In every system of morality which

[1] The nearest approach that Hume makes to indicating the process by which the idea of duty arose, or may have arisen, is the following: 'When men have found by experience that 'tis impossible to subsist without society, and that 'tis impossible to maintain society while they give free course to their appetites, so urgent an interest quickly restrains their actions and imposes an obligation to observe those rules, which we call the *laws of justice*. This obligation of interest rests not here; but, by the necessary course of the passions and sentiments, gives rise to the moral obligation of duty; while we approve of such actions as tend to the peace of society, and disapprove of such as tend to its disturbance.' *Of Morals*, II. § xi. (*Of the Laws of Nations*); vol. ii. p. 329. The same phrase, *obligation of interest*, occurs again, *ib.* II. § viii. (*Of the Source of Allegiance*), p. 309. It is apparently the connecting link by which Hume slides into the acceptance of *moral* obligation. But the very phrase betrays a strange confusion of thought.

I have hitherto met with, I have always remarked that the author proceeds for some time in the ordinary way of reasoning, and establishes the being of a God, or makes observations concerning human affairs; when of a sudden I am surprised to find that, instead of the usual copulations of propositions, *is* and *is not*, I meet with no proposition that is not connected with an *ought* or an *ought not*. This change is imperceptible; but is, however, of the last consequence. For as this *ought*, or *ought not*, expresses some new relation or affirmation, 'tis necessary that it should be observed and explained; and at the same time that a reason should be given for what seems altogether incomprehensible, how this new relation can be a deduction from others, which are entirely different from it.' [1]

It will be admitted at once that 'the observation is of some importance.' And in the light of the reasoning actually offered by the *Treatise*, it can hardly be denied that it is also not a little surprising. For, when it comes to the pinch, Hume neglects his own warning at every point.

Of all utilitarian systems, whether in Politics or in Morals, that of Hume is at once the subtlest as a piece of reasoning and the least out of harmony with the facts. So it was said at the beginning of our enquiry. And, as we are now entitled to add, the price that he pays for this distinction is uncommonly heavy. If he makes his system plausible, and more than plausible, that is only by surrendering, point after point, the cardinal principles with which he started. If he squares his theory with the facts, that is only at the sacrifice of all the hopes which he held out in his opening pages, of all that, in his heart of hearts, he was most concerned to uphold.

[1] *Of Morals*, I. § i.; vol. ii. pp. 245-6.

END OF VOL. I